Law's Anthropology

From ethnography to expert testimony in native title

Law's Anthropology

From ethnography to expert testimony in native title

Paul Burke
Research Fellow
School of Archaeology and Anthropology
The Australian National University
Canberra

E PRESS

Published by ANU E Press
The Australian National University
Canberra ACT 0200, Australia
Email: anuepress@anu.edu.au
This title is also available online at http://epress.anu.edu.au/

National Library of Australia Cataloguing-in-Publication entry

Author: Burke, Paul, 1956-

Title: Law's anthropology : from ethnography to expert testimony in native title / Paul Burke.

ISBN: 9781921862427 (pbk.) 9781921862434 (ebook)

Notes: Includes bibliographical references and index.

Subjects: Native title (Australia)--Law and legislation.
Judicial process.
Evidence, Expert.

Dewey Number: 346.9404320899915

All rights reserved. No part of this publication may be reproduced, stored in a retrieval system or transmitted in any form or by any means, electronic, mechanical, photocopying or otherwise, without the prior permission of the publisher.

Cover design and layout by ANU E Press

Cover image: Photograph of the claimants and their barristers at a reception during the Mabo hearing on Murray Island in 1989. Courtesy of Yarra Bank Films, photo by Trevor Graham. Left to right: Jack Wailu, Greg McIntyre, Dave Passi, Eddie Mabo, Brian Keon-Cohen, Bai Day and Sam Passi.

This edition © 2011 ANU E Press

Contents

Acknowledgments

This book would not have been possible without the cooperation of the lawyers and anthropologists who agreed to be interviewed. They are Jeremy Beckett, Nonie Sharp and Brian Keon-Cohen for the *Mabo* case study; Patrick Sullivan and Erich Kolig for the *Rubibi* case study; Craig Elliott and Ross Howie for the *De Rose Hill* case study; and Peter Sutton and Jon Willis for *Yulara*. Tim Wooley, the principal legal officer of the Native Title Unit of the Aboriginal Legal Rights Movement (South Australia), provided critical access to non-restricted documents and useful background explanation for *De Rose Hill*. The Crown Solicitor's Office of South Australia kindly provided me with a copy of the unrestricted version of Ken Maddock's expert reports.

In acknowledging the assistance of the participants in this research, I also acknowledge that they do not necessarily agree with the way I have presented them or the conclusions I have reached. All I can say is that I believe the current version presents the facts as fairly as I can, while remaining true to my assessment of those facts.

Ian Keen was my supervisor when this book started life as doctoral research. He has a deserved reputation as a good supervisor who knows when the wretched student needs praise, can offer practical escapes from seemingly dire entrapments and knows how to frame criticism in a way that gets under the guard of the most fragile ego. He has demonstrated all these qualities with me at various points, but mostly it has been a happy and productive collaboration. The doctoral research was really a group effort with my supervisory panel and the participants in the research. The other members of the panel—Francesca Merlan, Don Gardner and Gary Edmond—provided extensive feedback. As will be evident in the conclusion, the discussion of the draft chapters with the participants has been rewarding, if a little testing at times, and helped to clarify my thinking.

At the ANU, I have received special assistance and information from David Martin, Julie Finlayson and Kevin Murphy. Yasmine Musharbash spread good rumours about my work. Brendan Gibson helped me with theory over a Guinness. Moreover, Nic Peterson's unstinting support ensured the completion of this project.

I owe a special debt to my wife, Rosemary Budavari, and my children, Mark and Helen. It is not easy living with a husband and father who is physically present, but not there. Rosemary proofread previous versions of the book and translated some German articles for me. Moreover, her job and practical support kept the whole show on the road.

Lists of Maps, Tables and Figures

List of Maps

List of Tables

List of Figures

1. Towards an Ethnography of Anthropology's Encounter with Modern Law

Introduction

The bodies of anthropologists, bruised from their encounter with native title, are to be found recuperating all around Australia. Some, still wounded from humiliating cross-examination, swear, yet again, never to be involved in another native title claim. While they lament their lack of influence, others warn of native title completely engulfing anthropology and ruining it (see, for example, Morris 2004). One Aboriginal leader has made the opposite claim—that anthropology has engulfed native title law—blaming anthropology for the High Court's poor legal conceptualisation of native title.[1] After almost two decades of the native title era,[2] it is time to put these contradictory assessments to the test by a close examination of what happens to anthropologists and anthropology in some actual cases.

While the encounter between Australianist anthropology and modern law is not new in Australia, native title represents a distinct second phase following the era of land rights claims in the Northern Territory.[3] The central place of anthropology in land rights claims seems secure. The definition of 'traditional owner' appeared to be based on anthropological concepts, and anthropologists were given responsibility for compiling the key document outlining the case: the claim book. There were internal critics of the dual role that anthropologists played in the land claim process but there were also converts from an initial scepticism (Rose 1996). The new phase is characterised by a more marginal role for anthropologists in the formulation of cases, more vague legal doctrines, and a more direct exposure to formal legal proceedings. Thus, what is needed more than anything for a fresh examination of anthropology's engagement with modern law is for due emphasis to be given to the relative autonomy of the juridical field within the constitutional state.

---

1 Noel Pearson in *The Age*, 28 August 2002.

2 In this book, the phrase 'native title era' refers to the period following the High Court's judgment in *Mabo* in 1992 (*Mabo v Queensland (No. 2)* (1992) 175 CLR 1).

3 In this book, the phrase 'land rights era' refers to the period between the commencement of the *Aboriginal Land Rights (Northern Territory) Act 1975* (Cwlth) (the *Land Rights Act*) and the commencement of the native title era in 1992. This is a simplification made for ease of presentation. In reality, *Land Rights Act* claims continue up to the present in parallel with native title claims, although it is also true to say that the bulk of the *Land Rights Act* claims were heard prior to 1992.

The engagement of Australianist anthropologists with legal processes for land rights has a relatively long history, commencing with the appearance of Berndt and Stanner as expert witnesses in the *Gove* case in 1970.[4] Notwithstanding this relatively long engagement, the existing anthropological literature that attempts to explain it has yet to take advantage of the reservoir of literature on jurisprudence and the sociology of law.[5] In order to move to a more comprehensive, sociologically informed account of the current second phase of anthropology's encounter with modern law, I believe it is necessary to do two things. The first is to adopt a position of critical distance from the professional practice of both law and anthropology—that is, to describe them as social fields so that their internal workings can be exposed. The second is to examine the interaction of these fields, not just from the point of view of different practices, knowledge claims and power relations, but also through the medium of the interaction of the key actors: individual anthropologists, lawyers and judges.

Some have characterised the two fields at a very general level, such as Niblett's (1992) use of the concept of an 'interpretive community'. Others have emphasised particular features of the field of anthropology: Williams (1986:212) referred to 'swings in the pendulum of scholarly opinion'; Merlan (1998:173–4) referred to the 'theoretical revision' of the significance of the clan during the 1980s; and Gumbert (1984) made an opposite assertion of resistance to paradigm change in the preceding decade. In most of the previous literature, however, the social field of Australianist anthropology has been an implicit background that structures topics, methodology, references and orientation towards the intended audience. Thus one of the aims of this book is to thematise the implicit academic background and to give a more comprehensive account of its features. While histories of anthropological theory and institutional histories of anthropology might be relevant, they will not be the primary focus.[6]

---

4 *Milirrpum v Nabalco Pty Ltd* (1971) 17 FLR 141 at 160. Also see Berndt (1981); and Williams (2008).

5 Instead, in Australia, it tends to focus on the effect of participation in land claim processes on the anthropologists' informants—for example, the regimentation of customary practice (Merlan 1995), the objectification of tradition (Glaskin 2002; Merlan 1989), and the emotional trauma of those found lacking in tradition (Povinelli 2002). This demonstrates that judicial formulations of Aboriginal traditions do not match ethnographic reality—for example, Williams' *The Yolngu and Their Land* (1986) and Glaskin's (2003) analysis of the Ward decision. The literature also focuses on developing broad contextualisations in terms of a general political economy of Australia (Peterson 1985), state mimesis of Aboriginal tradition (Merlan 1998) or the pernicious limitations on the liberal state's recognition of Indigenous difference (Povinelli 2002); a narrower applied perspective that seeks to maximise anthropology's effectiveness in its allocated role by: a) asserting the need for the rigorous independence of expert witnesses, rather than advocacy (Kolig 1982; Maddock 1980a, 1998a, 1998b, 1999); b) addressing problems anthropologists have in responding to legal frameworks; and, more positively, by c) demonstrating that anthropology has the answers to the legal questions (Rumsey 1996; Sutton 2003); or collections of conference papers incorporating a number of these orientations and contributions to the ethnography of traditional land tenure (Hiatt 1984; Peterson and Langton 1983; Smith and Morphy 2007; Toussaint 2004; Weiner and Glaskin 2007). There is a similar body of literature arising out of the land claim experience in North America: see Cove (1996); Cruickshank (1992); Culhane (1992, 1994, 1998); Fisher (1992); Fiske (2000); Jones (1956); Kandel (1992); Lurie (1955, 1956); Manners (1956); Miller (1992); Mills (1994, 1996); Paine (1985, 1996); Ridington (1992); Rigsby (1995, 1997); Rosen (1977); Steward (1968, 1977); and Stewart (1966).

6 See Harris (1972); McCall (1982); Peterson (1990); and Stocking (1983, 1996).

The other part of the project is to overcome what could be called the anthropological cringe from sustained inquiry into modern law—that is, to find some position outside the framework of legal doctrine and legal procedures from which to develop a critical understanding of law. Williams' belated account of the *Gove* case continues to demonstrate difficulties in anthropological accounting for judicial practice. It is true that Williams effectively undermined some of the pretensions of judicial fact-finding through her ability to understand Yolngu concepts prior to their use by Yolngu witnesses, and to trace oversimplifying English translations and their eventual garbled reception by the judge. When it came to analysing the rule-finding work of the judge, however, Williams' approach tended to remain one of comparing legal doctrine with factual reality. But to say that the law does not reflect historical reality is a very preliminary stage of the analysis of law. It begs the question of the nature of judicial reasoning within the wider framework of the legal system.

Two significant works in the native title era—Mantziaris and Martin's *Native Title Corporations* (2000) and Peter Sutton's *Native Title in Australia: An Ethnographic Perspective* (2003)—appear to cover some of the ground of this book but they do not aim to provide a sociological account of the encounter of law and anthropology. The focus of this book will be the process by which knowledge, views, arguments and opinions that originate in the academically orientated field of anthropology are reordered into legal categories in the very different social field of law. I will commence with an account of Australianist and Torres Strait Islander anthropology as social fields, move on to the juridical field, then move to theorising the interaction between the fields of anthropology and the juridical field.

The social fields of the Australianist and Torres Strait Islander anthropology[7]

The word 'field' is used to evoke a Bourdieuian approach, which attempts to synthesise the analysis of structures and agency using such concepts as position

7 The distinct regional specialisations relevant to the case studies of this book require a distinction to be made between Australianist anthropology (the *Rubibi* and *De Rose Hill* case studies) and anthropologists specialising in Torres Strait Islander studies (the *Mabo* case study). In international anthropology, the term 'Australianist' is used to describe those anthropologists specialising in Aboriginal Australia. This usage does not recognise the culturally distinct Torres Strait Islanders within the borders of Australia and probably also reflects the low profile of Torres Strait Islander studies as a regional specialisation. One solution would have been to use the term 'Aboriginalist' instead of 'Australianist', but this would not reflect contemporary usage within anthropology. So when I use the term 'Australianist' I am referring only to those anthropologists specialising in Aboriginal Australia and not including Torres Strait Islander specialists. It should be acknowledged, however, that the term 'Australianist' might now be somewhat outdated and problematic since many anthropologists who specialise in Aboriginal Australia also investigate non-Aboriginal aspects of Australian society.

within a field, competition and habitus, which can be glossed as the ingrained dispositions and learnt, unwritten rules that facilitate interaction within the field with a degree of unconscious proficiency.[8] In Bourdieu's study of the Kabyle of Algeria, the field was one of small-scale, face-to-face interaction. The field of the academy does have some similarities, especially at the level of small regional specialisations in anthropology, such as Australianist anthropology and those specialising in Torres Strait Islander studies. In these specialisations, most of the participants would be known to each other, through physical collocation, conferences or virtual interaction through published works.

In approaching his broadest description of the field of the French academy in *Homo Academicus* (1988), Bourdieu took as his inspiration the distinction made by Kant in *The Conflict of the Faculties* between the higher faculties, which the government wanted to control because of their influence on the general populace (theology, law and medicine), and the lower faculties (everything else), where there was much more freedom of expression. Bourdieu comes to a similar conclusion, although he derived his hierarchy of the academic field from general indicators of social stratification of the professors in different disciplines. These indicators included such things as inherited social capital (status of father's profession), prestige of educational institutions attended, level achieved in the formal hierarchy of the university, general indications of status such as appearance in *Who's Who*, and indicators of intellectual celebrity such as invitations to contribute to mass-circulation newspapers or appear on television. His social hierarchy of the faculties in descending order is: medicine, law, arts (humanities and social sciences) and science (Bourdieu 1988:ch. 2). This structure also generally describes the characteristics of the dominant class since the 'field of power' and the university field reproduce each other. This reproduction is achieved by the success of the dominant class in the various induction processes such as competitive exams and professorial selection processes so that their inherited advantages are converted into 'earned' advantages.

Within this stratified field, Bourdieu distinguishes two kinds of symbolic capital: one based on 'scientific' competence and another based on social competence. These competencies acquire different kinds of power in the field: scientific power or academic power. Scientific competence relates to the mastery of a body of knowledge, the successful conduct of research, publication in prestigious journals and so on. Social competence relates to maintaining a privileged position in the general social field. In the academy, achieving academic power involves taking on administrative chores that go with senior positions, networking and

8 In truth, Bourdieu uses the idea of a 'field' in a number of different ways—for example, 'the field of power'. But it is 'field' in the sense of a relatively coherent shared habitus and competitive interaction that is relevant to the following analysis.

eventually securing positions that control the reproduction of the professional body and the cultural capital that can be acquired within the university. These would be positions that set entry requirements and exams, design curriculum and appoint staff. Broadly, the highest degree of social competence is to be found in medicine and the highest degree of scientific competence is to be found in the sciences. The science–social cleavage is, however, reproduced within faculties so that, for example, the professor of medicine might not do medical research personally, but will secure funding and arrange for the research to be done. In all faculties there will be people with meagre 'scientific' capital who nevertheless hold influential positions in the academic hierarchy through their clever playing of the game.

The position of the social sciences in the academic field so constructed is one of hybridity that represents the features of the whole field. The social sciences are drawn in the direction of science, where, in Bourdieu's—perhaps idealised—view, the logic of research sets the agenda and success in research provides a basis for hierarchy. They are also drawn in the opposite direction of the reproduction of the existing temporal order as in the role of some humanities disciplines in the transmission of legitimate culture through the consecration and conservation of a canon that, in effect, controls what is taught in secondary schools.

The other part of Bourdieu's account is the academic habitus and how it is reproduced. Here we encounter one of his central metaphors: the game. Those who have the necessary basic disposition—the desire for knowledge, for example—enter the game of the university. The price of entry is 'the visceral form of recognition of everything which constitutes the existence of the group, its identity, its truth, and which the group must reproduce in order to reproduce itself' (Bourdieu 1988:56).

Thus, although there is competition for 'scientific' capital, the competition is within limits that rarely challenge the fundamentals of the discipline. The social hierarchy is within the university field and internalised as ideal career paths. Pursuing a career involves entering into relations of dependency and domination with superiors—a kind of infantilising during which the professor can make the assistant lecturer wait. In the meantime the expectation of advancement requires reverence to the professor, citation of his work and public support of him. As with all games, the rules become so familiar through use that they become unconscious dispositions, a practical logic of automatically knowing what to do in a given situation.

To summarise, in Bourdieu's explanation, academic order is maintained by linking academic advancement to institutional control through co-option, and this linkage has somewhat stultifying effects.

While directed towards explaining the student protests in Paris in 1968, Bourdieu's description of the academic field and habitus is still suggestive of some of the general structures and tendencies in the academy of today, outside France (see Robbins 2004). In Australia, however, creeping managerialism and funding based on throughput of students and the resulting competition between universities must have had some transforming effect. A likely scenario is the strengthening of the hierarchy of prestigious universities and the weakening of the power of the master to direct the student and to demand the allegiance of the student. A more complex picture emerges in considering the discipline of anthropology within the general field of the academy.

The discipline of anthropology

In order to enable some assessment of how one acquires academic and 'scientific' capital within the complex contemporary situation of anthropology, it is necessary to give an account of some of the basic structures of the discipline. Three such structures are regional specialisation, an ethnography–theory divide, and a pure–applied divide.

Regional specialisation has been inevitable since the acceptance of long-term fieldwork as an essential part of professionalised anthropology.[9] As Fardon points out in *Localising Strategies* (1990), however, the development of each specialist literature has been far from predictable.

Fardon's contribution to the critique of the conditions of the production of ethnography was in part a response to the more high-profile critiques of ethnography as a form of colonial domination (Said's *Orientalism* [1978]; Asad's *Anthropology and the Colonial Encounter* [1973]) and the textually constructed authority of the ethnographer (Clifford and Marcus 1986; Marcus and Cushman 1982). His claim is that the textual critiques in particular have—for the purposes of deconstruction—essentialised the practice of ethnographic writing, imposing on it a homogeneity that does not reflect the way in which regional ethnographic literatures have developed. Fardon emphasises a dialectical process, usually commencing with an exemplary ethnography in a previously unstudied area. The initial exemplary ethnography associates that area with a theoretical problem, such as the problem of order in an acephalous society. Subsequent ethnographers then position themselves in relation to it,

9 In this book, I use the phrase 'professionalised anthropology' to refer to the period commencing roughly in the early twentieth century when anthropology was beginning to find a base in the universities and university qualifications were seen as a prerequisite for conducting fieldwork—that is, professional as opposed to previous amateur efforts by those without university degrees. The potential need for clarification arises since the phrase 'professionalised anthropology' is occasionally used in contemporary critiques of anthropological associations becoming too much like the professional organisations of lawyers and doctors, with 'applied' agendas overtaking those with an academic orientation (see, for example, Morris 2004).

by modification, contrast or filling in the gaps. In this way, a cross-referencing specialist literature is built up: 'Region, problem and descriptive values are established intertextually' (Fardon 1990:22).

The long-running debate about Aboriginal local organisation is a prime example of the growth of a cross-referencing literature within the Australianist specialisation. That debate provides one way of positioning particular anthropological works within the specialisation as a whole.[10] While the question of order and dispute resolution has been a fairly consistent feature of the Australianist specialisation, the inquiry into the law-like features of tribal societies has generally been associated with other regional specialisations. Early groundbreaking work in so-called primitive law tended to be located in regions with fairly specialised arbitral institutions, as in Africa (Bohannan 1957; Gluckman 1955), or among exceptional groups that had deliberative councils, as among some of the Plains Indians of North America (Llewellyn and Hoebel 1941). Melanesia and Polynesia also have their early ethnographies with a legal bent (Hogbin and Malinowski 1934; Malinowski 1926; Pospisil 1956). The debates that eventually emerged about the applicability of law as a universal category of cross-cultural comparison occurred outside the Australianist specialisation and, consequently, there was no ready-made Australianist literature on the ways in which Aboriginal relations to land could be encompassed by 'traditional laws and customs' when it re-emerged as a critical issue after the 1992 *Mabo* decision (see below).

Regional specialisation is sometimes enabling of an ongoing research program and at other times restrictive, as in the difficulty of moving away from what has become the established consensus of the key group of influential specialists about what is of interest in the region. National traditions of ethnographic writing—French, British or American—might coincide with anthropologically defined regions, but not always.

The existence of regional specialisations raises the question of how they relate to one another—what is the lingua franca; how do they distinguish themselves from other kinds of area studies? The answer is what Appadurai (1986) calls metropolitan theorising—that is, the attempt to transcend the local through generalisation, comparison and the framing of local data in terms of wider academic debates. Fardon himself notes that, in writing an ethnography, the

---

10 When I use the term 'local organisation debate' in this book, I am referring to the long-running debate over the most appropriate way to generalise, on an Australia-wide basis, about Aboriginal group relations to land in the pre-contact era. It is typified by Hiatt's 1962 critique of Radcliffe-Brown's generalisations and Stanner's 1965 defence and modification of Radcliffe-Brown's generalisations (Hiatt 1962; Stanner 1965). The debate has quite a long history and is ongoing. I did not have the heart to clutter this book with yet another rehearsal of the various positions taken in the debate; there are already many such accounts (see, for example, Hiatt 1996:13–35; Keen 1988:102–4; Maddock 1980b; Peterson and Long 1986:1–25; Sutton 2003:38–53, 68–70, 98–110, 140–58).

anthropologist has to weigh up the claims of the audience of fellow specialists and the interests of a more general audience of anthropologists. The relationship with the more general audience is not straightforward because it is mediated by simplified, and usually outmoded, metonymic linkages—for example, India = hierarchy; Mediterranean = honour and shame; China = filial piety; Australia = marriage systems. In order to be heard beyond the limited specialisation, the ethnographer must use the language of the metropolitan theorising and sometimes struggle to transform it.

The ethnography–theory divide

Thus far I have been using 'theory' in a relatively unspecified way, which implies a worldwide mapping of cultural particularity that fits into a rather general scheme for explaining the human condition in all its cultural variety. 'Theory' also has a different sense, which is reflected in the accounts of the long history of anthropological reflection, in abstract terms, about what inspires and guides the questions that anthropologists seek to answer. Sherry Ortner's article 'Theory in Anthropology since the Sixties' (1984) is illustrative of both the language of these accounts and the underlying anxieties about being left behind in the metropolitan theoretical debates.[11] She identifies various constellations of ideas and personalities as 'schools': 'symbolic anthropology', 'cultural ecology', 'structuralism', 'structural Marxism', 'political economy', 'practice theory', and 'symbolic interactionism'. The chief metaphor of her account is one of succession: the different schools capture the imagination of anthropologists at a certain point, are imitated and tested, and, either because of their inherent weaknesses or because something more interesting comes along, they slide from prominence. Assumed progress is a related theme as successive theories are presented as an answer to the defects in previous ones.

One of the unexplored assumptions of Ortner's paper—taken up in one direction by Appadurai (1986)—is the location of this drama of the rise and fall of theoretical schools. Although her topic is theory, it is also a piece of participant observation. It describes the metropolis of the field of anthropology: the United States of America. In simple demographic terms, the United States, with its thousands of anthropologists and hundreds of university anthropology departments, is the centre (see *American Anthropological Association Directory*; and Jolly and Jamieson 2002:69). From this perspective, it could be argued that the Australianists and those specialising in Torres Strait Islander studies—most of whom are located in universities in Australia—are doubly peripheralised: first of all, because of the relatively small number of academics in the Australian regional specialisations; and, second, because of its geographic and social

11 Also see Ortner (2006).

distance from the current centre of anthropology.[12] The internationalisation of ideas through publication should enable a democratising of chances to participate in metropolitan theory from any global location in anthropology, but the sense of periphery continues (see Beckett 2002:128) and not only in Australia (see Ribeiro and Escobar 2006).

There is a countervailing tendency in describing the contemporary multiplication of possible theoretical approaches and it was also present in Ortner's review. This tendency is to evaluate what each new school or proposed theoretical paradigm can and cannot do. Behind such analyses lies the question of what is an adequate anthropological explanation. Pursuing that question leads off into the realms of the philosophy of social sciences, into which anthropologists rarely venture. Analogous to the evaluative approach are survey courses—such as 'Anthropological Approaches to the Study of Social Life'—which perhaps represent the current *modus vivendi* between the insistence on a canon of great anthropological theorists and a more complete epistemological egalitarianism implied in some postmodern critiques. One way of presenting the new *modus vivendi* in a positive way is as the ever-expanding theoretical tool kit of anthropology. This captures some of the flavour of the egalitarianism and hides the underlying anxiety; there is still a high price to be paid for appearing to be out of date in one's theoretical inspirations. As June Nash (1997) complained, '"-isms" quickly become "-wasms"'.

The pure–applied divide

In America, the pure–applied divide has become institutionalised in a number of ways: applied anthropologists have become involved in a wide variety of jobs, have long had their own separate professional organisation (now under the umbrella of the American Anthropological Association) and have their own journals.[13] In Australia, the small number of anthropologists means that a separate association for applied anthropologists would be unsustainable, and tensions

12 As a result of several brainstorming sessions with colleagues at The Australian National University and Internet searches, I estimate that there are approximately 80 Australianists and 10 specialists in Torres Strait Islanders in anthropology in the academy worldwide. This compares with 550 listed in the *American Anthropological Association Directory* as members of the Society for the Anthropology of Europe, 375 members of the Society for the Anthropology of North America, 300 members of the Association for Africanist Anthropology and 745 members of the Society for Latin American Anthropology.

13 Some of the history of applied anthropology in America is set out in Chapter 2 of John van Willigen's *Applied Anthropology: An Introduction* (1993). The Society for Applied Anthropology was established in 1941 as a separate organisation from the American Anthropological Association (AAA) and had its own journal, *Human Organisation*. It ultimately rejoined the AAA umbrella in 1971 (see Spicer 1976). There is now a parallel organisation called the National Association for the Practice of Anthropology, with its own journal, *Practicing Anthropology*. For a recent collection of papers on applied anthropology in Australia, see Toussaint and Taylor (1999). For reflections on anthropologists in policy development/evaluation roles, see Palmer (2001); Finlayson (2001); and Altman (2001). For an independent overview of similar work undertaken by the Centre for Aboriginal Economic Policy Research, see Rowse (2002).

between the different orientations tend to be played out within the Australian Anthropology Society around proposals for greater professionalisation of the association (Martin 2004). At a superficial level, the tensions could be seen as simply a difference in employment orientations: the pure orientation is towards the academy—the pursuit of knowledge for its own sake; the applied orientation is towards the practical problem to be resolved by the employing agency. There are also hybrid bodies such as the Centre for Aboriginal Economic Policy Research (CAEPR) at The Australian National University. This centre has a largely applied focus—mostly the evaluation of government programs and policies towards Aboriginal people—from within an academic setting and via original research (see Rowse 2002).

But the differences between the two orientations run deeper. Many applied anthropologists must acquire new analytical skills and methods outside the usual canon of anthropological theory in order to complete their tasks successfully. The subject matter and findings of applied research tend to be of a practical nature, and, in Bennett's words, might be 'considered thin or trite by scholars' (Bennett 1996:S28). Both these factors tend to distance applied anthropologists from academic anthropological discourse.

There is no logical reason why the applied–pure divide should coincide with the ethnography–theory divide. It is, however, plausible that those who predominantly work outside the academy would not have an interest in valorising metropolitan theory and could therefore conveniently align themselves with the position that ethnography is independent of theory.

While these tendencies could be seen simply as different specialisations within anthropology (academic and applied), hierarchies develop that make it difficult for an applied anthropologist to engage in occasional work in the academy, but allow the academic to take on consultancy work during the semester break. The sense of relegation is in evidence in the sharp response of applied anthropologists to suggestions from their academic colleagues that applied work is ultimately dependent on long-term participant-observation fieldwork (pure research).[14] It can also be seen in the doubts about whether ethnographic information collected in the course of applied work adds significantly to anthropological knowledge (see, for example, Morphy and Morphy 1984:46). The response typically asserts that the applied researchers are in fact at the cutting edge—for example, of 'change theory', in Bennett's response (Bennet 1996:S30; also see van Willigen 1993:x).

---

14 See anthropologist Rod Hagan's letter to the editor in *The Australian* (17 January 1996:10), and the reply to Professor Weiner entitled '"The Devil take Hindmarsh": a reply to Professor Weiner', which was signed by Julie Finlayson, David Martin and Diane Smith—all anthropologists at the Centre for Aboriginal Economic Policy Research at The Australian National University at the time. Unpublished, copy in possession of the author.

For the moment, it should be noted that, unlike much applied work, being an expert witness in a traditional land claim brings applied anthropologists and academic anthropologists directly into competition over the same canon of anthropological theory and the same ethnographic archive, focused on the claimants and their claim area. This is because one of the constituting issues of the Australianist specialisation within anthropology—well before land rights and native title—has been local organisation and traditional land tenure.

Intermediate reflection on 'scientific' capital

From these basic elements of anthropology—regional specialisation, increasingly complex and self-referential metropolitan theorising and the pure–applied divide—it is possible to begin to build up a picture of how 'scientific' capital is accumulated in contemporary anthropology. One way is to find some anthropological 'green fields' that reveal some new cultural variation and enable an exemplary ethnography of a new region to be written. More likely is the ethnography of an existing region that fills in a gap, by choosing either a new location within the region or a new topic within the region, especially if that topic is a recognised specialisation within anthropology (gender, art, music, and so on). Such ethnography should demonstrate knowledge of the existing specialist literature and position its own new contribution within the literature. More risky and rewarding is to challenge or attempt to overturn the previously accepted wisdom of the specialist literature. Hypothetically, being able to demonstrate specialist skill—the accurate deployment of the extensive, specialist literature and an original contribution to it—in more than one established region should increase 'scientific' capital.[15]

As Appadurai implies, the other method of accumulation is by linking a regional specialisation to contemporary issues in metropolitan theorising—for example, by demonstrating how a particular field situation allows a new twist on a theoretical question. Bourdieu's own career could be seen as the ultimate form of the strategy: a particular ethnographic location and historical juncture inspiring a new general theory of society that can be seen as addressing shortcomings in previous theorising—in his case, Lévi-Straussian structuralism.

If theory, variously defined, is a key element of anthropology then the logic of competition would indicate that specialising in theory would be another way to gain 'scientific' capital in anthropology—and the more complex, the better (see Bourdieu 2000:36). Because of the difficulties of establishing 'scientific' capital

15 What I have called a strategy for acquiring scientific capital bears many similarities to Basil Sansom's 'lodge rules' for choosing a field site (Sansom 1985).

from applied research, it would generally have to be avoided by those ambitious for advancement in the field of anthropology unless it was undertaken from a secure position within the academy.

Because of the nature of the case studies to follow, I have so far emphasised the individual within the regional specialisation as the locus of the accumulation of 'scientific' capital and its conversion into academic capital. But it has to be acknowledged that the department, containing an assortment of different regional specialists, is the more typical unit of day-to-day socialisation within the anthropological field. This is where the tensions between teaching, research and departmental administration are played out. Departments also exist in a hierarchical field of status as evidenced by the occasional claims of elitism within anthropology.[16] Thus, as well as individual social capital there is institutional capital that gives an automatic advantage to the individual faculty members in prestigious departments. Similar pervasive prestige hierarchies apply to the academic anthropological journals.

The field of anthropology within the broader social field

Australianist anthropology has a low public profile and uncertain public support. From the high point of the establishment of the Australian Institute for Aboriginal Studies in 1964–65 and the invitation to W. E. H. Stanner to deliver the nationally broadcast Boyer Lectures in 1968, the situation has become more fraught (cf. Hamilton 2003; Hinkson and Beckett 2008). The Hindmarsh Island affair—however unfairly—probably created a negative public perception of anthropology: the naive anthropologist accepting the existence of restricted traditional knowledge, which had been fabricated by Aboriginal people for their own ends.[17] Moreover, there has been the rise of what could be summarised as the anti-colonial (sometimes 'post-colonial') critique of anthropology coming from internal critics (Asad 1973), from disciplines in competition with anthropology (Attwood and Arnold 1992; Hodge and Mishra 1990; Muecke 1992; Wolfe 1999) and from Indigenous people themselves. Thus, the task of gaining legitimacy and public support has become more complex. Arguably, the most successful contemporary strategy has been anthropology's repositioning as curator, decipherer, historian and commentator on contemporary Indigenous

16 See, for example, the various papers from a panel on 'Elitism and Discrimination within Anthropology' held at the 1993 Society for Applied Anthropology (Baer 1995; Cassell 1995; Harrison 1995; Johnston 1995; Nader 1995; Paredes 1995; Singer 1995; Smith 1995; Tashima and Crain 1995).

17 See Bell (1998); Brunton (1996); Clarke (1996); Fergie (1996); Hemming (1996, 1997); Kenny (1996); Lucas (1996); Simons (2003); Tonkinson (1997); Weiner (1995, 1999, 2001, 2002). Later accounts by some of the key Aboriginal participants indicate that there was probably a diversity of honestly held Aboriginal views about the disputed area, rather than a simple fabrication by one group (see Rowse 2006).

art, particularly the internationally recognised Western Desert art movement. From the legitimacy/public support perspective, land rights and native title would seem to play a critical role. They provide the highest-profile work that most anthropologists will undertake. They might also align anthropology with Indigenous interests, at least superficially, and could therefore be seen as a partial answer to the anti-colonial critique. This context no doubt puts pressure on anthropologists to become advocates for the Indigenous claimants—a role antithetical to the expectations of independent experts in the juridical field. The degree to which anthropology has succumbed to this pressure has become one of the major fault lines in internal debates about applied anthropology both in the land rights and native title eras.[18]

Anthropologists who specialise in Torres Strait Islander studies face similar issues, some of which will be canvassed in the first case study on the *Mabo* hearing.

The juridical field

When anthropologists enter the witness box, they know they are at the heart of the very different social field of law; a boundary has been crossed. Even before agreeing to undertake research for a native title claim, there must be a reorientation towards a strange world where the mastery of academic social situations or the consulting practice is suddenly discounted. Practical mastery of the seminar, the academic conference, the corridor discussion, departmental administration, or, alternatively, in the consultancy practice, and practical mastery of dealing with clients and helping them solve their practical problems, all count for very little. What counts is the mastery of the rules of evidence and the legal doctrine of native title, and these are part of the professional repertoire of judges and lawyers.

The juridical field and the constitutional state

The juridical field is part of the larger apparatus of the constitutional state and modern law. The foundational sociological theorists of modernity tend to put modern law at the end of a long social-evolutionary process, at the opposite end of the spectrum to small-scale, tribal societies.[19] They point to the positivity of modern law—that is, its objectified, contingent and explicitly conventional

18 See, for example, Kolig (1982); Maddock (1998b, 1999); and Sutton (1995b).

19 Here I am principally thinking of Weber in Chapter VIII, 'Economy and law (the sociology of law)', in *Economy and Society* (Weber 1925), but the same assumption can be found in Durkheim's proposal of a direct link between forms of law and forms of solidarity (mechanical and organic) (see Cotterrell 1999; Durkheim 1893).

nature, as opposed to charismatic revelation through law prophets. They also point to the formulation of rights in terms of citizenship within the state rather than rights attaching to group membership, law's reliance on a legitimate political order, its systematisation into complete codes, its use of relatively rational methods of fact-finding, its administration by trained specialists (the legal profession) and separate enforcement institutions (police).

The designated role of the judiciary, within the constitutional state, is one of the interpretation of the constitution and the independent adjudication of disputes by the application of legal doctrines to factual situations. Notwithstanding the constitutional distinction between law interpreters (the judiciary) and law-makers (the legislature), and the longstanding reluctance of the courts to admit their law-making role, judges do share law-making responsibilities with the legislature, particularly in formulating common law doctrines, interpreting the constitution and interpreting vague legislative provisions. The legal doctrine of native title demonstrates some of the complexity of this shared responsibility.

This doctrine sprang into being belatedly, in 1992, with the High Court decision in *Mabo*.[20] That decision contains a number of slightly different formulations of native title, although two other judges supported Justice Brennan's judgment. Brennan stated that traditional laws and customs, which give a clan or group an entitlement to land, may be recognised by the common law of Australia, provided that the traditional laws continue to be acknowledged and traditional customs observed as far as is practicable. Some change in traditional laws and customs was allowable provided that the general nature of the traditional connection to the land had been maintained. Brennan conceived of native title as a communal title. Despite inconsistent terminology in his judgment, he seemed to be pitching the legally relevant group—the native title-holders—at the intermediate level of the 'clan or group' (sometimes 'community, clan or group'). Membership of such a group was envisaged as depending on biological descent, mutual recognition and a system of traditional authority. Above the intermediate level was 'a people' who shared the same traditional laws and customs, and lower than the intermediate level were individuals (sometimes 'individuals and subgroups'), who exercised rights under the group's communal native title.

More recently, in the *Yorta Yorta* case in 2002, the terminology of 'normative system' and 'society' was introduced.[21] 'Normative system' appears to be a way of emphasising the need to demonstrate the obligatory nature of the relevant traditional laws and customs. The requirement to demonstrate a continuous 'society', out of which the relevant native-title groups and their traditional laws

20 *Mabo v Queensland (No. 2)* (1992) 175 CLR 1.

21 *Yorta Yorta v Victoria* 214 CLR 422.

arose, is a little more confusing. On the one hand it seems to be a restatement of Brennan's formulation, but on the other, it seems to cut across his distinction between his intermediate group and the higher level of 'a people' (Burke 2010). In any event, the effect of the *Native Title Act 1993* (Cwlth) (the *Native Title Act*) was to give back to the courts the problem of specifying the nature and extent of native title rights in Australia, case by case, in the usual adversary system of civil litigation—in other words, in the juridical field.

The core of the juridical field comprises judges, lawyers and, at lower levels, witnesses, performing their roles in a court case. This activity has a formal aspect recorded in court documents, transcripts and reasons for decision, and a less accessible informal dimension. The informal aspect would include the judge's private thought processes, corridor discussions with court staff, other judges and counsel appearing for the parties, discussions among the parties and their lawyers about the strategy of their case, the proofing of witnesses and what knowledge the lawyers might have gleaned about the idiosyncrasies of the judge, gossip, scuttlebutt and unflattering nicknames. Bourdieu includes legal academics in his description of the French juridical field, where he defines the field in terms of competition between judges, lawyers and legal academics over the creation of authoritative legal propositions.

But the judge really does not have to compete. The judge is in a position to pick and choose which propositions from academic commentary to accept. In Australia, especially after *Mabo*, judges have been relatively impervious to academic commentary about native title. New elaborations of native title doctrine tend to arise more directly from the professional competition of the adversarial process, in which new arguments can largely be understood as attempts by claimants to enlarge and strengthen the doctrine of native title and attempts by respondents to restrict it, and impose procedural orthodoxy via strict application of the rules of evidence. In this structured competition it is easy to see how the opposing sides could see 'normative system' and 'society' as simply a restatement of *Mabo* or, alternatively, as the addition of stricter requirements of proof.

At the higher levels of the juridical field—particularly the High Court and the Full Federal Court—the influence of decisions spreads outwards to related activities and fields, in a ripple effect, influencing the way in which lawyers advise their clients about native title, how governments formulate administrative guidelines for so-called 'connection reports' in lieu of contested hearings and how all parties make calculations in mediation and settlement negotiations—in short, what happens in the juridical field spreads to the legal shadow lands. At lower levels of the juridical field decisions about the application of native title doctrine tend to remain within the bubble of the particular case and its direct participants, although decisions about procedural issues might have a ripple effect too, through being carefully collected by legal practitioners as resources for procedural tussles in future cases.

Law-finding

Essentialist descriptions of the juridical field have long been made under the rubric of 'juristic thought and legal values'. Campbell (1974), for example, drew on Weber and others, to define juristic thought as

- an attitude of acceptance of the law as it is—in other words, limiting itself to the question of whether a proposition is a law or not (sometimes referred to as legal science)
- the use of abstract propositions conceived of as constituting part of a complete system
- a mode of persuasion that is rational but not conclusive in a logical sense
- a practical orientation towards making a decision and giving reasons
- particularistic, as opposed to the search for general rules—a process of matching complex factual situations with existing laws
- retrospective in orientation.

Another attempt to uncover the workings of the juridical field was through the close logical analysis of appellate decisions. This approach dates back to a remarkable intellectual movement in jurisprudence known as American Realism, which was sceptical of the denial of judicial creativity in legal doctrine and revealed widespread leeway and choices made by appellate judges (see Twining 1973). These so-called 'rule-sceptics' demonstrated a quite different aspect of law to Weber's broad-brush identification of modern law with occidental rationality (see Weber 1925:vol. 2, ch. 8).

While the focus of this book will be on fact-finding at the trial level, the way in which the legal doctrine of native title has been formulated impinges directly on that task. For the trial judge must adopt an attitude of acceptance of the doctrine and of the obligation to bring a case to a reasoned conclusion in the face of three major areas of indeterminacy: the precise nature of the group that holds the communal native title and the 'society' out of which that group arose; which practices and beliefs relating to land can be called 'traditional laws and customs'; and what degree of change of tradition is acceptable.[22]

In the field of the academy, there are ongoing debates in the sub-specialisation of 'primitive law' and its successors, 'legal anthropology', 'comparative law'

22 For an analysis of the indeterminacy of similar concepts in Canadian jurisprudence see Connolly (2006).

and 'legal pluralism' about whether law is a useful category for cross-cultural analysis. From the perspective of the academy, the High Court's native title doctrine takes a strong stand on one side of the academic debate. By judicial fiat it proclaimed an end to the discussion in the juridical field by institutionalising legal pluralism/primitive law in the doctrine of native title. Henceforth, for the trial judge, it became a question of finding those laws and customs in the facts of a case, not whether it was a feasible intellectual project.

It would be theoretically possible for the judge—either privately or in the course of the hearing—to seek in the philosophy of law, jurisprudence, sociology or anthropology some further specification of the indeterminate native title concepts. Tamanaha (1995), for example, refers to the anthropological literature that could be utilised to make a coherent distinction between 'laws' and 'customs'. 'Laws' could be confined to institutionalised norms—that is, those that have become objectified and named by the people of the society, and involve predictable procedures and enforcement. 'Customs' would then be the implicit norms that have no folk objectification but might become objectified in ethnography.

Similarly, it would be theoretically possible for the judge to draw upon the debates in legal anthropology to give a further specification to the combined phrase 'traditional laws and customs'. That phrase itself seems to arise out of a particular colonial and academic project associated with indirect rule in Africa and the attempt to integrate native courts into newly independent African states and hence the need to describe the traditional laws and customs that would be integrated (Roberts 1979:192–6). While this particular project might not have led to much reflection on the nature of law, the sub-discipline as a whole was involved in trying to craft a definition of law that would be applicable to all societies, including hunter-gatherer societies, and these efforts would seem to be particularly apposite to native title. For example, Hoebel in *The Law of Primitive Man* (1954:28) suggested that 'a social norm is legal if its neglect or infraction is regularly met, in threat or in fact, by the application of physical force by an individual or group possessing the socially recognised privilege for so acting'.

Adopting this kind of definition would lead to inquiries about social norms, enforcement of norms and authority.

In judgment writing, however, any explicit attempt to further define native title legal doctrine by reference to other bodies of knowledge would offend against the fundamental rule that legal doctrine must be sourced in legislation and the pronouncements of superior courts. Violation of this fundamental rule would risk a successful appeal on the basis that the judge misdirected himself or herself on the law of native title. This is why judgments in native title hearings typically commence with a formulation of the legal doctrine of native title drawn exclusively from the *Native Title Act* and the pronouncements of the High Court, then move directly to dealing with the typically voluminous transcript of the evidence of the claimants and experts and documentary evidence. It is also why the opportunity to clarify the phrase 'traditional laws and customs', by distinguishing law from custom, has not been taken up and remains, paradoxically, a unitary concept, at least in formal legal doctrine. This is not to say that there can never be an explicit engagement with other formal bodies of knowledge in the juridical field. But, like someone going into the library of another discipline and taking a book off the shelf at random, there will likely be a lack of comprehensive engagement (cf. Cotterrell 1986).

Fact-finding

The work of the judge at the trial level has long been conceived of as the application of law to facts. The formal institutions of forensic fact-finding could be summarised as follows

- pre-trial refinement of issues through the particulars of the statement of claim/application, the filing of defences by respondents and procedures for requiring further and better particulars (the pleadings)
- the hearing of witness testimony under threat of prosecution for lying
- rules of evidence aimed at adducing the most reliable evidence by excluding hearsay and opinions
- procedures for testing witness testimony in cross-examination.

When considering the fact-finding work of the judge, the legal doctrine of the fundamental distinction between fact and law must be acknowledged, but not taken at face value. The legal conception of a 'fact' tends to bypass the issues of the linguistically mediated nature of most evidence (see Jackson 1988:73) and the perennial philosophical difficulties with such a concept (see, for example, Hacking 1999:80–4). Instead, there is an unarticulated assumption or commonsense stance of the accessibility of the reality-in-itself of the fact.

The sceptical critique of appellate rule finding in American Realism was accompanied by a parallel scepticism about fact-finding, particularly in Jerome Frank's classic *Courts on Trial* (1949). What gives that book a lasting influence, aside from its debunking exuberance, is the fact that Frank himself was a senior judge. That fact cloaks the whole book with a confessional authenticity.

For Frank, the explanation of judicial process as the application of law to facts is nothing but a myth. Like the historian, the judge reconstructs the past from second-hand reports—the fallible sensory data of witnesses. Facts are guesses on which basic legal rights depend. He draws on the account of magic in Malinowski and Benedict to argue that the judicial process is nothing more than modern legal magic demonstrated by

- its pretensions to be able to see into the mind of another person
- its obfuscation of reality and projection of the mystique of the legal process by using ideal images of the judicial process in explaining itself to the public
- its denial of the extent of judicial discretion and social pressures operating unconsciously on the judge.

Frank's account is one of strategic judicial behaviour that is difficult to access because of the judge's mastery of the legal doctrines about admissible evidence and the giving of reasons that insulate a decision against successful appeal.[23]

Frank also drew on the language of Gestalt psychology to explain how frequently judges form an overall impression about a witness or a 'hunch' about the best result in a particular case. The judge's attention to the facts is then organised around supporting this overall impression or hunch. Although in Frank's experience this 'hunching' is ubiquitous, it is also contrary to the established norms of avoiding prejudgment of the facts, avoiding bias and contrary to the expectation of a methodical and even-handed approach to the resolution of disputed facts. Thus, there is a resistance to translate the Gestalt view about the preferred result into written reasons for decision. Instead, with the professional knowledge of the norms of judicial fact-finding and, with an eye to the appeal court, the judge formulates the written reasons in accordance with those norms, sometimes referring to an assessment of the demeanour of witnesses, which is obviously unavailable to the appeal court (Frank 1949:165–85).[24]

---

23 To support this proposition, he gives rare anecdotal evidence of explanations that judges have subsequently made to him about cases in which he was involved. For example:

> I will never forget one of my experiences as a young lawyer. I participated in a lawsuit, lasting a week, tried by an able trial judge without a jury. During the course of the trial, on every doubtful question concerning the admission or exclusion of evidence, the judge, to my great indignation, ruled in favour of the other side. To my surprise, a few weeks after the trial ended, the judge decided the case in my client's favor, with strong findings of fact. A year later I met the judge who referred to the case, saying: 'You see, on the first day of the trial, I made up my mind that the defendant, your client, was a fine, hard-working woman who oughtn't to lose all her property to the plaintiff, who had plenty of money. The plaintiff was urging a legal rule which you thought was wrong. I thought it was legally right, but very unjust, and I didn't want to apply it. So I made up my mind to lick the plaintiff on the facts. And by giving him every break on procedural points during the trial, and by using in my opinion the legal rule he urged, I made it impossible for him to reverse me on appeal, because, as the testimony was oral and in conflict, I knew the upper court would never upset my findings of fact.' That judicial conduct was not commendable. But the judge's story did open my eyes to the way in which the power of a trial judge to find the facts can make his decision final, even if, had he correctly stated his honest notion of the facts, his decision would have been reversed for error in applying the wrong legal rule. (Frank 1949:168–9)

24 For a realist critique of the evaluation of evidence using the demeanour of the witness, see Wellborn (1990–91).

Apart from Frank's challenge to the pretensions of forensic fact-finding, it is also clear from the examination of typical judicial processes that facts are moulded by legal doctrine and the trial process. For example, the legal doctrine of native title—particularly such concepts as 'communal title', 'traditional laws and customs', 'normative system', 'society' and 'continuing traditional connection'—guide the formulation and organisation of all the potential evidence that could be adduced, as does the list of rights in the proposed determination of native title.

Law and scientific expertise

In legal doctrine, expert evidence is characterised as exceptional because of its privileged exemption from the general rule restricting witnesses' evidence to what they saw or heard, rather than their opinions. The doctrine depends on the court's acceptance that the witness has specialised knowledge based on training, study or experience and that the opinions are based on that knowledge.[25] This wide Australian formulation allows for a variety of experts, although, in practice, expertise broadly overlaps with academic disciplines or professions based on the sciences or scientific methodology. This fundamental reliance on the institutions of science is reflected in the US law that refers to 'scientific, technical, or other specialised knowledge'.[26] Thus, judicial anxieties, pronouncements and guidelines, as well as academic commentary, tend to address the scientific expert and the interaction of science and law.

The general judicial anxiety is that experts tend to favour the parties who call them, especially if they have been requested to conduct new research specifically designed to resolve an issue in the case—disparagingly called 'research for litigation'.[27] In the United States of America, this anxiety was expressed by legal commentators as a concern to keep 'junk science' out of the courtroom and led to a readjustment of American legal doctrine about experts by the US Supreme Court in *Daubert v Merrell Dow* in 1993.[28] The judge was thereafter required to perform a gatekeeping role, evaluating the reliability of the scientific evidence using some factors that scientists themselves might use in evaluating their

25 See s. 79, *Evidence Act 1995* (Cwlth).

26 The relevant part of the US Federal Rules of Evidence states: 'If scientific, technical, or other specialised knowledge will assist the trier of fact to understand the evidence or to determine a fact in issue, a witness qualified as an expert by knowledge, skill, experience, training or by education may testify thereto in the form of an opinion or otherwise' (Rule 702).

27 The pervasive concerns about the bias of experts were recently confirmed by questionnaire research with Australian magistrates and judges (see Freckelton et al. 1999, 2001).

28 For the 'junk science' debate, see Huber's *Galileo's Revenge: Junk Science in the Courtroom* (1991); Bernstein's 'Junk Science in the United States and the Commonwealth' (1996); Black et al.'s 'Science and law in the wake of *Daubert*: a new search for scientific knowledge' (1994); Edmond and Mercer's 'Keeping "junk" history, philosophy and sociology of science out of the courtroom' (1997); and other references cited by Edmond and Mercer (1997:49–50).

colleagues' work, such as testability (falsifiability), peer review and publication, and the known or potential error rate. It was this move towards a more 'internal' scientific perspective that its critics saw as a discredited and naive attempt to formulate ideals or norms of scientific practice.

The most trenchant critics drew on the social-constructionist critique of the pretensions of science to demonstrate the enormous gap between the ideal criteria adopted by the US Supreme Court and the reality of scientific practice with its diversity, personal interests in research outcomes, secrecy, entrenched social networks and more circumspect claims about the benefits of peer review (Edmond and Mercer 1997).[29] Moreover, they argued that the prominence given to falsifiability as a key indicator of science—taken directly from the Popperian philosophy of science—ignores debates within that discipline that pose serious and widely accepted challenges to the centrality of falsifiability.

The unmasking of the pretensions of science becomes the unmasking of the authority of the judge. The judge who puts his faith in ideal images of science has no clothes. This, it is implied, allows a re-examination of what the judge is really doing. Jasanoff (1995:214), for example, sees the law's uncritical ideas of science as a concealment of its own jealous guarding of the power of courts to declare what counts as science for the purposes of law. As heirs to the realist tradition, she and others tend to see the wide leeway given to the judge by legal doctrine that is formulated with a high degree of generality or which contains contradictory elements. Contradictory elements allow different judges to emphasise different aspects of the doctrine to arrive at the desired result. Thus the *Daubert* formulation is not seen as absolutely determinative of a new approach to judicial decision making about scientific evidence, but more as a resource that a judge could deploy to justify a particular exclusion or inclusion of evidence.

What does this mean for the reception of anthropological evidence in Australia? Although legal doctrine in Australia about experts has not yet followed the American lead, it might be moving in that direction (Edmond and Mercer 1997). The Australian legal formulations of identifying areas of expertise have emphasised general acceptance by the scientific community but have also used the terminology of 'reliable body of knowledge'. More intrusive, *Daubert*-like criteria might enter Australian jurisprudence in the general rubric of reliability (see Freckleton and Selby 2009:ch. 4). More to the point, though, is that, in the juridical field, all expertise, including anthropological expertise, is likely to be viewed through the lens of ideal images of science. Compared with the specialist

29 In referring to the social-constructionist critique of the pretensions of science (see, for example, Latour and Woolgar 1979; Woolgar 1988), I am not necessarily aligning myself with it. There is also a valid critique of the pretensions of social constructionism: see Bohman (1991:ch. 3); and Hacking (1999:63–99).

jurisdiction of the Aboriginal Land Commissioner under the *Land Rights Act*, where virtually all experts were anthropologists, in the native title era, the anthropologist is just one kind of expert appearing before Federal Court judges. While addressing all experts, the rules and guidelines for expert witnesses tend to assume the scientific expert as a paradigmatic case (see Cooper 1997–98; Edmond 2004).

There is no in-principle decision in legal doctrine about whether anthropology should be regarded as a science. Accordingly, a question for this book is whether, in native title, the ideal of anthropological expertise will be modelled directly on ideals of scientific expertise or whether new ideal images will emerge to take account of anthropology's non-experimental methodology. In other words, will anthropological research for claims be rejected as 'junk anthropology'?

It might be possible to refine this question further because there has already been some harsh criticism of evidence given by anthropologists who have not done fieldwork with the claimant group. It could be hypothesised that, instead of ideal images of science, judges will utilise ideal images of anthropological methodology, perhaps forming around long-term fieldwork and all that it implies—intimate and extensive knowledge based on immersion in the society—as an evaluative criterion. This hypothesis is all the more likely as such methodology is not necessarily at odds with empirical ideals, even though it can never emulate the specifics of experimental methodology in the physical sciences. The question to be considered in the case studies, then, is what images of ideal anthropological research can be constructed from the judicial praise and criticism of the evidence of anthropologists and how those images relate to the idealised images of scientific expertise.

Legal habitus

To conclude this account of the juridical field, it is necessary to balance the sceptical critiques of fact-finding and ideal images of science with some of the constraints on judges. The sceptical critiques emphasise the wide leeway that judges have in formulating facts and in deploying vague or conflicting legal doctrines. These critiques tend to overemphasise the free agency of the judge and assume that all judges take a strong view of the most desirable outcome. It is equally plausible that the fortunes of the claimants' case rise and fall as the evidence unfolds—rising when the claimants' evidence is first presented, then falling when it is undermined by cross-examination or by the contradictory evidence of other witnesses. There are also the constraints of what Bourdieu (1987:833) calls the legal habitus 'shaped through legal studies and the practice of the legal profession on the basis of a kind of common familial experience'. Legal habitus incorporates Llewellyn's (1960) idea of steadying factors, such as an influential period style of judgment writing, which provides some predictability amid wide judicial discretion. Others have referred to it as the influence of the 'legal interpretive community' (Fish 1980; Niblett 1992). These shared values and experience tend to fill in the gaps left by formal legal doctrines, such as the actual standards of procedural fairness and courtesy in a hearing and the degree of reflexiveness expected in judgment writing, especially when justifying critical findings of fact.

Theorising the interaction of the social fields

Conceiving of anthropological expert testimony as an aspect of the interaction of specialised social fields enables a move beyond the centrality of Maddock's tension between independence and advocacy to a more complex explanation (see Maddock 1980a, 1998c, 1999)—for there are many ways of theorising this interaction.

Forming gestalt views of the other field

Frank's theorising about judicial fact-finding involving gestalts, in the sense of global assessments or hunches about witnesses and desirable outcomes, is suggestive of each field forming totalising assessments about the other. One particular example of this kind of assessment would be the decision facing the court in the first assertion of anthropological expertise in the juridical field in Australia in the *Gove Land Rights Case* in 1972.[30]

While in legal doctrine such decisions must be made afresh in each case, there is a sense in which the first acceptance of expertise in the field of anthropology makes it less contentious in subsequent cases. More generally, I have extrapolated from the science–law literature to predict the formation of ideal images of the anthropologist by judges. The corollary of this prediction is the adoption of ideal images of law and legal procedures in the field of anthropology.

---

30 The predicament of the trial judge in assessing expertise was captured by Justice Blackburn in the *Gove Land Rights Case*:

> In such a matter, it seems to me, there can be no precise rules. The court is expected to rule on qualifications of an expert witness, relying partly on what the expert himself explains, and partly on what is assumed, though seldom expressed, namely that there exists a general framework of discourse in which it is possible for the court, the expert and all men according to the degree of education, to understand each other. Ex hypothesi this does not extend to the interior scope of the subject which the expert professes. But it is assumed that the judge can sufficiently grasp the nature of the expert's field of knowledge, and thus decide whether the expert has sufficient experience of a particular matter to make his evidence admissible. The process involves an exercise of personal judgment on the part of the judge, for which authority proves little help. (*Milirrpum v Nabalco Pty Ltd* (1971) 17 FLR 141 at 160)

Swallowing

Luhmann's theory of law as an autopoietic system offers another model of interaction (Luhmann 1985:ch. 2; Teubner 1988, 1993). The autonomous, self-reproducing system of law recognises anthropology as part of its environment. When the law interacts with anthropology, however, it is not in a dialogue, but an act of digestion, in which law converts anthropology into what it needs for its own functioning. Thus anthropological knowledge is converted into a legal fact that sits alongside other facts, which are assembled by the judge into findings of fact, eventually reproducing law's unique binary code: native title/not native title. Free anthropology becomes enslaved and transformed into law's anthropology. The same conclusion could also be derived from the general asymmetries of power and status between the two fields and the relative inaccessibility of technical legal discourse.

Collusion and sharing responsibility

Bourdieu's passing reference to expert witnesses in 'The force of law' (1987) is suggestive of another way of looking at the interaction: collusion. In that article, it was the collusion of the professionals involved in dispute resolution who, through neutralising language, produce a misrecognition of the arbitrary and constructed nature of its pronouncements as autonomous and impartial. The science–law literature is also suggestive here, although the word 'collusion' is not used. It is more that judges look to science to share the burden of responsibility for difficult decisions, such as a costly finding of negligence against a powerful corporation. A finding that native title exists is similarly a costly finding against the interests of the state. Accordingly, in cases of positive findings, judges might accentuate the independence, professionalism and scientific nature of the expert anthropological testimony.

Competition

In *The System of Professions: An Essay on the Division of Expert Labour* (1988), Abbott argues that the chief organising principle among different professions is competition over the 'ownership' of a particular social problem. This proposition is suggestive of competition between anthropologists and legal experts, for example, over who is best able to discover and describe traditional laws and customs. Such competition typically emerges between anthropologists and lawyers about the best way to formulate the claim, particularly the key indeterminate concepts. In the juridical field of native title—more so than under the *Land Rights Act*—anthropology is structurally on the losing side of this competition.

The competition between archaeologists, historians and linguists, on the one hand, and anthropologists, on the other, is more amenable to Abbott's principal idea. In practice, under the *Land Rights Act*, the anthropologist was responsible for synthesising archaeological, historical, linguistic and anthropological knowledge into a claim book. In the native title era, aided by stricter policing of the legal doctrines restricting experts to their own field of expertise, archaeologists, historians and linguists have been able to carve out their fields from the synthesising dominance of anthropology.[31] This restriction suggests another possible aspect of collusion: anthropology enlisting law against its rivals to maintain its dominant position among the social sciences relevant to native title.

Notwithstanding these incursions, the scope of anthropology makes it the only discipline that can assert an overlap with all the issues facing the native title judge. This competitive overlap between expert and judge was originally subject to the conceptually confused legal doctrine requiring experts to somehow avoid addressing 'the ultimate issue' that is rightfully the sole prerogative of the judge. The doctrine, which was still applicable at the time of the *Mabo* hearing, has since been abolished in all federal matters including native title but seems to linger on in the legal habitus of some barristers who continue to object on this ground in native title matters.[32]

Hysteresis

In *Pascalian Meditations*, Bourdieu claimed that he had been misinterpreted by his critics and stated that he never intended habitus to be an inflexible concept based on a principle of repetition and conservation. Rather it should be seen as constantly changing and subject to mismatches, discordance and misfiring, especially when new situations are confronted (Bourdieu 2000:159–63). The constant mismatch of habitus and circumstance is the fate of the *parvenu* and the *déclassé*. In a similar way it could be anticipated that the academic habitus is subject to misfiring or hysteresis in the juridical field. An example of this, suggested by Professor Nicolas Peterson,[33] is the neophyte anthropological

31 For the claims of history, see Paul and Gray (2003); linguistics, Henderson and Nash (2002); and archaeology, Lilley (2000). Also see McCalman and McGrath (2003).

32 See Freckelton and Selby (2009:ch. 7).

33 Personal communication, 2004. Peterson is currently a Professor of Anthropology at the School of Archaeology and Anthropology at The Australian National University and has had a long career in Australianist anthropology. He has been a key figure in debates about traditional Aboriginal land tenure and an influential applied practitioner including involvement in the Woodward inquiry into land rights in the Northern Territory and involvement in numerous land claims in the Northern Territory and in native title claims (see, for example, Peterson 1976, 1983, 1985; Peterson and Long 1986).

expert witness, who, as if defending his/her conclusions at an academic seminar, steadfastly refuses to make any, even minor, concessions during cross-examination, thus giving the impression of inflexibility and bias.

A Bourdieuian perspective, or any simple class perspective, would also predict that those experts who occupy a similar social position to the judge—either because of their inherited social capital or because of their high academic and 'scientific' capital—would perform better because of their social 'ease'. Such experts might also receive a better hearing as the judge recognises 'one of his own'. Similarly, 'learning the game' of the juridical field through repeated appearances should reduce the hysteresis effect through the modification of the habitus.

Another implication of Bourdieu's insistence on the fundamental relevance of the relative positioning of law and the social sciences in the field of the university and in the wider social field is a possible underlying resentment in the courtroom confrontation. Law's position in the university field depends largely on its relevance to the reproduction of the temporal order, whereas, in Bourdieu's exposition, sociology must rely on its own limitless ambition to be able to explain all aspects of society, including law. Therefore, the appearance as an expert witness might for some involve a frustrating subservience, even if for a short time, to a discipline of inferior intellectual ambition.

Conclusion on theorising the interaction of fields

To what extent do these conflicting possibilities have to be resolved before proceeding? A partial resolution is to acknowledge the pervasiveness of asymmetrical power between the fields; anthropology has to submit to law, anthropology's ideal images of law do not matter and hysteresis effects are predominately of the anthropologist in the foreign juridical field. Yet, collusion and the sharing of responsibility also seem plausible. Moreover, both fields exist within broader societal entanglements exemplified in the ongoing need for legitimacy and public support.

I have come to the conclusion that it is not necessary at this stage to finally resolve the contradictory aspects of the preceding characterisations. They can be seen simply as alternative framing devices through which to consider the particular case studies. The question of which framing devices provide the most adequate explanation will be considered in the concluding chapter.

Judge and anthropologist as knowledgeable, reflexive actors

As human actors form the medium of the interaction of anthropology and law in native title, the question arises of how to conceptualise and describe the relationship between individual actors and both legal and anthropological corpora that the judge and expert witness are expected to draw on in performing their roles in the highly structured legal context of a court case. The challenge is to find a way through an encounter thick with rules and expectations that can adequately represent individual choices—one that does not fall into a naive voluntarism or a total subservience to structure.

Bourdieu's theory of practice has been an obvious place to start because of its self-conscious attempt to overcome the structure–agency dichotomy. He characterised his theory of practice as a middle course between the extreme of Lévi-Straussian structuralism and the extreme of agency represented by Sartre's existentialism. Bourdieu's resolution tends to be in terms of a variable but very limited scope for strategic action, within external constraints, and zero scope in certain instances, when dispositions are completely reducible to those external constraints (Bourdieu 1990:50). In the Bourdieuian social universe, this is frequently the case as people's expectations and desires are continually adjusted to their capacity to satisfy them, given the objective chances of a particular social positioning (see Bourdieu 2000:216–18).

The macro-structural constraints of social and economic class are brought into the face-to-face social situation via the habitus of learned dispositions. The most effective and controlling dispositions are those assumptions that are so widely accepted that they become part of a background commonsense. In this way, the arbitrary is misrecognised as natural—a process Bourdieu describes as symbolic violence because of the role it plays in domination. Interactions in a social field are also governed by different degrees of social competence and one's position in the social field, which is variable according to levels of accumulated material and symbolic capital. Instead of leaving structures at the abstract level of universal structures of the mind, symbolic structures are conceived of as embedded at the level of unconscious dispositions, which tends to structure interactions and thereby reproduce those very dispositions.

Another way Bourdieu avoids voluntarism is by emphasising the quick reactions to the field that depend on an implicit practical mastery, as opposed to the plodding, explicit nature of academic knowledge. Practical mastery—having a feel for the game of a particular social field—entails the exclusion of detachment and reflection. The logic of practice is the ability to organise all thoughts and perceptions by means of a few generative principles. In the immediate world of practical mastery, rigour is always sacrificed for simplicity, since a fuzzy generality is always easier to master. Theorising makes explicit the workings of thought, whereas practice excludes all formal concerns and understands only in order to act.

Bourdieu's emphasis on struggle, competition and the implicit rules of practical mastery has led some to suggest that his theory of practice speaks more to small-scale societies such as the Kabyle than to our own (see, for example, Bohman 1999:159–63). It is more likely that his work was a deliberate corrective to what he saw as the inadequacies of the dominant structuralist theoretical approaches of the day. While Bourdieu's ideas have been useful in describing the two fields under consideration in this book, they downplay the mediation of social interaction by language. The properties of language and the social aspects of speech acts have long been the concern of symbolic interactionism (see Mead 1934), ethno-methodology (Garfinkle 1967) and in Habermas's elaborate *The Theory of Communicative Action* (1984, 1987). What can be taken from these works is that it is the ability to imagine another person's position or the implicit validity claims in another's proposition, and to confirm it through objectifying language, that enables the development of an inter-subjectively shared life-world, with its stocks of objectified knowledge and the possibility of coordinated action.[34]

What we are dealing with in expert anthropological witnesses is an orientation towards a stock of objectified knowledge that has come into being through institutionalised reflexivity in the academy. In the courtroom drama of the presentation and reception of expert evidence, while the informal rules of the game remain in the background, the formal rules can easily be made explicit—for example, through challenges to the form of testimony based on legal doctrines of evidence. The judge's reasons for decision also require a high level of reflexivity about the formalities of what counts as a fact and what counts as law.

34 In making this move from practice theory to reflective social actors, I am aware that I am placing side by side strongly repelling theoretical perspectives—like holding together magnets of opposite polarity. Bourdieu was scornful of the possibilities of action orientated solely towards mutual understanding—the centrepiece of Habermas's magnum opus, *The Theory of Communicative Action* (1984, 1987)—as if it was an attempt to pretend that one could escape and stand outside the social world (Bourdieu 2000:65–7). But it is not necessary to read Habermas that way. All subjectivity is constructed in society and is relational in character. To focus on individual reflective actors is not to deny inter-subjectivity, only to momentarily bracket it. In native title claims there are a variety of reflexive moments arising out of quite different circumstances: the anthropologist's report, the anthropologist's answers to questions in cross-examination, the judge's written reasons for decision, reflections of the participants after the case, and so on. The different circumstances allow for varying degrees of critical distance. Having said that, a practice theory perspective is a salutary reminder of an implicit hierarchy in which academic research is assumed to be the apex of critical distance rather than the culturally positioned interaction of habitus and academic social field.

The medium of language and the possibility of reflexivity do not automatically overcome habitus or class position.[35] But it does mean that, to varying degrees, anthropologists are able to acquire some understanding of the legal doctrines involved in native title and the way in which the judge is likely to approach the task of fact-finding. It would then be possible for the anthropologist to compare the very different circumstances of the production of academic knowledge about the claimants. Finally, it would be possible for the anthropologist to conceive of the task of the anthropological expert witness as involving a deconstruction of the anthropological archive and its reassembly in terms that are relevant to the judge's task—that is, without for the moment overlaying it with the strong strategic action of the advocate.

An idealised model

This deconstruction/reconstruction process is also suggestive of a fundamental triangulation of the task of the expert anthropologist in native title (Figure 1.1).

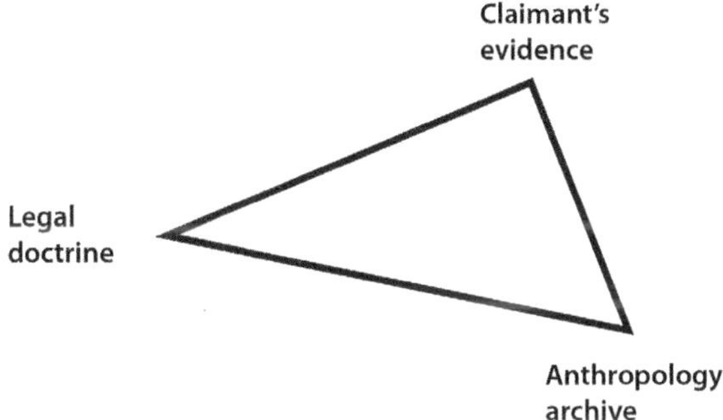

Figure 1.1 Idealised model of anthropological agency

It should be noted that this triangulation also describes the task of the claimants' lawyer—an indication that competition between the claimants' lawyer and the anthropologist will be an ongoing structural problem.[36] The triangle does not so adequately represent the judge's task, which, to oversimplify, is the resolution

35 Indeed, Bourdieu would probably see it the other way around—that is, that language incorporates and reproduces habitus and position within the social field (see Bourdieu 1991).

36 In a commentary on the US Indian Claims Commission process, Dobyns outlined two contrasting styles of lawyers:

> 1. Litigation directors who relegate the expert anthropologist to a service position of filling evidentiary gaps in the lawyer's theory of the case.
>
> 2. Team-leaders, who actively engage with the expert, explaining the legal requirements and seeking their advice on all aspects of the case. (Dobyns 1978)

One theory of the transition from land rights to native title would be of anthropologists having to cope with the change in their relationship with lawyers from the team-leader approach (land rights) to the litigation-director approach (native title).

of the two poles: legal doctrines and facts. In reality, the trial judge must also keep an eye to the appeal court and to public acceptance of the legitimacy of the judgment.

The anthropologist must manage this triangulation in a way that achieves maximum compatibility between the three elements, while projecting expert independence. One way of achieving this, without compromising the increasing theoretical complexity in the field of the academy, would be to confront interpretative indeterminacy directly, as in Bohman's approach to the philosophy of the social sciences (Bohman 1991).

In effect, this approach would mean saying that there is a complex, heterogeneous world of Aboriginal people, which anthropologists have sought to investigate and, inevitably, construct according to different theoretical approaches. The resulting archive and the claimants' evidence can be reconstituted and reinterpreted in a variety of ways, including ways that are relevant to the judge's task of assembling facts relevant to native title doctrine by

- explicitly discussing the consequences of choosing the title-holding group or the relevant 'society' from among the available groupings
- outlining the ways in which the traditional practices and objectifications in relation to land are law-like and the ways in which they are not law-like
- describing how current relations to land could be seen as continuous with pre-contact traditions and the ways in which they could be seen as discontinuous.

For ease of reference, this approach will be labelled the robust academic model—'robust' because of the strong conviction required to pursue it against typical expectations that the facts will always favour one interpretation over another and that the expert's role is to authoritatively resolve indeterminacies. It is also intellectually more robust in not pretending that there is always an easy fit between ethnography and legal doctrine.

Such an expert report would have the effect of throwing the responsibility for resolving central indeterminacies back onto the court. That this logical, if confronting, solution is rarely taken up is a further indication that there are triangulation decisions constantly being made, even though such decisions are difficult to uncover. These decisions are also based, either explicitly or implicitly, on some notion of the ideal expert witness and some positive ideal of the discipline that provides the expert with cultural capital.

Methodology

The subtle agency of individual anthropologists in the highly constrained situation of preparing expert reports and giving evidence in native title claims can be revealed only by a detailed analysis of the relevant anthropological archive, how it is reconstructed and how it is received in particular cases. An original review of the relevant anthropological archive will be undertaken, guided by Bourdieu (1988) (professional collusion and the game of the academy), Fardon (1990) and others (the historical development of regional specialisations in a dialectic with metropolitan theorising), Bohman (1991) (interpretative indeterminacy, matching of analytical tools to explanatory purposes), and Clifford and Marcus (1986) (textual deconstruction of ethnographic authority). Such a review will provide a more comprehensive account of the available material on groups, 'societies', normative systems, laws and traditional continuity before the process of deconstruction–reconstruction in an expert report has commenced. It deliberately moves in an opposite direction to the simplifying pressures in native title report writing by emphasising the theoretical frameworks of particular contributions to the archive and their position with the development of the discipline.

Comparing this review with the anthropologist's report should clarify where the decisions and choices were made by the anthropologist, both in reconstructing the archive in a way that is deemed relevant to the juridical field and in the degree to which the process of deconstruction and reconstruction is incorporated into the report or submerged. This textual analysis will then be supplemented with in-depth interviewing aimed at eliciting a subjective rationale for the choices made in the report, the construction of the legal doctrine of native title and the experience of giving evidence. The transcript of the hearing and interviews with participants should also balance the textual analysis with some evidence of the performative aspects of the encounter.

The immediate judicial response to the anthropologist's evidence is not as accessible and analysis must rely on the recorded interventions made by the judge during the hearing and a textual deconstruction of the judge's reasons for decision.

The case-study method[37] is the most suitable methodology to investigate the questions of this book because of the complexity of the variables involved in

37 The term 'case-study method' is used in a general social sciences sense without the particular resonance it might have in social anthropology. In the early period of professionalised anthropology, a case study could refer to a study of a large tribe, a country or even a continent. Within the so-called Manchester School, the 'extended-case method' referred to the tracing of a local village dispute from its origins to the development of the social relationships of those involved during and after the adjudication and settlement of the dispute. The current project has some broad similarities to the extended-case method, but is more accurately defined in Yin's *Case Study Research: Design and Methods* (2003). He emphasised the focus on contemporary decisions in real-life contexts where the boundary between the phenomenon to be studied and the context is not clear, where there are many variables of interest, where there are multiple sources of information and where theoretical propositions are developed prior to fieldwork to guide data collection (2003:12–13).

the interaction and the indeterminacy of the key legal categories. Multiple cases enable the testing, in different contexts, of the overarching generalisations proposed as well as the robust academic model of an expert report and the various ways of theorising interaction of the two fields. As Yin (2003:32) suggests, multiple case studies are not aimed at creating a bigger sample from which to generalise, as in surveying methodologies, but at building stronger theories by subjecting them to repeated testing.

Ideally, the choice of cases should be guided by some explicit design criteria. The difficulty of obtaining access to the critical anthropologists' reports meant, however, that I had to be satisfied with what was available. Nonetheless, there are some interesting variations in the contexts of the three cases chosen. These variations can be summarised as in Table 1.1.

Table 1.1 Important variables in the case studies

Variables	1. *Mabo*	2. *Rubibi*	3. *De Rose Hill*
Long contact history	X	X	
Relatively short contact history			X
Pre-Native Title Act claim	X		
Post-Native Title Act claim		X	X
Single expert anthropologist	X		
Multiple expert anthropologists		X	X
High academic capital of claimants' principal anthropologist	X		
Low to medium academic capital of claimants' principal anthropologist		X	X
High academic capital of State Government's anthropologist		X	X
Anthropological fieldwork conducted prior to lodgement of claim	X		
Anthropological research for native title litigation		X	X
Successful outcome of hearing for claimants	X	X	
Unsuccessful outcome of hearing for claimants			X

I invoked ethnography in the title of this chapter even though it is clear that this project did not involve participant observation in the typical sense of ethnographic fieldwork. Detailed accounts of native title hearings by participant anthropologists are rare. There might be many reasons for this, including the need to wait until the case is finalised because of ongoing obligations of confidentiality, the need to maintain good future relations with lawyers and Aboriginal organisations, the desire to avoid revisiting a demoralising experience, as well as the usual run of pressing concerns and other research interests. Moreover, it is possible for anthropologists to communicate some of their most urgent concerns publicly by obscuring the specifics of the case in which they were directly involved.

The transcripts of the court hearings do allow a virtual participation to some extent. But I also invoke ethnography in the sense of the search for knowledge through empathetic understanding. For I seek to draw on my own experiences as a lawyer in four claims under the *Land Rights Act*, as well as my experience of the field of academic and applied anthropology.[38] I believe that my dual background has facilitated a high degree of openness in the in-depth interviews. This was not without its ethical problems. As in all in-depth interviewing, there is the possibility of the subject misconstruing the role of the interviewer as one of collaborator or therapist (Johnson 2002; Warren 2002). Eventually, I decided to give interview subjects an ethical warning—that the interview was not a collaboration—in addition to obtaining written consent.

Outline of the book

To recap, the starting point of this book is the proposition that the formulation and reception of anthropological expert testimony depend on more than the specific roles of the interactants. It involves the complex interaction of separate social fields. While it is easy to imagine this interaction as a predatory digestion of anthropology by law, equally plausible interpretations, such as the sharing of responsibility for difficult decisions, need to be tested in actual cases. Parallels with the interaction of science and law suggest that judges will view anthropology through the lens of ideal images of scientific methodology, but a variation—ideal images of anthropology—might emerge.

In order to move beyond a simple expert–advocate dichotomy, the task of expert anthropologists might be idealised as the compelling triangulation of likely Indigenous evidence, the anthropological archive and legal doctrine. This perspective on the triangulation process involves the reformulation of expertise as an active deconstruction of the anthropological archive and its reconstruction in categories relevant to the judge's task. The question, then, is to what extent this deconstruction/reconstruction and triangulation model explains what

38 The claims were the Chilla Well Land Claim, Finke Land Claim, Western Desert Land Claim and North West Simpson Desert Land Claim during 1986–90. My experience of the field of anthropology includes my professional engagement with anthropologists on land claims, the completion of a Master of Letters in Anthropology at The Australian National University (1991–98) and doctoral research (2001–05), which is now the subject of this book; work as a consultant anthropologist researching native title claims in southern Queensland and the Pilbara region of Western Australia; and my current position as Australian Research Council-funded Research Fellow in the School of Archaeology and Anthropology at The Australian National University (2009–12).

happens in actual cases. An outline of the interaction of the two social fields indicates that, despite skilful triangulation, there will be factors outside the immediate control of the anthropologist that will be influential in the reception of expert testimony. These factors include the general social and academic capital of the anthropologist and his/her consequent ability to manage hysteresis issues, how the Indigenous evidence unfolds and the general disposition of the judge towards the case.

The first two of the case studies in this book consist of two chapters, one reviewing the relevant anthropological archive and the other covering the formulation and reception of the anthropologists' evidence. The first case study on the little-known evidential hearing in the *Mabo* case uncovers a gem of a performance by Jeremy Beckett (which has all but disappeared from public view) (Chapters 2 and 3). The second case study, on the first *Rubibi* claim to an Aboriginal reserve near Broome, introduces the element of conflicting anthropological expertise and how the judge resolved it (Chapters 4 and 5). The third case study consists of three chapters. This case study focuses on the *De Rose Hill* native title claim. It represents an extreme test for forensic anthropology, for it involves fluid traditional land tenure, multiple anthropologists with widely differing academic capital and a contentious political context (Chapters 6 and 7).

Following the completion of the main period of research for this book, the judgment in the native title compensation test case of *Jango v Northern Territory* (known generally as the *Yulara* case)[39] was delivered on 31 March 2006. Its treatment of a senior anthropological expert witness sent shock waves of disbelief and anger through the ranks of native title anthropologists. The problems hinted at in the *De Rose Hill* case became vividly foregrounded in the *Yulara* case—like acid on an etching. Rather than provide an account of the *Yulara* case as a postscript, I have decided to add it as a third chapter (Chapter 8) to the *De Rose Hill* case study. This will allow the reader to take full advantage of Chapter 6, the review of the anthropology of Western Desert land tenure, which fortuitously is the subject of both cases. Each case study will conclude with an intermediate reflection on how the theorising of this introductory chapter has been tested.

The conclusion of this book (Chapter 9) will explore what generalisations can be made from the case studies about interaction between the two fields and how best to characterise anthropologists' agency.

39 [2006] FCA 318 (31 March 2006).

2. Anthropological Knowledge of the Murray Islands Prior to the *Mabo* Case

The role of anthropology in the original *Mabo* decision has been obscured by a number of contradictory contemporary trends. The first is the lionisation of Eddie Mabo as the hero of the case, and that tends to overshadow the role of the other plaintiffs and the anthropologists. Despite the very negative reception of Eddie Mabo's evidence by Justice Moynihan in the Queensland Supreme Court, the case is associated in the public arena with Eddie Mabo. No doubt this flows from the naming of the case and the wide appeal of the heroic/tragic story of his dogged persistence in pursuing the case over 10 years, ending in his death before the final successful judgment of the High Court. His widow and family have actively promoted this image in numerous ways, including seeking a national Mabo day public holiday. The most detailed account of the case, by one of the lawyers representing the plaintiffs (Keon-Cohen 2000), also evokes the sense of Eddie Mabo and the lawyers together against the whole world. In Keon-Cohen's account, anthropology seems to be of minor importance.

In order to recover Beckett's contribution and the choices he made in formulating his expert opinion, it is necessary to review the anthropological archive that he had at his disposal. The chronology of anthropological research on the Murray Islands set out in Table 2.1 demonstrates that there were only a few major contributors to that archive: the members of Haddon's Cambridge expedition of 1898; Beckett himself, who undertook his initial period of fieldwork in 1959–60; and Nonie Sharp, who commenced her fieldwork in 1978–79. Laade's and Kitaoji's less prominent roles will also be mentioned.

The timing of Haddon's Cambridge expedition—less than 20 years after the assertion of British sovereignty over the Murray Islands—meant that the reports of the expedition were destined to become a critical source of information in the *Mabo* case to prove continuity of traditional land tenure over the period of colonisation. I now turn to examine those reports, under the broad headings that are relevant to native title: traditional title-holding groups and 'societies', laws and customs relating to land, and the transformation of traditional land tenure over time.

Table 2.1 Chronology of anthropological research on Torres Strait Islanders

Research	Year	Events
	1871	London Missionary Society (LMS) begins work
	1872	First annexation of islands by Queensland
	1879	Annexation of more islands (incl. Murray)
	1886	Government Resident appointed
Haddon's first visit	1888	
Cambridge expedition	1898	
	1899	Elected advisory councils introduced
Head-Hunters published *Reports* Vol. II published	1901	
Reports Vol. V published	1904	Islanders come under the *Protection Act* Papuan Industries established
Reports Vol. III published	1907	
Reports Vol. VI published	1908	
Reports Vol. IV published	1912	
	1914	Formal withdrawal of LMS in favour of Anglicans
	1914–18	World War I
	1920s	
	1930	
	1933	Ion Idriess's *Drums of Mer* published
Reports Vol. I published	1935	
	1936	Maritime strike
	1937	First Inter-Island Councillors Conference
	1939-45	World War II
Beckett's fieldwork	1959–60	
Beckett's PhD submitted	1963	
Laade's fieldwork	1963–65	
	1970	Lawrie's *Myths and Legends* published
	1972	Federal Labor Government, Border Issue
	1974	ANU Research Project
Kitaoji's fieldwork	1975–77	
Sharp's initial visits	1978–79	
	1981	First informal meeting of *Mabo* plaintiffs
	1982	Filing of *Mabo* writ
Sharp's PhD submitted	1984	
Beckett's *Custom and Colonialism* published	1987	
	1989–90	*Mabo* hearing before Justice Moynihan
	1992	High Court decision in the *Mabo* case
Sharp's *Stars of Tagai* published	1993	

Haddon's ethnology of memory culture

> In order to give the reader a substantially accurate idea of the Malu ceremonies, I do not propose to describe exactly only what we saw, but I shall endeavour, as briefly as possible, to resuscitate the past. (Haddon 1901:47–8)

Figure 2.1 Haddon's painting of an imagined Malo–Bomai ceremony in pre-contact times

Source: Haddon's *Reports* Vol. VI (1908:plate XXX).

Haddon's six-volume *Reports of the Cambridge Anthropological Expedition to Torres Straits* (1901–35) (the *Reports*) are imposing—like a huge artistic monument—impossible to ignore, intricate in detail, exasperating in their sprawling organisation, creating their own world of responses and providing a powerful resource for all subsequent generations of Meriam people, including Eddie Mabo. Parts of them were to play a critical role in the *Mabo* case. From the living memory of Meriam people who cooperated with Haddon and his fellow researchers during their five-month stay on the Murray Islands in 1889, the *Reports* document in extraordinary detail the life of the Meriam people about the time of the legal annexation of the Torres Strait Islands to Australia in 1879.

Some of the implicit claims to scientific knowledge in the *Reports* are to be found in their scholarly framing—notably the choice of authors with sound academic credentials, the publication under the auspices of Cambridge University, its reference to other scholarly journals in the text, its footnotes and its bibliographies. The claims to knowledge are also evident in the structure of the total work, the division of each volume into parts and in the nature of the exposition. In contrast with the populist, adventure narrative of Haddon's *Head-Hunters: Black, White, and Brown* (1901), with its grisly image of trophy skulls emblazoned in gold on the cover, the *Reports* announce their seriousness in the encyclopedic comprehensiveness under the enumerated topical headings. The impression of comprehensiveness is also reinforced by the exhaustive and unrelenting detail in which the folktales, genealogies, kinship terminology, rites of passage, social organisation, magic, religion and cults are recorded.

For Haddon's broadly comparative purposes, the thematic coherence of divisions was less important than applying the same categories to different populations. Only in this way could he contribute to the broad intellectual frameworks of the day: social evolutionism and diffusionism. Apart from the generally unreflective assertion of the universality of the categories chosen, the main interpretative focus for the whole of the *Reports* is the question of the immediate origin of particular cultural formations and their placement within a social-evolutionist hierarchy that had Australian Aboriginal totemism at the very bottom and European society at the apex. A key point to be made, though, is that there is not much sustained analysis and interpretation in the *Reports*. As James Urry (1998:220) explained: 'First the ethnographic cabinets had to be filled, the ethnographic maps completed and only then could a proper ethnological explanation be attempted. In the meantime, there was always more data to collect; data synthesis had to precede analysis and theory construction.'

The writing strategy adopted in the *Reports*—particularly the volumes dealing with 'Sociology, Magic and Religion'—is that of assembling the various sources on a given topic, whether from John Bruce, the long-serving teacher on the Murray Islands, their own informants, missionaries' stories or the meagre scholarly literature, and then, Frankenstein-like, assembling one authoritative account from the parts. This process can be most clearly seen in the recounting of the 'folktales'. The only exception to the approach of producing a single, authoritative account was the recording of a variation for part of the Malo–Bomai story.

The commitment to comprehensiveness and detail produces a mass of material that evokes an intense, multifaceted universe of myth, ceremony, sacred objects (*zogo*) and cults in this small, rather isolated population of the Murray Islands. The crowded islands are dense with individually named villages, shrines for particular purposes, and place names (both geographical features and the constellations in the night sky)—all of which refer to a rich corpus of myth. The writing strategy, especially in relation to the description of the typical life cycle and various rites of passage, tends to give the impression of a life highly circumscribed by the need to perform rituals to ward off evil spirits and to ensure success in gardening and fishing.

There is also material that evokes a competitive and intricate localism, with different spells, shrines, dances, songs, myths and associated paraphernalia distributed among the many small villages that were not part of a static tradition, but a humming, social factory, actively seeking out new dances, stories, and mysterious incidents and converting them into their own traditional rituals. It seems to have been a society in which there were many cults, some dwindling over time and others, like the Malo–Bomai cult, becoming dominant.

Most historians of anthropology see the results of the expedition as a sort of proto-anthropology. George Stocking saw the whole multidisciplinary approach as harking back to the great nineteenth-century maritime exploratory expeditions (Stocking 1983:24). James Urry notes Haddon's conversion from zoology to the emergent anthropology of the time and his preoccupation with asserting the scientific credentials of the new discipline and with the grand evolutionary theories of the time. This assessment leads him to describe Haddon's work as 'ethnology', understood as 'the reconstruction of the evolutionary and historical relationship between groups located within specific geographical and historical settings, based on evidence drawn from the analysis of "racial" types, languages, customs and material culture' (Urry 1998:201, footnote 3).

This is a neat summary of the *Reports*. To emphasise the point about the *Reports* being proto-anthropology, Urry compared the final volume of the *Reports* with Malinowski's *Coral Gardens and Their Magic*, both published in 1935, finding the *Reports* 'strikingly archaic' (Urry 1998:232).

Yet, there are also some striking continuities with subsequent anthropological practice. These include the genealogical method of kinship analysis, the importance given to understanding the local language, the acknowledgment of the superiority of long-term fieldwork and the trope of the ethnographic present in writing accounts of previous customs. Some of these claims might seem strange given that Haddon and most of his colleagues attempted to communicate with their informants in the local creole, referred to as Jargon English, and that their longest period of fieldwork was only a few months. In relation to language, what I am relying on is the thorough work of the linguist Sidney Ray and the use of his work in explaining key cultural concepts in the ethnography. In *Head-Hunters*, Haddon described Ray's near-obsessive application to his task, and the accuracy of his results has also been attested to by subsequent generations of linguists (see Shnukal 1998).

The claim about long-term fieldwork rests on the reliance of Haddon and his colleagues on John Bruce, the schoolteacher-magistrate; he had lived among the Meriam people for many years, had learnt the Meriam language and was intimately engaged with their lives. Direct reference to him as the source of information and adoption of his general assessments are as frequent as they are deferential throughout the *Reports*.

These continuities should make us wary of the broad periodisations of anthropological discourse used by Stocking and Urry, as an assumption of progress creeps in. Thus, especially if one includes the detailed account of his fieldwork experiences in *Head-Hunters*, Haddon provides greater transparency in his methodology, particularly his identification of the sources of his information, than the subsequent generation of anthropologists.

Groups

Haddon delegated the investigation of social organisation to Dr W. H. R. Rivers, then a lecturer in physiological and experimental psychology. His work on the expedition resulted in the methodological breakthrough of the genealogical method.

Rivers (1908) reported the results of his painstaking work on kinship terminology and genealogies in the Murray Islands in separate chapters and brought together his conclusions in another chapter entitled 'Social organisation'. In that chapter he identified four groupings. The first were those belonging to the same village—that is, village identity rather than residence. Typically, the village was also a single, named residential area, although some villages consisted of several named places. What I have called village identity was determined patrilineally and the group of people with the same village identity was exogamous. From the point of view of group exogamy, 22 separate village groups were identified.

The second grouping is a little more mysterious since it seemed to have been socially redundant. It is 'the district', which I would gloss as clusters of villages in a two-tier, nested hierarchy. Rivers identified seven districts on Mer, with one district having two subdivisions. Rivers does not assert the 'district' as having any particular contemporary social relevance; it is regarded more as a broad, regional identifier used as an alternative to village identity. From the memory of his informants, Rivers (1908:176) was able to assert that, in the past, certain funerary rights and increase ceremonies were confined to certain districts. Different kinds of magic, however, not practised by the community at large, are associated with a particular village or a particular district (1908:174).

Uncertainty at the margins about the constitution of some districts and villages is intriguing and suggests other, more flexible social processes at work. Whatever these other processes might have been, information about villages and districts is presented graphically in the form of a stable map that, like Tindale's tribal boundaries map, has gained iconic status in the annals of native title practice (see Map 2.1). It proclaims total traditional occupation at a glance.

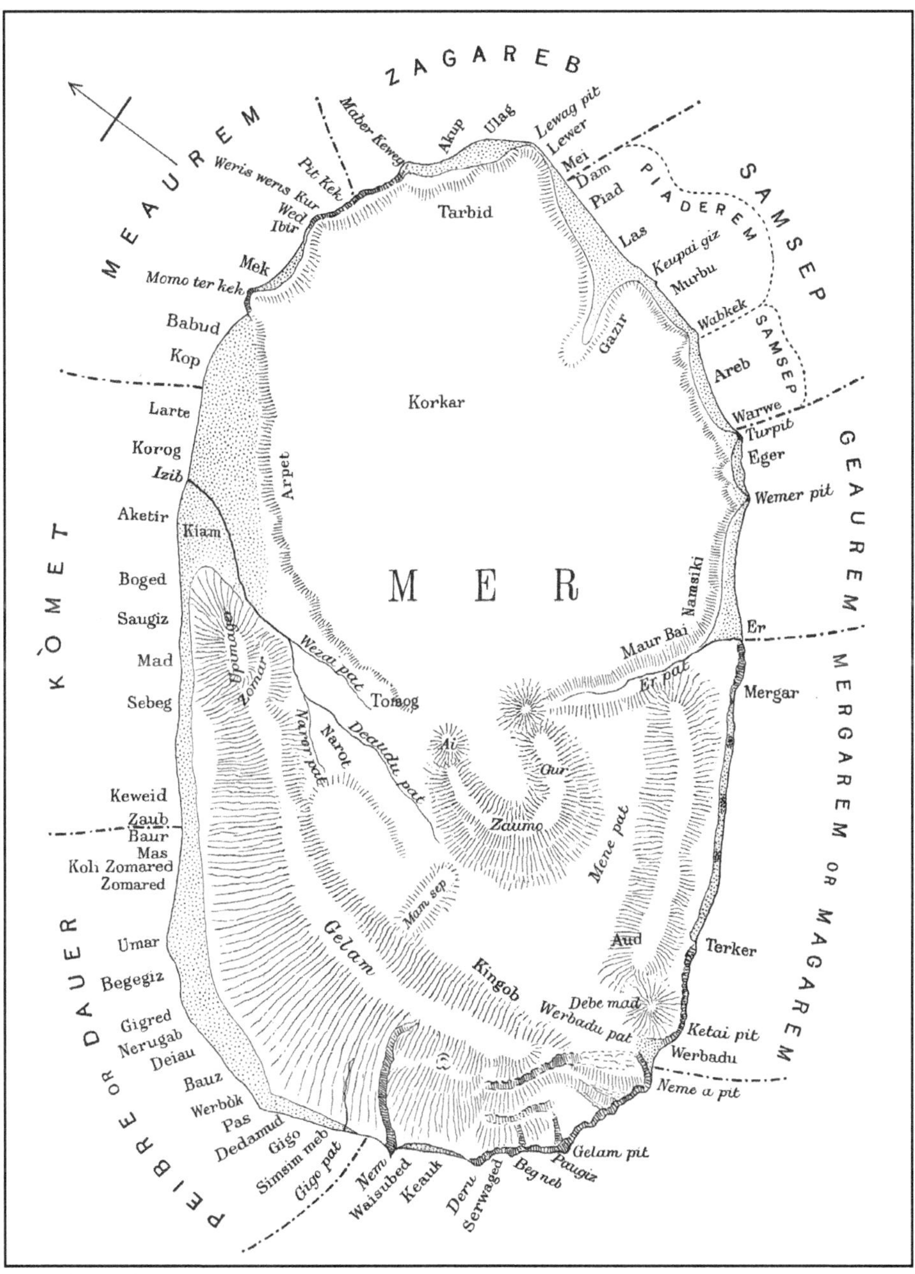

Map 2.1 Villages and districts on Mer

Source: From Haddon's *Reports* Vol. VI (1908:170).

The third grouping was a broad, dual division of all initiated Meriam men based on differing roles in the dominant Malo cult

1. the *Beizam le* (shark brethren), the leading members of the Malo fraternity
2. the *Zagareb le*, the singers and drummers in the ritual.

The fourth kind of grouping consisted of men who described themselves by reference to a particular animal—for example, dog men, pigeon men. There is no discussion of the social significance of this fourth group identity except to say that reference was made to it during their participation in the Malo dances.

Rivers' analysis of the interrelationship between the four identified groupings is preoccupied, and perhaps overwhelmed, by the interest in totemism and the evolution of social systems. Thus he stated: 'One of the chief interests of the social organisation of the Meriam is the complete disappearance of all traces of a totemic system which it is almost certain must have once existed' (Rivers 1908:174).

The remainder of his analysis attempts to reconstruct out of the available evidence a simpler, prior social organisation consisting of totemism, dual social organisation and exogamous districts that evolved into the 'territorial system' that the researchers observed (1908:174–7).

Rivers addresses island-wide social organisation in a section entitled 'Law and government'. It reveals an embarrassing gap—he simply forgot to question his informants about governance in the pre-missionary era. Thus, there is a very brief reference to the possibility of government by elders, the missionary Hunt's suggestion of hereditary chieftainship and the possibility that Hunt was referring to some government-like aspects of the Malo cult. Then the exposition moves quickly to the contemporary situation of 1889, outlining the composition of the court set up by the Queensland Government, the rival church court set up by Finau, the Samoan missionary, and examples of the criminal and civil actions brought before the court.

Other possible social groupings such as a hearth group or an island-wide community group were not explicitly considered by Rivers, although there is material in his chapter on social organisation and in other parts of the *Reports* that seems to assert the existence of such groupings or could be used as evidence of them. The inhabitants of one village on Mer had come from another island and were considered to be *Nog le* (foreigners), and as having 'no place in the more important institutions of the Island' (Rivers 1908:172). This designation would seem to indicate some sense of an island-wide identity. The linguistic research of Ray concluded that the language spoken on Ugar (Stephen Island), Erub (Darnley Island) and the Murray Islands was the same language. This is suggestive of an even wider Eastern Island identity and is implicit in the organisation of the *Reports* into a comparison of the Western and the Eastern islands.

Although there is no discussion of the hearth group as such, there is mention of the widespread practice of adoption and the problems it caused in relation to inheritance.

Laws, customs, traditions and practices

In the whole of the description of the Eastern Islanders in Volume VI of the *Reports* the chapter on 'Property and inheritance' contains the most explicit use of legal metaphors. It was written by Anthony Wilkin, a promising undergraduate, whom Haddon enlisted as the expedition's photographer, based on his published photography of Egypt. Wilkin died of dysentery in Cairo in 1901, seven years before the eventual publication of his chapter.[1] It was to become the focus of much attention in the *Mabo* hearing. In the chapter, the compiler's work is evident in the diversity of material collected and in a generalising tendency that looks for and finds rules. The opening paragraph must have delighted Eddie Mabo's lawyers:

> Queensland law has not affected native land tenure which is upheld in the Court of the island. In a few instances it is not impossible that English ideas—especially of inheritance—are making themselves felt. There is no common land, and each makes his own garden on his own land at his own convenience. (Wilkin 1908:163)

What follows includes a series of general, timeless, law-like propositions, sometimes supported by quotes in 'Jargon English' from informants, or quotes from Mr Bruce. For example, in relation to inheritance:

> 'Suppose brother he stop, girl he no get 'im garden belong 'im' was the remark of a native. Mr Bruce says 'The eldest son gets the lion's share—girls get very little, just enough for a marriage portion…'
>
> On the death of a wife the husband must give back her portion to her relatives—at least as soon as he contemplates remarriage…
>
> If a father is very angry with his children he is competent to disinherit them. Such action is very uncommon. (Wilkin 1908:163–4)

1 See Haddon's tribute in *Head-Hunters* (1901:vii).

Consistent with the tendency towards broad generalisations, the chapter also includes some broad cultural comparisons such as: 'Unlike the greater part of British New Guinea the Murray Islands are the scene of exchanges, sales, leases and loans of land and house sites' (Wilkin 1908:165).

But there are also other kinds of statements that tend to relativise the general applicability of the stated rules and their enduring quality. These include

- accounts of ignoring acknowledged rules—for example, moving fences to enlarge gardens in the absence of the neighbouring owner (1908:167), and the statement: 'Water holes are in theory the property of the finder, but in reality are common to all' (p. 167)
- accounts of strategic behaviour to use the rules for individual advantage or to circumvent the rules—for example, a self-appointed guardian of a child contriving to adopt the child so that he acquires the child's inheritance (p. 165), or the planting of vegetables on another's land as the basis of a future claim to ownership (p. 167)
- an account of the non-enforcement of rules for fear of sorcery (p. 163)
- descriptions of recent changes in land-tenure practice—for example, Finau, the Samoan missionary, stopping the practice of community voting on prospective candidates to be lent the gardening land of others (p. 166).

Overall, the promise of a systematic approach inherent in the title of the chapter gives way to the heterogeneity of the compiler's art. This is probably true of the *Reports* as a whole.

The question of laws and customs in the pre-contact situation is further complicated by the quasi-governmental role of the dominant cult of Malo–Bomai. This role has already been mentioned above in relation to the belated discovery of a gap in Rivers' questioning about traditional institutions of government in the Eastern Islands. In contrast, there is a relatively detailed description of chieftainship in the Western Islands outlining the names and lineage of chiefs and the districts over which they claimed authority.[2]

The cult of Malo–Bomai included an extensive body of myth describing the travels and activities of the cultural hero Malo. Haddon reveals in the unabashed style of the imperial scientist studying the distant primitive that Bomai was the restricted name for Malo. The main ritual activity of the cult was an elaborate, male initiation ceremony in which male youths were inducted into the secrets of the cult during ritual performances over a number of weeks at different locations on Mer. The ceremony was conducted by particular acknowledged leaders of the cult called *zogo le* (roughly translated as the sacred people). According to

2 See Chapter XI, 'Regulation of public life', in Haddon (1904:261–71).

Haddon's informants, there were three *zogo le* for the Malo–Bomai cult. The initiation ceremony involved all the families of the island, and there are some indications that its ritual framework provided opportunities for some of the clan groups to perform their own rituals. At one point in the initiation ceremony, the initiates were given severe and extended instruction in the proper conduct of their lives as adults. This instruction included the secrets of successful gardening through the use of particular methods and spells, exhortations against stealing other men's property and exhortations against bad behaviour in general, including the serious consequences of revealing the secrets of the Malo cult itself. Certain members of the cult adopted a policing role by taking on the identity of the malevolent spirit *Magur*. In taking on this role, they were responsible both for hazing initiates and for frightening non-initiates and women at certain times (Haddon and Myers 1908).

The claims of quasi-government for the Malo–Bomai cult could be justified by its dominance over other cults, the executive powers of its leaders and its specialised enforcement mechanism. The concentration of organisational power in the *zogo le* and their ceremonial status seem to have extended beyond the confines of ceremonial performance so that they could become dominant in other spheres of life and break rules with some impunity. On the other hand, since it was 'Malo's Law' that later became the exclusive reference to the old religion, it should be noted that, while Haddon presents the Malo–Bomai cult as the dominant cult, it was also one cult among others, including *Meket Sarik* and the licentious *Waiet* (Haddon 1908:280).

Elsewhere in Volume VI of the *Reports*, the idea of any specialised mechanism for the enforcement of rules is denied in favour of enforcement via public opinion 'as far as possible' (Haddon 1908:250). The qualification 'as far as possible' probably referred to the exceptional cases that were referred to the Island Court, then comprising Mr Bruce as assessor and the two Mamooses (or headmen) appointed by the Government: Harry and Passi. Rivers (1908:180–4) includes an account of one case involving a land dispute between adopted and natural kin. One wonders whether this case, and the other sections on adoption in the *Reports*, gave pause to Eddie Mabo's lawyers in pursuing his land claims based on adoption. For the case illustrated a certain pattern of behaviour: the early adoption of babies who are raised as natural children and not told of their adoptive status; their real adoptive status being revealed during some family squabble in later life; anger at the adoptive family for not telling them; and finally efforts to re-establish links with their natural family, thus leaving unresolved the question of whether these efforts amounted to renouncing any inheritance of land from the adoptive family.

Haddon on change

> [T]he people scarcely a generation removed from perfect savagery. (Haddon 1901:23)

Consistent with the aversion to theorising in the *Reports*, there is little sustained reflection about the contemporary processes of change that were observed on Mer and other islands in the Torres Strait. There is, however, a pervasive sense of urgency rooted in a broad, pre-emptory assessment of impending cultural loss based on a perceived vast gap in the detailed knowledge of traditions between generations and the apparent success of the missionaries in displacing traditional practices. Haddon attended a Sunday service on Mer and was almost deafened by the enthusiastic singing of hymns (Haddon 1901:9). He noted that, even at organised social nights, where families performed entertaining songs and dances for each other, the proceedings were concluded with prayers. On the other hand, he also reports a continuity of traditional beliefs. These beliefs contradicted Christian beliefs and caused some of his older informants, who were also leading church members, a degree of awkwardness.

There is a poignant account of Haddon's visit to Tomog, the site of a divination shrine:

> When I first discovered Tomog zogo it was considerably damaged as it had been burned by Jodiah [a South Sea Islander missionary of the London Missionary Society], Mataika's successor. In 1898 it was in a worse condition, and the encroaching vegetation and rubbish had to be cleared before we could photograph and make a plan of it. It was very suggestive to see the reverent affection the old men displayed for the zogo, and they seemed gratified at the care with which it had been cleaned and mapped. (Haddon 1908:266)

The shells and rocks of the shrine represented the various villages on the Murray Islands and the location of other islands. Divination had been performed by skilled men watching the shrine soon after dawn for the path of small insects across it and interpreting the events these movements foretold for the particular villages crossed. The day after Haddon had mapped the site, Arei, who had accompanied Haddon, performed a re-enactment of a divination ceremony, demonstrating that the old traditions were truly within living memory. The *Reports* include a photograph of the Islanders in their state of cultural uncertainty seated before the cleared shrine.

Figure 2.2 Photograph of Haddon's informants seated at the cleared Tomog shrine

Source: *Head-Hunters* (Haddon 1901:plate VII).

Despite their conversion to Christianity, the Murray Islanders initially refused to give Haddon the secret magic phrases of a rainmaking ritual and refused to part with associated secret stone figurines (*doiom*). Although they agreed to make models of the previously destroyed Malo mask, they insisted that it not be shown to women in accordance with previous taboos. There was also a degree of anxiety and divided loyalties provoked by the request for a revival performance of the Malo ceremony.

Haddon was also aware of the manoeuvrings of Finau, the Samoan missionary, against his expedition's inquiries into the old traditions and the missionary's fear of a 'recrudescence of paganism' (Haddon 1901:35). Some years earlier Finau had led the destruction of various traditional shrines on the island and preached against traditional dancing and charms. Thus, in Haddon's various descriptions, we find the raw material for an account of the dynamics of the interaction of traditional beliefs and the London Missionary Society's evangelising project—an account that is never developed by Haddon.

Beckett's competitive local politics

Beckett's position within the academy

When I interviewed Beckett in 2002, he had retired from his position of Associate Professor in the Department of Anthropology at Sydney University after a 28-year association, following four years in lecturing positions at other universities. He was still active on the editorial committees of both *Oceania* and *The Australian Journal of Anthropology*. In 2001, he had been honoured with an invitation to be the keynote speaker of the Australian Anthropological Society's conference to address the assembled anthropologists on the state of the discipline (Beckett 2002). He had published widely in academic journals over a long period, published a major book on the Torres Strait, which had been universally well received,[3] and he had been midwife to a major 'oral history' of the NSW Aboriginal man Myles Lalor (Beckett 1996, 2000). The simple conclusion from this incomplete list of achievements is that Beckett, at the end of his career, occupied a relatively senior position within the field of the academy. Yet his own account of his career emphasises marginalisation, as in the title of his recollection of anthropology in Australia between 1956 in 1970: 'Against the grain' (Beckett 2001).

There were two aspects to this perceived marginalisation—both concerning Beckett's position relative to the emerging structure of the larger regional specialisations: Australianist and Melanesianist anthropology. Beckett's initial research for his MA was with Aborigines in western New South Wales (see, for example, Beckett 1958, 1959, 1965). This field site placed him in a challenging relationship with the majority of Australianists at the time, who were orientated to recovering pre-contact Aboriginal traditions from Aborigines in remote areas, where the history of colonisation was much shorter. This divide has been one of the enduring features of Australianist anthropology—reflected in entrenched positions, bitter criticism and attempts to overcome it through multi-sited ethnography.

The other regional specialisation in which Beckett felt marginal was Melanesianist anthropology. The opening up of Papua New Guinea, with its exotic, largely unstudied cultures and mysterious cargo cults, made it a magnet for anthropologists worldwide. He was refused access to this country because of, he believed, his brief membership of a communist youth organisation years before (Beckett 2001:90). To his surprise, however, Queensland authorities agreed to his research among Australia's Melanesian minority in the Torres

3 See Dagmar (1989); Fitzpatrick (1989); Long (1989); Moore (1990); Nachman (1989); Sharp (1989); and Urry (1989).

Strait. In retrospect, Beckett felt that the ambiguous position of the Torres Strait Islanders within Australia seems to have been reproduced in his opportunities to publish within the larger regional specialisations: his work not anthologised in either Australianist or Melanesianist collections. As Beckett put it succinctly: 'one falls in the crack.'[4]

Torres Strait Research

> In 1958, 60 years after the Cambridge Expedition, I went to the Torres Straits to investigate the contemporary life of its indigenous inhabitants. (Beckett 1963:1)

In placing himself as successor to Haddon, Beckett wanted to acknowledge his debts to Haddon but not adopt his outlook. Anthropology had changed dramatically in the intervening period. In 1958 it was entering a period of consensus about its distinctive fieldwork methodology and unprecedented institutional security.

What Beckett found were Islanders obsessed by the politics of the local council, particularly who would win the elections for the three positions that comprised the council and doubled as the local court. Like the professional ethnographer who refuses to let the theoretical concerns of the day completely determine the course of his research, Beckett decided that local politics would be his central focus. Using Haddon's reports as a baseline, he also tried to give an account of the pattern of historical transformation in the intervening period—the decline from pre-missionary autonomy into colonial dependency. This dependency included fairly intimate administrative control over employment, morals, movement of the Islanders and communication with the outside world—most of these controls mediated by the local council. Islander experience of relative equality in fighting alongside Australian soldiers during World War II had the effect of intensifying the Islanders' sense of grievance at their relative position. The call was for freedom, in the sense of both removal of legal restraints and opening up of economic equality through access to equal wages. Freedom was to be achieved via the local council leaders asserting themselves against, or cooperating with, the existing state authorities.

These themes were explored by Beckett in his doctoral thesis and numerous published articles over the next 25 years, culminating in 1987 in his book *Torres Strait Islanders: Custom and Colonialism* (1987). The core of the book—the comparison of the different course of colonialism on Murray with that on Badu—

4 Jeremy Beckett, Interview transcript, 2003, p. 11.

comes more or less directly from his thesis. But it is recontextualised in the light of subsequent studies in historical anthropology, theoretical developments and substantial changes in the lives of the Islanders themselves over the period.

The book commences with a description of a tombstone opening on Murray Island in 1976—a ceremony that, for Beckett, had become the quintessential cultural event of island custom of the now widely dispersed Islanders. This description introduces Beckett's problematising of island custom and the linking of his work to the research and theorising of other anthropologists of dominated cultures in diverse settings, from Meso-American Indians, Pacific Islanders, and African slaves in America, to African slaves in the Caribbean, the New Guinea Highlanders and Newfoundland fisher folk. It is not only an attempt at a comparative description of his fieldwork location, but also an attempt to refine his own theoretical stance. He embraces Wolf's critique of anthropology's tendency to analyse local cultures as isolates (see Wolf 1982), as indeed this was his own original inclination 20 years before Wolf. He also uses the other anthropologists and historians to refine his original generalised assertions about dependent peoples still possessing a degree of cultural autonomy.

One refinement is the move away from explanatory frameworks that have economic exploitation at their centre. Thus the doubts about the general applicability of the theory of internal colonialism that he expressed in his 1977 article on the pearling industry give way to a more explicit adoption of Paine's terminology to describe the liberal era of statecraft towards indigenous people: welfare colonialism. Despite the adoption of welfare colonialism as an overarching description, it does not determine Beckett's approach. Paine's preoccupation in *The White Arctic* (1977) was predominately the contradictions and failures of government policy. Inuit subjectivity was not explored in any detail, but was assumed to exist as a coherent traditional culture waiting to express itself once the colonial restrictions were loosened. Beckett, on the other hand, tries to do much more, by adding a historical account of the Islanders' own conception of island custom, including the complex processes of interaction with colonial administration. He retains a degree of eclecticism in the explanation of the various conundrums of Torres Strait Islander history.

What is also new in the book is the sense of cultural evanescence. For example, in concluding the description of the tombstone opening ceremony by a returning diaspora, he states that 'their brief visit recreated for a few days the vital community that had existed up to the early 1960s' (Beckett 1987:2). More explicitly, in his concluding paragraph in the chapter on the Murray Islanders, he states:

> In 1967, when the Commonwealth Film Unit made its documentary The Islanders, Murray was able to master some eighty dancers in a magnificent display of their cultural heritage. Ten years later this would have been possible, if at all, only during the Christmas season when the emigrants made visits home. It is still possible to speak of the Meriam domain. But, as we shall see in later chapters, while Murray has greater bargaining power in external affairs it has reduced its capacity to regulate the lives of its citizens. (Beckett 1987:146)

In contrast, when justifying the focus of the book on his fieldwork between 1958 and 1961, he states: 'I found Torres Strait beautiful and its people welcoming. I was impressed with the vitality of island custom and captivated by the music and dancing' (Beckett 1987:21).

To be fair, Beckett, having posed the question of whether the island custom of the 1980s had degenerated into an 'alienated folkloric consciousness' or a private ethnicity, reviews the situation of the Islanders in his final chapter and comes to the conclusion that it had not reached that degree of degeneration. He thought island custom would survive, albeit in a different form (Beckett 1987:232).

Groups

Beckett was interested in the formation and dissipation of non-enduring action groups, principally the ones that formed as voting blocs or followings for particular candidates in council elections. This interest and its later development in his journal articles (for example, Beckett 1967) are reminiscent of later work by Sansom (1980) on the labile groups in Darwin fringe camps. These political followings formed around Christian religious affiliation, personal morality and other personal characteristics, political ideology (the radical–conservative divide) and perceived capacity to effectively deal with colonial institutions and administrators.

While his focus on local politicking led him to think about transient groupings, Beckett was always careful to distinguish the issue of the inheritance of land. There he observed that stable kinship groups had more explanatory power (Beckett 1963:195–6).

Less obvious, but equally relevant to the *Mabo* case, is Beckett's acceptance of an island-wide grouping based on a common language, custom and face-to-face interaction over a long historical period. Textually it is revealed in the use of the word 'Murray' as a shorthand description of a shared character trait or general disposition. While this is essentialising terminology, Beckett does historicise island identity. He sees the persistence of individual island identity, as opposed to pan-island identity, as partly the result of segmented, hierarchical church and state administration. He also suggests that the Murray Islanders' consensus about traditional land-tenure principles started to break down with the emergence of a resident versus immigrant cleavage (see below).

Laws and customs

Beckett's fundamental interests in local politicking, the articulation between local and broader systems, and historical transformation all seem antithetical to the description of practices, structures or rules that could be identified in a legal context as laws and customs. Beckett's adoption of the concept of the Meriam domain, however, provided a basis for arguing for a limited continuity with previous traditional laws and customs, particularly in land tenure. As a result, there always seems to be a tension between stability within this domain and radical transformation of the articulation with the encapsulating society. This is nowhere more evident than in Beckett's 1983 attempt to focus specifically on land tenure for a national conference on the theme of Indigenous land rights in Australia.

The significance of this article is that it is Beckett's only attempt to draw together his thoughts on traditional land tenure prior to the commencement of the *Mabo* litigation. With some prescience, he explained one of the probable driving forces behind Islander emigrants (who happened to include Eddie Mabo): 'Unable to influence local councils from a distance, some emigrants fear that their rights are being overridden by land-hungry stay-at-homes' (Beckett 1983:203).

Adopting his familiar pattern of analysis, he presents the broad historical sweep from the forms of traditional ownership reported by Haddon to the period of his own fieldwork and up to the recent past when the council on Mer approved the construction of an airstrip on the interior of the island—to the indignation of the traditional owners on the mainland, who were not consulted. Ultimately, his own concluding synthesis appears to emphasise historical transformation rather than continuity within a separate Meriam domain:

> While range was primarily a matter of economic use; estate was a matter of social solidarity, one of the means by which the Islanders maintained their ordered anarchy as well as giving social and historical meaning to the physical world. Under colonial conditions, land was used less intensively and for different purposes, while order and—to a degree—meaning were pre-empted by state and church. Estate was now a matter of the micropolitics of communities more isolated and embattled than they had been before contact. With the end of segregation and the move of more than half the population to the mainland, the principles on which the notion of estate has been based have come into question, not

> from the emigrants but from those who have stayed at home. Potential use, or actual—as in the case of the Murray airstrip—is now a basis for undermining traditional forms of estate. (Beckett 1983:208)

Change

Because Beckett's whole Torres Strait oeuvre is about the fluidity of local politics and historical transformation, it is sometimes difficult to distinguish between the narrative of change and his explanations of the reasons, causes and processes of change. He weaves his analysis into the historical narrative and avoids any extended theorising about his eclectic mixture of approaches. This style of writing is perhaps a product of his general approach to theorising: 'the way I have done my anthropology is to start with the ethnography first and then to say what helps one to understand this. In a sense, I find my theory in the street.'[5]

Neo-Marxist ideas, ecological adaptation, demographic change and strategic rational choice explanations are not used in a formulaic way, but are presented more as a background commonsense. The Murray Islanders' relative lack of commitment to the pearling industry is possible because of their fertile soil and the prestige of gardening. Faced with the realisation of the inferiority of their weapons in their early colonial encounters and the relief at the end of headhunting and warfare, the initial quick acceptance of the Christian missionaries was a rational choice. The Islanders chose leaders who could talk to white people because they saw this as the best way to eventually achieve their own objectives of improving their lot.

Some of his explanations of change also bring together ideas of essentialised cultural traits, strategic action and top-down changes in the ideology of the administering bureaucracy. This is particularly so in explaining Murray Island. The Murray Islanders are said to resent any outside interference and constraint on individual autonomy ('everybody *mamoose*'). These traits are then exemplified in their fractious and desultory engagement in the pearling industry, the resistance to the Anglican monopoly on Christian denominations, and the general tenor of their engagement in the political process. Beckett's PhD thesis integrates into this kind of framework individual personalities and their trajectories, including their learning experiences in the smaller organisations on the island.

Explaining the Islanders' embrace of Christianity, its pervasiveness and its misrecognition of exploitation is one of Beckett's central preoccupations in *Custom and Colonialism*, particularly Chapter 4, 'Reflections in a colonial mirror'. He states:

---

5 Jeremy Beckett, Interview transcript, 2003, p. 34.

> My companions seem to have relegated traditional forms of thinking to the edges of their minds, utilising them only rarely and discreetly for matters of purely local concern. The dominant modes of thought derived from mission Christianity and official teachings concerning the state, together with a work ethic that had its origins in the industrial revolution. What was lacking was a sense of the market or of *Realpolitik*: the world as the Islanders understood it was governed by a moral economy, and their place in it would finally be determined by their worthiness as Christians, loyal subjects and good workers. (Beckett 1987:88)

In explaining the rise of Christianity to become the dominant mode of thought among the Islanders, Beckett draws on more complex processes. These are described at the level of a generalised, essentialised subjectivity, such as 'the Murray Islanders', and include various feedback loops. One is between that generalised subjectivity and individual strategic actions—that is, the diffusion throughout the community of the experience of successful and unsuccessful attempts to alter their conditions. Another is a feedback loop between the everyday practices and the subjectivity in which taken-for-granted aspects of life are either reinforced or exposed to contradiction. Added to this is an analysis of the colonial ideology and potential reasons for its attractiveness in different historical periods. In attempting to draw these ideas together, he describes a transformation from initial pragmatic involvement to it becoming a medium of everyday life and being taken for granted: 'As Islanders came to live, and even more, think with their work ethic, their loyalty and their Christianity, colonial culture became hegemonic, "a lived dominance" (Williams 1977:108–14)' (Beckett 1987:91–2).

By the same token, some everyday experiences and practices draw attention to and magnify only faintly perceived contradictions within the hegemonic ideology. Thus the experience of relative equality of interaction with white soldiers during World War II exacerbated the feelings of contradiction between the assumption of equality of the King's subjects and God's people, as opposed to their actual inferior economic and juridical status.

The different kinds of explanations Beckett employed in his analysis of change make for a rich account. This brief overview also reinforces, however, the impression that Beckett is overwhelmingly concerned about explaining change rather than seeking instances of continuity. One imagines Eddie Mabo's lawyers, having read Beckett's works, wondering whether he would be the right person to help them prove their case, which was essentially asserting traditional continuity.

Laade

After Beckett, the next anthropologist to spend a significant amount of time in the Torres Strait was Wolfgang Laade. He was in the Torres Strait between 1963 and 1965, and during that time spent two and a half months on Mer. I have chosen not to describe his work in any detail because his main interest was in ethnomusicology and the recording of myths (see Laade 1971). He also admitted to not doing any systematic ethnographic work during his stay on Mer (see Laade 1969).

Kitaoji

After Laade, the next fieldwork research to be carried out on the Murray Islands was undertaken by Hironobu Kitaoji between 1975 and 1977. It was part of a larger research project initiated principally by Japanese human geographers and funded by the Japanese Ministry of Education. The project, entitled 'An Ethnological and Geographical Study of Fishing People in South-Western Pacific Islands', aimed to determine through studies of traditional fishing cultures the role of cultural diffusion and the process of acculturation in the Torres Strait Islands (see Yabuuchi 1977). Kitaoji, a senior lecturer in sociology at La Trobe University at the time, was recommended partly for his fluency in Japanese and was assigned to investigate acculturation in the Murray Islands since the time of Haddon.

For all Kitaoji's fieldwork on Murray, his published output is frustratingly meagre. It consists of a structural analysis of the Malo–Bomai myth (Kitaoji 1977), and a short article and interview on the theme of regional Torres Strait Islander identity (Kitaoji 1978). This material is also difficult to assess because he presents his conclusions in a summary way without marshalling the evidence that would support them and without a thorough engagement with Haddon's and Beckett's work.

Kitaoji's work seems to reflect a movement among the Islanders in the 1970s, particularly the Murray Islanders, to re-emphasise their cultural distinctiveness by asserting a traditional continuity through the Malo–Bomai myth. This movement coincided with the increasing influence of French structuralist approaches within anthropology, and a heightened awareness of ethical issues and the sometimes fraught relationship between anthropological representations and the political struggles of encapsulated informant groups. Kitaoji did not produce a widely influential body of work. His embrace of structuralism, broad cultural commonalities and a more politicised stance, which emphasised continuity of traditions, seems, however, to have been adopted by Nonie Sharp, the next anthropological researcher to do fieldwork in the Torres Strait.

Nonie Sharp's exemplary Islanders

Sharp's academic career commenced at Melbourne University, where she majored in psychology, before there was an anthropology or sociology course offered. She was initially an honorary research fellow in the Sociology Department at La Trobe, then on the teaching staff. She has always identified herself as a sociologist, although some of her intellectual influences—such as Marcel Mauss, Lévi-Strauss and the emancipatory politics of Stanley Diamond—were more clearly associated with anthropology.[6] It was only later in her career that the Torres Strait Islanders themselves would refer to her as an anthropologist.[7]

Sharp's concerns with the academy, with the impossibility of 'value-free social science' (Sharp 1980) and her broadly anti-colonial commitment meant that she struggled with the question of an appropriate theoretical framework and writing strategy for her own research. Inspired by some of Paul Radin's work (see Radin 1920), she ultimately opted for focusing on autobiographical narratives—the Islanders explaining their culture in their own words. This solution is highly reminiscent of the dialogic ethnography proposed by Dwyer and was the focus of some debate in anthropological circles about the time that Sharp was formulating her preferred approach.[8]

But there is a tension between allowing the narrators to speak for themselves and her project of demonstrating the continuing depth and coherence of Islander traditions against popular assumptions of their complete disappearance. Much oral history is impenetrable and requires background information, context and interpretation in order to effectively communicate its significance to an unfamiliar audience. Sharp attempted to resolve this explaining–speaking-for tension by organising the narratives into broad historical periods and by adding a structuralist interpretation of Islander custom and frame of mind. This approach allowed her to draw on the *Reports* and the historical archive to provide an explanatory context, which was fashioned as a commentary focused on the narratives and reflections of the Islanders.

The 10 exemplary Islanders are '"speculative philosophers", men and women of special knowledge, custodians of cultural traditions and mediators of non-

6 For a brief overview of the life and work of Stanley Diamond, see Gailey (1992), and for a brief version of Diamond's own vision for reinventing anthropology, see Diamond (1969).

7 Interview with Nonie Sharp, 11 November 2003, Tape 1, Side A.

8 See Clifford (1986); Dwyer (1979, 1982); and Rabinow (1986).

destructive change, our special Stars of Tagai' (Sharp 1993:11–12). Most were relatively highly educated people, who had held responsible positions in their working lives and were some of the key political activists, both in the critical actions of the past and in the instigation of the *Mabo* case during the period of her fieldwork and the writing up of her thesis. Others, however, were more closely aligned with the State Government administration.

Groups

One surprise in Sharp's account of the Meriam is the prominence given to eight totemic groups that correspond exactly with the eight (or is it seven?) district names that Rivers had described in the *Reports* and the famous map of Mer. Haddon (1908:254–7) was also explicit that there was no totemism in the Eastern Islands—one of their major distinguishing features compared with the Western Islands. It seems that Meriam totems (*lubabat*) were reported by Kitaoji (1980) in an unpublished conference paper.

Sharp is aware of the contradiction in the ethnographic record, since she discusses it in an endnote. Rather than pursue the idea of possible transformation since the time of Haddon, she tends to imply that the totemic groups might have been there all along, waiting for 'Kitaoji's pioneering work' (Sharp 1993:269, note 5).

The relationship between the eight 'tribes' and observable social organisation is unclear. As explained above, in Rivers' exposition of social organisation, there were 22 village-identified exogamous patrilineal clans. It was unclear to Rivers just what social function the district groupings performed, apart from being an alternative identifier in a taxonomic hierarchy. During Beckett's time, he identified 'families', small descent groups, as the basic units of social organisation, although he did comment that a 'number of adjacent clans were grouped into wider units, mainly apparent in ritual, which the Meriam now call by the English word "tribe"' (Beckett 1983:204). Sharp's narrators, however, particularly Sam Passi, insist on eight groups sanctioned by tradition: 'I have seen one seuriseuri [Malo ceremonial club] with eight points; those eight points stand for eight tribes of Murray' (quoted in Sharp 1993:174).

Sharp herself confusingly writes of 'eight clans' and equates the 'eight peoples' with clans (1993:30, 41). She might be simply repeating a folk use of the word 'clan', but in Rivers' exposition there was a significant difference between the level most like a clan—Rivers' 'village'—and the level of eight-part division of the Meriam: Sharp's 'people' and Rivers' 'district'. Unlike the 'district', the 'village' was exogamous.

The presentation of Haddon's material in her chapter on traditional Meriam culture is intended to suggest clear continuities with the past. Reading against the grain, though, it is also suggestive of the *Reports* possibly being another source of the eightfold 'tribal' identity, which was reported to Kitaoji and Sharp. Sharp appears to take the symbolic homologies even further than Sam Passi by implying that the eight tentacles of Bomai in his octopus manifestation represent the eight tribes. Drawings of Bomai in this form appear throughout her book.

Figure 2.3 Illustration in *Stars of Tagai* of Bomai in octopus form

Source: Sharp (1993:47).

According to Sharp, the link between the eight tentacles of Malo in his octopus manifestation and the eight Meriam 'tribes' had not been made by the Islanders during her initial research, but it was at a later time.[9]

Laws and customs

The compendious phrase 'laws, customs, traditions and practices' used in the Statement of Claim in the *Mabo* case (see next chapter) highlights, in comparison, the abstract quality of Sharp's account of Meriam culture. She is not necessarily concerned with observable practices, more the content and the interpretation of the Islanders' autobiographical narratives and the intellectual processes of her narrators in trying to achieve a 'psychic integration'. 'Law' is, however, prominent in her analysis because of the central position given to *Malo ra Gelar*—literally, Malo's taboos—glossed by her narrators as 'Malo's Law'. *Malo ra Gelar* is presented as a 'sacred code' or 'rule' embodied in a number of key sayings. According to Sharp these are:

9 Nonie Sharp interview, 11 November 2003, Transcript, pp. 15–16.

Malo tag mauki mauki:	Malo keeps his hands to himself; he does not touch what is not his.
Teter mauki mauki:	He does not permit his feet to carry him towards another man's property.
Wali aritarit, sem aritarit:	Malo plants everywhere—under *wali* [a creeping vine] and *sem*, the yellow-flowered hibiscus.
Eburlem, esmaolem:	Let it drop and rot on the ground.

(Sharp 1993:50)

How these sayings relate to the Malo myths, chants ('Malo has bad teeth') and the ceremonial songs, with their elusive, archaic language, reported by Haddon and Ray, is not something that concerns Sharp beyond a generalised assertion of continuity. It is possible that the sayings had their origin in the period of general instruction given to the initiates in the context of the lengthy initiation ceremony, following the revelation of the ceremonial masks. According to Haddon, that instruction ranged over various matters besides the general admonition against stealing and other disruptive behaviour, and covered specific instruction about gardening, including effective spells and the dire consequences of a breach of the secrecy of the cult. Now, Malo's Law is presented at a high level of generality with a decidedly moral, religious tone.

This change is probably due to Sharp's narrators specifically equating Malo's Law with the Ten Commandments of the Old Testament[10] and the Malo–Bomai cult with John the Baptist.[11] Thus, the synthesis that Dave Passi and others achieve is by seeing Christianity as the fulfilment of the old religion rather than in opposition to it. Sharp aligns herself closely with this view, which minimises the disruptiveness of the initial period of conversion, and she even goes a little further, summarising the situation as the Christian message 'rekindling a flame that already burned within the traditional religions' (1993:101).

Sharp does not explore some obvious alternative interpretations of this synthesis—namely, the selective incorporation of the old cults into Christian orthodoxy and the contradictory use of Christianity to revalue and Christianise the pagan traditions. Again, this is consistent with her approach of supportive commentary. Christianity did not swallow the Malo–Bomai cult. Instead, a pre-existing mythic consciousness—striving towards the joining of natural and cosmic circles—reordered mission Christianity. As this is not the way her

10 Sam Passi, quoted in Sharp (1993:82).

11 This link is made explicitly by Flo Kennedy at p. 254 and by implication in David Passi's narrative on p. 108: 'Malo came to prepare Murray Island for Christianity and it makes me very proud as a *Zogo le* to see Malo playing that role' (Sharp 1993).

narrators express things, explaining this reordering becomes a rather difficult interpretative task, but one from which Sharp does not shrink. Ultimately, Sharp seeks confirmation of her interpretation in homologies between symbols. She links the Christian crucifix with the Southern Cross in the Tagai constellation and with the four-pronged Malo ceremonial club (1993:125). The stars of Tagai not only point to the new religion, they incorporate it.

Encouraged by her reading of Eliade and the 'critical phenomenology of comparative religion', Sharp's approach continually leads her off into a theologising reverie expressed in generalised dualities. This approach means that the issues that later became central to the *Mabo* case—such as the nature of Meriam law—are not analysed from any critical distance. It is as if the proposition that Malo's Law is the basis of traditional land tenure must be accepted because of the force of the sympathetic exposition of the synthesising project of her narrators.

Change

In the introduction to *Stars of Tagai*, Sharp declared that she wanted to 'analyse the processes of continuity and transition' (1993:15). Yet in that same introduction, there are also indications that her approach would be one-sided. Her overall rhetorical stance is that Beckett's emphasis on radical transformation has gone too far and needs to be brought back into balance. Sharp's emphasis on continuity is perhaps dictated by her identification with the narrators, who all assert continuity in various ways. It is also present in some of the overarching metaphors in the book, her presentation of historical events and her general approach.

The subtitle of her PhD thesis is 'After the Storm-Winds the Leafing of the Wongai Tree'. 'Storm-Winds' is used consistently by Sharp as a metaphor for the non-reciprocal, disruptive force of the process of colonisation. Thus, traditional Meriam culture—like the living sap in the denuded tree—springs forth after the storm has passed in the late 1970s. She supplemented the idea of hidden reserves of traditional culture by interpreting the widespread reluctance of the Islanders to talk about some of the old traditions as proof of their continued subterranean existence. It is a theme also taken up in her account of the early missionary period up to the London Missionary Society (LMS) handover to the Anglicans (1993:103–6). She represented the first decade of the twentieth century as a period of disillusionment at the failure of the early utopian promises of the LMS missionaries to eventuate and disillusionment with LMS anti-traditionalism. Thus, under the more accommodating Anglican regime of the 1920s, the performance of Malo dances re-emerged. Similarly, the banned traditional mortuary practices re-emerged in the 1930s as the two-stage tombstone opening ceremony that continues today (1993:110–16). Continuity is also implicitly asserted in her general approach of weaving together material from Haddon and the contemporary narratives.

Sharp's theme of continuity is only slightly diluted by her reflection on the 'individuation' associated with Christianity, as opposed to her assertion of the essence of tradition as reciprocity and group orientation (1993:93). It is somewhat unclear what Sharp seeks to evoke by 'individuation'. It seems to be the new self-monitoring individual morality implied in the quest for personal salvation and the individual career. What is perhaps questionable is putting 'individuation' in such a radical opposition to traditional culture given, for example, the prominence of the three *zogo le*.

The promised analysis of the processes of change also fails to materialise in any explicit or detailed way. Instead, we have the familiar threading of narratives with material from the archives about segregated protection, working in the pearling industry and cooperatives, the 1936 strike and experience of World War II. Sharp's inclination is towards broad periodisations and simple polarisations: the decline of Islander autonomy with the coming of the protection era and the strike becoming a grand narrative of oppression and liberation, of 'becoming even', and showing the Islanders' deep-seated commitment to a reciprocity framework. At this level of interpretation, the contradictory figure of Tanu Nona of Badu is difficult to place because he not only cooperated with the authorities but also became a capitalist.

Conclusion

The aim of this chapter has been to survey specifically anthropological knowledge of the Murray Islands at the time of the hearing of the *Mabo* case.[12] The restricted focus allows for an exploration of the shaping of academic anthropological knowledge through the microcosm of Meriam studies undertaken at intervals, which could represent proto-anthropology (Haddon), the era of professionalised anthropology (Beckett), and the anti-colonial critique of professionalised anthropology (Sharp). This account challenges any simple notion of consensus about a clearly defined field of study that consistently expands and improves over time. Even the minimal commonality of fieldwork methodology was approached in divergent ways.

12 Perhaps arbitrarily, this focus means omitting the observations of early European mariners, the novelisation of Haddon's ethnography in Idriess's *The Drums of Mer* (1933), Lawrie's (1970) collection of Torres Strait myths and the work of marine biologist Robert Johannes on customary marine tenure (Johannes and MacFarlane 1984).

Beckett came closest to the ideal of long-term, localised fieldwork in the tradition of post-Malinowski, professionalised anthropology. Haddon was apologetic about his seduction by the prospect of reconstructing savage culture through the living memory of his informants, but he retrieves something of the ideal of long-term fieldwork vicariously through Mr Bruce. Sharp, a sociologist who drew selectively on anthropological theorists, went to various field locations for relatively brief periods. She does not expressly include her observations of people's behaviour since she is so firmly fixated on the narratives of her select group.

There are also different orientations towards empirical ideals of data description and transparency of exposition. Haddon makes the most straightforward claims for the possibility of objective description. Ray's systematic diligence in his research on Meriam language has already been mentioned, as has Haddon's commitment to a single, accurate account of previous traditions. While this kind of methodological rectitude continues to impress, its limitations are also obvious: there is no reflexivity about his role in creating an authoritative account and no investigation of the implications of diverse accounts for the comprehensive description of the social system that allows such diversity. On the other hand, it is Haddon's detailed description of his methodology that enables this belated critique of mine to be made. Sharp's critique of the pretensions of objective social science would seem to put her at odds with Haddon, but overall her attitude to Haddon is one of appreciation, perhaps reflecting the appreciation of her narrators, who seem to regard 'Dr Haddon' and the *Reports* very highly. Some of them are students of the *Reports*, copies of which were made available to them by Beckett during his period of fieldwork. Beckett, while critical of the frustrating gaps in Haddon, is also appreciative. Despite the obvious difficulties of Haddon's reconstructive enterprise, Beckett takes the *Reports* as a baseline for his own 1959–60 study that is partly aimed at filling in the 70-year gap since the Cambridge expedition from oral history and the archive.

Beckett's commitment to empirical methods and openness of presentation is somewhat buried under the generalisations and condensation required to fit his complete narrative of colonisation between the covers of one book. His careful methodology is more apparent in his PhD thesis. The apogee of his empiricism is the table of actual hours spent by individuals on certain activities over the course of a month. But even in *Custom and Colonialism* he asserts an authority backed by field notes, though actual quotes from informants are infrequent and typically consist of a single phrase confirming a larger narrative or analysis of his own.

Sharp's lengthy quoting of her narrators could, by itself, be seen as exemplary transparency. This must be weighed, however, against the elusiveness of her reasons for the choice of those narrators who would demonstrate her 'best of

Torres Strait culture', and her style of interpretation, which is unconcerned with any careful comparison of the differences between her own interpretation and what the narrators actually say.

The divergence between Beckett and Sharp should also be seen in the context of the similarity of their political orientations (anti-colonial, anti-paternalistic), and their initial interest in Melanesian cargo cults, their interest in state–local articulations and historical transformation. Both have seen themselves as outsiders in the academy at various stages. One would expect this similarity to magnify the perceived differences in their approaches and intensify academic competition between them. How have they managed this competition in practice? It seems on Sharp's part by explicit critique and on Beckett's part, with the exception of one notable dagger to her heart (Beckett 1994), by silence.

How are we to assess the competing interpretations in Sharp and Beckett? I have suggested that there is a gratuitous element in Sharp's critique of Beckett. She sometimes misrepresents the totality of his work. Moreover, time and the tide of history are on his side. The radical changes in the historical circumstances of the Murray Islanders over 100 years to the time of Sharp's fieldwork would be expected to result in major changes in any culture. But there is also a personal element here. Both Beckett and Sharp kept in touch with the Islanders after their initial periods of fieldwork, but Beckett has been able to observe the changes from a period well before Sharp's fieldwork. For example, there is a particular problem for Sharp's account of the Islander leader Marou Mimi and the 1936 strike. Sharp did not have direct access to Marou Mimi, but he was one of Beckett's major informants. Beckett rather wryly commented on what he saw as the *ex post facto* revising of history by later generations: 'The divisions of the post-war years have dissolved. Marou, who died in 1969, has undergone an apotheosis to become the father of Torres Strait freedom, while his old opponents seem to have forgotten that there were ever any differences between them' (1987:224).

It is not only Beckett's period of fieldwork that is a problem for Sharp's argument for continuity, but the much longer period of colonisation in which Christianity became a pervasive influence, as Beckett says, restructuring relations by becoming the basis on which the evaluation of the behaviour of others is made. In this way, Beckett's authoritative narrative spoils the simplicity of the narratives of Sharp's chosen informants.

Their respective defences of their informants and their periods of fieldwork are also suggestive of intense bonding between anthropologists and informants. Part of Beckett's negative reaction to *Stars of Tagai* was that it portrayed his Murray Islander friends in a way that made them unrecognisable to him. Thus, for Beckett, to acquiesce in the contemporary smoothing over of differences between Marou and his opponents in the current telling of history would be more than inaccurate; it would be a betrayal of his friend Marou. Likewise, Sharp's questioning of Beckett's assertion of the demise of the traditional culture keeps faith with her exemplary Islanders and their assertions of strong traditional continuity.

Although the foregoing seems to be suggesting the possibility of an authoritative evaluation of the relative merits of Sharp and Beckett's account, ultimately any such evaluation confronts the basic problem of interpretative indeterminacy and the oversimplified dualism of a continuity–change dichotomy that both Sharp and Beckett fail to confront explicitly. By interpretative indeterminacy, I mean the ability of the same evidence to support more than one interpretation (for an exposition of the problem, see Bohman 1991). I have already mentioned the divergent interpretations of the 1936 strike: a critical, unifying event according to Sharp, and, according to Beckett, in its isolation, an opportunity to reflect on the relative success of the administration policy of promoting individual island identity despite the many commonalities of all the Torres Strait Islanders.

Two further examples would be the latter-day performance of Malo–Bomai ceremonies and the issue of personal rivalry and competition. Beckett photographed a performance of a Malo ceremony in 1961, describing it as a re-enactment: 'It was one Island in the Strait where one could see an old cult re-enacted, albeit as entertainment' (1987:111).

The word 're-enactment' is probably intended to connote the transformation of what is implied by a performance from the pre-missionary period (initiation, gender restrictions, ceremonial leaders) to the 1960s (public performance by church-going Christians). From Kitaoji's description of the telling of the Malo–Bomai myth as deeply felt, it is possible to imagine that his or Sharp's interpretation of the performance would probably have been one of strong continuity. And these differing possible interpretations would all be using Haddon as the reference point.

The example of rivalry is more difficult to demonstrate as neither Beckett nor Sharp takes it up as an example of cultural continuity. The point is that they could have. Although not thematised by Haddon, there is material in the *Reports* and in *Head-Hunters* of rivalry and competition being pervasive—every new fad, such as top-spinning, quickly resulted in organised competitions that threatened to disrupt the routine of the whole island community (Haddon 1901:40–1). Sharp seems to be uncomfortable with intra-Islander competition and she does not know what to make of long-term council member George Mye's reflection that one of his own enduring motivations was competition with Tanu Nona, community leader of Badu Island. It is as if admitting to widespread rivalry would undermine her argument for the deep continuity of reciprocity as a guiding principle.

Figure 2.4 Beckett's photograph of a 1961 Malo–Bomai performance

Source: Beckett (1998).

Finding a way out of the limiting dualism of continuity and change has been the project of numerous thinkers in historical anthropology (Comaroff and Comaroff 1991; Sahlins 1981, 1983; Thomas 1989; Wolf 1982). Merlan has recently sought to bring various approaches together under the rubric of the 'inter-cultural'—'inter' being used in the same sense as in 'inter-subjectivity' (see Merlan 2002, 2005). We will have to return to that discussion throughout this book.

To conclude this review, the relevant material in the anthropological archive, which was available to Beckett in preparing his expert report in *Mabo*, could be summarised as in Table 2.2.

Table 2.2 Summary comparison of the *Reports*, Beckett and Sharp

Haddon, Rivers, Wilkin (1898)	Beckett (1959–61)	Sharp (1978, 1979)
	GROUPS, 'SOCIETIES'	
	Political followings	
	Family	
Village		
District	= 'Tribe'	= 'Tribe', 'clan', 'people', totemic group
The Eastern Islanders	The Murray Islanders/Meriam	The Meriam
	LAND, LAWS, CUSTOMS	
• Eldest male child inheritance • Marriage portions • Individual dispositions • Strategic behaviour	• Meriam domain • Traditional principles • Demographic change • Historical transformation	• Malo's Law as the religious foundation of traditional land tenure
	CONTINUITY/CHANGE	
• Fatal impact	• Ecological adaptation • Rational choice • Diffusion of learnt experiences • Naturalisation of foreign ideology through use	• Re-emergence of suppressed culture • Deep homologies with ancient traditions

What use Beckett actually made of this material will be the subject of the next chapter.

3. Beckett in *Mabo*

Also called for the plaintiffs was a senior anthropologist, Dr Jeremy Beckett. (Keon-Cohen 2000:926)

Involvement of anthropologists in pre-trial preparation

In order to understand the significance of Beckett's testimony in the hearing of the facts in the *Mabo* case, it is necessary to briefly outline how the claim to the Murray Islands was framed and what Justice Moynihan's role was within the High Court's adjudication of the case.[1]

The two key documents formulating the claim were the *Statement of Claim As Amended June 1989*[2] and the proposed statement of facts that the plaintiffs wanted Justice Moynihan to adopt. A statement of claim becomes the cardinal point of reference in any civil litigation. Around its assertions are marshalled evidence, counterevidence and conflicting final submissions. The *Mabo* Statement of Claim could be paraphrased as follows.

1. Since time immemorial, the Murray Islands have been continuously inhabited and exclusively possessed by people called the Meriam people who speak a distinct language.
2. The plaintiffs are members of the Meriam people and Eddie Mabo is a descendant of the traditional leaders known as 'Aiets'. They make their claim on their own behalf and on behalf of the members of their various family groups.
3. The Meriam people lived in permanent, settled communities under their own social and political organisation with community leaders and institutions that governed their affairs and included a system of laws. They had laws, customs, traditions and practices of their own for determining questions concerning the ordering of community life including the ownership of, and dealings with, land, seas, seabeds and reefs.
4. The particulars of the laws, customs, traditions and practices relating to land, seas, seabeds and reefs are

1 It would be superfluous to reiterate an account of the various events leading to the commencement of the *Mabo* case litigation as they have been covered in detail elsewhere (see Keon-Cohen 2000; Sharp 1996).

2 It is reproduced as Annexure A in Volume 3 of the *Determination by the Supreme Court of Queensland of the Remitter from the High Court of Australia dated 27th February, 1986.*

- numerous areas are separately owned by particular family groups; the members of the family groups have rights and duties in relation to their respective family group areas—for example, the head of the family has the right and duty to allocate portions of the family land to be used by individual members of the respective family groups
- some areas of land are individually owned but may be disposed of only to other members of their family group
- some areas have been granted collectively to the Meriam people and some areas have been acquired by the State of Queensland.

The plaintiffs continue to own and have rights in particular areas of land, and so on, according to the laws, customs, traditions and practices, and so on.

And the plaintiffs' claim

> A. A declaration that the plaintiffs are
>
> (a) owners by custom
>
> (b) holders of traditional native title
>
> (c) holders of usufructuary rights
>
> with respect to their respective lands.

Eddie Mabo's personal influence on the drafting of the Statement of Claim can be seen in the unusual identification of him among the plaintiffs as 'a descendant of the traditional leaders known as the Aiets'. This identification proved to be a fateful decision. Making this claim in an unqualified way could be seen as laying the foundations for undermining his credibility before Justice Moynihan in the Queensland Supreme Court—an undermining to which Beckett's evidence was to contribute.

The Statement of Claim had been filed in the High Court, which remitted the determination of the facts of the case to Justice Moynihan of the Supreme Court of Queensland.[3] Generally speaking, the Statement of Facts proposed by the plaintiffs before Justice Moynihan followed the Statement of Claim, but there

3 In this instance, the remittal means the transfer of the fact-finding part of the case, which was started in the High Court, to the Supreme Court of Queensland. Section 44 of the *Judiciary Act 1903* (Cwlth) allows the High Court to remit a matter commenced in the High Court, or part of a matter, to other Federal, State or Territory courts. In *Mabo*, this allowed the High Court to avoid the time-consuming hearing of evidence. According to Eddie Mabo's lawyer, Bryan Keon-Cohen, commencing the legal proceedings in the High Court was a considered strategy to ensure High Court supervision over the fact-finding process.

were some significant changes. One change was that the decisions of the Island Court relating to land became the example *par excellence* of the existence of customary laws[4]—an idea strongly contested by the Queensland Government.

The hearing before Justice Moynihan proceeded in much the same way as a trial. The plaintiffs called witnesses and presented documentary evidence in support of their claims, and the State of Queensland cross-examined witnesses and adduced their own evidence. Instead of making a final judgment, however, Justice Moynihan would present his findings of fact to the High Court for its ultimate decision on the law.

It would have been difficult for the plaintiffs' lawyers not to call Beckett. His book *Torres Strait Islanders: Custom and Colonialism* (Beckett 1987) was published two years earlier and it would have been obvious that, in terms of length of fieldwork on the Murray Islands, the number of publications and academic seniority, he was the best qualified to be the expert anthropological witness. If they had not called him, he could have been subpoenaed by the Queensland Government. But there were risks for the claimants. To oversimplify, Beckett had documented change but they needed his evidence to help prove continuity. How he negotiated his way through these expectations is one of the themes of the analysis of his performance as an expert witness.

Kitaoji was going to be called, but the lawyers changed their mind at the last minute.[5] It is apparent from the transcript of the hearing that the plaintiffs' lawyers had, at one stage, intended to call Nonie Sharp as an expert witness (T. 184).[6] Why this did not eventuate remains a little unclear. When I interviewed him in 2003, Keon-Cohen could not remember a specific reason. He thought that it was a tactical decision, possibly applying the same rationale as they did to Kitaoji: to avoid opening up variable accounts that would detract from the integrity of each.[7] In Nonie Sharp's recollection, the reason was her vulnerability to cross-examination on her radical politics.[8] Beckett shared her interpretation.[9]

4 Thus, proposed finding of fact 78J reads:

> 78. The Meriam People, including the Plaintiffs and their predecessors in title, have in the past and continue to…
>
> (j) Make and administer a system of customary laws including laws, customs, traditions and practices concerning rights in and dealings with the land of the Islands. Examples of such laws, practices and dealings are set out in Annexure D. [Annexure D being the Island Court records relating to the resolution of land disputes.]

5 See Keon-Cohen (2000:926, footnote 244).

6 'T' is the shorthand reference to the official transcript of the hearing of the facts before Justice Moynihan in the Supreme Court of Queensland in the *Mabo* case.

7 Brian Keon-Cohen, Interview, 7 November 2003, Tape 1, Side B.

8 Nonie Sharp, Interview transcript, 11 November 2003, pp. 8–9.

9 Jeremy Beckett, Interview transcript, 2003, p. 10.

Although Beckett had been involved in the preparation of the case, he was adamant that he had not been consulted on the drafting of the Statement of Claim.[10] If he had been consulted, he could have offered a radically different perspective on Eddie Mabo's claim to be a hereditary, traditional leader—an 'Aiet'. He recalled being startled by the way in which all Eddie Mabo's claims had been incorporated into the Statement of Claim.[11] Fortuitously, the Statement of Claim identified 'the family' as the social grouping relevant to land matters, rather than 'the clan' or 'the tribe'. This identification coincided with Beckett's view. It did not, however, make any reference to individual choice of owners in the disposition of their land.

Beckett had two jobs in the preparation of the case that involved him interviewing Murray Islanders who were living in Townsville. The first job was to produce a statement of his views, as an anthropologist, about the continuity of traditional land tenure on Murray Island. The second job involved directing potential Islander witnesses to the lawyers. Both jobs left Beckett somewhat estranged from the legal team. He eventually produced his statement, entitled 'Meriam Land Tenure', but received little feedback from the lawyers, except from Brian Keon-Cohen, who thought that it should have been more detailed. In Beckett's recollection, the areas that needed more detail were never specified. He thought that the statement had been dispensed with. He was surprised when it re-emerged, years later, to be tendered as part of his evidence. In relation to the search for potential Islander witnesses, Beckett had sent a very knowledgeable Islander friend of his to the lawyers. In response, he received complaints from the lawyers that his friend's evidence would have been extremely detrimental to the case as it was then framed.

The hearing

The plaintiffs' evidence

Given the overlap between Sharp's narrators and the claimants, much of the plaintiffs' evidence followed what could have been expected from the *Stars of Tagai* (Sharp 1993). This is largely true of all the evidence led by the plaintiffs' own lawyers. For example, Eddie Mabo emphasised the importance of the village of Las for the Malo–Bomai cult (reinforced by stories of the burial of the key ceremonial mask near Las [T. 129–30, 350]); the secret continuation of induction into the Malo cult during the period of the London Missionary Society (LMS), and extending, in modified form, into the period of the Anglican takeover, at

10 Jeremy Beckett 2003, Interview transcript, pp. 3–6, 31–2.

11 Jeremy Beckett 2003, Interview transcript, pp. 25–6.

least to the 1940s (T. 249–52, 800); the eight tribes of Mer with distinct tribal areas; the hereditary office of the Aiets, the Aiet being the leading law-maker and dispute resolver among the *zogo le* of the Malo–Bomai cult; Malo's gardening lore and law against property theft (T. 346–7); and the continuing significance of land previously occupied by shrines at Dam (T. 290) and Tomog (T. 352). What finds no counterpart in Sharp is Eddie Mabo's specific claims to particular plots of land. Nor does her book prepare us for Mabo's most extravagant claims in his written statement, tendered in evidence. Queensland Government lawyers made much of such passages as: 'My arrival on the Island rejuvenates hope amongst the people. I am their leader to be compared to the elected chairman. I am the leader in the people's memory according to tradition' (quoted at T. 1113).

In cross-examination, a more complex picture emerged that revealed the limitations of Sharp's account. Eddie Mabo had to admit that it was only his 'clan' that had the understanding that the word 'Aiet' refers to a hereditary title, as opposed to being simply a personal name. He attributed the lack of widespread recognition of the hereditary title to the 'petty jealousy' of other groups (T. 812). Similarly, he was forced to retreat from claims that his succession to the position of Aiet had been acknowledged in various ways by the Murray Island Council and, more fundamentally, he was forced to admit that it was no longer possible to become an Aiet, in the traditional sense of the term, given that no *zogo le* had been initiated into that position since 1925 (T. 823–7). Thus, the strong assertions made in the Statement of Claim and in his own written statement had to be pared back from an 'is' to a rather feeble 'would have been' but for the intervention of the LMS and subsequent colonial history.

Moreover, what might be called the politics of Eddie Mabo's assertion of traditionalism became increasingly transparent with the unfolding of the evidence. He had suffered under the power of the Island Council for many years. He had received the harsh sentence of banishment for one year for being caught drinking alcohol on Murray Island in 1956. Adding an intriguing note of complexity to Sharp's account of the exemplary Islanders, it was revealed that the Island Court that had sentenced Mabo was constituted by three other exemplary Islanders: Marou, Sam Passi and George Mye (T. 780). In addition, it was the Island Council—whether pressured by the Queensland administration or not—that had refused Eddie Mabo's formal requests for entry to Murray Island during the 1960s and 1970s. Following the cross-examination of Mabo's expansive assertions of his own executive decision-making power in matters of custom, Justice Moynihan summarised the obvious divergence of the bases for decision-making authority on Murray Island as a power struggle between the elected council leaders and those wanting the restoration of tribal authority.

Eddie Mabo's naive agreement with the Judge's summary—one of a number of moments of dangerous honesty—probably contributed to the negative impression being formed of his credibility. There was, however, an abundance of material on which Justice Moynihan could base such a negative impression of Eddie Mabo: the very large number of portions of land claimed on various bases; his insistence on recalling exact conversations with his grandfather when Eddie Mabo was only six years old; his insistence that only those adopted from close kin could base their claims to inheritance on adoption (thus conveniently disposing of a counterclaim to one of his claimed portions by another adopted Islander); and, generally, his defensive and on occasion hot-tempered, argumentative responses to cross-examination. Overall, the extraordinarily long and gruelling examination and cross-examination of Eddie Mabo exposed his claims to minute scrutiny, which was made possible by the mobilisation of the resources of the State of Queensland. Every government document relevant to the cross-examination was found, analysed and deployed, and other Islanders, who disputed some of Mabo's claims, were interviewed and presented as witnesses. Through this process, a much more complex and flawed character emerged. The Eddie Mabo of *Stars of Tagai* was revealed as an idealised portrait: Mabo before cross-examination.

Sam Passi, another of Sharp's stars, had experienced a serious decline in his health since the period of Sharp's fieldwork. He did give evidence and told the court some of the same things he had told Sharp, such as, 'If you want to be a real Murray Islander you follow Malo's Law' (T. 1115). His frailty, however, meant that the authoritative clarity of his narrative in *Stars of Tagai* was not apparent in his evidence.

David Passi, one of the plaintiffs, gave evidence about the Passi claims in terms that were also largely supportive of Eddie Mabo's claims. Consistent with Sharp's portrayal of him in *Stars of Tagai*, David Passi's evidence presented his project of synthesising Christianity and the Malo–Bomai traditions. Counsel for Queensland complained that his statement read more like a sermon (T. 1887), but generally his evidence seems to have been well received by the judge. His calm, reflective and direct approach to giving his evidence provided a direct contrast with Eddie Mabo's performance. It also led to some unguarded statements about the enforcement of property rights in the pre-colonial era: 'our understanding of the law was the club. The Gabba Gabba [club] was the justice' (T. 2007).

Beckett certainly thought that by the time he was called to give evidence—towards the end of the plaintiffs' case—the lawyers' initial breezy confidence in their case had been somewhat shaken. Not only had the judge made frequent criticism of the way in which evidence was being led, but cross-examination had successfully undermined some of their key witnesses and there had been evidence of the negative reaction of other Islanders to some of the specific claims made by the plaintiffs.

Beckett's examination-in-chief

Because of his task of writing his statement on Meriam land tenure, Beckett had been confronted at an early stage with the question of what general approach he should take to his evidence. As he explained to me in 2003, he thought that he had to chart a new course between the unrealistic traditionalism of the Statement of Claim and what he now saw as the excessive presentism in his own published work:

> [W]hen I was invited to become a witness I had to consider first the kind of framework in which my work had been done...My emphasis was on the present, recognising all the changes that have happened and that was the way I wrote my thesis. It stressed, perhaps excessively, the here and now, the post-contact...when I was in the witness box I realised the way in which the statement of claim had been made was very much in traditional mode...I thought firstly that it could not be assumed that either counsel or the judge had not read my material...that for me to simply present the warm inner glow of history...and to assert that nothing of significance had changed would simply go down...My strategy really was to anticipate all these objections and to say why I thought, nevertheless, the land tenure system was essentially the same.[12]

His recollection was also that in order to establish his own status as an expert witness, with his primary responsibility being to the court, he could not appear to be the mouthpiece of the plaintiffs' lawyers. From this perspective, his lack of involvement in formulating the Statement of Claim and his frustrating interaction with the lawyers might have assisted him. In any event, Beckett was duly called to Brisbane to meet with the plaintiffs' lawyers and prepare for his appearance as their expert witness.

In any model strategy for the successful conduct of litigation, the examination-in-chief is an opportunity to present the witness's evidence in the most advantageous way and to pre-emptively explain any obvious weaknesses or contradictions, so that they do not gain the credence of being concessions made during cross-examination. It allows for close cooperation between barrister and witness in the presentation of a methodically choreographed performance. Of course, historical contingencies tend to defeat such ideal strategies.

During his few days of preparation, Beckett read the transcript of proceedings up to that point and had productive preparatory meetings with Ron Castan QC, the plaintiffs' senior counsel. Beckett recalled that, on the day he entered the witness box, to his surprise, Brian Keon-Cohen, another of the plaintiffs'

12 Jeremy Beckett 2003, Interview transcript, pp. 14–15.

barristers, stood up to lead him through his evidence. Beckett remains baffled by this change of plan. He recalled that Keon-Cohen had a cold and that at various points Beckett could not quite follow where he was being led and what answer was expected. Having lost the thread of the questions, Beckett gave some answers that did not seem to respond to the apparent expectation of the questioner.

The transcript also reveals that Keon-Cohen's flow of questioning was interrupted fairly early by objections to the form of some questions. There was a certain sharpness and irritation on the part of the judge in dealing with the objections, as if he saw Keon-Cohen as a recalcitrant rule bender, surreptitiously trying to adduce evidence through Beckett that should have come from other witnesses. In the course of his research, Beckett had come across information supportive of Eddie Mabo's critical claim to adoption, and counsel for the plaintiffs could not resist trying to lead this evidence, provoking objection.

> HIS HONOUR: [Y]ou are not leading it as anthropological evidence. You are leading it as evidence probative of the fact that Eddie Mabo was adopted; that's got nothing to do with anthropology. (T. 2204)

This statement is revealing in the quality of its obscurity. In the background, there are legal doctrines about expert evidence that are not explicitly identified in the summary nature of the objection, the judge's ruling and the acquiescence of the plaintiffs' lawyer. That acquiescence could have been based on agreement that a legal doctrine had been transgressed or a pragmatic choice not to challenge this particular incorrect ruling. Why one may have an expert anthropological opinion about general principles of inheritance, including via adoption, but not about whether an individual was adopted according to island custom, seems to raise many arguable legal issues.[13] The judge's comment is also revealing of his conceptualisation of anthropology as a whole. Although somewhat elusive, the judge seemed to be expressing a preference for the anthropology of high-level, encapsulating generalisation, rather than the anthropology of intimate description or exemplary case study.

At the risk of smoothing over the disjointed unfolding of Beckett's evidence, the elements of his argument could be summarised as follows.

- Although the main focus of his fieldwork on Mer in 1959–61 was local politics, change and engagement with the wider world, he did carry out some research on land tenure. It was never published, but he felt the need

13 For example, in the Blue Mud Bay Native Title Claim (*Gumana v Northern Territory* [2005] FCA 50 (7 February 2005)), Justice Selway decided that, because of the long association of the anthropologist with the claimants in that case, he would accept his evidence both as expert evidence *and* as primary evidence (see paras 167–78).

to do it 'because the question of descent and inheritance was an important problem in anthropology at that time' (T. 2212).

- Continuity of land tenure can be seen at the level of 'principles' that operate against a background of the pervasiveness of the idea of ownership in Meriam culture that applied to ownership songs, dances and myths, as well as land (Exhibit 214, p. 2). Critically, Beckett stated: 'I would expect change of various kinds, but that doesn't necessarily mean that the basic principles... [of] the system of inheritance had been changed' (T. 2216–17).
- The principles can be stated as follows
  - current owners of land have the right to dispose of their land to whomever they wish
  - this freedom is, however, constrained by the legitimate expectation that the land will be disposed of to close kin, particularly descendants (including adopted children)
  - there is a legitimate expectation that males have stronger entitlements than females and that, if the inheritance is to be divided among brothers, the entitlement of the oldest brother is the greater. (Exhibit 214, T. 2218, 2223)
- The survival of the traditional land-tenure principles—albeit in a slightly modified form—is due partly to the particular colonial history of the Murray Islands, which focused on evangelisation, education and general governance for law and order, rather than a deliberate attempt at wholesale reorganisation of garden or village land. Thus, decision making about land could be seen to operate within a 'Murray Island domain' (T. 2221, 2236, 2334).
- On analysis, the Island Court, although a colonial institution, broadly supported traditional principles that operated largely outside the court system. It did this by resolving disputes at the margins, typically about boundaries, adoption and the real intentions of previous owners, and by not introducing any radical innovations (T. 2233, 2238, 2296).
- The advent of written wills was an innovation only in a 'technical sense' because most wills gave effect to the traditional principles as described (T. 2238).

What might not be apparent from this summary is a subtle shift in emphasis towards more anthropologically orthodox kinship explanations. As was noted in the previous chapter, although Beckett explored kinship in his original fieldwork, he specifically rejected it as an explanation of the political cleavages that seemed to dominate the island during his period of fieldwork. In his attempt to recover the world of the Meriam domain, however, kinship returned to prominence: 'kinship also organised in a general sense the peoples' understanding about how land could be legitimately occupied' (T. 2220).

This renewed prominence would not have come as a complete surprise to readers of his Torres Strait work, for he had always referred to the continuing relevance of kinship to matters of private concern, even if it was only in passing on to what he considered to be more pressing issues.

It should be noted that, in Beckett's conceptualisation of the system of land tenure, coherence is established at the fairly abstract level of 'principles', but at a lower level of generality than 'Malo's Law'. The level of 'principles' coincided well with the particulars of the laws and customs asserted in the Statement of Claim, but not necessarily with the claimants' insistence on the centrality of Malo's Law. Thus, Beckett's view of Malo's Law was potentially quite significant:

> DR BECKETT: I read Malo's Law or rule as a general precept rather than a statement of law in our sense of the term. (T. 2232)

In my view, his stance on Malo's Law became quite important in projecting his independence and connecting with the judge. It is also worth noting that Beckett's use of the opaque phrase 'law in our sense of the term' matched Justice Moynihan's comprehensive avoidance of defining his use of the critical word 'law' in his *Determination of Facts* (discussed below).

One of the notable features of Beckett's evidence is the eagerness of the judge to engage directly with Beckett, sometimes completely interrupting the flow of Keon-Cohen's questions. Many of the judge's interventions sought confirmation from Beckett of the judge's own questions and partially formed interpretations—in a sense performing a similar function to the Aboriginal Land Commissioner's anthropologist in land claim inquiries. For example:

> HIS HONOUR: Do you think that there is a risk, if that's the right word, that a redefinition under the sort of cultural forces that are operating on Meriam society now can be selective, the parts that are emphasised or even remembered are the ones that are most comfortable with the competing culture and which—?
>
> DR BECKETT: Yes, I think one of the things that happens, as I understand it, in cultural change, is a new situation arises, people have to devise new ways of saying things and doing things and what they do is to draw on the cultural resources which they have which may result in a new set of emphases, a bringing together of principles which haven't been brought together before. So, it is a kind of reworking of a culture...I think what we have now is that in what one might almost call a Murray Island nationalism—perhaps overstating it a little bit—the memories of the Malo–Bomai cult have been drawn on to articulate a new set of ideas for a new kind of audience. (T. 2248–50)

This interaction raises many of the issues considered in the course of this chapter. Is Beckett's historical contextualising of contemporary claims destructive of the success of those claims in this legal forum because it can too easily be assimilated to commonplace notions of inauthenticity? Did Beckett fall into Justice Moynihan's trap? Or does such contextualisation also have the effect of bolstering the appearance of independence and critical distance of the expert witness?

The judge also wondered about the shallow genealogical depth in the Haddon genealogies (T. 2250), the origin of the elaborate fish traps made of stone (T. 2265), how the traditional system would cope with land being unused for long periods (T. 2290), how 'tribe' related to 'clan' (T. 2309) and about enforcement of traditional rules prior to the existence of the Island Court (T. 2321). He proposed that the attitude of the Murray Island Council to land claims by long-absent Islanders might be a function of the perceived disruptiveness of the claims. Beckett diplomatically said that it could well be a consideration (T. 2302). The judge suggested that Europeans might have introduced the interest in genealogical depth beyond one or two generations. Beckett agreed (T. 2309). The judge wondered if the commitment of the Passi family not to divide their lands disproved the assertions that there is a system of individual ownership. Beckett said that he saw their commitment as an example of the rhetoric of the Passis about family solidarity (T. 2310). The frequency of such interventions gives the impression of the judge, at last, finding someone whom he could ask about matters that might have been troubling him. Generally speaking, Beckett was fulsome in his confirmation of most of the judge's ideas, Beckett's frequent response being 'Exactly so'.

Some of the judge's questioning of Beckett provided the most detailed evidence of the judge's thought processes at that point in the trial. They reveal a mind so preoccupied with his fact-finding task that it cannot admit to any interpretative indeterminacy:

> HIS HONOUR: This may be an inapposite way of thinking of it, but what in your understanding of Murray Island comes first; is it the garden or the land? In other words, is it the gardening which is important, and without sufficient land to garden, you're of little or no consequence, therefore you've got to have some sort of system to control access to gardening land, or is it rather that there's the land, you've got to do something with it and what you do with it is gardening. Do you understand the distinction? (T. 2235)

Beckett's answer was in terms of avoiding such a ranking. He mentioned fallow land as indicative of the value of land apart from immediate use value and land as a marker of one's prestige within the total social field (T. 2235–6).

Beckett's cross-examination

As part of her preparation, Mrs White, Counsel for Queensland, requested a private meeting with Beckett to discuss his evidence. As the legal maxim says, there is no property in a witness, so the plaintiffs' lawyers could not object.[14] The meeting occurred before her cross-examination of Beckett and was held in her chambers. In what appears to have been a pre-emptive attempt to find out how Beckett would respond to various questions, she covered a wide variety of issues. When her cross-examination in court commenced, she made full use of her familiarity with the plaintiffs' evidence as it had emerged in the weeks prior to Beckett's appearance. That familiarity precipitated moments of dramatic irony in which the barristers and the judge, but probably not Beckett, would have known the significance of a particular line of questioning and the probable use of his answers in final submissions. At the very beginning of the cross-examination, Beckett was asked seemingly innocuous questions about fieldwork methodology and oral history, particularly the tendency of informants to shape reminiscences to present purposes. Given the severe cross-examination of Eddie Mabo about his near-perfect recollection of childhood conversations with his grandfather, it would have been obvious, however, that this was the unstated reference in the questions (see T. 2316).

This interaction could be a metonym for the predicament of the expert witness in cross-examination. Should the witness concentrate on giving an answer to the immediate question? Should the witness think ahead to the ultimate issues in the case, so that the framing of the answer is made with sufficient qualifications, protecting it from misuse at a later date? Even if such complex thought processes are possible in the split second between question and answer, will too much second-guessing the ulterior purposes of questions detract from the appearance of frankness and honesty of direct answers?

Beckett had additional distractions:

> [The courtroom] was imposing and [had] a gallery at the back and I remember Eddie [Mabo] was there. I remember because during that question about Polynesia, Eddie caught my eye. One of the things we both liked was dancing from the island of Rotuma which was practised on Murray Island and he made a sort of dance gesture and I had to stop myself from cracking up.[15]

One technique of cross-examination is to lead the witness down a corridor, closing each escape door as they go, eventually leading to the last and only door that opens to a proposition that qualifies, undermines or contradicts

14 See Freckelton and Selby (2009:238).

15 Jeremy Beckett, Interview transcript, 2003, p. 8.

the witness's evidence-in-chief. Witnesses have to spontaneously create their own escape door or agree to the proposition and hope for some redress in re-examination.[16]

Mrs White attempted to lead Beckett down three such corridors. The first ended with the proposition that the principles of inheritance as described by Wilkin, and now by Beckett, are so flexible as not to amount to a system at all. This corridor commenced with gaining Beckett's assent to the proposition that Wilkin's description of inheritance principles—with its emphasis on the individual choice of the oldest male owner of land, including the possibility of alienation to non-family members (T. 2337)—was extremely flexible (T. 2318). Similarly, he had to agree that the widespread residence on land belonging to other families reflected a high degree of flexibility (T. 2340). There was also the story of one of the Passis' ancestors obtaining land on Mer through his supposed adoption, late in his life, by the unrelated owners of the land (T. 2346–7). Beckett's response was that one has to balance the assertions of individual choice with actual practice, which revealed much less flexibility—that is, overwhelmingly inheritance by immediate kin (T. 2318).

The second, related corridor led to the proposition that the rules of the traditional land tenure system did not act as any constraint on behaviour in relation to land. Instead, it was argued, such behaviour could be adequately explained in terms of shared concepts of looking after kin, shame, power relationships and strategic action. White pursued this proposition by asserting a distinction between 'social constraints' (such as shame) and 'system constraints' (presumably such as rules). Beckett responded, in effect, by rejecting the applicability of such a distinction 'in a community of this kind' (T. 2320).

In pursuing her second theme of land arrangements merely reflecting particular social interactions, Mrs White canvassed some indisputable material. This included Wilkin's chapter in Volume VI of the *Reports*, which describes the strategic action of particular 'land grabbers' asserting oral dispositions of land to them by deceased owners (T. 2321, 2345); a close analysis of the land cases reported by Rivers in the same volume of the *Reports*, which demonstrated the manipulation of the traditional rules of inheritance (T. 2342–4); reports of caretakers of land eventually becoming the owners (T. 2347); and the contemporary

16 I do not have the space in this book to review the extensive literature on techniques and strategies for cross-examining the expert witness. Freckelton and Selby's legal textbook on expert evidence provides an overview of such techniques and strategies (see Freckelton and Selby 2009:ch. 24) and there are whole books and academic careers devoted to the topic (see, for example, Imwinkelried 1997). Most of this literature addresses the scientific expert as the paradigmatic case. Had time and space permitted, it would have been interesting to systematically assess whether the established techniques for cross-examining scientists were used on anthropologists and how successful they were.

existence of Murray Islanders who had reputations as land grabbers (T. 2345). She then brought together the first two propositions and the inherent uncertainty of oral dispositions of land (T. 2345) in the following interaction:

> MRS WHITE: Would that cupidity, combined with a quite flexible system of inheritance, lead to instability in your opinion?
>
> DR BECKETT: A degree of instability, yes, I'm sure. (T. 2344)

The third proposition that Mrs White wanted to lead Beckett to was that the idea of an autonomous 'Meriam domain', in which traditional land tenure principles flourished, is unsustainable given the degree of change that occurred over the period of colonisation. The corridor leading to this proposition was quite long, since there is so much indisputable material—a great deal of it supplied by Beckett—indicative of historical transformation. The material she chose included

- early reports of interference to traditional gardening practices—for example, Wilkin's report of a competitive tendering process for the selection of gardeners at a public meeting (T. 2326) and the early intervention of colonial authorities to encourage the continuation of gardening through the organisation of competitions with cash rewards (T. 2333)
- Rivers' report of Mr Bruce imposing his commonsense and his understanding of custom in court decisions to do with land (T. 2328–9)
- the early building of a road around the island (T. 2332)
- changes to house design, dress and dance introduced by the South Sea Islanders (T. 2334)
- Beckett's own writing on the early abandonment of custom in favour of Christianity, the introduction of new dances, the outlawing of warfare and revenge killings, the rise of caretaking arrangements, the airstrip issue, and so on (T. 2354–67).

There are other aspects of Beckett's work that could have been used to similar effect but were not included. The prime example would be his many assertions of the pervasiveness of Christianity. In his paper 'Rivalry, competition and conflict among Christian Melanesians' (Beckett 1971), he speaks of Christianity not only structuring the Islanders' relationship with the dominant Europeans, but also as restructuring their relations with one another, so that their assessment of the behaviour of other Islanders is in terms of Christian norms. In *Custom and Colonialism*, he extended this idea by identifying underlying moral judgments as the basis for the rather naive political discourse that was pervasive during his period of fieldwork (Beckett 1987:especially ch. IV). This kind of pervasiveness is at odds with the maintenance of a traditional domain.

Thus, Mrs White asked:

> With all these things, which strike at the very fabric of one's community life, the kind of house you live in, the clothes that you wear, the dances that you perform, religion that you practice, how can one say that one's attitude to land holding remains the same?
>
> DR BECKETT: I think to try and make sense of this kind of puzzle, and that clearly in my writing I have made quite a lot of emphasis on the extent to which Murray Island did change in various areas of activity, I don't think we need to assume that all sectors change at equal speed or in equal degree, or that everything is so tightly integrated with everything else that so to speak, all aspects of life must change together. (T. 2334)

At the very end of the cross-examination, Beckett was asked questions about Aiets. This time he seemed well aware that his answer had implications for Eddie Mabo's credibility. Beckett could not help Eddie Mabo, and his answer—that he had seen the name 'Aiet' only in genealogies (T. 2368)—was all the more damning since Beckett had demonstrated over the course of the previous two days in the witness box that he had extensive knowledge of the Murray Islanders.

The account of Beckett's performance in the witness box has, thus far, focused on the content of his answers and how they relate to the relevant anthropological literature and its diverse theoretical inspirations. A more comprehensive account, though, must also examine all the ways in which his answers respond to the legal system's expectations of the independence and professionalism of an expert witness. Some of the most influential factors in meeting such expectations cannot necessarily be linked to the performance in the witness box. Here I have in mind the fact that his major period of research and many of his resultant publications had been completed before the case was contemplated, thus eliminating any grounds for suspicion of 'research for litigation'. This would not have been the case with Sharp's work. Similarly, although Beckett was presented as a witness for the plaintiffs, he seems to have had minimal involvement in the formulation of the claim and the proofing of witnesses.

Beckett reinforced this notional independence in his performance in a number of ways. The most important was his willingness to state views that were not necessarily in accordance with the plaintiffs' case, and even undermining of their case. Thus, he tended to put much less emphasis on the decisions of the Island Court, as demonstrating the traditional land tenure system, than did the lawyers representing the plaintiffs. He gave 'Malo's Law' a more diffuse position than the Islander witnesses. He demonstrated this independence by making appropriate concessions during cross-examination, such as admitting to a degree of instability in the traditional land tenure system. Similarly, Beckett admitted to being puzzled and unable to explain some contradictory facts, such as how a particular caretaker of land at Zomared had later become its owner (T. 2347) and the greater genealogical depth reported by Haddon in the Western Island of Mabuaig compared with Murray (T. 2330).

Moreover, Beckett projected circumspection about his interpretative claims. He was willing to say that there is insufficient material on which to base an opinion. This was the justification for his refusal to offer a definitive view on the relationship between the pre-contact Malo–Bomai cult and traditional land tenure (T. 2234). When he was willing to offer an opinion on meagre data, he was careful to identify it specifically as speculation.

Beckett was also more circumspect about the description of the Malo–Bomai performances, which he was previously content to describe as 're-enactments' and 'entertainment' in *Custom and Colonialism*:

> DR BECKETT: [T]he Islanders were also allowed to present dances from the Malo–Bomai cult as an entertainment, that was the way, at least, I think the church understood it. Now, the songs clearly survived, I recorded them myself in 1960, and they were recorded also by Haddon in 1898...So, these dances were revived from time to time. They could be presented as an entertainment. They were taken to Thursday Island I think in 1959 and performed for money. But one, nevertheless, has to say they were taken extremely seriously and there was some tension about the rights of certain individuals to play particular roles in the dances. (T. 2231)

Another possible way to demonstrate professional circumspection would be in identifying the limits of the field of anthropology as opposed to other academic disciplines. Beckett did this in minor, self-deprecating ways—for example, by not wanting to compare the accuracy of his measurements in his land survey with the accuracy of a professional surveyor, and in deferring to the specialisation of linguistics before offering a view on a language issue (T. 2353). There was, however, no such deferral to the expertise of historians when he presented a great deal of evidence about the period between the Cambridge expedition and his own fieldwork—nor was any objection or comment made about this.

Final submissions

Whatever might have been the lawyers' initial hesitation about Beckett's involvement in the claim, his evidence became central to the plaintiffs' final submission:

> It is respectfully submitted that the Court should find that a traditional land system exists. In identifying that system, in determining its nature, and the way in which the interests claimed by the respective Plaintiffs fit within it, the evidence of Dr Jeremy Beckett provides a coherent, sensible and pragmatic framework which, it is submitted, should be accepted by the Court.[17]

The lawyers specifically adopted Beckett's formulation of continuity at the level of principles and adopted his description of those principles as providing 'a coherent and compelling account of the survival and adaptation of a traditional or customary system of land tenure'.[18] On Beckett's view of his early marginalisation in the conduct of the case, the final submissions could be seen as a belated rehabilitation.

The Queensland Government's final submission also gave prominence to Beckett's evidence in the parts of their submission dealing with the pre-contact system of law and the survival of that system.[19] It argued, in relation to the pre-contact land-tenure system, that there was insufficient evidence to support Beckett's opinions. Consistent with its approach to Beckett's cross-examination, the Queensland Government argued that the degree of flexibility in the system was insufficient for it to be regarded as a regular or predictable system (p. 2), that Beckett's criteria for the survival of the system were too general and that there had been too much change for any traditional system to have survived (pp. 3–13).

Justice Moynihan's findings of fact

In the struggle for credibility, Justice Moynihan's *Determination of Facts* revealed Beckett to be one of the big winners and Eddie Mabo to be one of the big losers. The judge was scathing about Eddie Mabo, particularly his claims to be the hereditary Aiet: 'The claims are largely without foundation and Eddie Mabo must have known it' (*Determination*, pp. 71–2). It would seem that his negative assessment of Eddie Mabo coloured his whole view of the Islander witnesses, for the *Determination* reveals fairly deep suspicion of their evidence. In a chapter entitled 'Considerations bearing on the evaluation of the evidence of witnesses…', the judge made a sustained case against the possibility of a pure, Meriam oral tradition, uncorrupted by European written works, such as Haddon's *Reports* and the novels of Ion Idriess. In support, he drew on parts of Beckett's book and his evidence about the circulation of stories from Idriess

17 *Plaintiffs' Final Submission*, Ch. 8, p. 1.

18 *Plaintiffs' Final Submission*, Ch. 8, p. 22.

19 *Submission on Behalf of the State of Queensland*, Vol. 2, Parts I and III.

among the Murray Islanders. Much of this critique seemed to be aimed directly at Eddie Mabo, who in his evidence continually asserted his oral sources, such as his father and grandfather, over and above the written sources with which he was familiar. An extensive archive presents a conundrum for any literate Indigenous witness and a host of opportunities for the skilful cross-examiner. In theory, if the archive is consistent with the oral history, it could found an argument for mutually reinforcing accuracy. It could also be used for the purposes of arguing contamination through the illegitimate adoption of written material.[20]

The judge also brought various pieces of evidence together to suggest that the contemporary version of 'Malo's laws' had their immediate origins in a specific project of Marou Mimi, a significant Islander leader during World War II. In the 1940s and 1950s, Marou had been reworking Haddon's account of the Malo story (*Determination*:60–1). Finally, Justice Moynihan called on academic critiques of the reliability of oral tradition to conclude that 'When dealing with oral history it is necessary to be alert to separate "is" and "was" from "ought" or "ought to have been" and to be aware that "human memory the [sic] fluid memory is a marvellous instrument of elimination and transformation"' (*Determination*:62)

In this part of the *Determination* there was a transformation being effected by Justice Moynihan. Academic concern about accuracy was transformed through the use of such framing words as 'risk', 'extraneous sources' and 'corrupted' into a vague but pervasive question mark over the credibility of all the Islander witnesses.

The judge took his analysis even further, anticipating much later critiques by Merlan and Povinelli about the regimentation of customary practice in the land claim era:

> Thus many witnesses were in my view conscious, again in varying degrees, of the desirability of presenting Meriam society in a favourable light in the context of litigation and interested in establishing its relationship with the larger and dominant Queensland and Australian societies in terms which those societies are likely if not bound to favourably accept. (*Determination*:63)

The difference, of course, is that the Merlan and Povinelli critiques were aimed at the liberal state, whereas Justice Moynihan's introduction of Indigenous agency and selective memory of traditions was aimed at assessing the credibility of individual witnesses (see Merlan 1995, 1998; Povinelli 2002).

---

20 It is beyond the scope of this book to give a full account of the incorporation of written material into what was previously an oral tradition only and the reception of mixed sources in the courts, but see the discussion by Graeme Neate in the Queensland Land Tribunal 1994 report *Aboriginal Land Claims to Cape Melville National Park, Flinders Group National Park, Clack Island National Park and Nearby Islands.*

Given the judge's attitude towards the Islander witnesses, it can be seen that Haddon's work and Beckett's account of the contemporary situation assumed even greater importance to the outcome of the case. As might be expected from the nature of their interchanges during the hearing, Justice Moynihan's account of Beckett's published work and his evidence is a mixture of embrace and distancing, as exemplified in the general assessment of his evidence:

> His work may be accepted, for the moment if not totally, as showing that Murray Island society is resilient and adaptive to change. It is however, given the focus of his concerns, less useful in founding conclusions as to the position prior to the development of the responses and transformations which are his particular concern. (*Determination*:44)

Beckett is the most frequently quoted witness in the *Determination of Facts*. The judge quoted Beckett on the effect of the arrival of the LMS in 1871 (pp. 59, 64, 101–2, 141), the Islanders' knowledge of the literature on the Murray Islands (p. 60), and generally adopted Beckett's account of the history of the Murray Islands up to his period of fieldwork (p. 104; also see p. 142).

He also quoted Beckett on the importance of Islander gardening (p. 110), the interrelationship of 'clan', 'village', 'district' and 'tribe', and the Islanders' more recent interest in genealogical depth (pp. 116–19). He adopted, with a little alteration, Beckett's characterisation of Malo's Law as general precepts for conduct (p. 137) and described Beckett's work as giving a useful insight into the relationship between the Murray Islanders and their land 'in terms of distribution or sharing life-sustaining or socially advantageous resources in a potentially volatile social environment' (p. 170). He quoted Beckett extensively on the timing and pressures for the division of traditional lands between siblings and how the relatively unusual joint holdings approach of the Passi family related to the more typical situations (pp. 210–12).

In some instances, Justice Moynihan's apparent adoption of Beckett's material includes a subtle repositioning. One example is the use of the idea of a Meriam domain to justify circumspection in evaluating the Islanders' evidence—that is, because of the possibility of their evidence being strategically self-serving. This repositioning was done by selecting a passage from *Custom and Colonialism* that emphasised the Meriam domain as a conscious and positive strategy on the part of the Islanders to manage their relationship with the wider society with a degree of autonomy. In emphasising this aspect of the Meriam domain, the judge ignores those aspects of the Meriam domain that were beyond individual agency, such as the historical accident of there being no large-scale dispossession of the Islanders from their land (p. 65). Another, not-so-subtle example of the judge's repositioning is the use of Beckett's description of the traditional land concerns of the Murray Islander diaspora in Townsville to support his attack on Eddie Mabo's credibility (p. 69).

Justice Moynihan's main criticism of Beckett revolved around the question of what could be known about the pre-contact land tenure situation from the meagre evidence available. This was also a major point of criticism of Beckett in Queensland's final submissions (p. 87). In the *Determination*, Justice Moynihan used Beckett's acknowledgment of the difficulty of knowing the pre-contact land tenure situation to highlight the particular areas in which he believed Beckett had made that fatal step too far from expert opinion into the abyss of speculation. The first was the judge's imputation that Beckett was arguing that the *Magur*, who were associated with enforcement of the Malo–Bomai cult, had something to do with enforcing land tenure arrangements (p. 164). The transcript from which the judge wished to draw this imputation does not seem to support it—a rare error on Justice Moynihan's part. The second is Beckett's apparent reliance on the earlier reports of the existence of fenced household areas as confirmation of the existence of a land-tenure system (p. 164). Again, the implication—not made explicit—seems to unfairly isolate one piece of evidence to cast doubt on Beckett's conclusions about the pre-contact land tenure system, which he made from various sources, notably Wilkin.

A more general relativising of Beckett's evidence was achieved by pointing out that his evidence was subsumed in a larger body of evidence, which had to be assessed as a whole, and by asserting the formal superiority of judicial fact-finding within the legal system. Thus, even when praising Beckett's work, the judge adds such phrases as: 'although I should say the view I have expressed is a reflection rather of the whole evidence as I appreciate it' (*Determination*:170).

At the beginning of the *Determination*, Justice Moynihan adopted the words of a Canadian judge:

> Testimony in litigation...once admitted into evidence and interpreted by a Court, becomes fixed inter parties even though the same evidence out of the context of litigation could, as an intellectual exercise, be given a different interpretation by subsequent scholars or on other facts emerging to change the context. (Quoted in *Determination*:5)

This assertion of structural superiority also carries with it a certain anti-intellectualism, or, at least, an aversion to explicit theorising, which is often cast in opposition to fact-finding. Justice Moynihan expressed this anti-intellectualism in a number of ways. The first was in the context of his response to contradictory submissions about the general approach he should take to the evidence, which he glossed as an alternative between the 'thematic' approach and the 'historical' approach. The 'thematic' approach urged him to accept that various features of a society will change over time, whereas the 'historical' approach urged a comparison of the pre-contact society with the contemporary society. The judge's resolution is the dismissive assertion of fact-finding pragmatism: 'I have sought to approach the evidence free of such conceptual models while acknowledging that each may, on occasion, have its uses as an aid in reaching or evaluating a conclusion without the application of either (or for that matter both) being necessarily determinative' (*Determination*:13).

Another example of the judicial suspicion of the intellectual came in the terms of his warm embrace of Margaret Lawrie's evidence and her book *Myths and Legends of the Torres Strait* (1970): 'I interpolate here that it seems to me that one of Mrs Lawrie's advantages as a witness is that she went to the Murray Islands not for a scientific purpose but to collect the stories. To do this she immersed herself in the community' (*Determination*:122–3).

Another point of comparison with Justice Moynihan's close examination of Beckett's evidence was his relatively uncritical acceptance of Haddon, Rivers and Wilkin. The *Determination* includes five pages of quotations from Rivers' chapter on social organisation in Volume VI of the *Reports* (Rivers 1908) and much of Wilkin's chapter on 'Property and inheritance' (Wilkin 1908). Haddon is also quoted extensively. Initially, Justice Moynihan had proposed a fairly strict approach to the *Reports*, noting that they were beyond the reach of cross-examination and comparison with direct evidence of witnesses (*Determination*:52). He proposed that material in the *Reports* that could be classified as direct observation or expert opinion evidence should be accepted and weighed against the totality of other evidence. In relation to opinion evidence in the *Reports*, he stated: 'it is admissible in terms of the established expertise of the person proffering the opinion and to the extent to which necessary sustaining facts are established by admissible evidence' (*Determination*:54–5).

Such an analysis of Rivers', Wilkin's and Haddon's works would have been an enormous undertaking, and there is nothing in the *Determination of Facts* to suggest that Justice Moynihan had in fact carried it out in a systematic way.

In order to understand the full significance of the use made of Beckett's evidence, it is necessary to outline the judge's aims and methodology in drafting his *Determination of Facts*, as far as they can be ascertained from the determination itself and its general legal and political context. This is not an easy task because of some of the typical characteristics of judicial writing, in which a generally high level of reflexivity and precision are combined, usually at critical points, with obscurity and obfuscation. It also becomes apparent from the form of the determination that the judge himself was torn as to what the findings should be.

The plaintiffs' lawyers had prepared 116 paragraphs of specific findings of fact that they urged Justice Moynihan to adopt as his determination of the facts in response to the remitter from the High Court. The bulk of these findings described the history of the Murray Islands and was, more or less, uncontroversial. The critical findings, of course, were sharply contested. The plaintiffs had proposed a finding acknowledging a system of customary land law. Queensland's proposed finding was simply that no such system of customary law had been shown to exist. Instead of taking either of these positions, Justice Moynihan's formal findings (Volume 2 of the *Determination of Facts*) referred back to Chapters 8, 9 and 10 of Volume 1 of the *Determination*. These chapters resemble chapters of a book and are respectively entitled 'The people of the Murray Islands, their culture and society', 'Murray Islands society and land' and 'Claims by the plaintiffs to specific pieces of land'. They cover approximately 140 double-spaced typescript pages—in effect, circumventing the precision of the contending, alternative statements of proposed findings.

The potential confusion of the book-like approach to findings of fact was not alleviated in the text. In his discussion of the issues, the judge avoided the use of the term 'finding' when stating something that seemed positive for the plaintiffs. Instead, he used a range of words and phrases that implied different degrees of satisfaction with the evidence.[21] When he came to the chapter on claims to specific pieces of land, he was again ambiguous about whether firm findings of an existing system had been made or whether he was just assuming the existence of a traditional system for the purposes of dealing with specific claims (*Determination*:194).

Why Justice Moynihan would want to blur the precision of his *Determination of Facts* is hinted at in the *Determination* itself:

> I am conscious that much of the foregoing points of this chapter (or perhaps more of the Determination) are obscure and imprecise. I would like to think that this is as much a reflection of the state of the evidence as it is of any defect of mine. The point is it is the best I can do with the evidence. (*Determination*:172–3)

The conclusions he reached, which could be interpreted as positive findings, were expressed in a number of ways. For example, he stated: 'Entitlement in respect of a dwelling site within a village was and is usually regarded by [sic] inheritance from a direct male ancestor with an expectation that the person so entitled might pass the land on by the same means' (*Determination*:174).

Later, he stated:

> It is difficult, to the point of impossibility, to reach any conclusions precise [sic] as to the restraints on the disposition of village (or for that matter garden) land prior to European contact...

21 The qualifying phrases include: 'so far as the evidence reveals' (p. 145), 'there is a body of evidence' (p. 166), 'there was, and it seems that there is' (p. 175), and 'it seems clear enough however that' (p. 179).

> In more recent times an entitlement to dispose of land usually carried and carries a degree of expectation of disposition by descent to a blood relation by the male line, although this is now an extremely flexible concept.
>
> Adopted children might expect to inherit land in the same way as natural children, although this seems to continue to be a potential source of quarrelling and disruption.
>
> There was, and it seems that there is, an expectation that males have a stronger entitlement than do females and that as between brothers the position of the eldest was and is stronger. It may however yield to other considerations.
>
> It is difficult to determine how constraining these expectations were and are. In the chapter to which I earlier referred, Wilkin records Bruce as remarking to the effect that in the past a man could dispose of his land to whomever he chose and he remarked on the freedom with which land was dealt with on Murray Island, although in the context of there apparently being some constraints. These have certainly not increased.
>
> One is left with an impression that, as amongst themselves, it may be that the Islanders may dispose of land on whatever basis is acceptable to those directly affected and, to the extent to which a wider community may be affected, is acceptable to that community. Such acceptance is more readily attainable in terms of expectations relating to descent such as those to which I have referred. There do not, however, seem to be any qualifications on the disposition or acquisition of land which could be described as crucial. (*Determination*:175–6)

He also expressed conclusions as follows:

> It seems clear enough however that garden land was primarily acquired by inheritance in the sense previously spoken of in the context of village land and that that remains the practice. Daughters were, and perhaps are, given dowries of garden land. (*Determination*:179)

The *Determination* concluded with an unusual personal comment by the judge, in which he complained about the process of the remitter being unsatisfactory, principally because he was restrained from making findings of law. His view was that issues of fact and law were 'inextricably interwoven', implying that it is extremely difficult to evaluate the facts without reference to the law. Thus, his lack of precision can be seen as a response to his frustrations about his task in the overall judicial resolution of the issue by the High Court. The effect of the ambiguity of his findings, as opposed to the precision of the findings urged on him by the parties, was to transfer more responsibility for the momentous decision back to the High Court.

Anthropologists and lawyers reflect on the case

Beckett's article

Beckett's own account of the *Mabo* case (Beckett 1995) was written with the principal aim of responding to a conservative backlash by some newspaper commentators and legal academics. They drew sustenance from parts of Justice Moynihan's *Determination* in arguing that the High Court was in error and, in any event, the decision should be confined to the Torres Strait and not extended to the very different Aboriginal culture of mainland Australia. Another aim seems to have been to provide a concise account of all the anthropological issues in the case. Although these predominant aims tend to lead away from a personal reflection on his experience of being an expert witness, some of his concerns did come through.

One particular frustration was the exclusion of his own evidence, on technical grounds, confirming the adoption of Eddie Mabo. He felt that some of Eddie Mabo's statements that Justice Moynihan found dubious could have been proven correct by other evidence that was, for various reasons, never called.[22] As one might expect, this is part of a more fundamental complaint against the perceived artificiality of factual boundaries drawn by the rules of evidence in the contingencies of particular hearings. More generally, he felt that the whole process of searching for rules led to a radical de-contextualisation of the normative statements of the Islanders. These statements were used for rhetorical purposes in actual assertions of claims on the island, and were part of a complex and competitive set of relationships (Beckett 1995:21). It is apparent from the above examination of his evidence that he did try to bring some of this complex context back into view in his evidence. As with the subtleties of historical cultural transformation, however, he felt the dangers of doing this: 'Such subtleties can scarcely be risked in adversarial statements, and are hazardous in the courtroom situation, yet they are bound to arise' (1995:23). In an obvious departure from the authoritative stance required of the expert witness, he saw part of the problem—as I do—as stemming from anthropology's own difficulty in handling the question of historical transformation.

22 As explained in Footnote 13, Justice Selway has recently broken ranks with the more typical policing of the boundaries of the acceptable kinds of expert evidence to suggest that anthropologists with longstanding involvements with the claimants may also give 'primary' evidence.

Something he does not address is the seemingly central problem of the indeterminacy of 'law'. When I asked Beckett about this apparent omission in 2003—in the context of questioning his use in evidence of the opaque phrase 'law in our sense of the term'—he had a number of responses. The first was to say that he was prepared for the question of defining 'law' but was simply not given a chance to talk about it:

> He [the Judge] didn't ask me. I'm not sure what I would have done, dig out Radcliffe-Brown's essay in the *Encyclopaedia of the Social Sciences*—'Sanctioned Social Law'—it was an issue from Maine onwards that anthropology did address. Maine was not an anthropologist directly and the comparative analysis is crude but it is something that must have been addressed in the colonial literature...yet it was clear that one of the problems for Moynihan was, if you can wind back before the establishment of an Island Court, how did disputes get settled and how the decisions were enforced and, indeed, that is a significant question.[23]

Another kind of response was an understandable protectiveness towards encapsulated, small-scale societies. This protectiveness sees judicial attempts to distinguish 'their law' from 'our law' as inevitably being an unjustified assertion of moral and political superiority. This view often leads to a rhetorical deflection of the argument back to the pretensions of European law—typically identifying aspects of change and contingency in European law:

> She [Counsel for Queensland] was trying to say that what was done in relation to land was all a response to contingency and that there was very little, nothing hard in it, people responding to issues of the moment. And to a degree that is true. I would have said, had I been given the opportunity, that is also true of any law.[24]

Nonie Sharp's critique

The whole litigation saga, including Beckett's performance as expert witness, was given a lengthy treatment by Nonie Sharp in *No Ordinary Judgment* (1996). This book can be seen as the reassertion of the superiority of her presentation of Meriam culture in *Stars of Tagai*. Her presentation of Eddie Mabo, the witness, is still predominantly the Eddie Mabo of the *Stars of Tagai*. The devastating concessions he was forced to make in cross-examination might, however, have induced a new critical distance from her exemplary Islander: 'Were the Meriam to come to take his cultural authority seriously, as I saw it, he would have to seek their confidence in the process of face to face living over a period' (Sharp 1996:67).

---

23 Jeremy Beckett, Interview transcript, 2003, p. 23.

24 Jeremy Beckett, Interview transcript, 2003, pp. 24–5.

Otherwise, she continues to stress the centrality of Malo's Law, both as law and as religion, which 'gives sacred authority to rights in land' (1996:87). For Sharp, Justice Moynihan's lack of acceptance of Malo's Law—as law that can be recognised by the European legal system—was bewildering and a sign of his incorrigibility.

The whole experience of the court case does not lead her to any more fundamental questioning of the utility of such terms as 'religion' and 'law' as vehicles of cross-cultural translation. The thrust of her discussion is that Justice Moynihan should have been prepared to identify Malo's Law as law because it is equivalent to a religious law. Why she thought this equivalence should have been so persuasive is difficult to imagine, considering that Malo's Law did not specify rules of inheritance and, in Western societies, there has been a longstanding formal separation of law and religion.

One of the most interesting aspects of *No Ordinary Judgment* for this book is Sharp's assessment of Beckett's performance as an expert witness. She recounts and is uncritically supportive of Beckett's evidence relating to the continuity of traditional land tenure principles in a Meriam domain. But she is predictably critical of his unwillingness to see the Meriam witnesses' assertion of Malo's Law as the deep religious basis of their attachment to land (1996:132–4).

Sharp noticed that Beckett's evidence about the contemporary assertion of Malo's Law and his speculation about the pre-contact relationship between the Malo–Bomai cult and land tenure were at odds with some of the evidence of the Meriam witnesses, but highly influential with Justice Moynihan. Sharp's critique seems to be that Beckett could have aligned himself more closely with what the contemporary Meriam were saying about Malo's Law. In reinterpreting Beckett's evidence of the reality of traditional land boundaries and the pervasiveness of ideas about not trespassing on another's land, she suggests that it does not matter that Beckett's informants in 1959–60 did not make explicit reference to 'Malo's Law', because they had internalised it and acted instinctively (1996:142).

In her view, Justice Moynihan made the same mistake as Beckett. The judge's failure to see the continuity of a religious order 'was fatal to the process of understanding Meriam social life, Meriam meaning systems and the character of the Meriam people' (1996:154). Again, there is repeated assertion without engagement with the problems of her view: the underlying issues of cross-cultural translation, interpretative indeterminacy and the judge's forced orientation towards 'laws, customs, traditions and practices' of land tenure from time immemorial.

Keon-Cohen's article

From the apogee of the lawyers' acknowledgment of the significance of Beckett's evidence in their final submissions, there was a long way to fall. Just how far was revealed in Keon-Cohen's account of the case in which Beckett's role rates just one sentence—quoted at the beginning of this chapter. In contrast, when I interviewed Keon-Cohen about the case in 2003, he was full of praise for Beckett's performance, stating that it had helped to give some structure and coherence to the Indigenous evidence.[25] Keon-Cohen's published account of the case is rather like the often-reproduced photo below: a direct relationship with the plaintiffs, unmediated by expert knowledge.

Figure 3.1 Dave Passi, Eddie Mabo, Bryan Keon-Cohen and James Rice outside the Queensland Supreme Court in 1989

Courtesy of Yarra Bank Films, photo by Jim McEwan

25 Brian Keon-Cohen, Interview, 7 November 2003, Tape 1, Side B.

Conclusions about the *Mabo* case study

The encounter between law and anthropology in the *Mabo* case confirms some of the basic features of the two fields. In academic anthropology there is, ideally, a relative openness to what counts as evidence, a heterogeneity of approaches, and the continuing expansion of evidence and revision of interpretations. In contrast, the judicial process is essentially about drawing boundaries around the totality of evidence and constructing an interpretative finality about the enclosed material, at least with regard to the formal processes of the judicial hierarchy. This contrast is evident in the absence of Kitaoji's and Sharp's material from the court case, and Beckett's frustration that he was not allowed to express an opinion or simply provide relevant evidence about the issue of Eddie Mabo's adoption.

The legal system's attempt to include academic knowledge in the form of expert testimony became, in this case, the scene of a subtle competitiveness between the judge and the expert witness, as evidenced by the apparent close identification of the judge with the expert during the hearing and the judge's distancing from the expert's opinion in his *Determination of Facts*. Those moments during the hearing of Beckett's evidence when Justice Moynihan interrupted the flow of evidence—creating a space of mutual respect and the free exchange of ideas—are remarkable islands in the sea of suspicion, objection, and assessments of credibility. It is as if Justice Moynihan suddenly saw someone like himself trying to sift his way through a morass of strategic statements to some truthful reality beyond—a conversation between equals, the ethnographer as a sifter of informants' statements and actions and the judge as a sifter of witnesses' evidence and demeanour. On this island the adversarial system is temporarily suspended. The judge asks his own questions, responds to answers, exposes his thought processes and seeks confirmation of some preliminary conclusions.

At a later stage of the proceedings, the well-qualified, credible expert witness, such as Beckett in *Mabo*, represents a problem for the judge: how to differentiate his findings from the expert's opinion. This problem was particularly acute in *Mabo*, where the judge resorted to a retrospective undermining of the expert's evidence on some key points and by simply asserting his superior fact-finding role. This structural superiority is typically couched in time-honoured phrases asserting an assessment of the whole of the evidence (of which the expert's evidence is only a part), and occasionally by ignoring what the expert actually said in favour of an impression.

In Beckett's own account of his approach to being an expert witness, he embraced the idea of robust independence. This approach was at least partly as a defence against the unreasonable expectations of the lawyers, who he thought had exhibited a professional ruthlessness in disregarding evidence that did not support their Statement of Claim. But this declaration of independence did not absolve him of the necessity of reconstituting his body of work in a way that was relevant to the task at hand. This deconstruction and reconstruction of the anthropological material available to him will be examined under the previously identified headings of groups, laws and change.

The naming of 'family groups' in the Statement of Claim as the grouping of Islanders most relevant to landholding was remarkably fortuitous and remains somewhat of a mystery. Although Beckett was not involved in the drafting of the Statement of Claim, it matched exactly his own idea of the relevant grouping in the contemporary Meriam domain, in contrast with his labile, ideological groupings in council politicking. 'The family' also avoided the uncertainty of the re-emergent idea of the eight 'tribes' that was reported in, and possibly encouraged by, Sharp's writing.[26] The choice of 'family' probably emerged from the process of seeking instructions from the plaintiffs for the Statement of Claim. The Statement of Claim also mentions individually owned land, but asserts that only other family members could inherit this land.

The choice of the appropriate group to put forward was also a critical decision for avoiding the mismatch in the *Gove* case between the Aboriginal evidence and anthropological generalising. The Statement of Claim in *Mabo* addressed this problem by asserting that the islands were exclusively possessed by 'the Meriam people' and by presenting individual and family group ownership as particulars of the Meriam people's 'laws, customs, traditions and practices'. In effect, this approach provided some flexibility going into the hearing about the appropriate level of the title-holding group. Ultimately, the High Court's choice of the maximal grouping, 'the Meriam people', seems to have been influenced by the pragmatic factors of the generally negative factual findings about the specific claims of the plaintiffs and, mirroring Justice Moynihan's view, its unwillingness to become embroiled in the minutiae of resolving disputed claims over individual plots of land. Beckett and others did provide material that tended to support the idea of a maximal grouping as an anthropological reality, but it was always in terms of shared identity, shared history and a rather fractious commonality of beliefs, expectations and practices.

In the absence of a clear legal doctrine, Beckett's main challenge was to negotiate a course between his transformative account of Islander history and the absolute continuities asserted in the Statement of Claim, and to do so in a way that could

26 Recent events confirm Sharp's account of the contemporary importance of the eight 'tribes'. The rules of the Prescribed Body Corporate set up to help administer the native title rights won in the *Mabo* case are based on the equal representation of each of the eight 'clans' on the committee (see The Rules of Mer Gedkem [Torres Strait Islander] Corporation). On recent land disputes, including the contemporary significance of the 'tribes', see Burton (2005, 2007).

be supported by compelling facts and argument. In this, the notion of a Meriam domain, changing at a slower rate than other aspects of Meriam life, became critical to his presentation. It was a risky course because so much of his work was aimed at demonstrating how traditional concerns had been relegated to a private sphere, away from the dominant concerns of community life. The risks of appearing to tailor an interpretation to suit the plaintiffs' case were minimised to some extent by the fact that he had already raised the idea of a separate Meriam domain in his early work and he had retained the fieldnotes of his investigations into the layout and ownership of particular pieces of garden land.

The other important way in which Beckett was able to negotiate his difficult course was his conceptualisation of the systematic level of Meriam land tenure, within the Meriam domain, at the level of 'principles'. On analysis, these principles are two all-encompassing, broadly opposed tendencies. One tendency, which makes individual independence and autonomy paramount, is expressed in the opening sentence of the statement: 'owners have the right to dispose of their land, during their lifetime or at death, to whom ever they wish' (Beckett 1989:3).

The other tendency is acceding to the legitimate expectations of close kin, particularly of the eldest son, other sons and daughters. There is a cleverness about expressing these tendencies as a list of principles in a system since all instances of inheritance would fit into either category and thus support the existence of the system so described. When I put the 'cleverness' of his formulation to Beckett in 2003, his response was to revert to empiricist mode: the principles most accurately described the multitude of individual cases he had investigated.[27]

Beckett's use of broadly opposed principles is reminiscent of the fundamental antinomy introduced by Fred Myers in his *Pintupi Country, Pintupi Self*: the tension between autonomy and relatedness (Myers 1986). One of the consequences of this conceptualisation is that it extracts simple generalisations from the apparent complexity and appearance of haphazardness of individual decision making about inheritance. Myers, however, used the concept of 'negotiation' to integrate these broad opposing principles with individual action in particular circumstances. Thus, a possible alternative way to generalise about broadly opposed 'principles' by which such societies work would be to focus on the negotiation and renegotiation of everyday life, including inheritance decisions. It seems obvious, though, that 'negotiation' would not have evoked the stability of 'law' in the same way that 'principles' could.

27 Jeremy Beckett, Interview transcript, 2003, pp. 12–13.

Beckett did not deny the competitiveness and negotiability of everyday life in his oral evidence. That evidence presented a more complex picture than his summary statement, 'Meriam Land Tenure'. It became clear that what Beckett meant when he spoke about 'principles' and 'rules' were inter-subjectively shared values that can be legitimately deployed in traditional claims to land among Meriam people—in other words, all those traditional principles that had become objectified and would be raised in Indigenous justifications.

In demonstrating continuity, Beckett could, whether fortuitously or by design, point to Wilkin's chapter on 'Property and inheritance' in the *Reports* for the description of an identical tension. But by linking any strong claims of continuity to the identified principles, Beckett was then free to admit to his oeuvre on transformation and bring it into his evidence, not as destructive of the principles, but as demonstrating their resilience.

The absence of any legal doctrine of native title at the time of the hearing of the facts in *Mabo* is a challenge to the general triangulation model of anthropological agency proposed in Chapter 1. To some extent the formulation of a proposed legal doctrine in the Statement of Claim took the place of legal doctrine in guiding Beckett's deconstruction–reconstruction of the anthropological archive. He also seems, however, to have guided himself using more amorphous ideas of what would be required for legal recognition. He had, in reserve, anthropological theorising about primitive law, but did not have to use it. What he did use were general ideas of completeness (system) and generality (principles) that could be seen as transcending historical contingency. Although Beckett did not make explicit links to legal theory, this completeness (or gaplessness) and generality had long been identified by Weber as two of the distinctive features of modern law. The implication for the triangulation model is that the 'legal doctrine' corner of the triangle should be expanded to include vague conceptions of the legal system, perhaps anthropologists' ideal images of law, to match the judge's ideal image of the anthropologist.

The other apparent challenge to the triangulation model of anthropological agency is Beckett's distancing himself from the claimants' statements about the centrality of Malo's Law. I have suggested a need to harmonise the three elements, while projecting independence. On reflection, this distancing still fits the proposed model because Beckett was trying to harmonise their evidence with the *whole* of the anthropological archive, especially the period represented by his own contribution to it, when Malo's Law was not a prominent feature of public discourse. The benefits for the projection of his independence were also enormous.

Beckett did not take the path of demonstrating independence by explicitly confronting the indeterminacy of key concepts. This seems to have been his natural inclination ('I find my theory in the street') and a result of his general appreciation of likely legal fact-finding methodology, rather than any deliberate choice.

In Chapter 1, I admitted a certain impenetrability of written judgments because of the skilful obscuring of strong gestalts about the preferred outcome. Yet this very impenetrability allows other readings consistent with orthodox legal ideology. One illustration of the potential complexity is the judge's use of final submissions. There is some slight evidence that the judge, having rejected Queensland's ultimate conclusion that there is no system of customary land tenure on Murray Island, goes out of his way to adopt many of Queensland's other negative submissions—for example, that Beckett did not have any material on which to base his opinion about the pre-contact land tenure situation. This process of selection is suggestive of a broad-brush adjustment between the parties to demonstrate his own attempt at a middle course and has little to do with the evaluation of the minutiae of evidence. It is an attempt to give something to both sides. The problem is that this 'slight evidence' is also consistent with the judge having independently reached the same conclusions about the evidence as Counsel for Queensland.

One of the most difficult issues of interpretation has been in characterising Justice Moynihan's attitude to this very issue of interpretative indeterminacy versus the assumed accessibility and stability of the fact. Some of his interactions with Beckett indicate an awareness of the artificiality of the fact-finding process, which must abandon complexity of possible interpretations, to assigning a 'yes' or 'no' against particular assertions of fact. The judge's whole approach to the structuring of the *Determination* as a book rather than as specific findings is the most obvious example of this awareness. A possible interpretation would be that we have evidence here of a self-consciousness about the obligation of the judge to find facts rather than any deep belief that the science of fact-finding can be applied unproblematically to general characterisations of a whole society. Consistent with this interpretation is Justice Moynihan's sociological acumen in working through the implications of Indigenous agency in the contemporary reformulation of tradition, albeit under the rubric of the credibility of witnesses. A sociological imagination is also demonstrated in his description of how he thought the pre-contact society worked:

> It may be accepted that prior to the manifestation of the effects of outside contacts...the evolving Murray society, in common with most if not all human societies, had a bias towards social order and social cohesion. The ways in which this was implemented were many, diverse, complex and interrelated. Thus there was the complex system of social positioning by reference to descent and territory a perception of which is described by Rivers. Appropriate attitudes were inculcated into children from

> an early age by exhortation, example and reinforcing behaviour. The mechanisms were inchoate rather than specific and indirect rather than direct by comparison to what occurred after European contact although the former features remain in varying degrees. Social activities based on the interrelated groupings described by Rivers, magic and ritual all were designed to reinforce adherence to the social structure and the manifestation of appropriate patterns of behaviour. (*Determination of Facts*:190)

On the other hand, there is the seemingly misguided attempt by Justice Moynihan to find the one, true, dominant purpose of the Island Court, and similar themes in his conversations with Beckett about whether the land tenure system was in fact subservient to general notions of community harmony. An interpretation of Justice Moynihan's *Determination* that tries to incorporate the two different sensibilities would have to accept the heterogeneity of approaches evident in the *Determination* and be content to track the subtle switching of approaches at different points in his reasoning.

On my reading, Beckett's performance in *Mabo* was influential with Justice Moynihan, but his performance did not have any immediate ramifications within anthropology. It was the High Court decision itself that commanded wider interest and, as Beckett observed, 'after *Mabo*, the focus moved to the mainland'. Beckett's success remained obscure partly because of the form of the proceedings. The *Determination of Facts*, which gives the fullest account of his influence, was never published separately. By the time the various justices of the High Court had drawn what they wanted from the *Determination* and written their judgments, Beckett's input had completely disappeared from view. Moreover, like everyone else, anthropologists became focused on trying to understand the implications of the newly formulated legal doctrine of native title. This will be examined in the next two case studies.

4. The Anthropology of the Broome Region

By the time of the *Rubibi* claim hearing in 2000, the Aboriginal people of the region had suffered approximately 150 years of colonisation in various forms. The intrusion on the traditional life of the people started brutally in the 1860s–1870s with the recruitment of Aboriginal people to work on pearling luggers, and, in the hinterland, the direct competition with pastoralists over the resources of the land, sheep and cattle spearing and reprisal-killing expeditions. The 1880s saw the establishment of the Port of Broome as the centre of the pearling industry and the continued rise of pastoralism amid a legal regime that kept many Aboriginal people on pastoral stations in semi-feudal tutelage as rationed workers. In the same era, Catholic missions were established to the north of Broome, at Beagle Bay and Lombadina, and to the south, at La Grange. The town of Broome was booming with the market for pearl shell, and, in the early 1900s, there were about 1700 Japanese and Malay men associated with the industry living in town.

There was public concern about the prostitution of Aboriginal women, miscegenation and the spread of disease. The whole period had seen a dramatic decline in the Aboriginal population. Paradoxically, the harsh legal regime tying Aboriginal people to pastoral stations allowed some regrouping of the original inhabitants of the Broome region at Thangoo Station, to the south. But Broome tended to act as a magnet for Aboriginal people in the entire region. Following the disruption of World War II, when many Aboriginal people were moved to Beagle Bay mission, there was a gradual migration of Aboriginal people on Thangoo and other surrounding pastoral stations into Broome and various Aboriginal camps just outside Broome, including one associated with the claim area. This movement probably commenced soon after the war and continued in the 1950s and 1960s (see Hosokawa 1991:2–4). The migration from the surrounding pastoral stations and missions, as well as the migration of Western Desert people out of the desert towards the coast, resulted in a complex assemblage of different Aboriginal groups in Broome.

In Western Australia, the advent of native title was a revolution in Indigenous land rights. A proposed State statutory land rights scheme had failed in the WA Parliament in 1984, leaving security of tenure to the discretion of the Government under an outmoded system of reserves and leases held by a State-wide Aboriginal Land Trust. Following the *Mabo* decision, the assertion of Indigenous land rights did not have to await the pleasure of the Government of the day; they could be asserted immediately in court. For the hard-pressed Yawuru people around Broome, it meant identifying for claim those remaining areas where native title had not been extinguished by the grant of inconsistent interests as the town of Broome expanded. The Kimberley Land Council (KLC), representing the various claimants under the umbrella name of Rubibi, identified six such areas. For reasons that will be explained in the next chapter, the claim was split into two hearings, the first one dealing with a small Aboriginal reserve called Kunin (also known as Fishermen's Bend), about 5 km east of Broome, which had been set aside for Aboriginal ceremonial purposes.

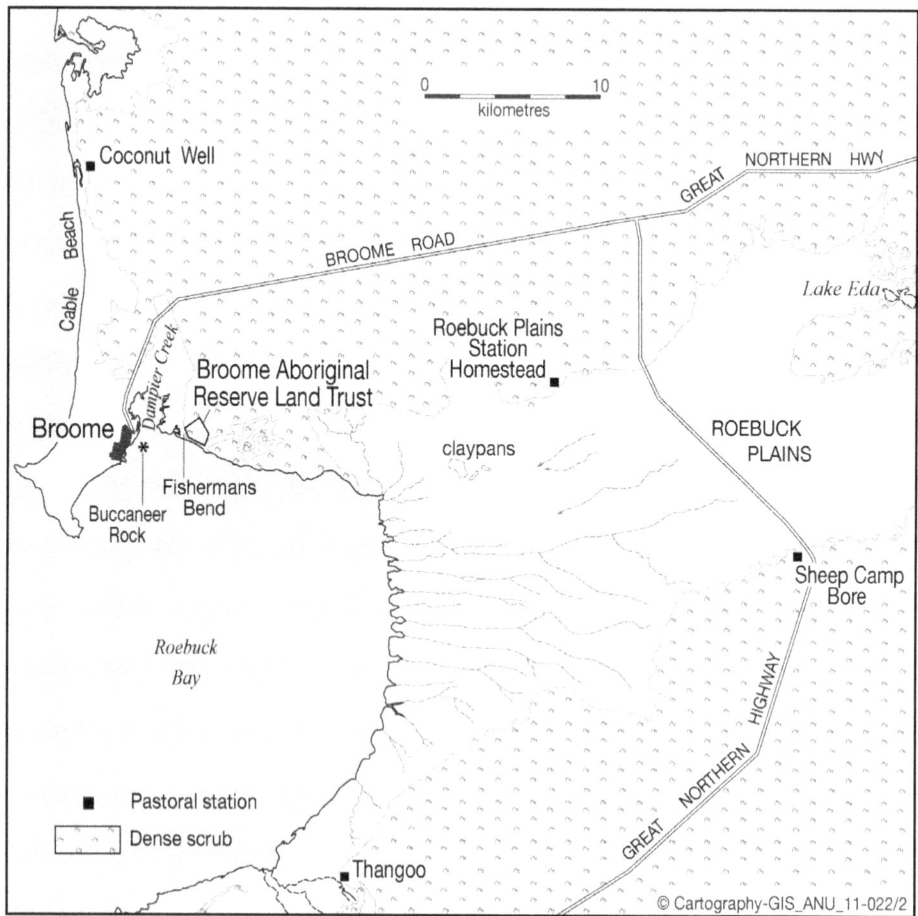

Map 4.1 The claim area (Broome Aboriginal Reserve Land Trust) in relation to Broome and Roebuck Plains

The claim was unusual in two respects: the area claimed was small (121 ha), and the rights claimed at the end of the hearing were limited to rights to perform rituals. In other respects, however, this claim might be more typical of the context of anthropological testimony in the native title era. There was no rich anthropological archive such as Haddon's *Reports* providing an anthropological baseline soon after the assertion of European sovereignty; there was no major ethnography arising out of classic long-term fieldwork completed well before legal proceedings were contemplated; and there was no single anthropological voice at the hearing. Instead, there was an extensive ethnography of the contemporary scene compiled by the claimants' anthropologist and, from the distant past, the uneven accounts of amateur anthropologists and the truncated accounts of professional anthropologists that were part of larger surveys. Thus we have a testing scenario for the historical imagination of the anthropologist: how to convincingly assert traditional continuity on the basis of a meagre anthropological archive.

In the hearing, there was also another typical feature of the native title era: the State Government retained an expert anthropologist whose job it was to offer a professional commentary on the report of the claimants' anthropologist. Usually, as in this case, such an anthropologist does not have the opportunity for extended fieldwork with the claimants prior to the case and their evidence begins to approximate a forensic peer review. The resolution of differences of expert opinion generated in the *Rubibi* case between Patrick Sullivan and Erich Kolig allows for a further insight into judicial fact-finding in native title. Well before this case, Justice Olney in the *Yorta Yorta* native title claim had taken the rather drastic approach of ignoring expert opinions in dispute, as if they cancelled each other out.[1] In *Rubibi*, a very different approach was adopted, as will become clear in the next chapter.

But first, in order to understand the differences between Sullivan and Kolig, it is necessary to give some account of the anthropological archive on which they both relied to form their professional opinions.

1 *Members of the Yorta Yorta Community v Victoria*—VG6001/95—18 December 1998, para. 62.

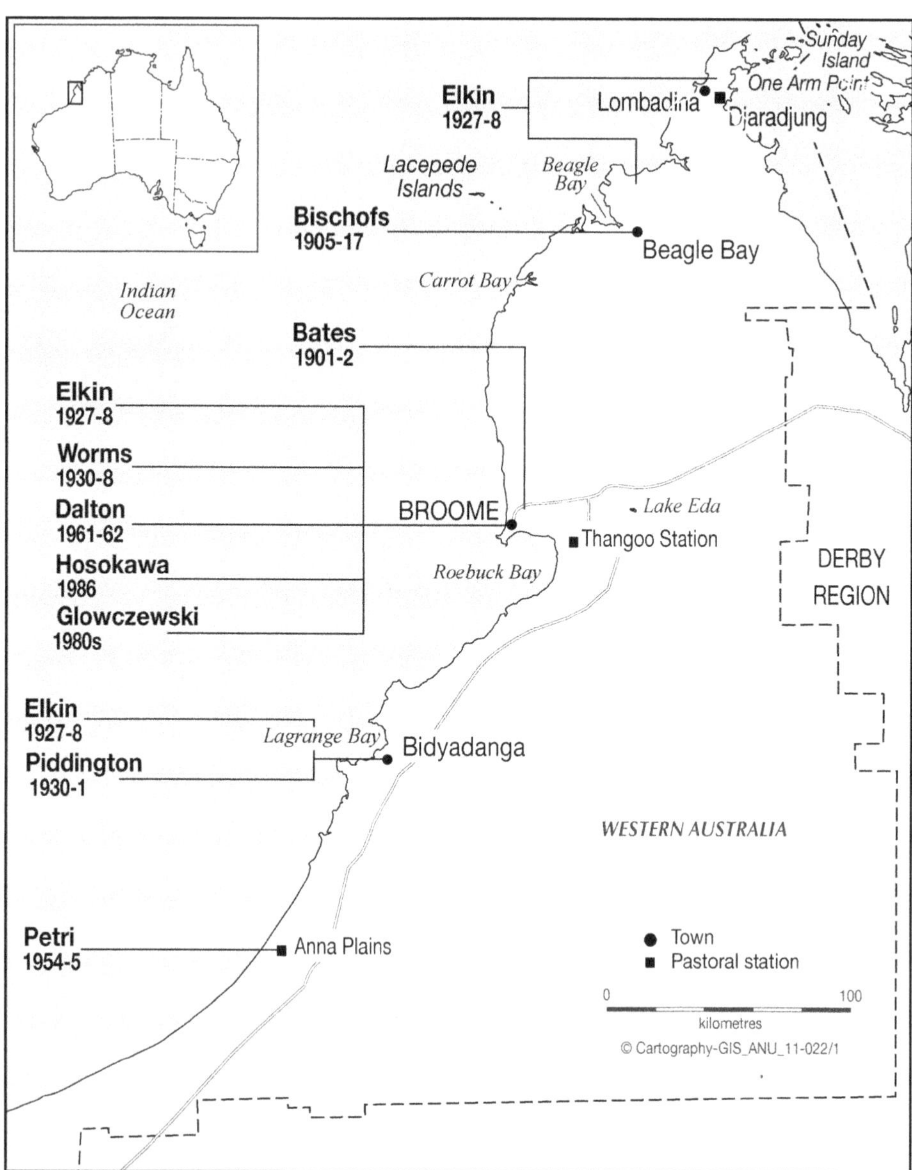

Map 4.2 Anthropological fieldwork locations in the Broome region

Bischofs

One of the first references to traditional ownership around Broome in the anthropological archive was made obliquely in a 1908 article in *Anthropos* on the Niol Niol (Nyul-nyul) tribe. It was written by Father Joseph Bischofs, the second Pallottine Superintendent of the Beagle Bay Catholic Mission (Bischofs 1908).[2] The Niol Niol traditionally occupied an area on the Dampier peninsula, well north of Broome, and this reference is included only because it became important in Kolig's critique of Sullivan's report for the claim. The article was mainly concerned with the survival of the remaining Aboriginal population and proposed that the Government purchase pastoral stations on which Aboriginal people could work. The early brutal period of colonisation would have been in the living memory of Aboriginal people at the mission. That experience is reflected in Bischofs' account, which refers to revenge expeditions, Aboriginal people being forced from their traditional lands to make way for cattle runs, labour exploitation, disease, and interracial sexual liaisons—especially with the Japanese and Malays—which were characterised as the trade in women.[3]

The article also mentions traditional land tenure in passing, and inaugurates a thematic tension that would continue up to the claim hearing in 2000. Bischofs asserted clearly defined tribal areas but also identified several different tribes living peacefully together on the mission and having friendly interaction with other tribes in the region. In his table of tribes with whom the Niol Niol had friendly interaction, there appeared the names *Yáwor, Káren, Ménger, Tjógon.* These seemed to be cognate words for contemporary places and identities.[4] Significantly for the claim area, Kunin, the table asserted a *Káren* tribe, with a *'Káren* bor' camping place (*Lagerplatz*), speaking the *Tjógon* language. In the light of the contested assertion in the native title claim of a Jugan identity separate from Yawuru, Bischofs' table is tantalising evidence. It would, however, have to be treated with some circumspection since the table was compiled before the era of professionalised anthropology and before the debate about Aboriginal local organisation. Moreover, little is known about Bischofs' qualifications or methodology.

---

2 The Beagle Bay Mission was founded in 1891 by French Trappist monks and taken over by the Pious Society of Missions (PSM, the German Pallottine Fathers) in 1901. Father Bischofs arrived at the mission in 1905 and took over as superintendent in 1908—also the date of his article in *Anthropos* (see Zucker 1994:31, 53, 75).

3 Compare with Daisy Bates' *The Passing of the Aborigines*, in which she gives an account of seemingly reluctant institutionalised prostitution in Broome under the guise of marriage to a 'Manilaman'. On the other hand, Bates (1938:12–13) also reported the unrestrainable enthusiasm of the Aboriginal women of Beagle Bay mission to be involved in such temporary liaisons with the 'Asiatic' crews of passing pearling luggers.

4 *Yáwor* (= Yawuru language, tribe), *Káren* (= Kunin, the Aboriginal name of the reserve under claim), *Ménger* (= Minyjirr, place name and dialect name), *Tjógon* (= Jukun dialect, tribe).

Daisy Bates

Daisy Bates commenced fieldwork in the era of the ethnological surveyors and compilers. Like those on Haddon's expedition, she could be seen as a proto-anthropologist in the history of the professionalisation of anthropology. Haddon's team achieved their transformation from the sciences to emerging social anthropology within the academy. Because of her lack of university qualifications and her gender, Daisy Bates risked being regarded as the female journalist aspiring to acceptance among the scientists of the academy, the mastery of the academic game continually out of her grasp (see Hamilton 1982a:94–6; White 1993).[5] The sensationalism of her autobiography, *The Passing of the Aborigines*, did not help in this regard—nor did her largely unfounded belief in widespread Aboriginal cannibalism of their babies.

As with Haddon's *Reports*, there were also some continuities with the later era of Malinowskian-style fieldwork. To be sure, Bates' magnum opus, *The Native Tribes of Western Australia*, belatedly published in 1985 due to the editorial labours of Isobel White, was organised under headings familiar from the turn-of-the-century ethnology of Spencer and Gillen, Howitt, and Matthews, as a broad survey work encompassing the separate topics of Origin, Marriage Laws, Social Organisation, Physical Characteristics, Arts and Crafts, Food, Initiation, Religious Beliefs, Magic, Legends and Folklore, and Totems (see White 1985:9–22). Some parts of that work resulted from a prolonged association with informants in the field, in the Aboriginal camps of Roebuck Plains Station in 1901–02, while she lived there with her husband, the manager of the station (see Salter 1971:90–9). These parts are presented in the detailed, insider's way that also adopted the literary conventions of modernist ethnography, such as the ethnographic present. One of these passages—the description of the stages of male initiation among Aborigines congregating on Roebuck Plains Station near Broome—would become a critical link for Sullivan in establishing traditional continuity 100 years later in the native title claim.

Groups

Daisy Bates conceived of Aboriginal groups in a variety of ways. At the highest level of generality were regional groupings that she called 'nations', defined as 'a collection of tribes with community of interests, with certain similar customs, ceremonies and beliefs' (White 1985:39). Other kinds of broad categorisations that appear in her work are those who share the four-section system and those who include circumcision in their initiation ceremonies. The next level down in her taxonomic hierarchy is the 'tribe', which, from the description of their areas, implies contiguous territories and ownership (1985:49).

---

5 For more on the life of Daisy Bates, see Blackburn (1994); De Vries (2008); Reece (2007); and Salter (1971).

Of interest to the *Rubibi* claim is Bates' description of the Broome area as forming part of the 'Kalarrabulu' tribal territory (White 1985:59), although, according to Glowczewski (1998:209), in her fieldnotes, Bates also spoke of a 'Joogan' language and the 'Yowera' people of Broome. In her description of other 'nations', she does describe lower levels in her taxonomic hierarchy as dialect groups or local groups (see, for example, White 1985:48–9).

Laws, customs relating to land, ceremonies

Bates' most poignant account of Aboriginal attachment to particular areas of land arose out of her horrendous encounter with diseased and dying Aborigines, who were forcibly transported from all over Western Australia (including some she knew from Broome) to the lock-up hospitals on Dorre and Bernier islands, commencing in 1910.[6] She described this experience in *The Passing of the Aborigines* under the chapter title 'Isles of the dead' (Bates 1938:93–104): 'silently for hours on a headland, straining their hollow, hopeless eyes across the narrow strait for the glimpse of beloved wife or husband or a far lost country' (at p. 100).

Much of her description of land affiliation is also consistent with the desire for the familiarity of known kin and country, and fear of the sorcery of unfamiliar Aboriginal people. With the exception of her description of increase ceremonies, the traditions that we would today see as tying individuals to particular places—such as conception totems, Dreaming stories and the sites of major ceremonies—are typically described in ways that de-emphasise place. Moreover, much of Bates' account supports the porous nature of tribal territories, especially her informants' description of various 'highways' of kin relations into neighbouring areas, intermarriage between different language groups, the inclusion of people from different tribes in initiation ceremonies and the long journeys of the initiates through the wider region.

The 'laws' she described were laws of marriage and laws about the proper performance of initiation ceremonies.

Change

'Culture contact' was not one of the established topics of ethnographic treatises of the times. Implicit in Bates' work, however, is an assumption of fatal impact or inevitable decline, presumably derived from her direct observation of the alarming effects of untreatable diseases on the Aboriginal population. These assumptions tended to be carried over to cultural matters as well. She variously

6 See Jebb (1984).

interpreted the appearance of half-caste children as the end of traditional marriage rules, and the physical relocation of Aboriginal people on pastoral leases and settlements as the dramatic end of the savage life.

Radcliffe-Brown

Although he did interview at least one Aboriginal person from Broome, Radcliffe-Brown did not do fieldwork in the vicinity of Broome.[7] Apart from Bernier Island and the notorious false start at Sandstone with Daisy Bates,[8] Radcliffe-Brown's WA fieldwork was confined to the Roebourne–Port Hedland–Fortescue River region, about 480 km south of Broome (Brown 1913). When he came to write his general survey *The Social Organisation of Australian Tribes* (Radcliffe-Brown 1931), he relied largely on the unpublished fieldnotes of Elkin and Piddington (see below) for discussion of the tribes around Broome (pp. 337–41). The exception is the Nyul-nyul tribe, where he also refers to his own unpublished fieldnotes of 1912.

Radcliffe-Brown famously asserted the horde—based on an exogamous, virilocal, patrilineal clan—as the basic unit of traditional landownership, occupation and exploitation for the whole of Australia (1931:35–6). This generalisation was part of his grand synthesis in the first part of *The Social Organisation of Australian Tribes,* which sought to construct both the commonalities of the existing localised ethnography and a general framework from which regional variation could be explored.[9]

The additional significance of this theorising about Aboriginal local organisation was in the influence it had over future researchers, particularly Elkin and, as we shall see below, Erich Kolig in the *Rubibi* claim in 2000. The reasons for Radcliffe-Brown's influence remain somewhat of a mystery, given his meagre publication record and how far his own fieldwork practices fell short of the

7 Elkin (1933:footnote 5 on p. 441, and the sentence commencing p. 444) refers to Radcliffe-Brown's fieldnotes of an interview with an Aboriginal man from the Broome district about certain Djukan words and concepts.

8 See Bates (1938:93–6); Kuper (1996:35–42); and White (1985:7–8).

9 For a recent overview of Radcliffe-Brown's theorising on local organisation and his critics, see Sutton (2003:44–53).

ideal of long-term, localised fieldwork that he tried to inculcate in his students.[10] Instead of fieldwork in the tradition of Malinowski, he dazzled with his ability to systematise and with his teaching.

The rhetorical strategies in his writing, perhaps because of their extremism, were destined to provoke a sense of intellectual excitement. His approach promised an end to speculative evolutionary theorising, the drawing of a line under previous amateurish, piecemeal accounts and the beginnings of solid scientific foundations based on careful observation. It was not only a promise. He delivered in *The Social Organisation of Australian Tribes* a compelling synthesis of diverse ethnographic detail into a few types and recovered from this mass of detail clear explanations of the relationship between types of kinship systems, marriage rules and classes (moieties, sections, subsections). This was an achievement of analytical perseverance, however, rather than fieldwork observation.

His millennial tone no doubt combined well with his confidence, his flamboyant personality and the academic capital with which he arrived in Sydney as Foundation Professor of Anthropology in 1926, to make the models proposed in *The Social Organisation of Australian Tribes* the reference point for all subsequent anthropological research. This agenda setting was not confined to the topic of social organisation, although this remained the privileged entry point into the Aboriginal world for a whole generation of researchers. It extended to local organisation, mythology and ritual, and their interrelationship with social organisation. He was obviously aware of a variety of rituals, including initiation ceremonies, but it was the widespread reporting of localised ritual sites, used for the increase of natural species or other natural phenomena, that provided a neat confirmation of interrelationship at the level of the horde (Figure 4.1).

---

10 Daisy Bates was not an unbiased observer of his fieldwork on Bernier Island and succumbed to occasionally making invidious comparisons with her own closeness to the natives and lampooning the Professor's distance:

> To question the poor shuddering souls of these doomed exiles was slow work and saddening, but as I sat with them in the darkness of their *mias* at night, the torture of the hospital routine was forgotten, and harking back to thoughts of home, they were, for an hour or so, happy. Of all the tribes there so dismally represented, from Hall's Creek to Broome and Nullagine, from the Fitzroy River to Winning Pool and Marble Bar and Lake Way, I learned much of infinite value in vocabularies and customs and pedigrees and legends. The scientists, I think, made intermittent headway…'Your two sons [referring to A. R. Brown and Watson]—why are they afraid of us?' I was asked more than once. The answer was obvious. Grant Watson was physically ill one day after taking a photograph. However, they helped him to collect shells and insects occasionally, and obligingly sang songs of *woggura* and *wallardoo*—crow and eaglehawk—into Professor Radcliffe-Brown's phonograph. He in return regaled them with *Peer Gynt* and *Tannhauser* and *Egmount*, to which they listened politely. (1938:101)

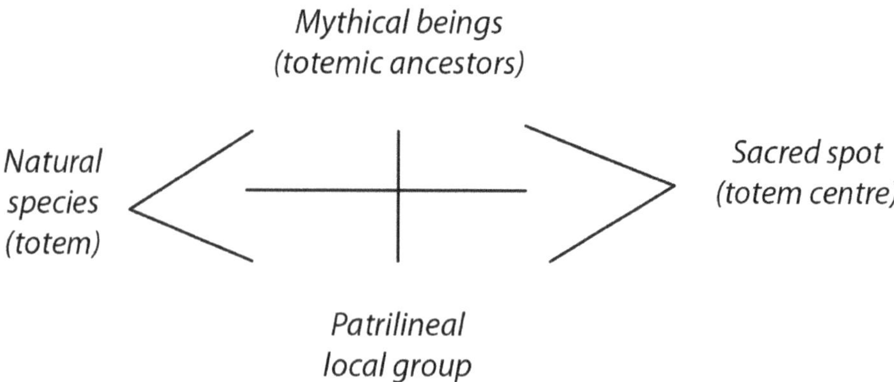

Figure 4.1 Diagram from Radcliffe-Brown's *The Social Organisation of Australian Tribes*

Source: Radcliffe-Brown (1931:61).

Elkin

Radcliffe-Brown had mentioned the possibility of Elkin doing fieldwork in the north-west of Western Australia when they first met in London, while Elkin was completing his PhD. Back in Australia, in 1927, Elkin became one of the first beneficiaries of the research funding that Radcliffe-Brown had secured from the Rockefeller Foundation. Radcliffe-Brown, the new Professor, made arrangements for Elkin, the newly qualified Doctor of Philosophy and novice fieldworker, to commence his field research. He lent Elkin some notes from his own previous fieldwork in Western Australia and sent him to the Kimberley to collect further information about kinship and social organisation before it was too late. Elkin commenced his fieldwork in Broome (see Wise 1985:47–55). During his 12-month fieldtrip in 1927–28, Elkin visited almost every settled area of the Kimberley. Why he should undertake such fleeting survey work, given Radcliffe-Brown's own previous surveys, admittedly further south, is a little mysterious. According to Wise, Elkin's biographer:

> Radcliffe-Brown had written to him urging that he stay in one place long enough to make an intensive study of one tribe, but Elkin was convinced his Kimberley-wide survey was a more important use of his time. He wanted to be able to pinpoint places where future anthropologists could

> fruitfully come for extended periods. An urgency to cover the entire region gripped him. What was more, by now he wanted to see the whole picture of the frontier contact situation. (Wise 1985:70)[11]

Elkin spent considerable time in Broome interviewing and taking genealogies of Aboriginal people from various tribes, including locals from the 'Jukan' tribe, the neighbouring 'Yauou' and some in the Broome jail from as far away as Halls Creek (about 645 km to the east). His most intensive fieldwork in the Broome region was done among the Nyul-nyul around Beagle Bay mission to the north and, towards the end of his fieldwork, 15 days with the 'Karadjeri' to the south at La Grange.

Groups

In his methodology, terminology and interests, Elkin closely followed Radcliffe-Brown in seeking the scientific bedrock of genealogy, kinship systems and formal social organisation. Radcliffe-Brown saw 'tribal' groupings as highly problematic, ultimately suggesting that unity at this level was primarily a matter of shared linguistic competence of a number of hordes (1931:36). Yet, he and Elkin were drawn into using the term 'tribe' in their general description of the distribution of Aboriginal groups, and they use 'tribal' names to identify particular types of social organisation. Accordingly, it is unclear to what extent Elkin's use of 'tribe', in this early work, implied clearly bounded territorial units.[12] He rather unquestioningly accepts Radcliffe-Brown's assertion of the 'horde' as the basic, reliable indicator of traditional ownership and exploitation of land. In his *Oceania* articles (particularly the sketch maps), field correspondence with his wife, Sally, and correspondence with Radcliffe-Brown, Elkin does, however, indicate a broad association between 'tribes' and tracts of land. The following sketch map appears in his 1933 article (Map 4.3).

11 Also see Gray (1997, 2007) for another account of Elkin's 1927–28 fieldwork.

12 In his mature synthesis in *The Australian Aborigines* (Elkin 1964), Elkin devoted a chapter to 'The tribe'. He opened the chapter with a seemingly strong statement of the tribe as a corporate and territorial unit: 'A tribe is a group related by actual or implied genealogy who occupy and own a definite area of territory and hunt and gather food over it according to rules which control the behaviour of the smaller groups and families within the tribe' (1964:56). But, taken as a whole, the chapter is more equivocal because of his acknowledgment of the greater importance of the local group, the frequency of imprecise boundaries, the social closeness of neighbouring local groups notwithstanding their affiliation to different tribes, frequent lack of a tribal name, strong intertribal ceremonial gatherings organised by the leaders of local groups, and the spread of customs between tribes.

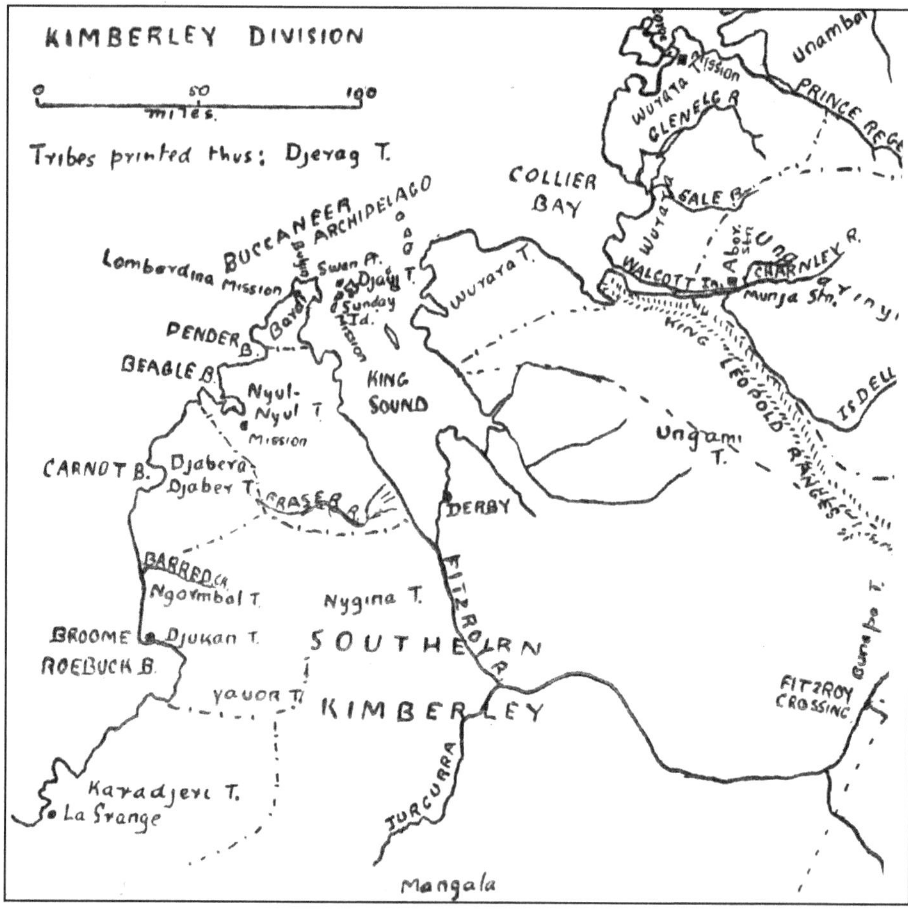

Map 4.3 Detail of Elkin's sketch map of the Kimberley Division showing the approximate location of tribes

Source: Elkin (1933:436).

Of interest to the *Rubibi* claim is the delineation of the 'Djukan', 'Yauor' and 'Ngormbal' 'tribes' in the vicinity of Broome. In a later publication Elkin (1964:57) wondered whether Djukan, Ngormbol and Djabera-Djabera were local groups of a single tribe.

The most suggestive of the field correspondence is quoted in Gray (1997:34–5):

> The Djukan tribe 'a quite small tribe with a coast line of few miles [was] almost a thing of the past. The Yauor people 'who swing around the harbour and join the Karadjeri, claim Broome'. There was one Djukan man left and Elkin was 'trying to track him down. But I have no doubt that the Djukan was similar to the Normbal at Willie and Bard Creeks and the Jabera-jaber [sic] at Carnot Bay and probably also the Yauor'.

There is also material in Elkin's articles that, on analysis, is supportive of the 'Djukan' and 'Yauor' being part of larger cultural blocs. All the identified tribes in the Broome region from the Karadjeri in the south, up to and including the Nyul-nyul in the north, shared the four-section system with the same names for the sections and had the same kinship system (1933:438, footnote 2). Elkin explicitly suggests that the shared section system facilitated intertribal sociality including arranging marriages (1932:325).

Laws, customs relating to land, ceremony grounds

Although his focus was on variation in social organisation, Elkin did venture some comments on local organisation. The 1932 article concludes with some generalisations about the whole Kimberley division. In effect, it recapitulated and enlarged upon Radcliffe-Brown's linking of horde-totem-totemic ancestors-totemic centre (Radcliffe-Brown 1931:61) to include the father's 'finding' the child's totem spirit (*rai*) in the horde country; and consequent strong affective relations to birth country, reinforced by the ceremonial life of the tribes and ritual increase sites (Elkin 1932:329–30). Elkin did complicate Radcliffe-Brown's model of patrilineal inheritance of horde country to the extent that, at least in the 1932 article, he saw totems as primarily attached to particular landscapes, implicitly suggesting that 'finding' or birth totems (*rai*) are not within the gift of a father, but might appear to be patrilineal only because children were in the past likely to be born in the horde country (1932:330).

Elkin's 1933 article on totemism is his most explicit examination of local organisation and, in theory, of great significance to the *Rubibi* claim because it deals with the 'Yauor' and the culturally similar 'Karadjeri'.

Elkin uses the rubric of totemism, yet argues that the simple group–natural species linkage is merely a starting point for further questioning. This terminology is another example of Fardon's analysis of the development of anthropological regional specialisations mentioned in Chapter 1. In particular, it exemplifies the tension between the need to participate in the metropolitan theorising of the time, which used the topic of 'totemism', and, on the other hand, to try to overcome the outdated simplicity of the metropolitan discourse in describing the latest ethnographic discoveries in the specific region. For the contemporary anthropologist looking to deconstruct such a strong theoretical framing device, the writing that results from this tension often leaves frustrating gaps and gives rise to the artificial fragmentation of cultural forms as different kinds of totemism (local totemism, conception totemism, cult totemism, moiety totemism, and so on) (cf. Lévi-Strauss and Needham 1973).

Elkin specifies the name of the 'horde-country' of all local groups in the 'Yauor' tribe and their associated totems/Dreamings (Table 4.1).

Table 4.1 Elkin's table of 'Yauor' local groups and Dreamings

YAUOR TRIBE			
No.	*ngura*	*Bugari*	(English)
1	Maramjuno	dzindzirmaning	Spring water
2	Langandjun (Djambarangandjal)	Mangoban wodarbin	A small marsupial Flying fox
3	Wondjeldjuno	Lan langur pargara	Stars Opossum Turkey
4	Daibineridjuno	Ingalua kulebil kungara nimanbur	A greenish rock-fish with a big head Green turtle A black berry off a prickly bush Flying fox

Source: Elkin (1933:271).

Despite this detail, there must be doubts about whether he had independently confirmed the existence of the horde in these tribes or whether his data have been allocated to the pre-existing category on trust. The text itself refers to his linguistic and methodological difficulties. The 'countries' were not visited, but described from the memory of his informants during the 15 days of intensive interviewing at La Grange Aboriginal Feeding Depot. Thus, it is not clear whether the names referred to specific sites or regions, or both. A further acknowledged difficulty was the polysemy of the word for country (*ngura*), meaning either the country of one's patrilineal inheritance or one's birthplace or conception site, or simply a camping place. He also noticed the sharing of totems between different 'countries' and the relaxation of permission-seeking requirements for access to the 'country' of certain kin (Elkin 1933:280).

The major problem with Elkin's account of the 'Karadjeri' horde-countries is that the much more extensive fieldwork of the Piddingtons (carried out shortly after Elkin's visit) failed to confirm the existence of horde-country in Radcliffe-Brown's sense of the term. The Piddingtons' research and Elkin's response to it are dealt with below.

The totemism article also includes details of both 'Karadjeri' and 'Yauor' increase rites and sites. Again, despite the limitations of his fieldwork, Elkin rather casually accepts and repeats Radcliffe-Brown's view that the increase ritual must be performed by members of the local horde (1933:284). Where this restriction does not seem to be the case, as in his material from the Forest River district, he attributes its absence to a rule being broken and the break-up of the tribe (1933:285). This commitment to the idea of the self-sufficient horde appears side by side with other material indicative of interrelationship and larger cultural blocs. For example, there is the fact that increase sites for important food sources are spread over a wide area, including in the country of distant local groups and neighbouring tribes (1933:283). Typically, these apparent contradictions are never explicitly discussed. Of interest to the *Rubibi* claim is his specific equation of Karadjeri and 'Yauor' increase rituals (1933:294).

Change

Elkin was acutely aware of the colonial circumstances of his fieldwork and the disastrous consequences of colonisation for the Aboriginal population, for he commences his account of social organisation with estimates of the dramatic decline in the numbers of each tribal group. Of the 'Djukan', 'Ngormbal' and 'Djabeera-Djaber' tribes, he says there were very few remaining and they were almost extinct (1933:271, 438). As with Haddon and Radcliffe-Brown, this realisation engendered a sense of urgency in the task of recovering as much as possible the pre-contact situation. Unlike Radcliffe-Brown, who thought that all theorising about social evolution and diffusion was speculative history that needed to be replaced with scientific comparative sociology, Elkin—perhaps under the influence of his old professor from London University, Elliott Smith—did engage in some diffusionist theorising about the likely spread of differing kinship systems and marriage rules in the distant past (1932:304, 319).

One of his few attempts at historical analysis of the contemporary situation came in his explanation of the prevalence of the patrilineal inheritance of totems. He saw the more pervasive and important 'local descent'—that is, conception site and its associated spiritual, sacred and mythological dimensions—as being displaced by patrilineal descent because Aboriginal children were being born outside their father's country as a result of white settlement (1932:330–1). His other major attempt at historical explanation came amid his critique of Piddington's findings that contradicted horde theory (see below).

Piddington

Ralph Piddington, a student of Radcliffe-Brown's, was the first anthropologist to conduct long-term fieldwork within the Broome region focusing on one tribe. Altogether he spent nine months around La Grange Government Feeding Station and two months at Beagle Bay mission in two field trips, one in 1930 and the other in 1931 (Piddington and Piddington 1932).

The amount of time he spent with the Karadjeri at La Grange marks a break with the survey work of Radcliffe-Brown and Elkin, and brought Piddington closer to the ideal of long-term fieldwork. It placed him in a unique position to give a more comprehensive account of one tribe. This he did in articles on Karadjeri initiation (1932a), the totemic system and social organisation

(1932b), and in his social anthropology textbook (1950). It was, however, a comprehensiveness enabled by, and limited to, the overriding interests and analytical categories of the day. Thus, he provides information on climatic and ecological background, and kinship organisation; a brief account of local organisation; detailed accounts of initiation ceremonies and related mythology, contrasting two different 'traditions' of circumcision ceremonies; and a very comprehensive account of various increase ceremonies under the rubric of totemism. As a convenient link to metropolitan theorising, 'totemism' seemed indispensable to the framing of Aboriginal ethnography. 'Totemism' persisted despite the fact that Piddington's elaboration of all the different implications of '*bugari*' (Dreaming) for the Karadjeri, as an interrelated cosmogony, ontology and religious law, demonstrated how awkward 'totemism' was as an overarching description (for example, 1932b:372–6).

One of the chief interests of Piddington's ethnography for the *Rubibi* claim is the implicit challenge to Radcliffe-Brown's horde theory. Given that Radcliffe-Brown was directing his research, it is perhaps understandable that Piddington diplomatically presented his own material on Karadjeri local organisation as an exception to the 'normal Australian type as described by Professor Radcliffe-Brown' (1932:351). But Piddington's exposition is frustratingly concise. Within the Karadjeri 'tribe' there are two sub-tribes or dialect groups that have slightly different kinship usages (1932:343) and who are associated with broadly differentiated tracts of land: the inland Karadjeri and the coastal Karadjeri (Nadja), who were his informants (p. 350). Among the Nadja sub-tribe, exogamous local groups did not exercise proprietary rights over their own territory:

> Certain small exogamous groups exist, but they lack the solidarity which characterises the normal Australian horde; small parties composed of less than a dozen individuals from any horde may go on hunting expeditions lasting several months, over the territory of any other horde, without asking the permission of the owners, who would not object. (1932:351)

And:

> On the whole, one is inclined to think that the Karadjeri never possessed a rigid clan associated with their local groups, but that there was a general tendency for the majority of men of one locality to belong to one or other of the two moieties, a state of affairs which was probably preserved by the predominance of patrilocal marriages. (1932:351–2)

Despite the length of Piddington's fieldwork, Elkin was not prepared to accept these conclusions. Instead, Elkin questioned Piddington by asserting a theory of historical transformation. Assuming that the horde theory accurately represented the pre-contact situation, he suggested that Piddington's informants, who had worked on various stations along the coast, had become accustomed to mixing freely on one another's horde-countries. He argued, therefore, that Piddington's informants, when questioned by Piddington, must have projected the contemporary 'decadent' situation back into the past (Elkin 1933:279). Elkin went on to suggest possible reasons why Piddington might have been in error, including the possibility of confusion between horde country and conception site country and the possibility of an individual with several totemic associations belonging to several totemic clans (1933:280-1).[13] There is no record of Piddington making a direct response to Elkin. This is probably due to the fact that about this time the two became involved in a notorious dispute.[14]

Apart from this undercurrent, it is tempting to see in Elkin's disbelief of Piddington's conclusions the effect of a straightforward academic hierarchy: Radcliffe-Brown, the international figure at the apex; then Elkin, the new professor in the colonial university; and, at the base, Piddington, the MA researcher. There is also Elkin's own investment in Radcliffe-Brown's theorising and the status it brought to the regional specialisation.

Piddington did make something of an indirect response, years later, in reply to similar criticism from Birdsell (see Piddington 1971). He repeated his assertion that the Karadjeri never had any horde boundaries and stated that the information he relied on for that conclusion was from older informants, who would have been in their late twenties in 1890. He also rejected Elkin's attempt to harmonise his material on increase rituals with Radcliffe-Brown's simple correspondence between increase site and horde (1971:243). Further, he warned against Australia-wide generalising and thinking in terms of European ideas of ownership. It is interesting that, even in this later article, Piddington does not directly criticise Radcliffe-Brown, although by then others had (Hiatt 1962, 1966; Peterson 1983; Stanner 1965). The disagreement between Elkin and Piddington in 1932–33 could be seen as the first skirmish in what was to become a more heated academic controversy, 20 years later, about the universality of Radcliffe-Brown's 'horde'.

---

13 Elkin presents the latter argument (multiple totemic associations of an individual) as some kind of caution against accepting Piddington's conclusion that the Karadjeri never possessed a rigid clan association with their local groups. Yet the crosscutting totemic ties would surely support Piddington's assertion, as I read it, of no simple correspondence between horde-country/clan/totemic sites/exclusive economic exploitation.

14 Briefly, after his fieldwork, Piddington made wide-ranging allegations in a newspaper article about the mistreatment of Aboriginal people in Western Australia. A. O. Neville, the Chief Protector of Aborigines, took it as an ill-informed and overgeneralised criticism of his administration and made counter allegations against Piddington of misconduct in the field. Elkin, as newly appointed Professor of Anthropology and Chairman of the Australian National Research Council's Committee for Anthropological Research, had to deal with the eventual fallout and the threat to future research in Western Australia. He took a negative view of Piddington's behaviour and, ultimately, Piddington did no further research in Australia (see Biskup 1973:94–5; Gray 1994, 2007; Wise 1985:115).

Of relevance to the *Rubibi* claim is Piddington's account of Karadjeri initiation (1932a). Together with Daisy Bates' material, it could potentially provide something of an anthropological baseline for the region in the vicinity of Broome. A comparison of the two accounts reveals the many structural similarities. These similarities include changing the name applied to initiates at different stages of initiation; food restrictions; and sex segregation of certain aspects of the ritual. A significant difference is what Piddington called the '*midedi* feast'—the ritual induction of initiates into an exhibition of long sacred boards, followed by a feast. The sacred boards were kept in a constructed storehouse or a specifically designated hollow tree. This ceremony and the ceremony surrounding circumcision were the two initiation rituals that survived strongly during the period of Piddington's fieldwork, while others had fallen away. They coincide with the terminology of 'first stage' and 'second stage' used in the claim in 2000 (see next chapter).

Worms

Father Ernest Worms, the German Pallottine missionary, spent an initial eight years in Broome (1930–38) as parish priest and part-time ethnographer. He is one of the intriguing figures of Australianist anthropology (Capell 1964:156). His academic oeuvre is very diverse, ranging from grand survey works on Aboriginal religion (Worms and Petri 1998), Aboriginal languages (Worms 1953), recounting of Aboriginal myths (Worms 1950, 1952), and comparison of initiation ceremonies (Worms 1938a), to more narrowly focused articles on Aboriginal onomatopoeia, sense of smell, placenames and particular petroglyph sites (Worms 1938b, 1942, 1944, 1954).

There are some indications that Worms saw himself as part of the *Kulturkreis* school (see Marchand 2003), which he portrayed as a scientific reaction to evolutionism (see Worms 1947a, 1947b, 1947c). This association was a potential problem for the acceptance of his work, since the regional specialisation of Aboriginal Australia was dominated at the time by British anthropology in the structural-functionalist mode, which had, in effect, rejected *Kulturkreis* and diffusionism as conjectural history (Harris 1972:382–92; Heine-Geldern 1964; Sylvain 1996:483). Worms did navigate these differences with some success, at least in having numerous articles published in *Oceania*. His technique seems to have been to focus on common ground—ethnographic description—and to leave theorising in the background, to be taken up by the master theorists in Vienna. The presentation of uncontroversial facts and broad surveys also dovetails with another concern: to dispel misconceptions and ignorance about Aboriginal people among a German readership, who did not have easy access to the specialist English-language anthropological literature.

Groups

Worms adopted the terminology of 'tribe', 'tribal country' and 'clan'. It is not clear from his usage, however, how he saw the relationship between clan and tribe, and whether he accepted the clan as the basic unit of traditional ownership of land. The use of the terminology of 'clan', without further explanation, is exemplified in his article on Kimberley placenames. That article seems to have been an attempt to reassert the Aboriginal heritage of the European-dominated landscape by explaining the Aboriginal significance of settled places. In doing so, he provides his most detailed account of the extent of Yawuru country (Worms 1944). Of direct relevance is his description of the claim area (assuming *Ganen* = *Kunin*):

> 32. Ganen, or Malngologon (Y.)
>
> A short stretch of land on the south bank of the inner Roebuck Bay, opposite Broome. It belongs to the Yaoro tribe, Walmandyano local clan with the turtle (golebel) totem. A big oval stone on the beach represents this local totem. High middens extending along the shore bear witness to a large population of earlier times.
>
> (a) Ganen, lit. 'the shore', from ganen (Y.), 'land, partially or entirely surrounded by water: shore, cape, island.' (1944:295)

Also mentioned as Yaoro clans are the Langandyono (places east and south of Broome = Elkin's 'Langandjun'?), the Menyerdyano (places in Broome township = Minyjirr the place, Yawuru dialect?) and the Dyolbaidyano (places to the south-east extending to Thangoo Station). He had given some slightly different totemic associations for the clans in a previous article (Worms 1940). How to interpret the differences between the two articles became an issue in the native title claim in 2000.

Ceremony

Worms' article for the Vatican ethnological journal *Annali Lateranensi*, comparing stages of initiation among various Kimberley tribes (Worms 1938a), is the most relevant from the point of view of establishing continuity of ritual in the native title claim, for it includes an account of Yawuru initiation. There are no details of his source of information, or the participants, or the circumstances of the rituals he might have observed personally.[15] Trying to recover his methodology and original data through the text is made more difficult because of the adoption of an ethnographic present for describing the pre-colonial past. Of significance is his clear association of the shore of Roebuck Bay and the land surrounding Broome with the Yaoro (Yawuru) and the continued distinctiveness of their initiation ceremonies despite their depleted numbers (1938a:164). It is also interesting to compare his six-stage account with Daisy Bates' 10-stage account of initiation.

Worms did not have access to Bates' material, yet there are remarkable similarities of structure, content and terminology. The sheer mass of detail in Bates' version, despite her amateur status, lends verisimilitude to it and leads one to wonder, again, whether Worms' account, probably truncated for the purposes of comparison, was based entirely on the recollection of informants. Another difference is the complete absence in Worms' account of the significance of particular kinship relationships, moieties and sections in the organisation of ceremonies—all of which permeate Bates' account.

Worms also mentioned the '*mideđi* feast'. He published an explicit account of a Two-Man myth told to him by an old Karadjeri man (Worms 1949). It contained the esoteric details of the Dreamtime inauguration of circumcision and the '*mideđi* feast'. Curiously, Worms did not make the links with Piddington's earlier material.[16]

Change

The Yawuru are typically presented by Worms as 'the most detribalised natives of the Western Kimberley' and deserving of pity: 'It is rather touching to observe the persistence of the remaining fifty Yaoro who try to keep up the old traditions. This tendency can be attributed in part to the effect of the frequent visits of the neighbouring tribes' (1944:298–9).

---

15 Some details of the account and references in other articles seem to indicate direct observation. For example, in a footnote in his 1957 article on the poetry of the Yaoro and Bad, he states:

> In August 1950 and in February 1953 the Yaoro invited Europeans and Malays regardless of age and sex to their initiation ceremonies. The initiant, in one case, was armed with a rubber sling ('shanghai') tinned meat and insect DTT powder. Such bathos was unheard of twenty years ago, at which time I described their rites for *Annali Lateranensi*, 2, 164–168. (Worms 1957:214–15)

On the other hand, it is a very condensed account (five pages) and it includes subincision, which, according to other reports (see Piddington 1932a:62), was less frequent at that time.

16 Piddington's 'southern tradition' of Karadjari initiation is associated with a 'two-brothers' mythology called 'Bagadjimbiri'. The two brothers perform a similar inauguration function as in Worms' account. At the end of Piddington's account, he refers to two other cultural heroes who seem to have cognate names with the 'two great men' of Worms' account (1932a:51).

Worms had quite a long association with Broome and that put him in a position to observe historical transformations. For the most part, he tended to theorise change as loss—both loss of people and loss of traditional culture defined in objectivist terms of language competence, knowledge of myths, ritual performances and adherence to marriage rules. In his contribution to a 1970 collection of papers on Aborigines and change, he continued his objectivist focus on changing residential patterns (the mixing of tribes), clothing, housing, hygiene, material culture and so on. He also demonstrated an adeptness at formulating less obvious arguments for cultural continuity in drawing links between the immediate distribution of killed game in the past and the contemporary aversion to saving money (1970:371–2).

Dalton

Peter Dalton's unpublished MA thesis on social stratification and racial–ethnic groups in Broome provides a vivid and intimate portrait of the town circa 1961–62 and what might today be called the intercultural space and sexual politics (Dalton 1964). It was for anthropology an innovative topic, closer to sociology in its subject matter and theoretical inspiration. It was also ambitious. The project sought to describe the internal dynamics of the Japanese (2 per cent), Malay (5 per cent), Chinese (5 per cent), Indonesian (2 per cent), Coloured (part-Aboriginal) (19 per cent), Aboriginal (31 per cent) and European (34 per cent) groupings, as well as the relative social position and interaction of the different groups. Based on a total of five months' fieldwork in Broome, the thesis is peppered with picaresque characters, extremes of cruelty, exploitation and salacious gossip of grog parties, gambling and illicit, interracial sex.

Groups

With so much ground to cover in his thesis, it is doubtful whether Dalton spent much time with the Aboriginal group. This seems to be confirmed by his seemingly total reliance on Elkin, Piddington and other anthropologists to provide the explanatory background for his description of the contemporary situation of 'The Aborigines—The Low Status Group'. On the other hand, Dalton thought that the experience of some of the older Aboriginal people with previous anthropologists had facilitated the understanding of his role (1964:vi). Whatever the depth of his fieldwork, he does provide some intriguing details of the internal stratification and location of different Aboriginal groups.

Dalton found that the location and composition of the Aboriginal camps in the town broadly represented an orientation towards the traditional country of Aboriginal groups who had migrated into Broome. The position of the camps also represented differing degrees of 'Europeanisation'. Thus the Bard from the north lived in camps facing the north, and the Karadjeri, Yawuru and other groups from the south and south-east established camps on the southern side of the town. The more 'traditionally orientated' lived further out of town at the 'One mile' camp, the 'Four mile' camp and at 'Eight mile' camp, Fishermen's Bend (in the vicinity of the *Rubibi* claim area) (1964:117–18).

Ceremony

The old men from Eight Mile camp had strong links with The Hill camp, within the township of Broome, and, together, the Aboriginal people of the two camps formed a relatively cohesive in-group of closely related Karadjeri and Yawuru people. In a place that was a crossroads for different ritual traditions, including the importation of new cults from the east (specifically the *gurangara* cult), they maintained a separate identity. They kept their own traditional ceremonies separate from the northern Bard and some of the inland tribes. In practice, this meant the continuation of their circumcision ceremonies, in association with the Two Men song cycles and a continuation of the revelatory rite described by Piddington as the *midedi* feast. Dalton gives an account of both ceremonies, demonstrating some remarkable continuities with Piddington's description. Of particular importance for the *Rubibi* claim is the identification of the *midedi* ground, being some little distance from Fishermen's Bend, and of it being used for other rites to do with the sacred 'birmal' boards (1964:146–7).

Dalton's theories of change

Despite the constraints on his fieldwork, Dalton does present various theories of historical change and possible trajectories. These are in broad terms of the breakdown of traditional culture, intergenerational conflict about adherence to tradition and Europeanisation.

His assumption of the inevitability of the direction of change is based on some quite contradictory evidence, which could equally suggest continuity of traditions within an unassimilated Aboriginal underclass. For example, while Dalton reported some instances of the disrespect of the younger generation for some of the older traditions, there appeared to be shared beliefs about the power of sacred objects and ceremonies, and the effectiveness of sorcery. It is never clear whether the derogatory opinions expressed to him privately would have been repeated in the presence of the 'old traditionalists'. Moreover, he reported the continuation of initiation ceremonies. The fact that the timing of the ceremonies had been adjusted to suit the European economy was seen by Dalton as evidence of a weakening of commitment to them. But that evidence is really more ambiguous. It could equally be interpreted as a commitment to continuing the ceremonies in difficult circumstances. Dalton also provides myriad evidence of the lack of integration of the Aboriginal group into the class of stable wage labourers. It involved an increased contribution to Aboriginal income from prostitution, social security benefits, the ubiquity of gambling, the absence of saving and a general resentment of European prejudice and power over their lives. Contrary to Dalton's assumption about continuing Europeanisation, all these factors could also indicate a trajectory towards continued Aboriginal identity in a distinct stratum of Broome society.

Tindale and the map makers

Norman Tindale's position within Australianist anthropology will be examined in more detail in Chapter 6. For the purposes of the present review, it is necessary only to note that, for his tribal map of Western Australia, he collaborated closely with Worms. Tindale's magnum opus, *Aboriginal Tribes of Australia* (1974), is dedicated to Worms, 'whose active encouragement...led to the preparation of this work in its present form'. One of the curiosities, then, is that Tindale's map (Map 4.4) shows a separate Djukan tribe for Broome, whereas Worms consistently wrote of the Yawuru alone. Tindale never explained this part of the map in any detail, so we must assume that he thought earlier accounts, such as Elkin's, were closer to the pre-contact situation that he was trying to represent (1974:142–53, 241).[17]

Tindale's map of Djukan tribal territory has been reproduced in all subsequent maps of tribal areas.[18]

17 His description of the Djukan tribe refers to Bates (1914, 1915); Bischofs (1908); Capell (1940); Connelly (1932); Elkin (1933); Petri (1939); some of his own fieldwork; the notes that Worms had given him and the work on languages by Nekes and Worms (see Worms 1953). He stated: 'Some informants prefer the term Tjunung. This tribe virtually is extinct' (Tindale 1974:241).

18 See Davis and Prescott (1992) and the Australian Institute of Aboriginal and Torres Strait Islander Studies (AIATSIS) tribal boundaries map and critiques of such maps (Sutton 1995a:99–101).

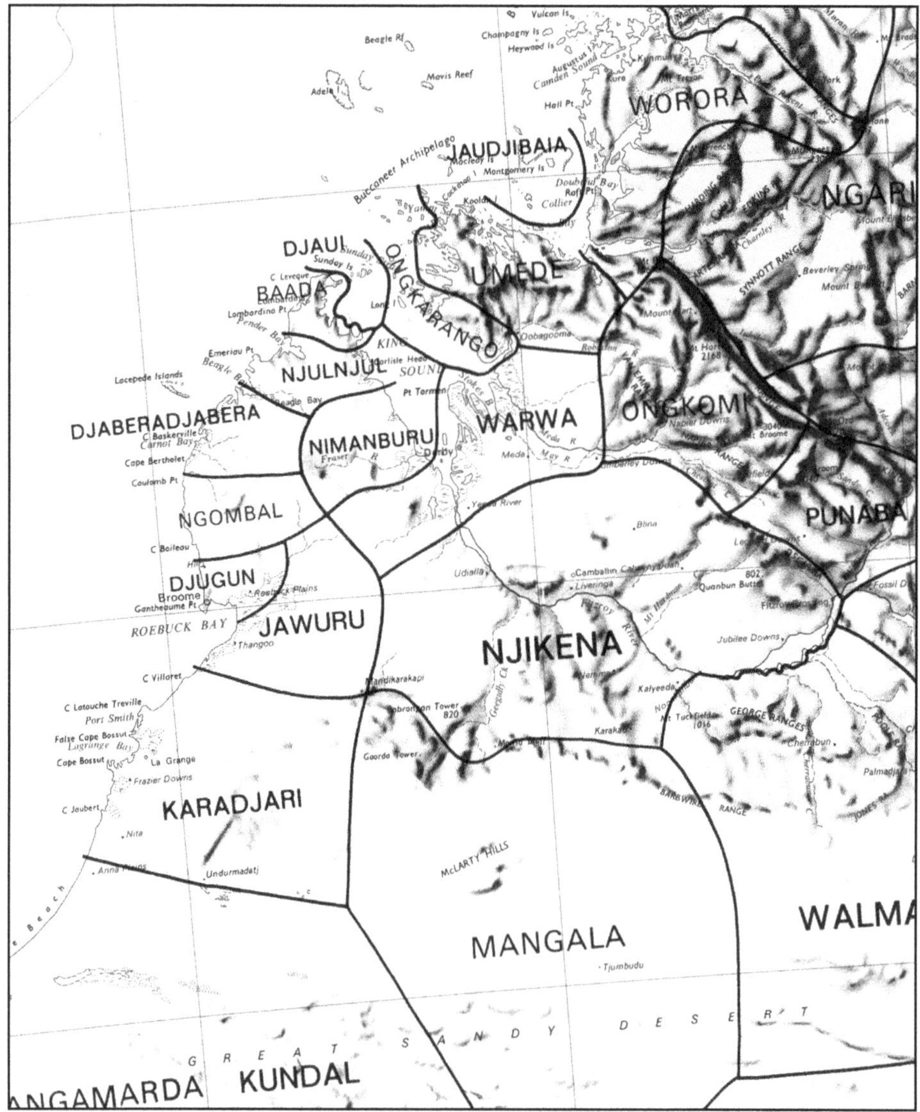

Map 4.4 Detail of Tindale's tribal map of Australia showing the Broome region

Source: Tindale (1974).

Hosokawa

Strict adherence to the task of delineating the anthropological archive would mean excluding the linguist Hosokawa. But subsequent reliance on his work by a number of anthropologists means that we must draw him into this review. His lengthy fieldwork, taking up most of 1986, punctuated the long, post-Dalton gap in anthropological studies of the Yawuru. Also, his work, while mainly a conventional linguistic analysis, did venture into sociolinguistics (see especially Hosokawa 1994). Critically, in his PhD thesis, he declared Djukan to be one of three dialects of the Yawuru language—a language that could be described as 'sick', with less than 20 speakers, all over fifty years of age (1991:11). Hosokawa also seems to have recovered 11 names of Yawuru local groups or territories (1991:45), and he identified a broad contemporary social grouping that he labelled 'Southerners' (Yawuru, Karadjeri and Nyangumarta), who spoke a similar kind of Aboriginal English dating from their co-residence at Thangoo Station in the 1930s and 1940s (Hosokawa 1994).

Glowczewski

About the same time as the linguist Stephen Muecke was enlisting Paddy Roe in his post-structuralist inspired analysis of narrative (see Benterrak et al. 1984), Barbara Glowczewski, a French anthropologist more inspired by the tradition of Lévi-Straussian structuralism, arrived in Broome and also found Paddy Roe a willing informant. She had done her main fieldwork among the Warlpiri of Lajamanu (Hooker Creek) between 1978 and 1984 (see Glowczewski 1991). In 1980, she recorded Paddy Roe's recollection of the ritual that he had observed at La Grange years before. She recognised it as having strong similarities with a Warlpiri ceremony (*Juluru*), which she had witnessed in 1979 (Glowczewski 1983). Glowczewski eventually moved to Broome permanently and married local Aboriginal filmmaker Wayne Barker, whom she met in Paris. They lived in Broome for most of the late 1980s and 1990s.

She was never engaged directly by the Kimberley Land Council to research traditional land tenure around Broome. In theory, this meant that she was a free agent on the outside of the claim. In practice, she was drawn into the research process through her genealogical research for a women's oral history project. Her genealogies were used as the starting point for KLC researchers in producing genealogies for the native title claim (T. 557).[19] Glowczewski takes credit for the realisation that, for all the differing traditional names being used to distinguish different groups, the genealogies revealed 12 longstanding, closely related family groups (Glowczewski 2000:416). Moreover, her research on identity, which took place between 1992 and 1998, coincided with her informants being intimately involved in working through the implications of new native title law for Broome.

19 'T' is a shorthand reference to the official transcript of the hearing of the first *Rubibi* claim, *Felix Edgar, Frank Sebastian & Others on Behalf of the Rubibi Community v The State of Western Australia*, No. WG 90 & 91 of 1998. It was produced by Transcript Australia.

Her major paper on contemporary Aboriginal life, 'The meaning of "one" in Broome' (Glowczewski 1998), inevitably overlapped with the issues that would have to be covered in the expert anthropological report for the claim. They include

- the contemporary fluidity and the diversity of Aboriginal connections to land around Broome
- the local intra-Indigenous complications precipitated by the need for a single incorporated claimant group
- the reanalysis of the anthropological archive in terms of continuity–discontinuity and fluidity–boundedness
- the critique of the land claim process and the formulation of the legal doctrine of native title.

One of the things that could have alarmed the land council lawyers was Glowczewski's presentation of the contemporary Aboriginal scene in Broome as one of cultural revival (1998:208). The legal doctrine of native title, as formulated by Justice Brennan in *Mabo*, required substantial continuity and explicitly rejected the possibility of the revival of the legal right, once it had been extinguished through the abandonment of the acknowledgment of traditional laws and practice of traditional customs relating to land. Yet her entry point into the issue of contemporary Aboriginal identity was her collaboration with Yawuru women, who were undertaking a cultural history project to determine whether Broome was rightly conceived as Jugan or Yawuru country. That project seemed to acknowledge that they no longer had the immediate cultural resources to resolve the issue. Another motif is the resurgence of Yawuru identity against the 'regency' of Paddy Roe, who had in the 1970s and early 1980s asserted custodianship of an extensive coastal strip including Broome (under the overarching name of Gularabulu),[20] which he said had been entrusted to him by the now extinct traditional owners. In Glowczewski's narrative of recent history, this resurgence involved the holding of an initiation ceremony at Kunin in 1991, with the help of neighbouring tribes, after a gap of about 10 years, during which Yawuru boys were taken away to be initiated on the country of those neighbouring groups. The resurgence was further galvanised by a threat to the integrity of ceremonial grounds by a proposed crocodile farm in 1992, which was eventually thwarted through Commonwealth Aboriginal heritage protection legislation. In Glowczewski's history of this period, the Aboriginal women of the Jarndu Yawuru played a critically supportive role in both actions.

The rather fraught dynamism of Aboriginal identity about this time, especially in relation to traditional connection to Broome, comes through graphically in

20 Also spelled 'Goolarabooloo'.

Fred Chaney's (1994) report for the minister about the traditional significance of the crocodile farm site. Chaney quotes at length the affidavit of Brian Saaban, who details the circumstances of his involvement as an initiand in the reconvened initiation ceremonies at 'Kunan' (Kunin) in 1990, referring to it as the continuation of Yawuru Law with the help of neighbouring tribes. In the report, reference is made to the Yawuru Aboriginal Corporation and its President, Francis Djiagween, the leader of The Hill camp in the 1960s, according to Dalton (1964:130), and grandfather of Patrick Dodson, who became a key witness in the native title claim. The Yawuru group had been angered by the apparent approval given by Paddy Roe and his Goolarabooloo Group Incorporated for the crocodile farm site. Before this incident, they seem to have been content for him to field the increasing amount of heritage consultation work coming from various government agencies. Eventually, Paddy Roe came to oppose the crocodile farm proposal. Other groups emerged to present their views to Chaney separately. Tajuko Garstone made a submission on behalf of the Jugan Aboriginal Corporation, asserting an interest through her grandmother, who had told her she was 'a Jugan woman' (Chaney 1994:22–3).

In Glowczewski's account, the harnessing of the identity dynamism in Broome was pursued by the KLC, which tried with some success to convince the disparate groups of the need for a *modus vivendi* between them in order to make the most advantageous strategic response to the opportunities that were arising out of native title law. These opportunities were principally the possibility of native title claims and a site clearance/planning role in urban development around Broome (see Jackson 1996).

The new native title claim process—particularly the requirement to name an applicant and to eventually nominate an incorporated body that would manage the native title rights—provided a direct, legal justification for the land council's coalition-forming approach. The resulting meetings agreed on a process that institutionalised the main groups—Yawuru, 'Djugan' and Goolarabooloo—in an overarching new body under the name Rubibi, the name of a soak in Broome.[21] Glowczewski traced some of the early challenges of the new Rubibi Working Group

- the increasing apprehensiveness of some of the Aboriginal people of Broome, who could not establish their own traditional rights to the town, and who became more firmly wedded to government programs, such as leases from the Aboriginal Lands Trust and State housing projects, which did not require proof of traditional connection

21 Patrick Sullivan explained that he had suggested the name 'Rubibi' specifically because it was not identified with any of the three groups in the coalition and thus would not favour the claims of one group against the other two (Transcript of interview with Patrick Sullivan, August 2005).

- the heavy workload of the working group dealing with the multitude of development applications
- internal tensions about appropriate negotiating positions and delays in the distribution of negotiated monetary compensation
- attempts to rationalise the approval process and develop regional agreements
- the difficulty of finalising the constitution of the Rubibi Aboriginal Corporation, particularly disagreement about defining the Council of Elders[22]
- the realignment of personal and family alliances following the deaths of some elders.

She concluded, rather ominously for the native title claim, that the 'conflict is currently tearing apart the whole community, but as some locals wisely say: "you know us mob we hit first and then we talk"' (1998:220).

Another strand of her paper is the analysis of the anthropological archive in an effort to help the Jarndu Yawuru women's group resolve the Jugan–Yawuru question and, more generally, the issue of the traditional ownership of the Broome region. Following a very condensed survey of the contradictions in the anthropological archive, she adopts Hosokawa's resolution (Jugan as a dialect of Yawuru). She supports this resolution with her own observations of her informants, referring to the Jugan as 'Big Yawuru' and the willingness of Jugun-identifying people to join the Yawuru Aboriginal Corporation.

Glowczewski noticed that contemporary Yawuru formulated their traditional claims to land in terms of large tracts of Yawuru country and entitlement through either a male or a female Yawuru ancestor. These formulations led her to ponder Elkin's confirmation of Radcliffe-Brown's patrilineal hordes. As I have done, she also wondered about the implications of flexible *rai* (conception Dreaming) in Elkin's work for his inflexible conclusions. Glowczewski observed the continuing cultural practice of *rai*. It remained a central idiom of traditional connection to place. It involved discussion among older people about a baby's true *rai*, dreams about *rai* and reported sightings of *rai* spirit children. The relative flexibility of choice of *rai* leads to a multiplicity of possible connections to country within the one patrilineal group and she wondered why it should not always have been this way.

The most interesting and intricate reassessment of the archive, however, 'against all anthropological tradition' (1998:214), is her challenge to the prominence given to matrimoieties and patrimoieties, as opposed to generational moieties, in the

22 Membership of the Council of Elders was defined in terms of authority to speak about Aboriginal Law, but this seemed to exclude many senior Aboriginal people. Sullivan, in his account of the same events, saw the definition of the Council of Elders as a particularly positive feature, in that it recognised traditional authority centred on male initiation ceremonies (Sullivan 1997b).

transmission of traditional rights to land. Again, these arguments are presented all too briefly (1998:214–15) and only slightly expanded on in a later paper published in the journal *L'Homme* (Glowczewski 2000:418–22). At least the later paper makes some sense of the phrase 'against all anthropological tradition' as directed to an Anglo audience. Her critique is directly inspired by the longstanding critique of descent theorising by, principally French, alliance theorists. One of these, Louis Dumont, seems to have alerted her to the potential significance of certain kinship terms and marriage rules that seemed to be invisible to descent theorists (see, for example, Dumont 1971).

Glowczewski's critique of the claim process crystallised in her *L'Homme* paper—coincidentally published in the same year as the hearing (Glowczewski 2000). For her French audience, the rhetorical temperature is turned up to furious, as she decries the injustice of the Government requiring Indigenous people, who were devastated by colonialism, to now prove the continuity of their authentic traditions as the only means of regaining their traditional lands (2000:414). In framing the native title question as one of authenticity, she bypasses the ambiguities of the legal doctrines to go directly to her critique, omitting any reference to that part of the legal doctrine that allows an indeterminate degree of change of tradition.

Glowczewski implicates anthropology in this injustice. Because of the lack of historical records, the early ethnographic research of Radcliffe-Brown, Elkin, Tindale and others takes on an exaggerated importance. In particular, it overemphasises patrilineal descent and small landowning groups, at the expense of fluidity and networks that, by the way, would have been more apparent if they had known more about French theorising of kinship (2000:415; cf. Gumbert 1984). Glowczewski concludes:

> The Aboriginal genius consists in having always supported a great circulation by rites and alliances, while redefining local identities distinguished by their languages, their land attachments and their systems of kinship. Today, the phenomenon of family segmentations by connection to tribal (language) groups is a new way of creating local identities. Unfortunately, the expert anthropologists of the Australian land claims do not seem ready to translate these phenomena in a positive way, because that would require conceiving the tradition as dynamic and not reified, following the example of the artificially closed models that are required to be produced to legitimate the restitution of the country. (2000:426, my translation)

This judgment was far too pre-emptory—for, as we shall see in the next chapter, Patrick Sullivan was developing quite similar arguments for his expert report.

The state of the anthropological archive prior to the hearing

Groups

The various approaches to Broome landowning groups are summarised in Table 4.2.

The table does reveal that the closest alignment of anthropological theorising and the question asked by native title doctrine occurred in the local organisation debates of the 1930s (Radcliffe-Brown, Elkin, Piddington). For others (Bates, Worms, Petri, Dalton), vaguer concepts, such as the assumption of the tribal homelands, were sufficient as their interests lay elsewhere—in myths, rituals, the dynamics of the spread of new rituals, and ethnic stratification. For these purposes, territory-identified groups were not so obviously relevant; individuals could recount myths, and initiation ceremonies seemed to involve diverse territorial groups, even if internal protocols distinguished between those on their own homeland and those invited from elsewhere. Dalton's broad social group analysis did not require a traditional land tenure perspective, even though some elements intruded, such as the spatial orientation of town camps towards home countries.

Table 4.2 One hundred years of describing traditional landowning groups around Broome

	Maximal			Minimal
Bischofs	Tribe/camping place/language			
Bates	Nation	Kalarabulu tribe	Dialect group	Local group
Radcliffe-Brown	Same social organisation, kinship systems	Shared language competence (his tribe)		The horde
Elkin	As above	Jukan, Yauou tribes		4 Yauor hordes: 1. Maramadjuno 2. Langandjun (Djambarangandjal) 3. Wondjeldjuro 4. Daibineridjuno
Piddington (on Karadjeri)		Language-named tribe, Karadjeri	Dialect groups, coastal Karadjeri, inland Karadjeri	
Worms		Language-named tribe, Yaoro		4 Yauor clans: 1. Walmandyano 2. Langandyono 3. Menyerdyano 4. Dyolbaidyano
Dalton	Regional Aboriginal commonality, networks	Racial–ethnic groups: Coloureds, Aboriginal	Town camps of same language, tribe	
Hosokawa (linguist)			3 Dialect groups: 1. Jukun 2. Julbayi 3. Marangan	Local groups: Jukan, Minyjirr, Walman, Marangana, Kardarru, Marrmarrma, Burrany, Julbayi, Garraljunu, Lankanjunu, Birrmanan and others
Glowczewski		Language-identified collection of cognatic descent groups, Yawuru, 'all one'	Dialect groups ('little' and 'big' Yawuru)	Confirmation of Worms' 4 'localisations' plus Lake Eda and Yajugan groups

At a superficial level, the table does seem to assert a continuity of a tribal group, with the exception of Radcliffe-Brown, who tended to be dismissive of the coherence of the tribal level. I have suggested that the use of the word 'tribe' is partly the pragmatics of having a convenient referent to a collectivity. In Tindale's case, it was an under-theorised and dogged attempt at reconstruction. Yet, the 'tribal' level appears again in the 1990s in Glowczewski's work, in a dialectic of identity between an all-inclusive language-identified group (Yawuru) and identities based on dialect, traditional toponym or family. By the time Glowczewski was writing, there had been much debate in anthropology about the utility of the concept of tribe and tribal boundaries (Berndt 1959; Peterson and Long 1986; Sutton 1995a), the appearance in land claims of so-called 'language groups' (Rumsey 1989) and, more generally, the relationship between language, social identity and land affiliation (Merlan 1981). Merlan's and Rumsey's work, in particular, is suggestive of possible further fine-grained research into the language referents in traditional myths, particularly those involving travel beyond Yawuru country, to see whether they contain assumptions about the identification of land with a particular language.

Laws, customs and ceremonial sites

Simple patrilineal inheritance of a clearly bounded horde territory comes closest to the unstated ideals of law-like stability and uniformity. In a similar vein, but on a larger scale, Glowczewski's 'all one family' is suggestive of a large Yawuru tribal or language-group area, defined by consensus with neighbouring groups, traditional historical association and a rule of cognatic inheritance. Then there are other cultural practices such as *rai* that tend to cut across such simple notions. It is difficult to see how the constellation of beliefs and practices that makes up *rai* could be codified in a way that would accurately predict future links between individuals and land—a neat example of the incommensurability of different systems (see Mantziaris and Martin 2000:29–35).

The narrow question of the first *Rubibi* claim—traditional laws and customs requiring certain places for particular ritual performances—does not precipitate as many possible answers from the archive. The sites of increase ceremonies, the *midedi* feast and similar ceremonies involving the revelation of sacred boards, stored at a particular storehouse or hollow tree, are perhaps the quintessential models of a traditional rule linking places and ceremony. Even these rituals proved to be, to varying degrees, detachable from place. Sullivan (1998:101) reported that, in the 1990s, songs from increase ceremonies were still sung to ensure successful hunting or fishing expeditions, but they did not have to be performed at a particular location. Although it is somewhat unclear whether Hosokawa had the ceremony of the *midedi* feast in mind, he did describe the movement of Yawuru ceremony grounds within the Thangoo pastoral lease in the 1950s and then from Thangoo to its current location at Fishermen's Bend. Notwithstanding that this passage and most of his introductory chapter were incidental to his linguistic study, it became a point of contention between the anthropologists in the native title claim.[23]

There is nothing in the archive to suggest that the exact location of an initiation ceremony was mandated in the Dreamtime. It is possible, however, to imagine how a convenient place such as Kunin could become, through habitual use, a consistently preferred site for ceremonies. First of all, the location of the storehouse would link it to various Dreaming stories associated with nearby geographical features; the storehouse itself would attract the *midedi* feast ritual, and the objects would relate to the content of initiation ceremonies.

As we have seen, the early accounts of Yawuru initiation ceremonies (Bates and Worms), but also later accounts of neighbouring groups (Piddington), used the grammatical device of the continuous present in order to evoke a sense of what invariably happens at all such ceremonies. Thus, observation of one performance is transformed into a model of all performances, and observations of many performances are synthesised into the one ideal performance. This generalising approach is reinforced by the emphasis in these accounts on structure, both in the sense of identifying distinct stages of initiation and in identifying the classes of kin performing various roles in the ritual.

Aboriginal agency, historical specificity and local politics are thereby submerged. These aspects of ritual were explored by Keen (1994) and Dussart (2000) in other Aboriginal groups. Their work is highly suggestive of how ritual performance can cover multiple individual identifications, classifications and subsequent interpretations, and is always an achievement of the key participants, who might have a fraught relationship. Ritual can provide an arena for advancement of the ceremonial status of leaders (a kind of career path). Also, the choice of performance

23 The passage reads:

> [T]he exodus from Thangoo may also have been related to the urbanisation of Broome as well as the war-time relocation. It is known that a successive shift of ceremonial sites (from south-west to north-east) took place in the Thangoo Yawuru country. In order to successfully perform the ceremonies such as *yurna, kuramirdi, dyamunungurru, bungana* (all related to circumcision and other stages of male initiation) and *dyulurru* 'Fire Dance', the host lawmen needed to invite people of the neighbouring and even far distant groups. As the Aboriginal population of the West Kimberley generally tended to gather in the area around Broome, the ceremonial sites shifted several times, gradually getting closer to the township of Broome. In the 1930s, the main initiation ground was a place called *yarlanbarnan*, south of Mararr Hill, approximately 8 miles west of the present Thangoo homestead. By 1950, it had shifted to *mirda-yirdi* (or Tea Tree Ground) just east of the homestead. The most recent ceremonial site was located in the Fishermen's Bend area (traditionally called *walmanburu* or Walman country), east of Broome, just on the other side of Dampier Creek (*karlkarlgun*). (Hosokawa 1991:4)

from a diverse repertoire can either emphasise the distinctiveness of the local group or be inclusive of a wider regional grouping. The flexibility and negotiation implicit in this approach rarely surface, however, in accounts of Yawuru initiation.[24]

Change

Early contributors to the anthropological archive on Broome rarely covered historical transformation as a distinct topic. Radcliffe-Brown was opposed to any attempt to reconstruct the past. Apart from some tentative diffusionist theorising, Elkin was drawn into theorising about historical transformation only in his critique of Piddington. All, however, used concepts such as 'detribalisation' and 'loss', particularly their own lost opportunity to observe genuine local organisation because of sedentary life on pastoral stations and missions.

Dalton's theorising about Europeanisation harks back to the earlier loss paradigms. But he also uses the earlier contributors to the archive in a new way—like Beckett's use of Haddon—as a baseline from which to measure loss.

It was the appearance of native title doctrine and the desire of her Aboriginal women collaborators to resolve the Djukan–Yawuru issue that drove Glowczewski towards a kind of historical anthropology, with the aim of demonstrating continuity of a contemporary landed identity with the past. As we have seen, this demonstration involved a deconstruction and critique of those elements of the anthropological archive that suggested sharp discontinuity. Perhaps being concerned that an exploration of discontinuity could be mobilised in a critique of contemporary Aboriginal authenticity, all aspects of historical transformation between the 1960s and the 1980s tended to be obscured. It would seem obvious that the internal dynamics of the Yawuru would change as a result of the increasing fragility of some traditional practices and the societal revaluation of Aboriginal tradition in general.

Because the anthropological archive is so sketchy for the period between the 1960s and the 1980s, possible themes can only be suggested from the snapshots taken at the beginning (Dalton) and at the end of this period (Hosokawa, Chaney, Glowczewski). I have suggested above that Dalton's use of the racial–ethnic group as the unit of his analysis probably predisposed him to underestimate the links between the traditionally orientated Aborigines (principally living in the town camps) and the 'Coloureds' (principally living in the town). Nevertheless, we cannot dismiss his general observation that the two groups led quite different lives. In addition, he reported a generation gap among the

24 An exception would be Dalton's report that Paddy Djaguin (= Djiagween) liked the new 'gadrania' song cycle so much that he was trying to incorporate it into the stages of initiation as a prerequisite for the *midedi* feast (1965:89).

traditional Aboriginal group, in which the younger generation's belief in some of the traditions faltered. We know that, in the period that followed, access to alcohol became easier with citizenship rights, and there was a period of 10 years during which no distinctively Yawuru initiation ceremonies were held — facts that seem to confirm Dalton's imagined trajectory.

For those who were interested in pursuing initiation, however, it was available among the other tribes of the region, and this choice is perhaps symbolic of a strategic direction available to those Yawuru wanting to continue their traditional ceremonies. They could emphasise the aspect of regional cooperation, rather than the distinctiveness of the Yawuru. This route would be hard to bear for some of the key Yawuru lawmen, and it will be recalled that Worms thought the competition with other tribal groups was one of the sustaining factors for the continuation of Yawuru initiation ceremonies in the 1940s.

One can imagine the effect of this decline on the Yawuru ceremonial leaders such as Paddy Djiagween, and the custodians of intimate knowledge of Yawuru country, such as Paddy Roe. It seems that one reaction was to attempt a preservation of the old traditions in a different form—a sort of heritage protection impulse that can be seen in Roe's work with Muecke and his involvement with the Lurujarri Heritage Trail north of Cable Beach (see Glowczewski 1998:208). This might have been the impulse behind Paddy Djiagween's cooperation with oral historians[25] and giving Dalton the details of the Two-Men songs (Dalton 1965).

The decline in traditional observances seems to have also put strains on the relationship between some of the key traditionalists, who had cooperated in ceremonies and in preserving the storehouse of sacred objects at Kunin (Fisherman's Bend). Dalton (1964:130) reports the cutting criticism of Paddy Djiagween by Paddy Roe and Butcher Joe Nangan. Kevin Keeffe, Patrick Dodson's biographer, states: 'The cultural identity and position of Patrick's grandfather, Paddy Djiagween, was hotly contested in a dispute that had divided both the small town and his extended family' (2003:326).

Again, it is unclear just how open the feud was or whether a certain degree of cooperation was still possible. The awkward dynamics between the traditionalists were publicly exposed in the crocodile farm episode and were laid bare in Chaney's report to the minister (Chaney 1994).

The period would also see a dramatic reordering of the relationship between Dalton's 'Coloureds' and the traditionally orientated Aboriginal group. The juridical infrastructure maintaining this distinction was dismantled and replaced with a more inclusive definition of Aboriginal. Towards the end of the period, the traditionalists—whom Dalton painted as a marginalised and declining group

25 Wendy Lowenstein's tape recordings referred to in Keeffe (2003).

compared with the dynamism of the 'Coloureds'—moved back to the centre as key players in heritage protection, as the sources of culture in a newly valued multiculturalism and the pivotal players in the native title revolution in Broome.

The implication of this reordering for the native title claim research, as confirmed by Glowczewski, was the need to deal with a volatile claimant group, which included vastly different orientations towards, and knowledge of, Aboriginal traditions. As Glowczewski pointed out, there were also perceived conflicts of interest within the group about land. These conflicts were between the traditional owners and those Aboriginal people who had land interests under pre-native title legislative schemes (housing commission homes, leases and reserves). The latter felt threatened by a potentially radical change to ownership based on Aboriginal tradition. Added to this was the public exposure of the fragility of the continuation of Yawuru initiation ceremonies. In a way, the grand opportunity of native title came at the most difficult time for the Yawuru.

5. The Anthropology of Broome on Trial

Background

Patrick Sullivan was a convert to anthropology from modern history and Asian studies. During 1983–84 he did fieldwork at Halls Creek in Western Australia while working as the coordinator of an outstation resource agency. This high-pressure job allowed him to observe at close quarters some of the irrational and counterproductive interventions by government agencies in the traumatised lives of Aboriginal people in Halls Creek (Sullivan 1986). It also provided him with a privileged vantage point for the subject of his thesis: the interface between Aboriginal and non-Aboriginal culture in the Kimberley region, both in administration and in less formal processes (T. 821).[1]

Sullivan's thesis included an account of the origins and development of the Kimberley Land Council (KLC), his future employer. He was critical of a larrikin political style among the Aboriginal leaders of the time, although he saw a new maturity emerging with involvement, via the Aboriginal and Torres Strait Islander Commission (ATSIC), in welfare funding decisions and negotiations necessitated by the recognition of native title (Sullivan 1996a:ch. 4). This anthropology of black–white interaction, bureaucracy and intercultural organisations was an innovative thesis for anthropology at the time. But when Sullivan took up the position of in-house anthropologist at the KLC, most of his assigned tasks took him back to a more conventional focus on traditional culture and land tenure. A few projects—such as the need to establish native title corporations and KLC's entrepreneurial policy development on regional agreements—did provide some continuity with his initial interests in intercultural organisations.[2]

Pre-claim research in Broome

Sullivan's initial professional encounter with traditional land tenure around Broome was through the Aboriginal Development Commission, which commissioned him in 1989 to produce a report on the traditional ownership of Broome. There followed a long and intensive association with the Aboriginal people of the area. Prior to the native title claim, he had appeared as an expert anthropological witness in a fishing prosecution case, involving the defence of

1 'T' is a shorthand reference to the official transcript of the hearing of the first *Rubibi* claim, *Felix Edgar, Frank Sebastian & Others on Behalf of the Rubibi Community v The State of Western Australia*, No. WG 90 & 91 of 1998. It was produced by Transcript Australia.

2 See Sullivan (1988, 1995a, 1995b, 1996b, 1997a).

a traditional right to fish in the sea adjacent to Broome. He was also intimately involved in the efforts of various Aboriginal groups to resist a proposal to build a crocodile farm close to the Kunin Aboriginal Reserve (the claim area). Sullivan's report about the traditional significance of the crocodile farm site featured prominently in Chaney's report for the Commonwealth minister on the Aboriginal heritage protection application (Chaney 1994). The repeated use of Sullivan's formal title (he is always Dr Sullivan) reminds the reader that he alone, of all the consultants used by the various parties to the dispute, had attained that academic level. Chaney also made full use of Sullivan's enumeration of the various aspects of the significance of the site.

Sullivan's long association with the claimant group provides an interesting contrast with the other expert anthropologist in this case, Erich Kolig. In comparison, Kolig had done no fieldwork with the claimants, although he knew them. He had to rely on his superior academic capital. This is not to suggest that Sullivan was a stranger to the academy. Sullivan had done work as a tutor and lecturer while completing his academic qualifications, and had held a lecturing position at Edith Cowan University and a fellowship at the North Australian Research Unit of The Australian National University between his two periods as in-house anthropologists at the KLC. To focus on his consultancy work and position with KLC would not, however, do justice to the non-applied aspects of his career. He had ambitions to theorise the whole colonial encounter in the Kimberley and, through publications and conference attendance, kept his academic options open. As we shall see, however, in *Rubibi*, the battle over the interpretation of the anthropological archive was between anthropologists of quite different levels of academic capital. Kolig was older and, when the confrontation between the two anthropologists occurred in 2000, he had devoted 20 years to his academic career, centred on his position as senior lecturer in anthropology at the University of Otago. He had been an examiner of Sullivan's doctoral thesis. Did Kolig's relative seniority in the field of the academy play a role in the reception of his opinions? Or do we see a balancing out of academic position with Sullivan's superior knowledge of the claimants?

Anthropological research for litigation

Prior to finalising his report for the *Rubibi* native title claims, Sullivan published a paper in a collection on customary marine tenure in Australia (Sullivan 1998). That paper provides an insight into his preliminary ideas and tentative formulations about traditional land tenure around Broome. He describes the continuing use of the land by Aboriginal people, who had a rich, contemporary ecological knowledge of species, habitat, seasonal variation, traditional hunting and fishing techniques and traditional pharmacopoeia, although the number of knowledgeable people is unclear (1998:98). Outlining actual use of natural resources allowed him to conveniently introduce the concept of *rai* in all its manifestations, as would be expected from its prominence in the anthropological archive (1998:102).

Rai can justify a claim to a particular place as home, or a claim to be from there, 'while still enjoying rights over the combined land and sea of the wider group' (1998:103). As I have done, he reads back into Elkin's account of *rai* the flexibility of linkage to place that Elkin resisted. Sullivan also found an ideology of descent, which is a legitimate claim to 'come from' or 'belong to' the place of a parent. These kinds of identification with place were, however, subject to a broader consensus usually achieved via the authoritative pronouncements of a respected elder. As articulated by Sullivan, in this social process of assertion and response, not all arguments are of equal weight. He identified the most influential as

1. descent or inheritance through the male or female line
2. place of birth
3. conception spirit (*rai*)
4. knowledge of the mythology and ritual associated with an area.

The picture then emerged of a people whose members each have particular attachment to a relatively small area of homeland—an attachment they might have achieved by a number of means, and which they share with close kin, as well as those who might not be directly related. They hunt, fish and perform ceremonies over a wider area of the land, where they feel themselves to have rights in common with a larger group (1998:105).

Sullivan admitted that the set of factors mentioned above, especially *rai*, produces a highly flexible situation. With an eye to the task of working out how legal recognition might be achieved within this flexibility, he turned his attention to a maximal grouping. If such a grouping could be identified with sufficient clarity, the means of identification to particular places within the overall territory of the wider group could be more easily presented as internal questions that did not require resolution by the court.

At this stage of his research, Sullivan seemed to be groping for something rather elusive: the maximal grouping that could be considered to hold a right of possession, as opposed to a mere right of access or use.[3] He found Berndt's use of 'society' a promising concept. In his critique of the use of 'tribe' for Western Desert Aborigines, Berndt had proposed, instead, the idea of 'a

3 Sullivan commented: 'I don't think I'm groping for it. I think I'm trying to convince the judge that it is inherently elusive, it doesn't exist in the terms required of it for formal recognition' (Sullivan's comments on draft chapter, 2005).

society'. He defined society as those who meet regularly and consistently, even if intermittently, and who are closely involved in reciprocal duties and obligations and make up the widest functionally significant group. This concept allowed Sullivan to incorporate the broader connections based on Dreaming tracks and shared ritual life, which were still an important prerequisite in order to be acknowledged as a traditional elder in Broome. Perhaps anticipating the potential for his formulation to objectify and solidify relations, he expresses some hesitation about his own suggestion:

> The concept of 'the land/sea-holding society' is an abstraction from the actual practices of assertion of affiliation to the named tracts, demonstration of knowledge, socially accepted lines of descent, and assertion of competence in and rights over linguistic domains. These are socially determined, sometimes by consensus and sometimes in dispute. (1998:106).

In any event, to ensure that all the members of the Rubibi coalition, including the Goolarabooloo group, would be recognised as native title holders, a grouping at a more inclusive level of generality than a clan, dialect group (Jukan) or language group/tribe (Yawuru) needed to be identified.

Strategic choice in formulating the *Rubibi* claims

Sullivan prepared an expert anthropological report to cover all the traditional country of the Rubibi community. At some point, however, a critical tactical decision was made by the lawyers and Sullivan to split the *Rubibi* claim, so that the first hearing would be for the Fishermen's Bend Reserve, Kunin. Initially, the rights claimed were for full native title rights. But, for reasons that will be elaborated below, it was eventually decided to limit the rights claimed to ceremonial purposes, so that the disputed use of the reserve would be resolved. The claim to all the other available Yawuru traditional country would not be so limited and would be heard later (in fact, in 2004).[4]

Although the details of the reasoning behind this decision remain confidential, the benefits can be imagined: the history of the use of Kunin as a ceremony

4 At the time of concluding the research on the *Rubibi* case study, the second *Rubibi* hearing had been completed but the legal proceedings had not been finalised, pending the outcome of late mediation negotiations between the claimants and the WA Government. In an unusual move, Justice Merkel delivered reasons for decision on some of the issues (principally, which of the competing groups would be found to be the native title holders), ostensibly to assist the mediation: see *Rubibi Community v Western Australia (No. 5)* (2005) FCA 1025, 29 July 2005. For legal commentary on the unusual procedure, see McKenna (2005). Following the failure of mediation, a final determination of native title was made in 2006: see *Rubibi Community v Western Australia (No. 6)* [2006] FCA 82 (13 February 2006) and *Rubibi Community v Western Australia (No. 7)* [2006] FCA 459 (28 April 2006).

ground was well documented; the claim would be supported by regional ritual leaders; and it coincided with a folk understanding, possibly shared by any judge, of ritual as quintessential traditional culture. Objectifying culture in this way would perhaps also coincide with the juridical need for objective facts of traditional laws and customs, ritual being more law-like in the normative aspect of law as an enforced uniformity, and less likely to appear flexible and negotiable. Moreover, the sensitive subject matter would keep the *Rubibi* claimant coalition unified and enforce some discipline on the potentially disruptive Aboriginal groups outside the Rubibi coalition. Of course, on the negative side, the fragility of the continuation of specifically Yawuru ceremony would be exposed.

The claimants' evidence

At the time of the hearing in 2000, it had been nine years since Paddy Djiagween's death. Paddy Roe was still alive but apparently too old and frail to give evidence (see T. 841). A senior Yawuru elder had disappeared a few years earlier, having walked out of an aged-care hospital in Derby. To avoid mentioning his name, the participants in the hearing referred to him as The Man Who Disappeared. The most senior surviving Yawuru elder was Felix Edgar, who gave evidence from his wheelchair, having suffered a stroke some time before. After the fluency of the opening address of Mr Kevin Bell QC, the Yawuru claimants' barrister, the evidence of Felix Edgar descended into tragi-farce. Technical difficulties with the court public-address system compounded the obvious physical and language difficulties. Also, his untrained interpreter, another claimant, occasionally gave inaccurate translations, sometimes adding his own evidence and suggesting answers to the witness. All this meant that highly contradictory evidence was left unclarified, despite the tortuous efforts of all involved. The next witnesses, Frank Sebastian (Gajai) and Francis Djiagween (Lulga) (Paddy Djiagween's son), fared a little better.

In contrast with the truncated, hesitant and sometimes contradictory evidence of the other Aboriginal witnesses were the relative clarity of Joseph Nipper Roe's evidence and the articulate expansiveness of Patrick Dodson, partly reflecting their level of Western education. Nipper had been taken away to Perth for schooling and returned to Broome to work as a trained carpenter. In later life he worked in government services as an interpreter and cross-cultural consultant. In this capacity, he produced various documents aimed at explaining Yawuru culture to white service providers. These auto-anthropological cross-cultural manuals became the focus of the presentation of his evidence about the concepts of *lian* (emotional centre, being), *rai*, *bilyurr* (spirit from within) (T. 157–9), the section system, kinship terms, avoidance relationships, joking relationships and respectful relationships and so on (T. 160–5).

Patrick Dodson had been on a remarkable journey since his birth in Broome in 1948. He grew up in Katherine in the Northern Territory, suffered the premature death of both his parents in separate accidents in 1960, attended a Catholic boarding school in Melbourne and was ordained a Catholic priest in Broome in 1975. Following a long interval, he returned in 1989 as the director of the KLC. That journey had taken him to the height of national prominence as one of the key Aboriginal leaders of the land rights movement and reconciliation (see Keeffe 2003), and in 2000 he appeared as Aboriginal claimant and witness approved by the Aboriginal lawmen of the region to give evidence about secret ceremonies at Kunin.

> PATRICK DODSON JAGUN: Well, the significance of the stories is that it belongs to the Bugarrigarra, the beginning of time. It belongs to the ceremonies that young man start off with initiation and gradually get up to a stage where there's a clarification or xx...[restricted part of transcript excised]...xx. And that's only for men. It's not for women. It's serious, serious law. It's not just talk. (T. 268)[5]

He also explained the idea of *lian* in relation to ceremony (T. 293).

A feature of Dodson's evidence was the centrality of the Aboriginal vernacular word 'law' in his explanations: the subsection system is a Bugarrigarra law (T. 283); ritual leaders are lawmen; a ceremonial ground is a 'law ground'; some rituals are 'law'; shared rituals and Dreaming stories are a 'common system of laws' (T. 350); and sacred objects are 'law'. While this seemed to reflect the Aboriginal vernacular use of the word, its polysemy did require untangling at times—for example, in clarifying that 'law', in the sense of ritual shared with neighbouring tribes, did not necessarily imply shared country—since people could not speak for another's country and Yawuru was a separate country (T. 349–52).

Five of the senior male Rubibi claimants gave evidence, as did six of the senior female claimants. Patrick Dodson and Nipper Roe gave evidence in a restricted session at Kunin in the presence of the ceremonial leaders from neighbouring tribes, including Mangala, Nyangumarta, Walmajarri, Nygina and Karrajarri (T. 265–6). Through these witnesses, the main elements of the case emerged.

- All Yawuru have rights to all traditional Yawuru country.
- Yawuru are descendants, through the male or female line, of the original Yawuru, irrespective of whether those ancestors identified as Yawuru, Djukan or Goolarabooloo.

---

5 Note: I did not make the judgment about excising the restricted material. This is a direct quotation from the unrestricted transcript, which is all I had access to.

- Kunin is now the principal Yawuru law ground, ordained in the Bugarrigarra (Dreamtime), not just a site of historical convenience for ceremony.
- The current Yawuru senior lawmen are the five Rubibi witnesses and they are responsible for Yawuru law (in every sense) at Kunin.
- This position is supported by neighbouring senior lawmen.

Another Yawuru group opposed this generalised formulation of the title-holding group and the extent of the law ground at Kunin. They argued that the land in the vicinity of Kunin belonged to their Yawuru 'clan' called Leregon after the name of a soak adjacent to the reserve. What emerged was a bitter, longstanding family dispute. Paddy Roe and others had originally pursued the formal reservation of the area as a ceremonial ground and a place to store sacred objects. The original declaration in 1971 stated that the reserve was for a ceremonial site. A reorganisation of reserve administration resulted in a change of purpose of the reserve to more general 'Aboriginal purposes', paving the way for the leased area to be used for other purposes, such as housing and possible commercial development of a crab farm. At one point, those pushing for the lease seemed to have obtained the agreement of some of the influential Yawuru leaders of the time but there was also significant opposition from others, particularly Paddy Roe. He initiated legal proceedings to stop the Aboriginal Land Trust issuing a lease, on the basis that the whole of the reserve was required for ceremonial purposes. Because of the controversy, a lease was never issued. Nevertheless, members of the Leregon group, including Jacky Lee (now deceased), built houses near the edge of the reserve and just inside the reserve overlooking the law ground. The impropriety of that action was a festering dispute among the Yawuru up to the time of the claim.

The dispute was exacerbated in the early 1980s when sacred objects in the storehouse at Kunin were stolen. That theft caused great distress among the Yawuru and throughout the region. Jacky Lee's son, Colin Lee, was eventually charged with having one of the objects unlawfully in his possession. He said that another man, who had since died, gave him the object. Thus, the native title claim became the vehicle for a historic settling of scores. The stakes were high. On one side were the five remaining senior Yawuru lawmen asserting their continuing traditional authority to decide what is appropriate in the vicinity of Kunin. If their position was endorsed by the court it would mean the removal of the Lee houses. On the other side, the Leregon claimants challenged the idea that traditional title was held at the level of the Yawuru, instead asserting their own traditional ownership at the level of the 'clan' that would give them the necessary rights around Leregon to construct permanent dwellings. As we shall see below, these contrary positions broadly coincided with the opposite views that Patrick Sullivan and Erich Kolig took of pre-contact traditional land tenure.

The Leregon group was unsuccessful in obtaining funds for a lawyer and was represented by a family friend, Mr Johnson. He did not appear to have a sound grasp of the legal doctrine of native title or legal procedures—a problem that also undermined other Yawuru people who wanted to intervene in the hearing. For the Leregon group it meant that opportunities to effectively cross-examine the Rubibi witnesses were never fully realised. It also meant that the feuding between the groups clouded their appreciation of their own need to prove traditional continuity in order to succeed. A clear example of this was when one of the Leregon senior witnesses, Rosie Charlie, declared: 'our law is dead, it went with the old people' (T. 628).

She seemed to be basing her claim to the land on a number of factors including the place of birth and residence of her mother's mother, agreements between a previous generation of Yawuru elders, and the blunt assertion of 'clan' and of the white kangaroo 'totem' (T. 594–633). Their other main witness, Colin Lee—the man convicted of the unauthorised possession of the stolen sacred object—also asserted connection through 'clan' and 'totem' (White Kangaroo), and in his statement to the court drew support from a translation of an article by Father Worms (T. 684–5).[6]

Despite their inept representation, a relatively clear position emerged.

- A previous generation and some of the present senior Yawuru leaders approved the location of the houses.
- The sheds storing the sacred objects could be moved without breaching traditional law.
- The ceremony ground was a much smaller area than suggested by the boundary of the reserve and was well within the reserve, away from the boundary.

Notwithstanding their oppositional stance to the Rubibi claimants and their doubts about the traditional propriety of Patrick Dodson's and Nipper Roe's induction into the 'second stage' of initiation, the Leregon witnesses did, at times, acknowledge the traditional seniority of some of the other Rubibi claimants and, in various ways, demonstrated that they still complied with traditional prohibitions on women and uninitiated men speaking about secret male-only ceremonies—for example:

> MR BELL: You don't speak for that ground, do you?
>
> ROSIE CHARLIE: No, that's not my business, that's men's business. (T. 601)

6 The translation was probably of a story in Worms' 'Fifty legends' paper (1940).

In Colin Lee's case, he implied that he would have supported the concerns of the previous generation of ceremonial leaders about Kunin as they had been initiated according to his own high standards of traditional continuity:

> MS WEBB: Colin, you said you refused to take part in law ceremony. Can you tell us why?
>
> COLIN LEE: Well, it was explained to me at that time by the late Jack Edgar that they could do a lot of cheating as far as going through Aboriginal law. They don't have to go through full initiation to be a lawman. And that's when I didn't want any part of it. (T. 737)

The other impression from their evidence is the shifting alliances between key players and family fragmentation, as key elders passed away. What appears to be a *modus vivendi* of previous generations—the give and take between the traditionalists and their 'Coloured' relations, who chose not to follow that path—is taken up by later generations as increasingly inflexible positions. Family honour requires that the family's version of the *modus vivendi* of the previous generation is preserved and, with fewer opportunities for celebrating their commonality with other families—for example, in shared rituals—these differences take on an entrenched bitterness. The insularity of family versions of history is then reinforced by separate incorporation of associations. At the time of the hearing there appeared to have been five such bodies: Leregon Aboriginal Corporation, Walman Aboriginal Corporation, Djukan Aboriginal Corporation, Yawuru Aboriginal Corporation, and the older Goolarabooloo Association Incorporated.

The outcome of the conflicting Rubibi and Leregon claims was not a foregone conclusion. There was a great deal of evidence about cultural change that could be interpreted as demonstrating the fragility of specifically Yawuru ceremony continuing at Kunin. When asked about the future initiation ceremonies, Joe Nipper Roe said that he thought young Yawuru men would have to learn about Aboriginal culture before being considered for initiation. That comment gave the impression of a profound distancing of the younger generation from traditional culture (T. 172). Patrick Dodson spoke of how a drinking man would not be trusted with the secrets revealed in various stages of initiation and thus might not be considered as a candidate. Nipper Roe and Patrick Dodson had been put through the law in 1994 amid concerns about who would look after the law when the few remaining senior Yawuru men passed away. On their version of events, they were inducted by the senior lawmen of the time in the tradition of being 'grabbed' in order to be put through the law. But they were also cross-examined about embarrassing entries in Patrick Sullivan's field notebooks, which referred to Nipper Roe as pestering his father for initiation and that Patrick Dodson's inclusion was an afterthought. These suggestions were denied, but they were potentially undermining of their credibility as witnesses.

There was also the fact that there had been no ceremonies at Kunin since 1994. Patrick Dodson tried to explain this gap as being the result of various factors, including the theft of the sacred objects, the disappearance in Derby of the senior Yawuru lawman, who had put them through the law, and the continuing encroachment of the Leregon houses. But it was not clear whether there were any suitable Yawuru candidates for initiation being considered after 1994. The regional picture of the continuation of initiation ceremonies seemed to be much stronger.

Cross-examination by representatives of the State of Western Australia was predictably based on inconsistencies in both the governmental and anthropological archives. The State had engaged Erich Kolig to excavate the anthropological archive and, as we will see below, he was a defender of the 'horde' and was quite impressed with Hosokawa's work. Thus, the cross-examination of the Aboriginal witnesses tended to seek out a clan level of traditional ownership, explore the nature of Djukan identity and confirm the movement of sacred objects from Thangoo pastoral lease to Kunin.

Sullivan's evidence

Sullivan explained that the first part of his expert report stated the nature and extent of the various Rubibi claims in plain English and the second part was a very detailed review of the anthropological archive. The aim of his review was to demonstrate that, because of the various inconsistencies, weaknesses and contradictions, and the lack of consensus, none of it could be relied upon.[7] Not having access to the report, I am unable to give an independent assessment of it and my account of Sullivan's contribution to the case will inevitably be biased towards his court performance.[8]

The ideal of the choreographed performance of the barrister leading his expert witness—absent in *Mabo*—also failed to eventuate in *Rubibi*. Bell referred to

7 Sullivan's comments on the draft chapter, December 2005.

8 I received word via a KLC lawyer that the claimants had refused my request for access to the non-restricted parts of Sullivan's report. This seemed to have had a domino effect, as the WA Crown Solicitor's Office refused me access to the non-restricted parts of Kolig's written report for no other reason than I had been refused Sullivan's report. The KLC did not give me any reasons for their refusal. Consequently, the factual basis of this case study is incomplete. Ultimately, I decided to proceed, judging that there was sufficient detail—in the transcript (including extensive cross-examination of Sullivan and Kolig), the judge's reasons for decision, the interviews with Sullivan and Kolig, their written reflections on the case and their responses to my draft chapters—to enable me to complete the case study.

Sullivan's report as 'rather complicated' (T. 814) and so justified leading evidence from Sullivan to summarise the main points. Some of Sullivan's responses were unhelpfully taciturn—quite the opposite of Beckett's expansiveness—and sometimes gave the impression of lack of coordination between expert and counsel. In my interview with Sullivan in 2005, he confirmed that there had been a basic misunderstanding: Sullivan thought that he would have another opportunity to expand on his answers. Bell bluntly corrected him during a break: 'If you have got something to say, say it now.'[9]

Tensions between barrister and expert had been simmering. Sullivan thought that Bell, who had no prior experience with Aboriginal people, did not appreciate the KLC's achievement in convincing the Djugan and Goolarabooloo groups to give up their separate legal representation in favour of the KLC, and did not appreciate the continuing significance of the Rubibi coalition for the whole Aboriginal community of Broome. More fundamentally, Sullivan found himself defending the complexities of the on-the-ground situation against the simplifying tendencies of the whole process, which seemed to be imposing the false uniformity of a Yawuru linguistic–tribal grouping. This tendency would marginalise the members of the Goolarabooloo group, who were fundamental to the Rubibi coalition and the ceremonial life of the region.

Sullivan also felt other conflicting pressures that made it difficult to choose the most effective register for his oral evidence. He explained:

> Firstly, I wanted to talk to the judge in the most comprehensible manner possible, non-academic, and was not sure how to do this. Secondly, and much more difficult, I simply could not switch to academic mode to describe the people I'd known so well who were sitting behind me. It seemed to me a gross insult and a breach of our relationship to represent them thus while in their presence, though I did this in my report.[10]

As anticipated in Sullivan's 1998 paper, his general approach to traditional land tenure was as follows.

- A relatively large area of land (defined at T. 830–1) is held in common by the Rubibi community, who have a shared history, language, kinship system and understanding of the natural world (T. 834). Membership of this group depends on descent from the previous generation of Yawuru. Traditional authority within this group is a question of a person's claims to be Yawuru through descent and *rai* affiliation, then knowledge of the country, its traditional ceremonies and songs, and whether there is a high degree of community consensus about the person's status (T. 847–8).

9 Transcript of interview with Patrick Sullivan, August 2005, p. 26.

10 Sullivan's comments on draft chapter, December 2005.

- Subgroups within the Rubibi community have particular interests in smaller local areas. The subgroups might be defined by a variety of criteria, sometimes overlapping, but rarely is there an exclusive identification with one small area (T. 831, 838). The two principal kinds of affiliation to specific places within the Yawuru country are via descent or *rai* (T. 850). Other criteria for the formation of subgroups include different dialects of Yawuru (for example, Djukan), attachment to named locales (for example, Leregon, Yardugarra, Walman), association with the practice and custodianship of different ritual complexes (for example, the Goolarabooloo with its 'northern' ritual as opposed to the rituals associated with Kunin) (T. 836–42, 851–3).
- This situation is substantially in accordance with the pre-colonial past in which there were no exclusive, small horde territories (T. 848) but flexible land tenure patterns that are seen in other arid regions of Australia (T. 831, 837).
- The existence of traditional Rubibi community authority structures, the continuation of ceremony and the seriousness with which the current senior lawmen take their traditional obligations demonstrate 'in the face of considerable adversity Yawuru culture being alive and well, vigorous and vibrant and in good hands' (T. 869, 874–5).

In relation to Kunin, his evidence could be summarised as follows.

- Dreaming stories can specify the kinds of landscapes or vegetation that link those stories to particular places for the performance of related ceremonies. The physical features of Kunin and the stories from ceremonies performed at Kunin are so linked and the details were given in a restricted session of the hearing (T. 826, 916).[11]
- The earliest anthropological records (the fieldnotes of Daisy Bates made in either 1902 or 1907) link Kunin with the seclusion of initiates, using an Aboriginal term that was also reported by Worms and is still in contemporary use (T. 828, 912).
- Given the centrality of ritual to traditional Aboriginal life, it is reasonable to infer a continuity of ritual at Kunin since the assertion of European sovereignty in 1829 (T. 829).
- The ceremonies performed at Kunin are of significance to the wider Yawuru group—even if most do not participate—because the ceremonies are part of their cultural inheritance (T. 843–4), and they are the key to the traditional authority structure among the Yawuru (T. 866), 'the backbone of authority' (T. 946).

11 Kolig later claimed that evidence of such specific links was never presented (Kolig 2003:216–17). Sullivan rejected this in my interview with him in 2005.

- Kunin is central to the continuation of the Yawuru as a separate identity because it is the only site where Yawuru secret ceremonies are carried out, especially the 'second stage'.
- The claimants asserting to be the senior Yawuru lawmen for Kunin are in fact the senior lawmen and their assumption of that role was made in an orderly fashion in accordance with tradition (T. 867–8).

As with the cross-examination of the claimants by the barrister representing the WA Government, Ms Webb's cross-examination of Sullivan appears to have been inspired by Erich Kolig's report. Her line of questioning pursued the following arguments.

- Sullivan's focus on the contemporary Yawuru situation resulted in a highly flexible and negotiable membership of the Yawuru community that de-emphasised primary attachments to particular places within Yawuru country.
- These primary attachments are consistent with a clan model of traditional ownership described by the early ethnographers.
- Sullivan is too dismissive of them for supposed internal inconsistencies, especially Worms.
- The Broome region is not really arid; therefore, the argument for the ecological necessity of flexible land tenure arrangements is not sustainable (T. 896–7).

In pursuit of these conclusions, Ms Webb made much of apparent inconsistencies in Sullivan's fieldnotes. Some entries indicated that several families apparently rejected the idea of holding Yawuru land in common and instead suggested that it was subdivided into land held by different families, described in his notes as 'primary attachment' (T. 888–9, 892). In a similar way, extracts from Sullivan's fieldnotes reporting a preference for 'following the father' were raised (T. 893). Sullivan tended to parry the implications of these questions by characterising the notes as the incomplete evidence of an early phase of his research. But they do raise questions that will need to be considered at the conclusion of this chapter about how Sullivan conceived of his task. Did he see it as constructing a model from all the divergent, inconsistent positions that would express a general proposition that encompassed the divergent views, but was not reducible to them? If so, did this not risk proposing a model that included everyone, but that few strongly supported? Sullivan later commented that he was acutely aware of these issues, and had discussed with the KLC's in-house lawyer the prospects of using the differences of opinion as evidence of an underlying system.[12]

Inevitably, Sullivan was confronted with his note of a conversation with The Man Who Disappeared in which the revered leader seemed to have been quite

12 Sullivan's comments on draft chapter, December 2005.

dismissive of the last two recruits to 'second-stage' initiation (Nipper Roe and Patrick Dodson). Acutely embarrassed, Sullivan stated the obvious, averting to the pressure towards a new level of juridification of fieldwork practice in the native title era: 'I've not written it with the intention that it should do anything other than inform me of that. So certainly if I had felt that it was going to receive this level of scrutiny these words [would] never have appeared' (T. 904).

Sullivan also had to respond to similarly awkward passages from his fieldnotes of private conversations with a senior claimant, in which the claimant contemplates the end of Yawuru culture if The Man Who Disappeared was no longer around, and canvassed the possibility of some ceremony continuing because of its similarity to Karadjeri ceremony (T. 905–6).

It might have been the discomfort of cross-examination that focused Sullivan's mind, because, for whatever reason, his re-examination provided an opportunity for him to give some of his most coherent evidence and to make a concession that would, in my view, prove critical to the claim. He explained the precise aspects of the continuity he was asserting:

> DR SULLIVAN: It's received knowledge and knowing themselves to be members of a language community, whether or not each one has competence in that language, they're members of that language of that language community...More fundamentally, the knowledge of a shared law in the sense of shared ritual, ritual specific to that group there, their origins in the Bugarrigarra and their own rituals on their own land. The operation of the kinship system that they believe to be—may be shared with other groups but they believe it to be a particular defining characteristic of themselves. Other beliefs such as *rai* belief, practice of using the land in a way that they feel is appropriate for Yawuru people, including talking to the spirits of the land when they go into an area, and dealing with the natural species of the area in the appropriate way, the way that's appropriate for Yawuru people. All of these things.
>
> MR BELL: All of these things. The conduct of ceremony in lawgrounds?
>
> DR SULLIVAN: That's what I intended to say when I said the ownership of—I think I said fundamentally, the ownership of Yawuru ritual and carrying out of Yawuru ritual, yes. (T. 946)

He also explained his own testing of the clan estate hypothesis and the reasons he rejected it as an inadequate explanation of the contemporary scene. Critically, he conceded the possibility of a historical transformation from a clan estate of the past to the ambilineal descent community of the present (T. 944).

This concession should not have been difficult to make since the process of transformation from patrilineal to cognatic reckoning of group membership had been posited in many parts of settled Australia (see Sutton 1998:45–53).

Erich Kolig

Kolig completed his doctorate at Vienna University and was researching an Islamic topic in Afghanistan when an opportunity arose to do fieldwork at Fitzroy Crossing in the eastern Kimberley in 1970. Helmut Petri had given occasional lectures at Vienna University and kindled Kolig's interest in Aboriginal Australia. Kolig's Kimberley research, consolidated in his book *The Silent Revolution: The Effects of Modernisation on Australian Aboriginal Religion* (1981), can easily be seen as a continuation of Petri's interest in the dynamics of the religion of Western Desert peoples moving out of the desert and re-establishing themselves in the former country of other tribes on the fringe of the desert. In Petri's case, the movement was north-west to Anna Plains Station and La Grange, and in Kolig's case, the movement was north to the Fitzroy River Valley.

The Silent Revolution is an ambitious and original work of historical anthropology. It sat provocatively alongside his contemporaries' ethnographies, which were dominated by synchronic generalising. It was ambitious in its attempt to imagine a transition from pre-contact to contemporary Aboriginal consciousness. It was also original in that it applied to the Aboriginal people of Fitzroy Crossing, less than a generation removed from their hunter-gatherer life in the desert, Weberian and Durkheimian themes of modernity, especially the fragmentation of consciousness accompanying the division of social spheres into work, leisure and religion—a sort of microwave modernisation of the Western Desert diaspora. The 'silent revolution' refers to his argument that, although Aboriginal ritual life around Fitzroy Crossing seemed to be effervescing with cultic imports, its significance was fundamentally changing. The original total world view supported by broad consensus, strict enforcement, a strict hierarchy of knowledge and ritual austerity was becoming more a vehicle for ethnic awareness associated with more liberal attitudes to enforcement, a flatter ritual hierarchy and eutrapelia in ritual performance.

Kolig's account of the dynamics of religious change is much more comprehensive than anything achieved by Petri. There are, however, still some difficulties in his exposition. His key descriptive concept, 'consciousness', is left at a high level of generality. This means that the mechanisms through which changes in material circumstances and practices transform 'consciousness' remain impressionistic, rather than systematically analysed. Moreover, the broad scope of the historical narrative means that there is little detailed marshalling of the evidence for his conclusions. Some of these conclusions are relevant to the native title claim. They include the following.

- Pan-Aboriginality in traditional law is a new development (Kolig 1981:11).
- Clan identities were stronger in the past (1981:30) and there was a more straightforward inheritance of patriclan lodge sacra in the past (p. 35).
- There is a generalised trend among Aboriginal people towards rethinking traditional cosmology along the lines of Western thought (1981:38).
- With the move out of the desert, there has been a general decline in the need for topographical authentication of mythological incidents (1981:46).

Most of these propositions seem plausible, but, because of Kolig's writing strategy, it is simply impossible to see how they arise out of his data. His older informants could have helped him reconstruct their life in the desert, but we simply do not know.

His assumptions about a simpler past compared with the complex, degenerate present continued in his subsequent book, *The Noonkanbah Story* (1987). He acknowledged that all accounts of pre-contact traditional land tenure are to some extent speculative. This does not, however, cause him to hesitate and methodically justify his acceptance of the prior ubiquity of the patrilineal clan and his interpretation that vague clan boundaries are evidence of severe disruption (1987:84–5). To be fair, Kolig's level of disclosure of his methodology is not unusual for anthropology and he has continued to wrestle with issues of changing ritual practices and world views/consciousness that were first raised in *The Silent Revolution*.[13]

His published oeuvre and the few available biographical details allow us to construct his approximate positioning within the field of anthropology. Following his postdoctoral research based on Fitzroy Crossing (1969–72), he worked for a few years as the Regional Anthropologist for the WA Aboriginal Affairs Planning Authority. Then in the early 1980s he secured the position of senior lecturer in the Department of Anthropology at the University of Otago in New Zealand—a position he still holds. He has maintained his links with German and Austrian anthropology through several publications in German (see, for example, Kolig 1973–74a, 1979b), publishing in the journal *Anthropos*, and through visiting professorships at Vienna University. He is a major contributor to the regional specialisation of Aboriginal Australia and the subregion of the Kimberley in edited collections of papers and leading journals. There is some evidence that

13 See Kolig (1972, 1973–74a, 1973-74b, 1977, 1978, 1979a, 1979b, 1980, 1989, 1995a, 1995b, 1996, 2003). Most recently, he has made a contribution to the expanding literature on the historical anthropology of the Pacific (Kolig and Mueckler 2002).

he feels a little marginalised within the regional specialisation and does not receive sufficient acknowledgment for his early contribution to historicising Australianist anthropology. He complained, with some justification, that the papers on the change of traditional ownership in the Peterson and Langton collection *Aborigines, Land and Land Rights* completely overlooked his previous work on the topic (1987:155, endnote 7). In summary, apart from the brief interlude of full-time applied work with the Planning Authority, he has pursued an academic career based on research and academic publications.

His involvement in the high-profile political confrontation of the Noonkanbah affair convinced Kolig of the need for strict independence and detachment in applied anthropology (1987:10).[14] He expressed this sentiment much more forcefully in his response to Marcia Langton's suggestion in 1981 that anthropology must now work at Aboriginal direction and for Aboriginal interests: 'I think it is time that Anthropology makes it clear to everybody that as a discipline of some intellectual integrity and ambition, it intends to be nobody's whore' (Kolig 1982:27).[15]

Kolig's evidence

Kolig was quite clear about the limits of his research for his expert report. It was a desktop literature review and critique of Sullivan's report. He deferred to Sullivan's account of the contemporary Rubibi community (T. 958), but he was not a complete neophyte regarding Broome. When interviewed, he said that, because of his extensive contact with the Aboriginal people of the Kimberley, he knew the Aboriginal people involved in the claim and the general background of local Aboriginal politics ('the political constellation').[16] He concentrated on establishing 'the historical presence of group identities and to trace ancestral continuities' (T. 957), and he claimed to be doing this in an objective and detached way that would not take oral history at face value and would assume the likelihood of historical change (T. 958). Elsewhere in his evidence, he expanded on the ideal of objectivity, but in a way that risked appearing disingenuous or naive about drawing conclusions from a very uneven anthropological archive:

> MR BELL: You've expressed rather firm views about the presence of the Djugan—
>
> DR KOLIG: Again, I would want to correct you there...I have not expressed views, personal views—I've simply recorded what I've found in the literature. (T. 1011)

---

14 Compare this with his views on other issues—for example, Christian Missions, grog, and land rights—in Kolig (1973a, 1973b, 1974, 1988).

15 For Langton's original comments, see her article in *Identity* (Langton 1981).

16 Transcript of interview with Erich Kolig, 14 September 2005, p. 5.

He concluded from his literature review that, although the evidence is slight, it is likely that the Djukan 'tribe' was in the past a separate group and not simply a subgroup of the Yawuru. The evidence included the fact that the Djukan have long been mentioned as a separate group in the early ethnographic accounts of Bischofs, Bates, Elkin, Radcliffe-Brown and Petri. Bischofs' listing of 'Karnen' (= Kunin) as the 'bor' of the speakers of 'Tjogon' (= Djukan) is particularly significant because 'bor' is a clan estate. A Djukan identity persists into the present according to the more recent researchers: Dalton, Hosokawa and Glowczewski. Moreover, he argued, several of the earlier researchers and, later, Dalton speak in a general way of cultural differences between Djukan and Yawuru (T. 959–60).

Kolig thought that the early ethnographers should be taken as correct in asserting the patrilineal clan as a landowning entity. He explained:

> DR KOLIG: [T]he presence of clans or clan structure in this area has been quite unambiguously recorded in the older literature. That it has been recorded and maintained by fieldworkers who are widely respected in the anthropological profession and that in the meantime, as far as this area is concerned, nothing has been said, nothing has been produced bar Dr Sullivan's report and a paper of his map [sic] would soundly disprove the findings of Elkin which in turn are based on the findings by Radcliffe-Brown. Radcliffe-Brown is widely criticised in anthropology as having got it wrong. I would disagree. I think basically his contention, based on fieldwork, based on the help by Daisy Bates, for instance and also by Elkin, his findings are of a clan structure, are sound, correct. What had to be done in later years was to make some corrections, some fine touches, some elaborations, but basically and I repeat, for this area here, there's no doubt in my mind that, especially Elkin in the way he portrayed the situation here, was absolutely correct. (T. 961–2)

Kolig then argued as follows.

- Primary rights to the clan territory, including the right to exclude others, belonged to the clan. Secondary rights may derive from matrilineal linkage, spirit origin on the clan estate, and rights in a Dreaming track that passes through the clan estate. Clans were embedded in a large network of relations that are not identical to tribal awareness (T. 964).
- Worms' overlapping identification of the claim area with the Leregon and Walman sibs (= clans) is not a reflection of unreliable fieldwork, but of the 'highly disturbed' state of the society (T. 960).
- The adoption of land tenure models from arid regions, especially Berndt on the Western Desert, is questionable because the coast is not arid in the same way as the desert, and despite Berndt's scepticism about the concept of tribe in the Western Desert, he still believed the clan structure to be the core of land attachment (T. 962–3).

- Sullivan's proof of cultural continuity, by reference to essential features of a culture, is problematic because it is never possible to describe the totality of a culture, and what is considered to be essential by the people themselves might change over time and, thus, there is an arbitrariness about essential features (T. 956–7).
- Because of inadequate records there is no conclusive evidence in the genealogies of descent of any kind, only 'hearsay family tradition' (T. 969).

When I interviewed him in 2005, Kolig was even more direct in his assessment of Sullivan's report: he thought it was a poor piece of advocacy anthropology.

Kolig also introduced the idea that there was an anthropological consensus about what would be 'reasonable change', implying that a move away from group membership according to patrilineal descent would be a move beyond reasonable change (T. 970). Paradoxically, this judgment seemed to assume that there were, in fact, some essential features of traditional society.

The possibility that Kolig's idea of 'reasonable change' incorporated an 'essential features' approach was confirmed the next day after the judge had pressed Kolig to think overnight about what he considered to be the traditional criteria for membership of the Yawuru:

> DR KOLIG: I think there are two criteria that were relevant here. The first is membership of a clan by descent, through patri-filiation, and the second criterion is that this clan is recognised as part of the speech community of Yawuru, speech or language being used here in a wider sense referring also to culture. Traditionally Aborigines would have regarded language as a vital part of their culture. (T. 978)

Kolig thought that, with the loss of language, a vital building block of culture would be missing and that the language connection to the Dreamtime would be broken. He imagined that, with few Yawuru speakers, the traditional culture would become an elite culture in which only a few could participate (T. 1033).

Kolig made several other points on the subject of change.

- The current degree of sharing of ritual between the different tribal groups involved in Kunin ceremonies, which includes implanting and incorporating religious patterns from a neighbouring group into another group (presumably Karadjeri into Yawuru), is of recent origin (T. 988–9, 1031).
- Not conducting initiation ceremonies more frequently than every 10 years could be a breach of traditional law (T. 1033–4).
- The permanent absence of sacred objects from a law ground would make it doubtful whether it continued to be law ground (T. 1035).

It is difficult to say how critical the cross-examination of Kolig was to the applicants' case. It was evident that the judge was becoming a little exasperated with Kolig's apparent reluctance to give straightforward answers to the key questions of the case, such as how he, as an anthropologist, would resolve the continuity–change dilemma. On the other hand, if the judge accepted Kolig's standard of traditional continuity, the claim would be defeated. No doubt, in an attempt to make him seem unreasonable, Kolig was systematically led by the claimants' barrister through the claimants' evidence and forced to agree that many aspects of their evidence showed continuities with ancient traditions—for example, belief in the Bugarrigarra, the use of ceremonial grounds, kinship, sequential initiation processes, restricted sacred knowledge, sexual division of labour in ceremonies, sharing of law with neighbouring groups and the consequences of disclosure of secret sacred information (T. 980–91). In response, Kolig asserted, on behalf of anthropology, a higher standard of evidence:

> MR BELL: But these individuals, nearly 20 in number, men and women, have told you about their life, about their customs and ceremonies as they observe them, so that evidence is evidence of what they do.
>
> DR KOLIG: It is not evidence from an anthropological point of view; you have to see these things in operation; you do not rely—and this is no disrespect to the people who have made these statements—you cannot rely on what people say, you have to see that in operation, and the reason is not because there's a profound distrust that anthropologists have for what people say, but the reason is the fact that there's often a discrepancy between what people say they do and what is actually being done. (T. 992)

The paradox of this stance is that the extremely limited observation of systems in practice was exactly the fieldwork situation of Radcliffe-Brown and Elkin, on whom Kolig relied in support of his reconstruction of pre-colonial local organisation. Kolig's answer might well have been a turning point for the judge, who felt obliged to point out what could count as evidence in the court hearing:

> HIS HONOUR: Your qualification is understandable but because the Court can't go out and live in the community, and maybe it should, but it's not the way it operates at the moment, the only way these matters can be established is through evidence of the kind that has been called. (T. 992)

Kolig's similarly high standard of proof of traditional continuity of ceremony was also revealed:

MR BELL: And where you find it among communities, observing that structure in a particular place by reference to particular tracts of land you have community title in that land by those groups, do you not?

DR KOLIG: If you do not take regard to content; if you just refer to structure.

MR BELL: What is an item of content in your view, separate from the structure?

DR KOLIG: For instance the ceremonies that are being conducted on that law ground; the particular myths that are being cultivated... The particular details of kinship and marriage obligations; the stories associated, particular stories associated with particular sites; the contents of rituals performed; the designs being used in ritual procedures. (T. 996)

One of the most interesting episodes in Kolig's cross-examination was how an academic argument within anthropological discourse about traditional land tenure became the subject of direct cross-examination. One of the ways for the claimants to undermine Kolig's claim of objectivity was to demonstrate that he had taken an extreme position within the academic field of anthropology. The only way to do this effectively, given Kolig's academic seniority over Sullivan, was through Kolig's own concessions in cross-examination. Thus, we had the unusual spectacle of Kolig being confronted with the details of the subsequent anthropological critique of the position taken by Radcliffe-Brown and Elkin, including Hiatt's direct assault (Hiatt 1966) and the relevant passages from Piddington's work on the Karadjeri, which I have quoted in the previous chapter:[17]

DR KOLIG: I'm aware of that, and with respect it doesn't mean anything. In fact, this very passage [Piddington's suggestion that the Karadjeri never possessed a rigid clan associated with their local groups] was rebutted by Elkin by saying that this is a post-contact alteration, or innovation.

MR BELL: I see. So the passage is the subject of anthropological dispute?

DR KOLIG: Not really.

MR BELL: We have Piddington on one side and Elkin on the other, with you? You are the disputants?

17 The material for this part of the cross-examination had, of course, been supplied by Sullivan.

> DR KOLIG: No-one has followed that dispute to my knowledge. (T. 1004–5)[18]

Later, in response to the suggestion that Elkin's account of land tenure in the Broome region might have been compromised by lack of time:

> DR KOLIG: Some people are able to produce sterling work within a short period of time; others can spend a lifetime and produce nothing.
>
> MR BELL: But you'd have to admit that to try to describe the richness and intensity of cultural life of an Aboriginal group in 15 days is an extremely difficult task?
>
> DR KOLIG: It is. Some people are qualified to do that task in a reasonably short time. (T. 1010–11)

The judge

To attempt to position Justice Merkel within the juridical field and the broader social field is to immediately step outside the formal discourse of the hearing and take up a stance that might be seen as contemptuous if repeated in the formal hearing. But to raise Merkel's impeccable liberal credentials is not necessarily to suggest reprehensible bias, because actual motivations still remain relatively impenetrable. These credentials are part of the wider background that judges inevitably bring to the task of resolving the various indeterminacies in native title doctrine in particular cases.

Merkel was appointed to the Federal Court in 1996 from the Melbourne Bar, where he had been a Queen's Counsel for some years. At the beginning of his career, he had worked as a lawyer for the Victorian Aboriginal Legal Service and in 1986 had helped to establish the Koori Heritage Trust. He was one of several prominent barristers, including his friend Ron Castan, senior counsel in the *Mabo* case, who had become involved in both the Council for Civil Liberties

---

18 Note: his answers in this passage are confusing because he was well aware of the debate and had written about it in 1973:

> The problem of traditional local organisation, which linked to aspects of land tenure, was initiated into Anthropology by Radcliffe-Brown and his concept of the 'horde' (Radcliffe-Brown 1913). The 'horde' remains a Danaidean gift to the present day. As the literature accumulates on this topic, the scholarly opinions sulkily diverge (For a brief abridge [sic] of the 'horde'-conflict vide: L. R. Haitt 1962; W. E. H. Stanner 1965; L. R. Hiatt 1966.).
>
> Other anthropological contributions aimed at the elucidation of land-tenure itself and actual landholding groups. They seem to make the point that profound variations existed in Aboriginal Australia, provided all of the scholars, or most of them, are right in their assumptions. While some anthropologists still hold to the conventional notion of 'tribes' in Aboriginal Australia, others speak of much smaller landholding units and less clearly defined 'territorial' organisation. (See, for instance, R. M. Berndt 1959). (Kolig 1973a:63)

and Aboriginal legal rights. His continuing association with the Koori Heritage Trust led the Victorian Government to challenge his inclusion in the Full Bench of the Federal Court assembled to hear the appeal from Justice Olney's original decision in the *Yorta Yorta* claim. He stood aside and was replaced with another judge for that appeal. It was perhaps sensitivity to these issues that prompted his statement at the beginning of the hearing of *Rubibi*:

> HIS HONOUR: Just before we call the first witness, there is one matter I overlooked mentioning first thing this morning. I notice that Mr Dodson is now an applicant and also a person who is giving evidence. I had met Mr Dodson over the years on one or two occasions at one or two functions at which he spoke, and therefore I have some passing acquaintance with him from the past. (T. 47)

No application was made for the judge to disqualify himself and, unlike the Victorian case, here it is difficult to see how it could have succeeded.

The *Rubibi* hearing was Justice Merkel's first native title case at the trial level, although he had been a member of the Full Court that heard the appeal from Justice Olney's decision in the *Croker Island* case. His relative inexperience might explain the many interventions he made during the hearing, or they could simply reflect a judge approaching his task in an efficient manner by trying to clarify issues at the time they arise. As in the *Mabo* case study, these interventions are revealing in a way that the tight formality of judgment writing never is.

Judicial interventions

Some of the interventions were simply questions of clarification, with Sullivan taking on a role that would be performed by the anthropologist assisting the judge in NT land rights hearings. Thus, the judge wanted to know how 'clan' was defined (T. 884), why it was that *rai* attachment to land cut across descent attachment (T. 936), and, more generally, the nature of the part–whole relationship between Kunin and the whole corpus of Yawuru sacra and country (T. 833–4). More interesting, though, is the judge's paradoxical concern about legal concepts contaminating anthropological evidence:

> HIS HONOUR: Dr Sullivan, I must say you've lost me on your answer… the problem may have stemmed from the question, because the question related to who was holding this land, and what's crept into a lot of the discussion is European concepts of land-holding and ownership which may have nothing to do with what we're talking about in this case. (T. 832)

He was also concerned that Sullivan was being too traditionalist in his identification of subgroup affiliation to place and not considering groups that were constituted by their co-residence on pastoral stations, such as 'the Thangoo mob' (T. 837).

In a similar vein, the judge seemed worried about the claim of traditional continuity of the broad Yawuru community as opposed to the possibility of a transformation from more strictly defined clans (T. 849). He seemed relieved when Sullivan made concessions about the inevitable evolution of tradition (T. 850).

One consistent feature of the judge's questioning of Kolig was his attempt to find common ground between Kolig and Sullivan. A hot-tubbing session for the two anthropologists did take place, as required by the Federal Court guidelines for expert witnesses.[19] It was brief, with both experts agreeing to disagree. The judge, on the other hand, took on a kind of shuttle diplomacy between the two experts. Having the previous day received some evasive answers from Kolig on the question of discontinuity versus evolutionary cultural change, the judge pressed him again, this time using the example of Nipper Roe, who under a strict patrilineal clan model could not have primary traditional rights to Yawuru country, but who could have such rights in a descent system modified because of the increasing number of non-Aboriginal fathers:

> DR KOLIG: The focus would have shifted away from purely patrilineal descent as conferring primary rights to ambilineal descent and possibly other mechanisms. But if we consider that primary rights, landholding rights, were probably not simply bound to descent, but depended also on the assumption of religious responsibilities, taking care of clan land, not just for the benefit of the clan, but for the benefit of related clans, surrounding clans, then possibly the perception of the unit that meets those responsibilities may have shifted away from the focus on patrilineality, first to matrilineality or ambi-lineality and possibly in further consequence to other units who could meet that responsibility, and by virtue of meeting that responsibility of caring for the land, to assume actually under traditional Aboriginal rules, title to that land. (T. 1025)

19 'Hot-tubbing' is the nickname, widely used in legal circles, for the meeting of all experts to attempt agreement on the issues in the case. For an account of another hot-tubbing experience in a native title claim, see Brunton and Sackett's 'Anthropologists in the hot tub' (2003). For the legal framework of the hot-tubbing, see Federal Court Rules, Order 34A (Evidence of Expert Witnesses) and Federal Court Practice Note CM7 Expert Witnesses in Proceedings in the Federal Court of Australia.

Then:

> HIS HONOUR: The difficult task one has sitting as a Judge in a native title case is to ascertain what is an evolving of a tradition and what is a new tradition. Your definition this morning in respect of traditional society and the resistance you had to answering some of Mr Bell's questions seemed to raise that issue very starkly. I'm trying to understand how the court can draw the line between what you yourself said is a cultural response to changing needs in a society which is an evolving tradition as I understand it. Is that correct?
>
> DR KOLIG: Yes.
>
> HIS HONOUR: And maybe starting something totally new, which is not an evolving tradition, but if you want, some new social or cultural practice which isn't based in tradition.
>
> DR KOLIG: Possibly for opportunistic motivations. (T. 1026)

Subsequently, referring to the difficulty of reconciling Kolig's critique of Sullivan's 'essential elements' approach with Kolig's 'isolable traits' approach to continuity, the judge challenged Kolig by saying:

> HIS HONOUR: I suppose what I'm really putting to you is—this may be a very difficult question to answer, but given your acceptance of cultural change as part of a continuing tradition and you say, I think, at page 78 that
>
> *no one cultural feature is apt to establish cultural continuity. It's the sum total of isolable traits.*
>
> That's like a weighing process, an evaluation process. I'm not sure in what precise way that differs from what Dr Sullivan was putting. He seemed to be saying there's a whole lot of factors that you put into the balance and you have to measure them and evaluate them and look at it in terms of the tradition and the evidence in the particular case, but no one factor can be determinative and he had a very—I raised with him his very broad criterion. I raised with you your very narrow criterion. It seems to me once you introduce cultural change into the model, you both may not differ at all in any significant respect. I'm trying to understand what is the difference between you and Dr Sullivan on that point.
>
> DR KOLIG: Only to the extent that Dr Sullivan rationalises the existence of—or the basis of this view without reference to the past and presents the picture as one—or the situation as one that has always existed like that, that there wasn't an evolution, that there was no change. (T. 1027)

It seems to me that this answer provided the judge with the means of reconciling the two experts. In effect, Kolig was saying that Sullivan had got the pre-contact land-tenure system wrong and had overemphasised continuity. Taking this view of Kolig's evidence would allow the judge to formulate the common ground by allowing Kolig to be right about the pre-contact situation, Sullivan to be right about the contemporary situation, and to link the two by legally permissible historical transformation that would accept some of Kolig's critique of Sullivan and settle on Sullivan's fallback position—that is, the transformation from a strictly patrilineal to an ambilineal system.

The judgment

Justice Merkel delivered his judgment in Broome on 29 May 2001. It commenced and ended in a slightly unusual way by addressing a wider audience than the parties. He introduced his reasons by quoting previous judicial acknowledgment of the strong spiritual attachment of Aboriginal people to their homeland (adopting Stanner's formulation in his Boyer Lectures) and concluded with a plea for greater understanding between Aboriginal and non-Aboriginal people in Australia (paras 1, 198). Between these bookends of liberal sentiment is a concise judgment, of which only 117 paragraphs cover the entirety of all disputed factual issues. This perhaps indicates that the overriding judicial task is one of simplifying and condensing.

Our chief interest is how he presented and resolved the differences of anthropological opinion. The first dispute deals with the difference of interpretation about the use of Kunin as a ceremonial ground prior to the sacred objects from Thangoo being moved there in 1947. After reviewing the documentary evidence, Justice Merkel comes to the conclusion that, by itself, it is not decisive:

> [52] While there is some substance in Dr Kolig's criticisms of the conclusions drawn by Dr Sullivan, ultimately the material must be weighed in the context of the totality of the historical and ethnographic records, as well as the oral history provided by the local community.

But he also briefly turns his mind to what weight should be given to the meagre archival evidence in the circumstances:

> I would add that because of the highly secret nature of the second stage ceremony, during which important and esoteric aspects of traditional law are revealed, it is not surprising that little appears to have been written or disclosed about its occurrence at Kunin. (Para. 60)

He then moves to oral history evidence and legal pronouncements, including his own in the *Croker Island* case, encouraging judges to give due weight to oral history in native title cases. He was able to draw on the recent leading Canadian case, *Delgamuukw*, which turned on this very point. He reviews the evidence of the childhood memories of the current claimants and what had been told to them by now deceased ancestors and the early agreement, dating from the 1960s, about establishing Kunin reserve for ceremonial purposes. He felt able to conclude, on the balance of probabilities, that in the 1890s Kunin had been used as a law ground (paras 76–8). What we see here is not just the authoritative finality of legal proceedings, but an implicit assertion of the superior synthesising capability of judicial methods.

The issue of whether the gap in the performance of ceremony at Kunin was a fatal break in traditional connection was dealt with by reference to long passages of Patrick Dodson's evidence. In what could perhaps be the signature quotation of Merkel's judgment, he simply states, 'Mr Dodson's evidence was not seriously challenged and I accept it' (para. 93).

The claim of the Goolarabooloo group to be part of the Yawuru community was fairly summarily dismissed by Merkel (para. 100). During the hearing, there had been a change of terminology used by the claimants' lawyers from 'Rubibi community' to 'Yawuru community'. This change is emblematic of Sullivan's difficulties with the claimants' lawyers. He felt that they had unnecessarily abandoned the Goolarabooloo and endangered the future of the Rubibi coalition. The lawyers and the judge were partly responding to the way in which the evidence unfolded, especially the prominence given to descent and *rai* as the critical criteria for belonging to the Yawuru community. The exclusion of the Goolarabooloo group highlights, in a dramatic way, the disjuncture between social reality and the judicially endorsed models. Paddy Roe's inclusion in the Rubibi coalition reflected his knowledge of Yawuru country and ceremony and his fighting to preserve Kunin reserve. Legal models, however, require consistency at the level of the principle of inclusion and apparently cannot abide historical anomaly, no matter how compelling. It was Sullivan's attempt to include Paddy Roe's group that skewed his model towards a greater emphasis on knowledge of ceremony and the consensus of elders as a criterion for inclusion in the Yawuru community.[20] In the give and take of the judge's mediation between Kolig and

20 In response to this paragraph in a draft of this chapter, Sullivan commented: 'There is much more to it than this. Paddy's involvement in Kunin is very important, but was historical. Of more importance is current Goolarabooloo knowledge of the land, associated ceremony (though of an alternate tradition) and continuing active nurturance of significant parts of the land under claim. They have all the classic attributes of a traditional owner group except use of the Yawuru language. This is why I continue to challenge the ethnic model of native title' (Sullivan's comments on the draft chapter, December 2005).

Sullivan, the exclusion of the Goolarabooloo was also something about which the judge could agree with Kolig (see T. 961) and something he could 'take' from Sullivan, because of the sheer lack of Aboriginal evidence.[21]

As formulated by Justice Merkel, the most important dispute between Kolig and Sullivan was whether the current Yawuru community, as defined by Sullivan, was sufficiently continuous with the 1829 community, or whether, as Kolig asserted, in moving away from strict adherence to the patrilineal clan having primary rights to land, they had lost something essential. Justice Merkel's mediating style of engagement with the anthropologists in the witness box came to the fore here:

> [136] Ultimately, the substantive dispute between the two anthropologists was less than it might appear to be. Both accepted that it is not possible to have a definition of a traditional community that is frozen in time. Rather, they agreed that the definition must recognise the process by which a community's traditional laws and customs evolve, respond and adapt to change. That approach finds substantial support in the cases.

There follows the reassertion of legal doctrine and the final acceptance of the judge's responsibility to resolve indeterminate legal criteria:

> [139] Although Dr Kolig accepted that allowance must be made for 'reasonable' change and presented substantial criticisms of Dr Sullivan's analysis, he offered no clear guidance as to why the matters relied on by Dr Sullivan do not fall within the concept of reasonable change to the interruption to traditional life. Dr Kolig conceded that, on the question of continuity, the evidence is in general unclear and suggests that it is 'impossible to say just how much "culture" had been "lost"' before the recent cultural revival and how much had to be 'imported' or 're-learned' in order to revive or revitalise at least a semblance of the old culture. When Dr Kolig was asked whether a change from a patrilineal clan group to an ambilineal group would fall within his concept of 'reasonable' change, Dr Kolig said:

21 The mystery of the absence of Goolarabooloo witnesses was partly explained by Sullivan in his interview with me in 2005. It seems that it was a deliberate decision, and had to do with ritual etiquette and the rapprochement between the Yawuru and Goolarabooloo groups in the Rubibi coalition. Not asserting a ritual interest in Kunin was consistent with Goolarabooloo's focus on the 'northern Law'—that is, Dreamings not associated with Kunin and ceremonial grounds to the north of Broome. Also, by staying away from the hearing, the claim of the Yawuru group would not be complicated by reviving, via cross-examination, pre-Rubibi disputes between the Goolarabooloo and the Yawuru about who was really following and defending the Law. In other words, he saw it as a selfless gesture that backfired on them (Transcript of interview with Patrick Sullivan, August 2005, pp. 14–16).

> 'I think there would be consensus in the anthropological community that such changes might not be considered unreasonable. Whether this then constitutes a break in continuity is a different matter. But the changes in themselves would be considered reasonable, I think.'
>
> [140] The problem with Dr Kolig's approach is that the concept of 'reasonable' change is problematic and requires some unstated value judgment to be exercised on a question that essentially is one of fact and degree.

Finally, the judge concluded that a change from a patrilineal group to an ambilineal group was an evolutionary change of traditional laws and customs, which was consistent with substantial maintenance of traditional connection (para. 142).

Kolig reflects on the claim

In 2005, Kolig was keen to correct a misapprehension I might have received from the written record: that he disagreed with the result of the hearing. Ultimately, he thought that the judge made the correct choice between the contending Aboriginal groups. He was, however, sceptical of the process. The depth of his scepticism about the Aboriginal evidence and the judge's assessment of credibility was revealed in an article he published in 2003, in which he brought together the Noonkanbah confrontation, the Hindmarsh Island affair and the *Rubibi* claim as examples of 'Legitimising belief: identity politics, utility, strategies of concealment, and rationalisation in Australian Aboriginal religion' (Kolig 2003). Now, after the event, he felt free to express his concerns about the absence of a viewing of sacred objects at Kunin, the unspecified link between the Two-Men mythology and the topography of Kunin,[22] and Patrick Dodson's dominant role. In relation to the first two matters, he concluded: 'When obvious vested interest is involved in the claim of sacrality, as was the case here, adducing empirically accessible detail seems to be of paramount significance in rendering credibility' (2003:218).

In relation to Patrick Dodson, whom he does not name, but clearly identifies, he states:

> Imposing his own stamp through his interpretation of traditions, his role invites analysis as to how traditional or authentic, or alternatively utilitarian and opportunistic the circumstances of presenting a dominant 'official' view is. It also raises the question as to how cloaking of traditional diversity and dissonance is achieved. (2003:219)

22 This is disputed by Sullivan, who stated that the link had been made in the restricted evidence.

Kolig also explored a paradoxical traditional continuity of 'the traditional protection and privileging of pieces of knowledge which are considered of great significance and potency' (2003:222). In earlier times, this knowledge would have been esoteric details of Dreaming stories and the deeper significance of certain rituals. Kolig thought that the potent secret among the Aboriginal claimants was that the genuine present, in reality, diverged significantly from the past. It is difficult to know how to interpret this observation, given his ambivalence about the claim process. If taken literally, it suggests deep continuities. As irony, it is a critique of Dodson's traditional credentials and Justice Merkel's gullibility.

Kolig's article is also a contradictory mixture of sophistication about the general effect of the claim process on the previous subtleties of cultural practices and high expectations about judicial methodology.[23] He makes the general observation:

> Advocate anthropology (in putting forward an official version) and court session then tend to function very much like the consensus-forming, 'orthopractical' medium of the joint ritual performances. However, while ritual orthopraxy of old was temporary and ephemeral, the legal process has more lasting gravity, as belief once recorded will remain in a legally binding version. (2003:221)

Towards the end of the article, he states: 'Perhaps, if it were not practically impossible what it [the legal process] should ethically be obliged to do is to distinguish between sincerely held views and crass forms of insincerity. In this distinction the concept of historical continuity would play only a small role' (2003:224).

Of course, the judge is already obliged to assess sincerity, as part of 'the credibility of the witness' and the 'weight' to be given to a witness's evidence. Furthermore, no participant, including the judge, can avoid the problem of historical continuity because that is what the legal doctrine of native title requires. Kolig, it seems, would have made different assessments of credibility.

---

23 On the traditional instability of orthodoxy, Kolig states:

> Differences are embedded in what is no more than a thin veneer of vague agreement, made for momentary convenience, about a fleeting 'orthodoxy' and ritual 'orthopraxy'. Yet different understandings of myth and ritual, never expunged or suppressed, do not in most cases prevent co-operation, nor does this fact usually invite open censure or mutual recrimination (although that, in my experience, does happen, though very rarely). Little attempt is usually made to remove ambiguities as this would increase the likelihood of confrontation. Such a crisis is usually avoided among peers and played very cautiously by persons who considered themselves, or are considered, to possess superior knowledge. (2003:220)

Sullivan reflects on not educating the judge

Sullivan has chosen not to write about the details of the first *Rubibi* claim until all the *Rubibi* claims are finalised. He did, however, present a paper entitled 'Don't educate the judge: court experts and court expertise in the social disciplines' at a native title conference (Sullivan 2002).[24] The title refers to some instructions from a lawyer who was preparing for the next *Rubibi* claim. The instruction not to attempt to re-educate the judge seems to be a reference to Justice Merkel's summary dismissal of the inclusion of the Goolarabooloo group in the determination and what appears to be a request not to re-argue the point in the next *Rubibi* claim. Such a request represents the most acute tension between lawyers and anthropologists, ostensibly working for the same side. The pragmatics of managing a court case might require jettisoning weak or counterproductive aspects of the case to maximise the overall chance of success—like a surgeon lopping off a diseased limb. But the proposal for Sullivan to drop the Goolarabooloo, if it was that, also had its problems. Such a change of expert opinion would risk compromising the perception of the anthropologist's independence, which is also important for the overall success of the case.

Sullivan tried not to personalise his response in the paper, using it as a launching pad for a reflection on why 'courts' and 'the legal process' have difficulty in accepting the real-world fluidity and complexity of groups. In doing so, he touches on many of the issues covered in Chapter 1 of this book. Despite his obvious understanding of the legal process, one also senses the angst of being part of a process that recognises the rights of some and disenfranchises others:

> It would not be surprising for legal counsel for the claimants to feel that the construction of the claimants' case in a manner already familiar to the judge would be most likely to result in recognition of the claimants' rights. I think, on the contrary, the rights of claimants to be themselves are being curtailed. (2002:6)

Conclusion of the *Rubibi* case study

The singular articulateness of Patrick Dodson and, to a lesser extent, Nipper Roe raises the issue of the redundancy of anthropology, or at least competition between anthropologists and claimants for the authoritative presentation of Yawuru tradition. In the clarity, force and expansiveness of Dodson's evidence, we see a powerful combination in one person of the usual roles of claimant,

---

24 Sullivan has since removed the paper from the Australian Anthropological Society web site, feeling that the original provocation, which he felt was justified for a conference presentation, was becoming known to a much wider audience than was originally intended.

lawyer and anthropologist. And in Nipper Roe, we find a claimant creating an archive of his own objectifications of his culture in the form of cross-cultural manuals. Their success as witnesses, exemplified in the extensive quoting of Dodson in the judgment, could be contrasted, in a cautionary way, with the fate of Eddie Mabo's testimony in the original *Mabo* hearing. In that case, being articulate about ancient traditions might have reinforced the judge's suspicion that Mabo had learnt much about Meriam traditions from books, rather than through traditional mechanisms. So one wonders whether a different judge might have interpreted Dodson's articulateness and Nipper Roe's objectifications as further evidence of the attenuation of Yawuru traditions as a lived experience.

The most dramatic example of possible competition between claimant and anthropologist involved Sullivan's fieldnotes rather than his testimony. Although Sullivan was able to deflect some potential harm by pointing out the incompleteness of the passages quoted back to him, the more insoluble problem was the sheer length of his fieldwork—10 years of fairly dramatic transformation. The relatively small number of senior Yawuru lawmen meant that any consensus among them might be dramatically altered with the death of one or two. This might have been the situation with The Man Who Disappeared. At the beginning of Sullivan's fieldwork, this man was a key player and could afford to be offhand in his private conversation about Dodson and Roe. At the end of Sullivan's fieldwork, Dodson and Nipper Roe had assumed key traditional leadership roles and needed to consolidate the position without the help of The Man Who Disappeared.

The fact that Sullivan's fieldnotes provided an intimate account of the internal dynamics of the Yawuru over 10 years is a metonym of the larger problem of the relationship between the complete anthropological archive and the objectives of the current generation of Yawuru—both enabling and constraining them in their native title aspirations. The Aboriginal witnesses, with the exception of Colin Lee, who referred specifically to Father Worms, scrupulously avoided mentioning this archive. Patrick Dodson and Nipper Roe's anthropology was of their own experiences. It was Sullivan who had to deal with the archive.

The strength of Sullivan's evidence was in the ability of his model to reflect the likely evidence of the claimants. The most skilful part of this was in combining the maximal grouping (all Yawuru land for all Yawuru people) with particular attachments of individuals and families to particular places. This formulation allowed the evidence of those who strongly opposed the consensus reached among the Rubibi claimants to be at least partially consistent with the Rubibi model. Moreover, it relieved the judge of the need to totally disenfranchise opposing groups. In a similar way, by defining traditional activity largely in terms of authority in the ceremonial sphere, opposing claimants, even if they challenged the traditional propriety of Dodson's and Nipper Roe's induction into the 'second-stage' initiation, were forced to defer to some aspects of shared traditional etiquette.

From this angle, there are striking parallels between Sullivan's approach to his model and the politics of the KLC representation of the disparate Yawuru groups. For the political logic of representation demanded a coalition of Yawuru groups to present a joint front for maximum strategic advantage, even if some disparate groups could not bring themselves to actively be a part of the formal Rubibi coalition, or even to make themselves known to the KLC before the hearing.

Given this kind of argument and Sullivan's actual employment by the KLC over a long period—much of which was specifically devoted to preparing for the claim—it is a little surprising that he did not come under more direct questioning of his professional independence.[25] Beckett avoided such an attack by having completed his research well before the *Mabo* case had commenced. In Sullivan's case, such an attack could have been anticipated from the science–law literature on the discrediting of 'research for litigation'. This probability occurred to Sullivan only in hindsight. An attack did come, but in a more subtle form: it was that Sullivan made the mistake of looking at the archive through the lens of the contemporary Yawuru community and consequently saw more continuity than there really was. This critique came from Kolig. It was the interpretation of the archive, particularly in imagining historical transformation, that was the main area of conflict, since Kolig had already deferred to Sullivan about contemporary Yawuru ethnography.

In doing so, Kolig could be viewed as choosing an arena in which he had an advantage: a superior place in the field of the academy. This superiority did count for something. He was able to speak fluently and coherently, as one would expect of a long-time senior lecturer. He was also able to convince the judge that there was an anthropological discourse about historical transformation using the concept of 'reasonable change'. There is a discourse of historical anthropology, but it has never used 'reasonable change' as a technical term and certainly not one in which there is any measure of consensus.

In other respects, his position in the field of the academy did not help him, and he seems to have misconceived the expectations of him as an expert witness. I have already referred to his confusing disavowal of expressing opinions about the archive. But he also seemed to want to confine his role to one of academic critique of Sullivan's report, without appreciating how much his own position would need coherent justification as well. Because continuity–change is a classic example of interpretative indeterminacy, coherent justification is

25 Sullivan noted in his comments on a draft of this chapter in December 2005 that he also worked on the claim while he was at the North Australian Research Unit and as an independent consultant.

elusive, unless an orientation is first chosen towards demonstrating continuity *or* discontinuity. Sullivan did choose one of these orientations—continuity—at the risk of compromising the appearance of independence. Kolig had not sufficiently resolved his thinking about the problem to avoid proposing yet another indeterminate concept, 'reasonable change', as if it could provide a solution. The indeterminacy of 'reasonable' is well known to lawyers through the use and critique of the concept of 'the reasonable man'. Therefore, Kolig's lack of regard for the legal doctrine of native title did not help him in the way that Beckett thought it helped in distancing himself from the unrealistic traditionalism of the *Mabo* claim, as formulated by Eddie Mabo's lawyers.

Sullivan had been working on the *Rubibi* claim throughout the period of the native title revolution in Broome and was forced to develop an understanding of the legal doctrine. His approach was firmly orientated towards the relevant aspects of the legal doctrine. Again, this did not seem to assist the acceptance of his evidence. Justice Merkel was concerned about European concepts of ownership prejudicing ethnographic accuracy. Also, while not mentioning it directly, the judge would have recognised in the form of Sullivan's conclusion about continuity ('substantial continuity') the identical terms in the formulation in Justice Brennan's judgment in *Mabo*: 'their traditional connection with the land has been substantially maintained.'[26]

While the triangulation model proposed in Chapter 1 of this book does seem to coincide with the basic tensions in Sullivan's presentation of his expert opinion, in one important respect it is wanting. Sullivan felt strongly constrained by other considerations, which were outside the simple calculus of the best alignment of legal doctrine, archive and claimants' evidence. Those considerations could be summarised as: how the presentation of the claim would remain true to the hard-won Rubibi coalition and on-the-ground complexity. In these concerns, he felt very much alone among the team representing the claimants, as if he was the only voice representing the ideals of the coalition against the win-at-all-costs professional predilection of the lawyers.

This kind of conflict represents something more than I anticipated in Chapter 1. There, I predicted that the worst disputes between anthropologists and lawyers working for the same client would be over conflicting assessments of the best alignment of the triangle of basic factors. In this case study the lingering bitterness was more about certain other issues, such as the legal team ruling as irrelevant the question of how presentational decisions would affect the community after the claim.

26 *Mabo v Queensland (No. 2)*(1992) 175 CLR 1 at 59.

Justice Merkel's mediating approach to the differences of anthropological opinion contrasts with his approach to the historians. With them, he was prepared to examine the key historical documents—for example, the original dedication of the reserve as a 'ceremonial site'—and form his own opinion of them, much like Justice Olney in *Yorta Yorta* forming his own opinion of Edward Curr's autobiographical account of his early encounters with Aboriginal people in his *Recollections of Squatting in Victoria* (1883). Where he differs from Olney is in his reserve when it comes to the anthropological archive—admittedly more clearly a product of the academy in the *Rubibi* case than in *Yorta Yorta*. The complexity of the anthropological archive and the academic capital of some of the contributors might have been a factor in the judge's inclination to mediation, rather than the dismissal of experts in dispute. But it also seems likely that he was aware that the acceptance of his liberal stance—hidden within the legal formula of 'a question of fact and degree'—would be enhanced by sharing the responsibility for his judgment with an expert consensus that he identified.

The judge's mediation of conflicting expert opinion in this case study allows a reconsideration of how to characterise the interaction of the fields of law and anthropology, raised in Chapter 1. It tends to confirm that, within the overall process of law swallowing and digesting anthropology for its own ends, there are circumstances in which sharing of responsibility is equally plausible.

In the next case study we shall see how anthropological 'research for litigation' fared when there was no broadly liberal judicial background to appeal to and no active judicial mediation at work: the *De Rose Hill* native title claim.

6. The Enigma of Traditional Western Desert Land Tenure

Introduction

This case study examines the formulation and reception of anthropological expert testimony in the *De Rose Hill* native title claim that was heard in 2001–02. It was a claim to De Rose Hill Station, which abuts the eastern boundary of a large block of Aboriginal land in the north-western corner of South Australia, known as the Pitjantjatjara Lands (see Map 6.1).[1] The controversial judgment of the High Court in the *Wik* case in 1996 allowed native title claims to residual native title rights on pastoral leases on the basis that those leases did not grant exclusive possession and, therefore, did not extinguish all native title rights. This decision made for a contentious and hard-fought legal battle between the pastoralists in occupation of the lease and native title claimants, who, if successful, would be granted some limited access rights. In South Australia these access rights would overlap with existing statutory access rights, but the *Native Title Act* would also give successful claimants a right to negotiate in the event of mineral exploration or mining.[2]

The claim—being the first native title claim to proceed to hearing in South Australia—had a strategic role to play in relation to the many other native title claims lodged in South Australia. In various ways, the possibilities of successfully negotiating agreed determinations in those other claims rested on the outcome of the *De Rose Hill* claim. On the other side, a finding that *Wik* did not apply to SA pastoral leases would relieve all pastoralists in the State. From the point of view of the State-wide native title representative body, the Aboriginal Legal Rights Movement (ALRM), which represented the claimants, the choice of De Rose Hill as the 'test case' was also strategic. The Aboriginal people from that part of the State probably had the strongest claim to traditional continuity.

---

1 The claim was over the three separate leases that are run as a single enterprise and commonly known as De Rose Hill Station. The three leases are Agnes Creek, Paxton Bluff North and Paxton Bluff South.

2 The Right to Negotiate in ss. 25–44 of the *Native Title Act* is a potentially valuable right in areas that are prospective for minerals. Under the Right to Negotiate, exploration and mining companies must negotiate with native title holders and, failing an agreement, be subject to arbitration by an independent body, which will set the conditions to apply to the exploration or mining. The Right to Negotiate is available before a hearing and successful determination of a claim, provided the claim passes the registration test (ss. 190B–190C). But, generally speaking, any compensation determined under the Right to Negotiate procedures would not flow to the native title holders until they are successful in obtaining a determination that native title exists (s. 52). A determination of native title would also ensure that the freedom from certain government regulation of traditional hunting rights guaranteed by s. 211 would apply, but, again, a determination is not strictly necessary to assert rights under that section.

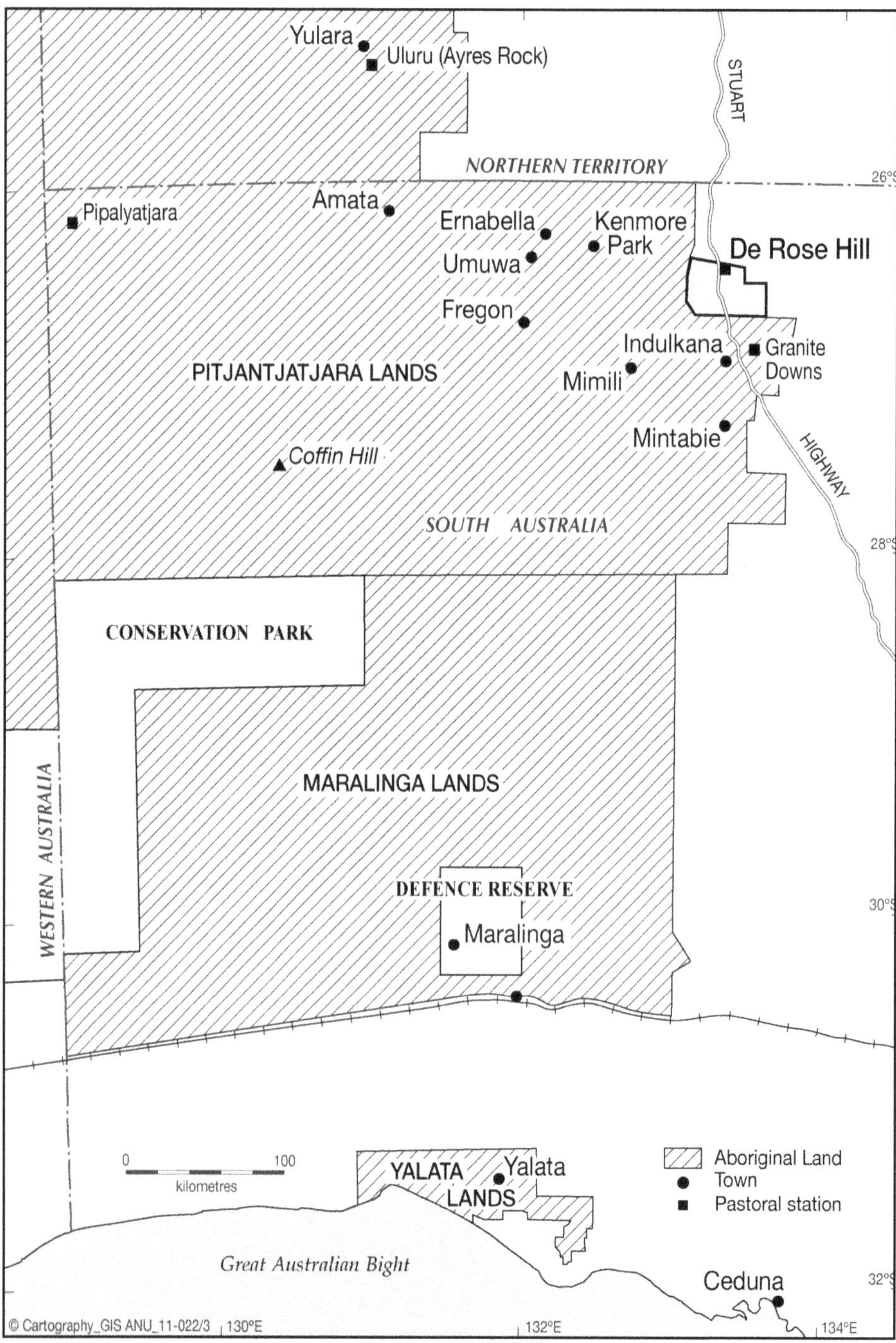

Map 6.1 Location of De Rose Hill Station in relation to the Pitjantjatjara Lands

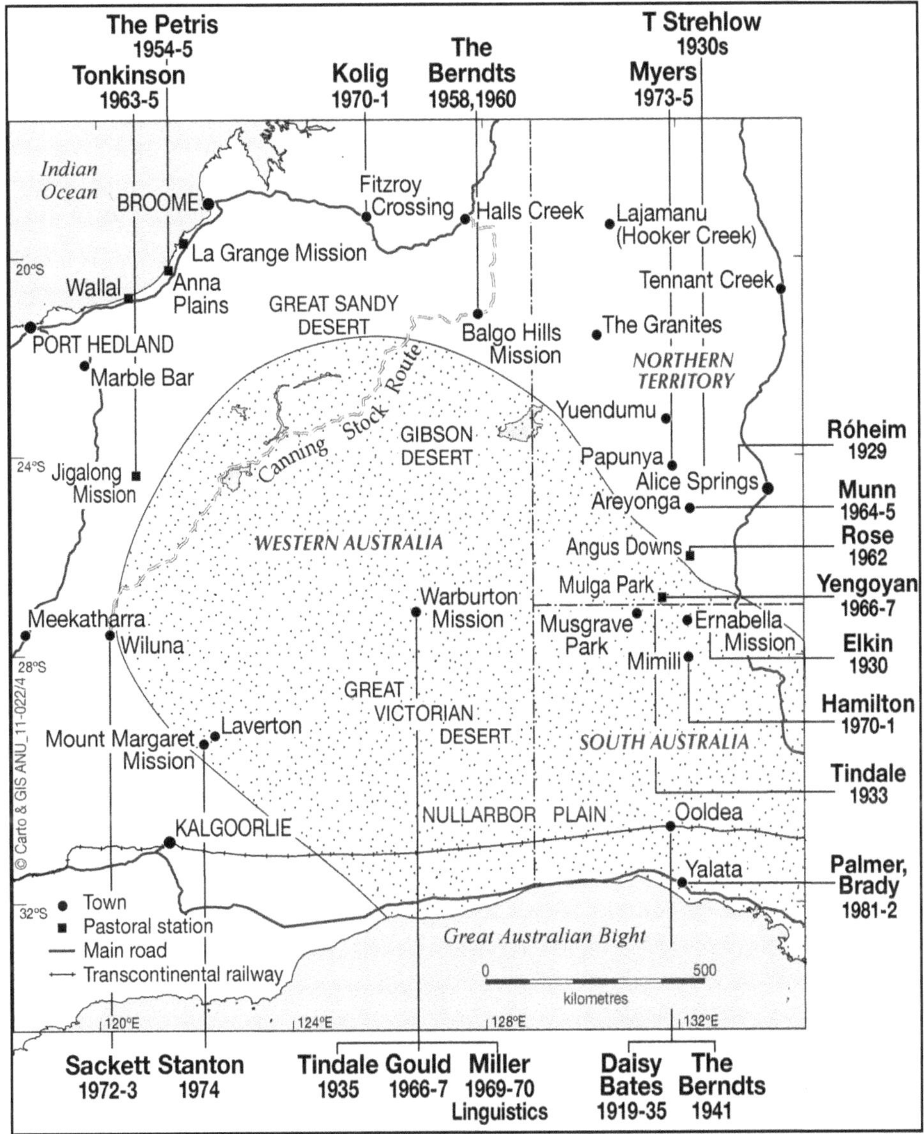

Map 6.2 Selected fieldwork sites of anthropological research on Western Desert peoples

For reasons that will become clearer in the course of this chapter, the claimants in the *De Rose Hill* native title claim should be considered as part of the larger Western Desert cultural bloc. This group of people, who share a language and their original habitation of the vast deserts of inland Australia, has intrigued anthropologists for generations, since they represent Aborigines in an extreme environment and with a comparatively shallow contact history. When, in 1930, Elkin made his extraordinary field trip to the vicinity of the claim area, he travelled beyond settled areas to work with Aboriginal people who were still living an independent, nomadic, hunter-gatherer life, with quite limited contact with white people. In 1933, Tindale's expedition could still film the unclothed natives as they went about their daily routine, travelling from waterhole to waterhole in the Musgrave Ranges. According to Fred Myers (1986:11), the last family moved in from the remote stretches of the Gibson Desert only in 1984.[3] For many anthropologists, the Aborigines living in, or only recently migrated from, the desert provided a privileged window into the pre-contact Aboriginal world. The Western Desert cultural bloc, then, became synonymous with traditionalism. It was also associated, however, with an unusual flexibility of group identification and fluidity of relations to land. As well as openness to new ritual and myth, there is conservatism about compliance with the 'Law'. This juxtaposition suggests a sort of avant-garde traditionalism. Stabilising a group of traditional owners for De Rose Hill Station within this cultural bloc represents an extreme test for forensic anthropology and, thus, a fitting finale to the case studies of this book.

Elkin

The risk of commencing this review with Elkin is the unintended confirmation it gives to professionalised anthropology's myth making about itself as a dramatic break with previous ethnographic investigation. All anthropologists drew on the work of earlier researchers. It is, however, beyond the scope of this chapter to include an account of the encounters of Carl Strehlow, Herbert Basedow, Daisy Bates and Géza Róheim with Western Desert Aborigines.[4]

---

3 A detailed account of the various sightings of Western Desert Aborigines continuing their nomadic life is contained in Peterson and Long's *Aboriginal Territorial Organisation* (1986:100–41).

4 Pastor Carl Strehlow was a Lutheran Missionary at Hermannsburg between 1894 and 1920, during which time he made extensive ethnographic investigations of Aboriginal people on the mission, mainly the Western Arrernte, but also some of their southern neighbours, to whom he referred as the Western and Southern Loritja (see Hill 2002:31–86; Veit 1991). One of the key organising principles of his encyclopedic work 'Die Aranda- und Luritja-Stämme' (Strehlow 1907–20) is the separation of the two culturally distinct groups, Arrernte and Loritja, although the Arrernte tend to take a central place in the comparison. His deep interest in recording myths, but without much reference to the location of places referred to in the myths, makes his work of limited value to this review. Similarly, Géza Róheim's nine months in Central Australia in 1929 enabled his creation of a psychoanalytical anthropology, but little linking of people to land (see Morton 1988). A prospector and science student at Adelaide University, Herbert Basedow was one of the first Europeans to systematically record something of his encounters with Aboriginal people in the vicinity of the claim area as part of the SA Government prospecting expedition in 1903 (Basedow 1904, 1914). Of interest is his reporting of an initiation ceremony being held near the claim area (1914:67) and the unusual names he attributes to the tribes of the area—names that were never used by later researchers. Most of Daisy Bates' ethnographic notes from her time spent tending to the natives at Ooldea between 1919 and 1935 remain on various scraps of paper in her manuscript collection at the National Library of Australia. Her account of her time at Ooldea in *The Passing of the Aborigines* (1938) is useful only in confirming the migration of Aboriginal people from the north to Ooldea. She did have the wit to notice that the kinship terms she obtained were almost identical to the list of kinship terms for the Loritja in Spencer and Gillen's *The Native Tribes of Central Australia* (1899), so Bates could be seen as the first to identify the potential scale of what became known as the Western Desert cultural bloc (see Bates 1918:163).

Elkin's 1930 fieldwork in South Australia continued the short-term survey method of his Kimberley expedition, outlined in Chapter 6. In his accounts of his remarkable journey beyond the newly established sheep stations north-west of Oodnadatta, there is a barely disguised excitement at leaving behind 'settlement', and encountering Aboriginal people 'living in a totally uncivilised manner' (Elkin 1931:45–6). He was accompanied by two (unnamed) local Aboriginal men, who spoke some English. They proceeded by 'bush bashing' along old camel tracks in a truck driven by a prospector (1931:44). His first encounter with the 'wild natives' was at Ernabella Soak in the Musgrave Ranges. The expedition then travelled east, roughly along the South Australia–Northern Territory border, interviewing three small groups of Aboriginal people at three unnamed homesteads on the way, visiting ceremonial grounds, and interviewing more people from the Musgrave Ranges, who were at Finke Siding. Thus he travelled around and probably through the claim area. The genealogical method again yielded detailed accounts of formal kinship, social organisation and totemism (Elkin 1931, 1937, 1939).

Groups

Elkin's painstaking analysis enabled him to identify a large 'Western Group' incorporating a bewildering array of 'tribal' names, and 'characterised by a remarkable unity of language, mythology and social organisation' (1931:60). It included Aboriginal people who were the original inhabitants of vast areas of the interior of Western Australia, northern South Australia and the southern part of the Northern Territory. Although Elkin was clear on the nature of their commonality, he still tended to use the terminology of 'tribe' to identify a dialect group or a broad regional grouping within the 'Western Group'. His own material suggested complex naming practices, which included temporary, contingent names and friendly or derogatory nicknames used by neighbouring groups. But Elkin did not pursue the implications of such naming practices for his own attribution of 'tribe'. He simply suggested that some reported tribes were, in fact, single hordes or groups of hordes. He was more interested in identifying the commonalities of the 'Western Group', which he listed as follows

- an absence of dual organisation, and instead, generational lines that grouped alternative generations together[5]
- a kinship system that was much simpler than that of the surrounding groups
- totemic association with the place of actual birth (rather than, for example, conception)
- belief in the 'Djugur' (Dreaming)

5 Note: his terminology is somewhat confusing here since alternate generation levels are a kind of dual organisation, just in a different form to what was then known (see White 1981).

- belief in a place where all spirit children live
- a pattern of cicatrisation (slightly curved parallel scars on the back of the shoulders) (Elkin 1931:69–71).

He later proposed the term 'the Aluridja Group' instead of 'Western Group', following the Arrernte identification of their southern neighbours.

As with his previous surveys, here, the 'horde' is assumed, without explanation, to be the indestructible atom of social organisation and traditional land tenure (1939:203).

Traditional laws and customs

Despite his own observations that reported tribal names as often being dialect or horde names, or convenient nicknames, Elkin persisted with the terminology of 'tribe' to map broad locations, as demonstrated on the following sketch map (Map 6.3).

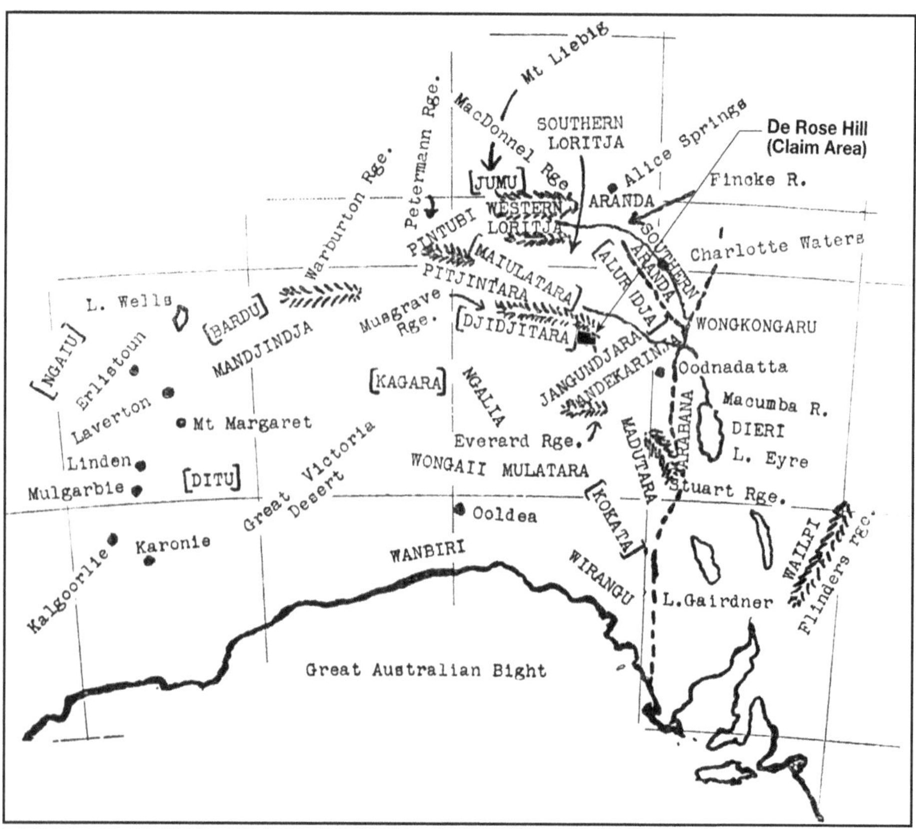

Map 6.3 The location of De Rose Hill Station on Elkin's sketch map of Western Desert tribal areas

Source: Elkin (1939:202).

This sketch map would locate De Rose Hill Station in the vicinity of Elkin's Andekarinja (today's Antakirinya) and Jangundjara (today's Yankunytjatjara). But Elkin never explained exactly what he intended to convey by his map. Perhaps it was simply a pragmatic simplification for the purposes of introducing the region, using some existing terminology. His preoccupation with formal kinship, social organisation and totemism did eventually lead to a brief consideration of local organisation via marriage rules. According to Elkin, marriage rules included a rule of local exogamy based on local 'country', which he equated with 'horde' (1939:218–19). Throughout his discussion, Elkin assumed a definitive horde country, circumscribed by ecological imperatives: 'one never asks the name of a person's camp or *ngura* but of his water, *kapi*. Man is tied from his birth to his death to the rockholes and soaks, and to the tracks between them, and so too were the heroes of mythology' (1931:49).

Here we see the tentative beginnings of economic-determinist and ecological-adaptation explanatory approaches that inevitably become part of anthropology's attempt to theorise the cultural effects of the extreme physical conditions of the desert.

Change

The theme of historical transformation was also provoked by the long-distance migrations of Western Desert people out of their original homelands. Generally speaking, this migration was seen as a methodological problem in reconstructing the pre-contact past, but occasionally it led to attempts to imagine its cultural implications, as in:

> [T]he Aborigines of western South Australia have been in a continuous state of migration southwards for some decades; a movement which I believe was in progress before the coming of the white man. This explains the similarities of dialects, kinship systems and mythology over such a vast area, and also the difficulty of fixing definite tribal boundaries and names. (Elkin 1939:203)

Closely related to the theme of historical transformation was the appearance of what we would now call rational choice explanations, within accounts dominated by structural functionalism. Thus we have Elkin also explaining the migrations in terms of Western Desert people taking over the more hospitable country of neighbouring tribes on the fringes of white settlement when those tribes die out (Elkin 1931:49).

Tindale

After Elkin, the next scientific recorder of Aboriginal people in the vicinity of De Rose Hill was Norman Tindale, who participated in the joint University of Adelaide–SA Museum Anthropological Expeditions to the Musgrave Ranges, Ooldea and the Warburton Range in 1933, 1934 and 1935.[6] Placing Tindale within Australianist anthropology requires the characterisation of the field given in Chapter 1 to be modified somewhat. For Tindale held various positions at the SA Museum, commencing in 1919 as an entomologist, but he eventually assumed responsibility as an 'ethnologist' (Bicchieri 1972:217). What were his original academic qualifications in America remains unclear, although at some point he received a Bachelor of Science degree at the University of Adelaide. If he can be claimed for anthropology, it would be anthropology in the American sense of the four pillars of anthropology, encompassing physical anthropology, archaeology, cultural anthropology and linguistics.

His formal qualifications and his diverse publication record, which covers botany, geology and archaeology, indicate that his approach to social anthropology would be steeped in the methods and assumptions of the physical sciences. His institutional security at the SA Museum preceded the institutional security of social anthropology at Sydney University. That security could be seen as providing some competition with Radcliffe-Brown and Elkin at Sydney University in the search for American funding and conducting research in remote areas. Birdsell, Tindale's friend and collaborator, added credence to this sense of competitiveness during the local organisation debate by labelling those who questioned Radcliffe-Brown's model as 'the Sydney school' (Birdsell 1970).[7] The perceptions of a polarisation between Adelaide and Sydney around personalities and disciplinary backgrounds seems to have become so pervasive in anthropology's own folklore that Ronald Berndt felt he had to respond to it in his 1982 reflection on the first 50 years of anthropology in Australia (Berndt 1982:50). He identified the perception as competition between the professionals (fully qualified social anthropologists at Sydney University: Radcliffe-Brown, Elkin and his students) and the amateurs (the physical scientists and fieldworkers centred on the Adelaide Museum: Tindale, Mountford).

Despite this mild competition, Tindale was always respectful of Elkin's work and seems to have had no problem in having his own work published in *Oceania* and obtaining some supplementary expedition funding from the Australian National Research Council—Elkin's domain. Respect for Elkin's protégés, Ronald and Catherine Berndt, was another matter, as we shall see below.

6 See Tindale (1934, 1935, 1936, 1937); and Jones (1987).

7 He included Elkin, Hiatt, Meggitt and Berndt in 'the Sydney School'.

Groups

The enduring theme of Tindale's published work on the Western Desert was his unshakable belief in the tribe, traditional tribal territory and the sociological reality of tribal boundaries. This belief distinguished him from Radcliffe-Brown's dismissiveness of 'tribe' as a mere collection of hordes and of little significance to traditional local organisation. It also distinguished him from Elkin, who tended to use tribal names as convenient approximations. For Tindale, tribal boundaries were clear and would be defended by the members of the tribe.

Yet Tindale simultaneously adopted Radcliffe-Brown's terminology of the 'horde', and usually in a way consistent with the minimal, landowning and land-exploiting group (see, for example, Tindale 1972:224). His apparent acceptance of horde theory might explain his lack of interest in testing it among the people still living a nomadic life in the Musgrave Ranges. For whatever reason, neither Tindale nor Elkin sought to ask where their informants had just been and who exactly constituted the group on those journeys and at the various camping places.[8] Their interests lay elsewhere.

In his 1972 synthesis of his Pitjantjatjara material for the collection *Hunters and Gatherers Today*, Tindale revealed for the first time an intermediate grouping between the tribe and the horde: 'named regional units', which occupied certain areas within the tribal territory in non-drought times of the year. He named five such regional groupings (Kurujulta, Maiulatara, Wirtjapakandja, Pibiri and Mulatara), but he rather confusingly concluded that they were not true sub-tribal groupings, but generalised names associated with smaller regional groups within the whole tribal area (1972:227–8).

Tindale never explored the relationship between his hordes, his regional groups and his tribes. His presentation is suggestive of a nested hierarchy. The meaning of 'tribe' and its sociological implications are nowhere given a systematic treatment, save belatedly in his magnum opus at the end of his career in 1974. This is surprising given that one of his lifelong projects was a comprehensive tribal map of the whole of Australia and that he used the concept of 'tribe' for other analytical purposes, such as his analysis of intertribal marriage (Tindale 1953).

There are probably two reasons Tindale thought it plausible that tribes occupied discrete areas of the Western Desert: ecological and physical constraints, and Aboriginal self-identification at the level of dialect. With some justification, he imagined desert people as if they were in an ecological trap, which annually shrank to a few permanent waterholes in dry times, and expanded in times of

8 Later researchers did embark on this fine-grained reconstruction through questioning older informants about the details of journeys in their previous nomadic life: see Myers (1986); and Yengoyan (1970).

higher rainfall to a larger circuit of relatively ephemeral water sources within the tribal territory, when 'everywhere is camp'.[9] Thus, apart from affective ties to one's own totemic waterhole and the fear of the sorcery and savagery of distant strangers, it was physically difficult to walk out of a tribal territory because of the general scarcity of reliable water sources and the vast distances. Tindale never expressed the effects of the ecological constraints so bluntly. But expressing the effect of the ecological constraints in this way allows us to see more clearly how such approaches can de-emphasise the wider networks based on commonalities of language, kinship, shared Dreamings and ritual. Activating such networks could easily have opened up a much larger area of land for survival.

Tindale's published work never explained exactly how his informants spoke about dialect identity and traditional territory. To be fair, Tindale was a meticulous recorder of certain kinds of details. But whether his informants ever said words to the effect of 'I am Pitjantjatjara and the extent of Pitjantjatjara tribal territory is…', we will never know. Tindale's own material suggests that they said 'I am Pitjantjatjara and my waterhole is…'. Perhaps, because of his strong assumptions about tribal territory, he never explored how dialect identity related to other possible ways of self-identification and the range of practices for naming groups. Tindale was certainly aware of a variety of group-naming practices throughout Australia. But these were elaborated only to demonstrate that Tindale believed, with proper scientific methodology and knowledge, it was possible to winnow past mistakes from true tribal names (see Tindale 1974). He apparently did not explore the relationship between language competence and personal identity, or whether there was any direct identification in myth and song between country and dialect.[10]

On Tindale's information, the area now covered by the De Rose Hill Station was in the pre-contact territory of the Antakirinja tribe (see Map 6.4).

Change

As could be expected from the terms of Tindale's grand reconstruction project, his account of change tended to emphasise demographic movements resulting from basic environmental factors, expressed at the level of tribal identification. For example, in his catalogue of tribes, under Jangkundjara, he states:

> In 1917 (dated by the annular eclipse of 30 July 1916) a portion of the tribe moved south to Ooldea in company with a few Antakirinja at the end of a major drought, under threat of the attacks of Pitjandjara; their western and northern areas are now usurped by Pitjandjara. (1974:212)

9 Sutton described this seasonal expansion and contraction as a pulsating movement (see Sutton 1990).

10 See Merlan (1981); and Rumsey (1989).

The idea of Yankunytjatjara and Pitjantjatjara hostilities about this time was originally reported by Tindale in 1940, and was recycled by later anthropologists such as Berndt (1941:5). Other anthropologists reported confirmation of the story from their informants.[11] The idea of usurpation, based on Tindale's theorising about tribal territories and oral histories taken during his fieldwork, was to become extremely significant to the lawyers opposing the *De Rose Hill* claim.

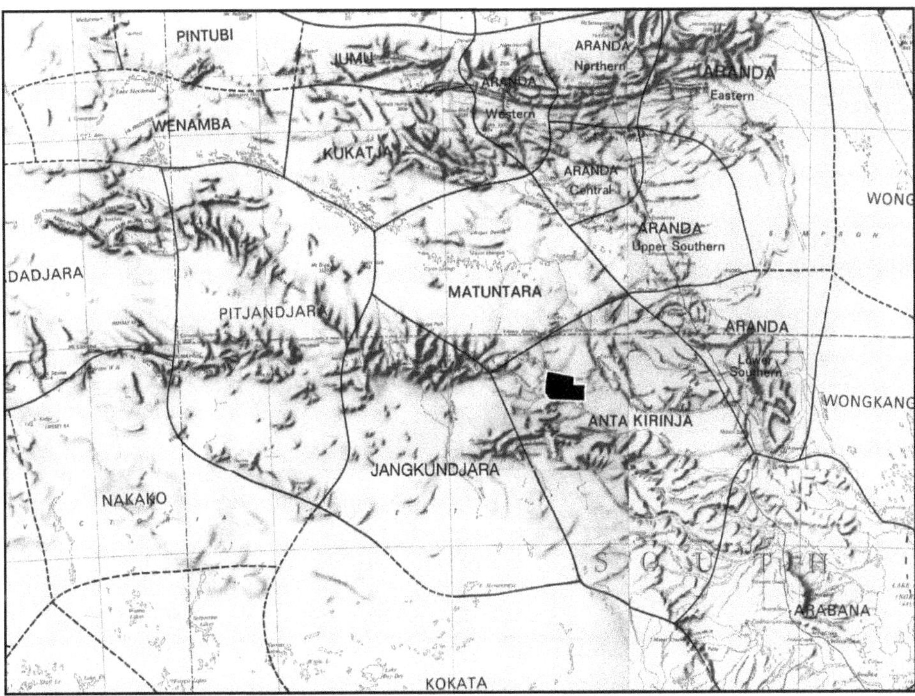

Map 6.4 The location of De Rose Hill Station on Tindale's tribal map

Source: Tindale (1974).

The Berndts

Ronald and Catherine Berndt were academic protégés of Elkin. They did their first fieldwork together at Ooldea Soak in 1941 (for six months), after Ronald's preliminary work there in 1939.[12] Most of the Aboriginal residents at the time originally came from the vicinity of the claim area and identified themselves as 'Antakirinja'. The published reports of this fieldwork deferred to Elkin's

11 See Hamilton (1979:5); and Vachon (1982:487, endnote 9). In *Aboriginal Tribes of Australia*, Tindale also made a cryptic reference, under the heading 'Antakirinja', to even earlier Antakirinya movements associated with violence: 'Earlier movement was from west after massacre by them of some previous inhabitants of Mount Chandler district; they are closely related to the Jangkundjara' (1974:210).

12 For an outline of their careers, see Sutton (2001).

description of kinship and social organisation, and tried to cover what was left: history, myth, ritual and their current circumstances (Berndt 1941; Berndt and Berndt 1945).

Like Elkin, the Berndts refer to 'tribal' units, notwithstanding their own evidence of historically contextualised, disposable group names such as 'railway mob' to refer to those who had moved out of the desert when the transcontinental railway was being constructed, and crosscutting broad topographical identifications such as 'spinifex people' for those who had come from the desert sand dunes to the west and south of the Petermann Range.[13] It was perhaps assumed that there was a rigid distinction between these kinds of naming practices and traditional-sounding names. Like Elkin, they defined as a cultural bloc a population sharing a common language, kinship system, myths and rituals, including, it was revealed, a travelling collection of sacred objects and relics that moved through the whole Western Desert region (1945:134–40).[14] Yet, it was not until 1959 that Berndt seriously questioned the use of 'tribe' in the Western Desert (Berndt 1959). In their earlier reports on fieldwork, he had generally equated the level of the 'tribe' with a dialect group. Uncertainty about just what degree of cohesion and territoriality was intended by their use of the term 'tribe' makes it difficult, however, to assess some of their interim assertions. Land tenure is touched on with a specific denial of the relevance of the tribe, confirming Elkin's assertion of a strong link to place of birth:

> A tribal area is ever varying, although a group of people do, through the passing of many years, become associated with a particular stretch of country...mentioning the water-hole at which he was born a native will say, 'That's my "gabi" there, my country'—and he is not very interested in the tribal names. It is these people within a certain stretch of country, associated intimately with one totemic gabi who constitute the group. Nearby are other people just as intimately associated with their own water-holes, they also are groups. Each group is the guardian of a particular section of a great religious myth associated with the physiographic sites. (Berndt and Berndt 1945:23)[15]

Berndt's 1959 challenge to the applicability of the concept of tribe in the Western Desert represents one of the first examples of the way in which Western Desert ethnography has provoked Australianist anthropology to a heightened reflexivity about theoretical constructs. These constructs, which were originally developed in other regions, proved to be inadequate to explain Western Desert peoples and recall Barnes' earlier objections to African models in the New

13 As to the longevity of the name 'spinifex people', see Scott Cane's book of the same name (Cane 2002).

14 Originally published in *Oceania* (vol. 14:32–8).

15 Originally published in *Oceania* (vol. 12, no. 4:327).

Guinea Highlands (Barnes 1962). Berndt's sustained analysis in his paper was a marked departure from his usual reporting of data. It was a direct challenge to Tindale in arguing that there was no sociological reality corresponding with a dialect-identified tribe, that there were no strict boundaries within the Western Desert cultural bloc, and that movements of so-called 'tribes' were relatively frequent.

These assertions were based on

- a review of the wide variation in the naming and locating of 'tribes' by successive researchers (Elkin, Tindale and the Berndts themselves)
- the Berndts' experience of the widespread practice among Western Desert Aborigines of identifying with more than one dialect name
- a review of the evidence and conceptualisation of observed social groups that revealed that membership of the clan, the horde and the totemic lodge were in no way dependent on prior membership of a dialect group (Berndt 1959:83–93).

He concluded by suggesting that the maximal, face-to-face, functional grouping in the Western Desert could be called a 'society'. It would be defined as a group with sustained interaction between its members, possessing broadly common aims and with effective and consistent communication between them (1959:105). This group would include a variety of clans, hordes and dialect units.

Berndt's article was seminal in some respects, but it was limited in others. Notwithstanding his willingness to countenance the likelihood that the observed movements of dialect-identified groups also occurred in the pre-contact past (1959:89), he shared Tindale's belief in a relatively stable association between people and country. It was only that, for Berndt, the pre-contact stability occurred at the level of the local patrilineal descent group, tied by birth to a particular waterhole, not at the level of Tindale's 'tribe' (also see Berndt 1972).

At the end of the article, Berndt suggested that his critique of the supposed territorial stability of dialect groups could be used in other regions of Australia to re-examine groups identified as tribes. But reanalysis in the other direction—of the assumed stability of local groups—was not considered. It was as if there was a need for a stable building block—an atomic social unit. The splitting of this atom did not occur systematically in Western Desert studies until Yengoyan's 1970 reconstruction of constantly recombining local groups and Myers' pioneering work on the individual land affiliation among the Pintupi (see below).

Following Berndt's 1959 challenge to the notion of the tribe in the Western Desert, Tindale made a belated response, in 1974, in *Aboriginal Tribes of*

Australia, in which he finally adopted Elkin's fivefold definition of tribe (1974:115).[16] Despite having had so long to formulate it, Tindale's response does not engage with Berndt's arguments in any detailed way and, infuriatingly, seems to miss the point altogether by questioning the accuracy of Berndt's tribal names. Overall, Tindale dismissed Berndt's argument as a reading back into pre-contact history the complexities and confusions that, in his view, resulted from culture contact. It can be noted that this is the same rhetorical strategy that Elkin used against Piddington's challenge to horde orthodoxy: the deflecting of conceptual challenges into assumed historical transformation from ancient stability and simplicity into contemporary, degenerate complexity and fluidity.

Strehlow

Barry Hill's comprehensive biography of Strehlow, *Broken Song* (Hill 2002), suggests that his life's work was to demonstrate the profound 'literary' qualities of Arrernte songs through translation. This theme was always in tension with Arrernte ethnography, which had its home in anthropology, where Strehlow was an academic outsider. Nevertheless, anthropology held great potential for Strehlow to acquire 'scientific capital' given his fluency in Arrernte and his long-term contact with Arrernte people. He was born at Hermannsburg and spent his childhood there (1908–22). He had also conducted field research for his doctorate on the Arrernte language (1932–33), as well as during his work as the first patrol officer in Central Australia working for the Department of Native Affairs (1936–41), and in various research capacities after that.

His awareness of his outsider status is revealed in his considerations of Western Desert culture (Strehlow 1965, 1970). There, he deferred completely to Berndt and Meggitt on 'the relationship between local groups, the dialectical units, the hordes, and so on' (1965:127). One also senses that he might not have completely mastered the anthropological literature, since he alone included the Warlpiri as part of the Western Desert cultural bloc and seemed to have misunderstood anthropological theorising about moieties, sections and subsections; he seemed to think that it implied moieties, sections and subsections were separate kin groups or residential groups (1965:125, 134).

16 Elkin's definition as summarised by Tindale is that they

a) inhabit and claim a definite area of country

b) use a dialect or language peculiar to themselves

c) possess a distinctive name

d) have customs and laws differing in some measure from those practised by their neighbours

e) possess beliefs and ceremonies differing from those held or performed by others (see Elkin 1943:57).

The aim of the 1965 article was to make a broad ecological and cultural comparison of the Western Arrernte and their southern Western Desert neighbours, the Loritja, as the basis for a consideration of the ecological determinants of cultural forms. In this comparison, we find some familiar themes: the extreme environment, hunting skill, the 'weakness' of the section system, and the importance of the traditions relating to the wanderings of totemic ancestors. But there are also some new themes. Strehlow was keen to emphasise the strong emotional attachment of the Loritja to their own local group area and a norm of hospitality, which was more than delayed self-interest, rather 'an inescapable obligation laid on the hosts by immemorial "tribal" tradition' (1965:128). More significant, though, is the thematising, for the first time, of the relative openness of the Western Desert peoples to new cultural forms despite a strong ideology of cultural conservatism:

> Unhindered by the rigidity of outlook that results from centuries of residence within safe hunting grounds, the Western Desert people borrowed religious concepts, social norms, and artistic practices freely, even if the extent of their borrowings was often limited, and adversely affected by their material poverty. They also diffused these borrowings to tribes living on the coastal periphery of the Western Desert area, as the writings of Elkin, the Berndts, Worms, and others have shown. (1965:31)

Perhaps the most innovative aspect of Strehlow's article, for present purposes, was the use of his linguistic prowess to interpret the cultural and ecological differences embedded in the geographically anchored songs of long-distance Dreaming tracks—in this case, the *tjilpa* (native cat) track from Port Augusta, north through Central Australia and beyond. At a precise geographical point referred to in the song cycle, as recounted by Strehlow's Yankunytjatjara informant, the *tjilpa* ancestral heroes begin to address each other in Arrernte skin names, and looking back to the south they say, 'Stay on, covered by night,—you who do not have any form of address'; then they create a barrier of sandhills:

> In other words, the Central Australian subsection and class systems were *based on the land itself*: for it was the same wandering horde of ancestral beings which had validated the 'classless' kin-grouping system of the Western Desert groups south of the sandhills barrier that marked the Aranda–Matuntara border. (1965:134)

This passage is suggestive of further research that could have been undertaken on the sociological reality of Tindale's proposed tribal boundaries within the Western Desert bloc (cf. Merlan 1981; Rumsey 1989).

Hill demonstrates that Strehlow was writing a grand epitaph for the Arrernte, and there is something of this theme of terminal degeneration in the few passages to address historical transformation of the Western Desert people:

> I am, of course, writing in the past tense. Within the past twenty-five years most of the tough but lovable inhabitants of the Western Desert regions have gone to stations and government settlements on the fringes of their former homelands. Droughts no longer have the same menace for their descendants. But far too many of the young folk have lost the pride, the purposeful energy, and the independence of spirit of their elders; and with them has departed the ready capacity for laughter. (1965:132)

Tonkinson

Robert Tonkinson, a student of the Berndts, was the first anthropologist to do sustained, long-term fieldwork, approaching the Malinowskian ideal, among Aborigines in the Western Desert bloc. Between 1963 and 1970, he spent a total of 16 months at Jigalong and made five brief field trips deep into the Western Desert for the Department of Native Affairs, contacting some of the remaining nomads (Tonkinson 1974:9–10). His most intensive work at Jigalong was in 1963–66 for his MA thesis (Tonkinson 1966). At that time, Jigalong, which had been established as a small depot station for the Canning Stock Route and later for the rabbit-proof fence, was a mission station run by a small Christian fundamentalist sect. They had been spectacularly unsuccessful at converting the 200 or so Mandjildjara and Gadujara people, who had been coming in from their nomadic life in the desert to the east.

Tonkinson pursued two broad directions in his research and writing: reconstruction of the pre-contact situation and culture contact. Later, he introduced a comparative perspective from his fieldwork in Vanuatu. *The Jigalong Mob* (Tonkinson 1974), his first published culture contact study, could also be considered one of the first 'community studies' exploring the formation of a new Aboriginal social unit and the interaction of the Aboriginal people and the resident whites.[17] Tonkinson was caught in the middle, passing messages between the mission and the Aboriginal camp. In his reconstruction study, *The Mardudjara Aborigines* (Tonkinson 1978, revised 1990), he aimed for comprehensiveness in the range of topics covered, like Meggitt's *Desert People*. He has maintained intermittent contact with the community throughout his career, reporting and analysing changes up to the present.

17 Compare with the 'new-type grouping' in Petri and Petri-Odermann (1970).

Tonkinson had great success in converting his 'scientific capital' into academic capital through the arc of his career, which eventually saw him replacing Ronald Berndt as the Chair of Anthropology at the University of Western Australia in 1985. There was no symbolic patricide here, but tutelage, patronage and the bonds of mutual respect and affection.[18] Tonkinson also played a continuing leadership role in the Australian Institute of Aboriginal and Torres Strait Islander Studies.

Groups

Tonkinson made repeated modifications to his presentation of 'local organisation' from his MA thesis in 1966 to the revised version of *The Mardudjara Aborigines* in 1990. These modifications were made in dialogue with the intensification of the local organisation debate within Australianist anthropology. In his earliest work (Tonkinson 1966, 1974), he was content to identify himself with Berndt's 1959 critique of the 'tribe' and with Stanner's 1965 distinction between estate (area of main religious connection) and range (larger area of economic exploitation). In his later work, however, he abandoned the terminology of 'horde', 'local descent group' and 'clan' in favour of the more precisely defined 'family' (nuclear family plus additional wives), 'band' (actual land-exploiting group, avoiding the ambiguities of 'horde'), and the Stanner-inspired 'estate-group' (Tonkinson 1978, 1990). The 'estate-group' replaced the previous 'clan' and Berndt's 'local descent group' and Radcliffe-Brown's 'horde' with the concept of an overlapping, loosely defined group that consists of a core of patrilineally related men and women, with the primary, but non-exclusive, religious rights to the sacra of a particular area, based on one or several sacred sites (1990:67).

Tonkinson also modified Berndt's 'language unit' to a 'dialect-named unit' (1990:66), and reference is made to Rumsey's assertion of a direct link between language and country (Rumsey 1989). Tonkinson's discussion of this possibility is a little unclear. For on the one hand, his general reconstruction of 'Mardu' territory (for example, in Tonkinson 1990:12–13) associates dialect groups and tracts of land, even for dialects that no longer have speakers. On the other hand, he tends to deny a direct link with country, at the level of dialect, because people usually identify themselves at the more specific level of major waterhole–totemic site and describe regions in terms of clusters of sites, not tracts of land. This lack of clarity—perhaps a by-product of the reworking of an already condensed account—might also be an attempt to avoid resurrecting and dealing with Tindale's defined tribal territories at the level of dialect group.

18 See Tonkinson (2002); Tonkinson and Howard (1990); and Tonkinson and Tonkinson (1991).

Despite the refinements of terminology, there is also a sense of unease in the presentation, as if it is going against the grain of the Mardu perspective: 'Not surprisingly, considering the great uncertainty of rainfall in their homelands, Mardu local organisation is notable for its flexibility and fluidity and the lack of stress on boundaries and exclusiveness of group membership' (1990:65).[19]

Tonkinson illustrates the relative fluidity of his 'estate-group' by describing one such group: the estate-group whose 'main place' is Giinyu. There is an elaborate dingo myth associated with Giinyu, which is also linked to the comprehensive, long-distance Dingari Dreamings. The several families making up the bands associated with this focal place were referred to by others as the 'dingo mob' and were all closely related in the male line, although apparently not all were born at Giinyu or had their conception site there. Individuals are not named, but Tonkinson suggests the nature of individual claims in terms of other 'criteria for membership' of the estate-group. These include: descent from mother or father who is acknowledged to be from that place; circumcision at Giinyu; or participation in the Midayindi revelatory ritual.[20]

He explains: 'Obviously, the more of these criteria that coincide, the stronger the primary attachment, but because the full congruence is rare, every individual is entitled to membership in more than one estate-group through bonds of shared spirit and substance' (1978:52).[21]

Tonkinson then goes on to explain that the main religious responsibilities of the estate-group are to ensure the safety and integrity of the sacred objects stored near the main site (in the pre-contact era), and to lead the 'Yinirari' (dingo Dreaming ritual) and increase rituals associated with the site. So it becomes apparent that the corporate-ness of the estate-group revolves around the acknowledgment by others of the group's custodianship of sacra and the group's actual performance of associated ritual. But the multiple pathways to such custodianship and performance, and multiple pathways to other estate-groups, would seem to make the corporate-ness of an estate inherently unstable, and perhaps fleeting. It would be unstable in the sense of having no simple formula as the criteria for membership, and fleeting, in the sense of acting jointly only in the actual performance of ritual, which in turn depends on the available performers and a host of other practical contingencies. Tonkinson suggests the possibility of group instability and fleeting corporate action when he switches to the perspective of anonymous individuals at the end of his explanatory

19 And later, in relation to the estate-group, he states: 'Like the larger dialect-named unit, the entity here referred to as "the estate-group" has no reality as an exclusive, on-the-ground collectivity, so it can be difficult to identify' (1990:67).

20 Compare with the *midedi* feast of Chapter 4.

21 The idea of the sharing of 'substance' is never elaborated by Tonkinson. A similar idea of the sharing of the spirit essences of the Dreaming (*kuranitja*), including through eating food imbued with such essences, was to play a part in the *De Rose Hill* claim through the evidence of Jon Willis (see next chapter).

example: 'Because of the existence of multiple criteria of attachment to estate, no two Giinyu people name exactly the same set of sites when asked for their *manda* ("country"). Every individual imbues some places with special meanings and significances that are not shared by many others' (1978:53).

That pregnant sentence, which seems to largely undermine the notion of a stable estate-group, is left hanging with a footnote reference to Myers' more individualist approach to the same question (see below).

Laws

The bulk of Tonkinson's research and writing was conducted well before the native title era, and thus there is little explicit theorising about traditional laws and customs relating to land, although his criteria for membership of an estate-group would have been a starting point. Like many Western Desert researchers, he did occasionally comment on the Aboriginal adoption of the word 'law' to describe aspects of their traditional culture. Tonkinson thought that they saw it as an appropriate way to describe their Dreaming because of similar notions of 'obedience to a set of powerful dictates, and of punishment for non-conformity' (Tonkinson 1988:409, endnote 2).

Change

Tonkinson's writing about change is very reminiscent of Beckett's. There is the intimately observed period of fieldwork in the early to mid 1960s, then accounts of observable changes gained from shorter periods of later, intermittent fieldwork. Typically, this enables him to construct broad comparisons between: 1) the pre-contact era based on his own reconstructions; 2) the mission era; and 3) the period of his later visits. His sustained period of involvement also meant that, towards the end of his career, he could provide a condensed narrative of the broad sweep of history of the Jigalong mob over a 50-year period.[22] There is, however, little explicit theorising about change of traditional land tenure.

22 Briefly, it covered the emergence of the 'Jigalong Mob' and Jigalong as a law centre and focus for regional ceremonies (the annual 'big meetings'); the end of the mission and, with the imposition of community self-management regimes, the breaking down of a clear distinction between a Blackfella and a Whitefella domain that had previously assured their independence; competition with the so-called Pindan (socialist–traditionalist) movement; the fragmentation of the Jigalong Mob along the dialect lines to Strelley and outstations; concerns about the threat of mining to sacred sites; the rise of a regional land council and the surprising re-emergence of Warnman identity based on the outstation in country previously associated with Warnman; and increased funding and competition for resources (see, for example, Tonkinson 1996). Tonkinson also undertook a major retrospective in 2007, of course, well after the *De Rose Hill* hearing (Tonkinson 2007).

Hamilton

Annette Hamilton undertook long-term fieldwork at Everard Park Station (Mimili) in 1970–71 (see Hamilton 1979). The main focus of her research was the implication of sex segregation in economic and ritual activities, especially from an Aboriginal woman's perspective. In 1982, however, she published a surprisingly inconclusive contribution to the local organisation debate (Hamilton 1982b). Referring to Tindale and Berndt, she states:

> Both writers have been in the field intermittently but frequently since the thirties (Tindale) and early forties (Berndt). There is no reason to assume bad faith on either of their parts; they are both careful and meticulous scholars, they are both familiar with Western Desert languages, they are both interested in 'the truth' about Aboriginal local organisation. Why then should there be this disparity?
>
> In my own fieldwork I fluctuated between their two views. Berndt's reconstructions made intuitive sense, in the social context of the area where I was working. Nonetheless people repeatedly referred to the Everards [Ranges] as 'Janggundjara' [Yankunytjatjara] in everyday contexts, contrasting the area with Amata and Ernabella, which they said were 'Bidjandjarra'. In addition they referred to people as having one or other language, and they did indeed seem to refer to an idea of 'ngura'. (1982b:96–7)

Hamilton attempted to make some headway towards a resolution of the two positions by inquiring into the social use of dialect names. I would summarise her account as saying that her informants used dialect names in different contexts to expand or contract inclusiveness—that is, to emphasise commonality of identity or alternatively to emphasise difference. From this observation, she derives the notion of there being only a de facto relationship between a tract of land and resident people who grew up learning and identifying with one dialect. Unfortunately, she does not explore whether the dialect–land identifications are reflected in song cycles that traverse large areas.

Her interpretation of the social meaning of dialect identity would seem to align her with Berndt's formulation, but she is sceptical about his stretching of the concept of ownership. She asks 'in what sense is it "land-owning" if others have free access to the land and there are no boundaries' (1982b:99). She also noted in Berndt's account an unresolved ambiguity about how one becomes a member of a local group—by birth at a particular place or by being fathered by a person who already has totemic association with a particular place. She wondered about the inherent improbability, even in a pre-contact situation, of fathers' and sons' birthplaces overlapping. For Hamilton, this and other evidence of men seeking spouses on the same Dreaming track indicate the primacy of place of birth and question the validity of Berndt's identification of the local group as a 'patrilineal descent group'. More important, in her view, is the symbolic descent from the totemic ancestors that depends on place of birth.

In conclusion, Hamilton suggested that it might be heuristic to conceptualise the system of land affiliation as having been in a state of transformation in pre-contact times and to imagine 'the system as it was straining to become'. The internal contradictions to be resolved are between a place-based and a father-based system of defining rights to ritual property.

Hamilton suggests that the impetus for her imagined pressure for transformation is the attempt by Aboriginal men to find more secure ways of ensuring the transmission of rights to ritual property from father to son (1982b:106). Why mothers would not also equally support this attempt is not explored. What is hinted at, but still quite problematic, is a contradiction between the economic base and superstructure: the power of men to exploit the labour of women.[23] Thus a move to patrifiliation is a pre-emptive attempt by men to block the potentially disruptive economic power of women: 'There is the possibility that the shift to an ideology of patrifiliation is a de facto, although covert, method of removing any ambiguities regarding the father–son transmission of identity which might be introduced by the mother's choice of birth-site for her child' (1982b:102).

Again, there are problems of how this 'objective' exploitation would ever become part of an explicit ideology or motivating force, if men and women shared strongly held views about the reproduction of the religious sphere—for example, that men's religious activity was sustaining them and their whole world, not exploiting them.[24]

One of the interesting features of Hamilton's contribution to the local organisation debate was her challenge to the utility of Stanner's distinction between religious and economic groups, in his attempted resolution of the debate in terms of estate (religious) and range (economic). She suggested that, in tribal societies, it is better to consider the religious sphere to be all encompassing and determining of other spheres of activity, and, thus, it is more profitable to consider differentiations within the religious sphere rather than make global, categorical distinctions between religious and economic spheres.

23 Unfortunately, she does not refer to the seminal article by Bern (1979) and the ensuing debate.

24 It is interesting to note that Elkin covered similar ground by simply asserting the historical explanation that the process of sedentarisation away from home country would lead to re-emphasising patrilineal descent as opposed to local descent.

Myers

During 1973–75, and intermittently since then, Fred Myers has conducted fieldwork among Western Desert people who referred to themselves as Pintupi. They had migrated or had been moved east to Haasts Bluff, then Papunya, then smaller settlements near Papunya (Yayayi and New Bore) and finally, in the 1980s, they returned to the west at Kintore and Kiwirrkurra, closer to their home country. His thesis (1976) and numerous articles (Myers 1980a, 1980b, 1982) culminated in the book *Pintupi Country, Pintupi Self: Sentiment, Place and Politics Among Western Desert Aborigines* (1986). The articles and the book were, with one notable exception, very well received within Australianist anthropology as original and penetrating.[25] Peterson described the book as an instant classic.[26] Its articulation of a central tension between individual autonomy and relatedness in Aboriginal societies was adopted by numerous others as an overarching framework. There were also rumours that some researchers, who had been labouring for a long time on similar Western Desert material, gave up because Myers had finally 'cracked it'. Even the dissenting voices were admiring of some of his insights (Michaels 1987; Rose 1987).

The main dissident, Eric Michaels, appeared to be questioning the ethics and intellectual integrity of holistic ethnography in the light of recent anti-colonial and postmodern critiques (Michaels 1987). Any contemporary ethnography could have been subjected to much the same critique, but the stakes in 'scientific' and academic capital for both parties were higher because of the prestige of the book within the specialisation. Myers' furious response was understandable (Myers 1987). The Michaels critique seems to have had little effect on the process of Myers converting his 'scientific capital' to academic capital. Myers was eventually appointed to the Chair of Anthropology at New York University and, having been present at the very beginnings of the Western Desert art movement, he was ideally placed to take advantage of the enlarged international profile of Western Desert art and renewed interest in the anthropology of art and material culture generally (Myers 2002).

Groups, laws relating to land

Unlike Tonkinson, Myers explicitly thematised ownership of land and movable property. Part of his defence of the ethics of his work was that a holistic account would be of greater benefit to the Pintupi in land claims. It is, however, easy to see from Myers' exploration of the Pintupi view and his constant use of 'ownership' in quotation marks that Pintupi concepts of ownership are far removed from, and even antithetical to, European notions of stability, exclusivity and precision.

25 See, for example, Morton (1987); Munn (1987); and Sutton (1987).

26 Personal communication, 1996.

There is a seductive power in Myers' writing that flows from his unique synthesis of what I would call a phenomenological sensibility, and the more typical analytical tools and categories of anthropological theory: local organisation, kinship, life cycle, economy and religion. Additional communicative force is added by his writing strategy of encapsulating his syntheses in pithy phrases or key Aboriginal concepts such as 'always ask', '*ngura*' (country), 'one countrymen', 'relatedness and differentiation' and '*kanyininpa*' (looking after, holding). This power continues up to the present day and is exemplified by Ralph Folds' critique of Aboriginal welfare policy towards the Pintupi in *Crossed Purposes* (Folds 2001) and Brian McCoy's examination of the health of Aboriginal men at Balgo (McCoy 2008). Folds in particular falls on *Pintupi Country, Pintupi Self* like a hungry man falling upon a feast. It seems to block out any original insight into the Pintupi that he might have gained in the 15 years since the publication of Myers' book. Folds' story of Pintupi material failure–cultural success is essentially identical to Myers' account.

What I have labelled Myers' phenomenological sensibility consists of his insistence on the relevance of individuals' perspectives, and attention to the process and idiom of everyday interaction—mostly glossed as emotion (happiness, grief, homesickness, pity) and also as norms (generosity, compassion). Of course, much of this description of process and idiom is consistent with the central concern of most ethnography: to recover the emic perspective of others. For Myers, it is, however, the need to adequately explain this particular ethnographic context that requires the individual perspective. In the desert homelands of the Pintupi, ecological factors make any sociality problematic. Thus the process by which Pintupi social networks are maintained is particularly relevant and can be adequately explored only from the individual perspective.

Before proceeding to an account of the results of his methodology, it is worth noting that Myers' grounding of his approach in regional cultural and ecological specificities is strictly unnecessary. He seemed to be surprised that researchers in other regions had used his approach to similar effect (1986:128, footnote 1). He should not have been. The idea of the individual perspective is context independent. It reminds us again of Bohman's insistence that interpretative indeterminacy can be resolved only by reference to the purpose of an explanation, and Myers' purpose—principally to uncover the cultural logic of the Pintupi way—is a fairly common aim of most ethnography. Why Myers would want to conflate a theoretical approach with a regional cultural specificity would appear to be a product of the way in which the ideas occurred to him—through the long grind of trying to make sense of his complex data that did not fit existing socio-centric categories and theorising. But it also must relate to the dynamics of the Aboriginal specialisation in anthropology. As with all regional specialisations, new work must position itself in relation to the existing archive—for example, as bluntly corrective of previous work or, more deferentially, as an incremental refinement or, diplomatically, as simply adding an account of a new subregion for comparative purposes.

All these possibilities reveal how deftly Myers handled the potential sensitivities to criticism of other specialists. He had a definite contribution to make to the long-running local organisation debate and a trump card to play: the detailed recounting of the journeys of his informants when they were leading a completely nomadic life.

He has often presented his contribution to the local organisation debate as a middle course between the extremes of the abstract structuralism of the Radcliffe-Brownian horde theory and the ecological determinism of Lee (1976) and Lee and De Vore (1968), which he saw as making cultural constructs epiphenomenal (Myers 1982:174–5). What individual life stories demonstrated was a highly mobile band, of changing composition, that regularly encountered new persons and places. Yengoyan's analysis of his Pitjantjatjara life histories had already suggested this flexibility in the composition of the band, especially the recomposition of bands after large gatherings (1968, 1970). What Myers now integrated into his own account were the basic cultural imperatives and the specific mechanisms through which they worked. Thus, he asserted that there was an overriding imperative to extend one's acquaintanceship and affiliation to far-flung places. The diversity of individual networks of people and places tended to be subsumed under concertina concepts such as *ngura* and 'one countrymen', which could have a wide or narrow reference depending on the context: 'It seems most reasonable, following the Pintupi concept of "one countrymen" as people who share a "camp", to argue that bands are largely the outcome of individual decisions, and the actual composition can be explained only through understanding the processes of individual affiliation' (1982:183).

Multiple individual networks mean that so-called estate-groups, based on Stanner's distinction between estate and range, are in fact overlapping. What is rhetorically powerful in this individualist perspective is its demonstration that previous attempts to stabilise local organisation were oversimplifying a more complex underlying reality. Thus Myers could be interpreted as synthesising previous approaches and surpassing them. By taking an individual perspective, he was able to demonstrate the likely basis for the socio-centric models and also why they were so unstable.

One of Myers' approaches to 'ownership' is via resource use, and here he takes as his encapsulation of the Pintupi view a remark of a Western Desert man, quoted by Tindale: 'My country is the place where I do not have to ask anyone to cut wood for a spear thrower.' Myers then goes through the subtleties of 'asking' such as lighting fires to announce one's presence and the idea of a standing permission for close kin and co-residents.

How one becomes a person who must be asked is bound up with the economy of religious knowledge about places. This status is not simply a matter of father–son inheritance. It has much to do with actual cooperation of co-residents, enabling people to become 'one countrymen', through shared experience, helping each other and enabling the teaching of the esoteric aspects of the local manifestations of Dreaming stories. In keeping with the multiple individual networks of affiliation and the lack of any arbitral body to legitimate particular claims, 'ownership' is the product of negotiation through assertion and acceptance or rejection of individual claims to affiliation made on various inter-subjectively shared principles that Myers has helpfully codified:

> There are numerous reasons for referring to a place as one's 'own country'. If the place is called A, the following possibilities may constitute bases for such a claim:
>
> 1. conception at the place A;
> 2. conception at a place B made by and/or identified with the same Dreaming as A;
> 3. conception at a place B whose Dreaming is associated mythologically with the Dreaming at A (the story lines cross);
> 4. initiation at A (for a male);
> 5. birth at A;
> 6. father conceived at A or conditions 2–5 true for father;
> 7. mother conceived at A or conditions 2, 3, or 5 true for mother;
> 8. 'grandparents' (*tjamu, kaparli*, including all kin types so classified) conceived at A or conditions 2–5 true;
> 9. residence around A;
> 10. death of close relative at or near A. (1986:129–30)

This is why 'ownership' is invariably in quotation marks in Myers' account: any list of owners is merely a snapshot of an ongoing process that is dated as soon as it is taken. It also tends to be expansive, including those co-residents who have proved through their generosity that they are close kin and 'one countrymen' (1989:30).

Myers and change

To raise the question of the historical transformation of traditional laws and customs relating to land is to pinpoint one of the central contradictions of Myers' oeuvre. For although context, process and the achievement of sociality through action are at the heart of his approach, his explanatory aims are invariably conceptualised as context-independent, synchronic generalisations such as 'the Pintupi way', 'Pintupi cultural logic', Pintupi ontology and the shared meaning of key terms. This approach means that his account of the various claims to the country of their exile at Haasts Bluff and Papunya, and the Pintupi approach to cars, health services, the community council and meetings generally, are all examples of an underlying logic that is continuous with the pre-contact past. In this respect, he takes an opposite approach to Tonkinson, who tended to describe such things as new, transforming developments.

It would be possible to develop a narrative of historical transformation from his generalisations; however, because land ownership depends so much on actual residence, which continually changes, the subtle to and fro of claim and acceptance or rejection, and on who is present at any one point in time when the question is being asked, it would require an impossibly intimate and panoptic view to construct a socio-centric account of ownership transformations. That realisation is itself instructive and salutary. It grounds an expectation of change within ancient tradition. It also anticipates that the outstation movement would not be simply a return to a previous consensus about the ownership of their homeland, but a critical step in the reproduction of claim, counterclaim and acceptance or rejection. Although not explicitly thematised by Myers, there are indications that he anticipated the dramatic expansion of 'one countrymen', with improved transport and communications, to the extent of the whole of the Western Desert cultural bloc becoming a social reality, particularly in matters of ceremony. Again, these developments mean that the process of claim and acceptance or rejection would spread to a highly dispersed bloc and the continual transformation of affiliation to country would be extremely difficult to monitor.

There is material in Myers' work that is suggestive of more fundamental cultural transformation, but exploring this seems to have been antithetical to his main purpose. I am thinking of the change from the constant fear of revenge attacks ('It was like the army all the time') to the imposition of *Pax Australiana*; from the relentless discipline of the daily search for food to the rations of Haasts Bluff and the relative abundance of the mess hall of Papunya; from being masters of their own world to being derided as myalls by other Aborigines in the same mess hall (see Folds 2001:30–9); and, more subtly, from a world where many aspects of their everyday practices and beliefs could remain implicit, to a world that, for example, required lists of traditional owners. Of course, these changes were not quite as simple as this. I have sharpened the contrast to make the point that some transformation should be expected to result from these dramatic historical changes and that an approach of uncovering a cultural logic tends to obscure these cultural transformations.

Myers does hint at a new level of objectification of the Pintupi, by the Pintupi, in relation to the colonisers, in such quotations as 'You white people are always worrying for money. You don't think about who will cry for you when you die' (1989:24). Typically, for Myers, the historicity of this kind of discourse—that is, the historical appearance of defining one's essential self in opposition to an essentialised alien other, a kind of folk orientalism and occidentalism—is ignored in favour of it confirming the correctness of his account of the social imperative in underlying Pintupi logic. He discusses changes in the processes of custodianship in a similar way:

> It seems clear that the introduction of new elements into the procedure of custodianship of sacred sites—inaccessibility of sites, the separation of persons who had previously lived together into various settlements, the need to formally list 'owners' for white records, concern over payment and filming, and so on—have added dissonance to the traditional context in which ownership was defined. These elements do not, however, necessarily represent an alteration in the substance of ownership. (1986:143)

Conclusion on the anthropological archive prior to the claim

What I have been suggesting throughout this selective review[27] is that Fardon's idea of a dialectic between the development of regional specialisations and metropolitan theorising has taken on a particular nuance in Western Desert

27 Once again, to keep this review within reasonable bounds, I have had to make invidious choices. The most worrying was to omit any separate treatment of Gould's work. He presented the most detailed and cogent account of the ecological imperatives of local organisation in the Western Desert based on fieldwork around Warburton and beyond in 1966–67 (see Gould 1969a, 1969b). His work could be seen as foundational for later anthropologists such as Tonkinson and Myers, who extended it to include cultural imperatives. There has also been significant ethnomusicological research among the Pintupi (Moyle 1979) and Pitjantjatjara and 'Andagarinja' women (Buckley et al. 1967, 1968; Ellis and Barwick 1989). In matters of traditional land tenure, these works tend to rely on the authors I have dealt with in detail. The same is largely true of the historian–anthropologist team of Bruce Shaw and Jen Gibson, who did work around Oodnadatta in the mid 1980s (Gibson 1989; Shaw 1995). Mountford (1937, 1976) did early innovative fieldwork among Western Desert people, obtaining crayon drawings of Dreaming stories that could rightly be seen as a precursor to the Western Desert art movement. His monumental collection of the details of Pitjantjatjara myths and ritual, *Nomads of the Australian Desert*, angered some Aboriginal people with its disclosure of some secret rituals, and they successfully applied for an injunction through the Pitjantjatjara Council to limit the circulation of the book. I have not attempted to cover it in my review as it does not make any particularly original contribution to the question of traditional land tenure. Kolig's *The Silent Revolution* (1981) is a major ethnography of Western Desert people who identified themselves as Wolmadjeri. Its focus, however, is on ritual and change in religious consciousness. Ideas about traditional land tenure are present to the extent that he discusses the way in which Wolmadjeri people settled in the Fitzroy River Valley, in effect achieving a traditional succession of ownership. Woenne (1977) and Palmer (1984) have made contributions to the ethnography of Western Desert traditional land tenure at Docker River and Yalata respectively, but lack of space prohibited any detailed account of their contribution. Following the claim, several significant works relevant to Western Desert ethnography appeared. These include Cane (2002); Holcombe (2004); Peterson (2000); Poirier (2005); and Vachon (2006).

anthropological studies. The relative accessibility of the pre-contact era, and the fluidity of Western Desert local organisation, as reconstructed, allowed for a powerful contradiction of Radcliffe-Brown's horde theorising about the whole of Australia, and strained Stanner's reformulation. The polarisation of those who would defend Australia-wide generalisations about local organisation and those seeking to undermine them has been so persistent that it has become an enduring feature of the Australianist specialisation within anthropology. What is surprising is that Western Desert ethnography has not led to a heightened reflexivity about explanatory purposes and analytical tools. Tonkinson tended to update his terminology to keep pace with the debate as it unfolded. Hamilton's interesting suggestion for collapsing Stanner's distinction between economy and religion, in favour of examining an economy of an all-encompassing religious sphere, was never taken up seriously. The potential radicalising effect of Western Desert ethnography was also blunted by Myers, who tended to ground different analytical tools in the requirements of adequate ethnographic description, and ultimately in the people themselves, as in his light-hearted suggestion that the Pintupi, with their pervasive concern with immediacy, were natural phenomenologists rather than structuralists (1986:294). This kind of comment tends to mystify the process of fitting analytical tools to explanatory purposes, especially when those purposes are not fully articulated. For it seems that one of his explanatory purposes was to disturb the emerging consensus in the local organisation debate, which, for all its antagonism, was still being waged in conceptualisations based firmly in structural functionalism.

Groups

When we ask the question 'what groups could be considered as the title-holding groups in a Western Desert native title claim?', explanatory purposes are immediately brought to the foreground and the superiority of Myers' individualist–phenomenological account is relativised. For this task, the superseded socio-centric accounts of groups—the ones of Tonkinson, Tindale, Berndt and Elkin—come back into their own.

Myers is still highly relevant, but not as a direct response to the requirements of the legal doctrine of native title, which assumes a stable title-holding group. Myers is highly suggestive, however, of the need for widespread consultation, meetings and travelling around the claim area in large groups before the hearing, so that the process of individual claim, counterclaim, and acceptance or rejection can take place and so that a contemporary snapshot can be presented to the court—a snapshot that will align closely with what the claimants will say in the witness box.

Possible title-holding groups from different researchers are summarised in Table 6.1.

Table 6.1 Potential title-holding groups in the anthropological literature on Western Desert peoples

	Maximal				Minimal
Elkin	Western Desert Cultural Bloc—'the Aluridja group'		'Tribe'?		Horde
Berndt	Western Desert Cultural Bloc	'Society'			Patrilineal, local descent group
Tindale	Western Desert Cultural Bloc		Tribe, based on dialect identity	Regional groups?	Horde
Strehlow	Western Desert Cultural Bloc				
Kolig	Groups involved in exchange of rituals	Groups sharing excitement about same new ritual	Dialect-identified tribe	'Mob' = loose landowning group based on residence	Patrilineal descent group
Hamilton	Western Desert Cultural Bloc		Dialect group's de facto link to region		Those born at a place
Late Tonkinson	Western Desert Cultural Bloc	'Big meeting'	Dialect-named unit		Estate groups with a variety of bases for membership
Myers	Western Desert Cultural Bloc	Context-dependent 'one countrymen' comprising a bilateral, descending kindred with a variety of claims to country			

It is interesting to note from this table that the 'Western Desert cultural bloc' is the most stable identification between land and people. Although it has no Indigenous corporate name, the group does possess many commonalities typically associated with tribes, using Elkin's definition, and there are some indications of it functioning as a 'society', in Berndt's terms, of face-to-face interaction in certain shared rituals (see, for example, Peterson 2000). The demography of the Western Desert diaspora makes it totally impractical to be named as the claimant group or as a title-holding group in a determination. It would trespass on fundamental principles of not claiming traditional affiliations to country that one does not, in any sense, know. It would also obscure regional cultural differences within the Western Desert cultural bloc, such as the adoption of sections (western side), subsections (Pintupi in the north) and involvement in different trading networks for new rituals (for example, Wolmadjeri in Kolig 1981).

The dialect-named tribe as a possible title-holding group raises all the doubts, expressed throughout this review, about Tindale's view of tribal names and tribal territories in the Western Desert. Tindale's faith that the existence of corporate names contributed to the proof of the existence of tribes has been continually undermined by later anthropological and linguistic research. Dialect identifications tend to be highly contextual and multiple.[28] There are also examples in the archive of seemingly stable dialect identities changing with circumstances. Tonkinson reported the case of people whom he knew as Mandjildjara and Gadudjara from Jigalong starting to refer to themselves as Wanman in the mid 1980s, when they set up an outstation near country that was traditionally associated with Wanman speakers, who had since died out (1989:111–13). Brady (1986:44) reported that the Western Desert people of Yalata, who had for decades identified themselves as Antikarinya (including to the Berndts) all referred to themselves as Pitjantjatjara in the 1980s. The most that can be said for the 'tribe' is that some researchers have noticed the persistence of the identification of tracts of land with particular dialects, but in the Western Desert this identification seems to be merely a de facto one arising out of actual occupation and use (Hamilton, Tonkinson) and subject to change. On the other hand, some dialect-named identities, such as Pitjantjatjara and Yankunytjatjara, seem to have been more robust over time than others. It seems likely that the persistence and popularity of these identifications owe something to the adoption of Pitjantjatjara as the language of instruction in Ernabella's bilingual school and its use as the masthead in successful land rights struggles in the 1970s. Antikarinya seems to have declined as an identity at Yalata, although it seems to have persisted among Western Desert people at Oodnadatta, Coober Pedy and Port Augusta (see Ellis and Barwick 1989; Gibson 1989).

That brings us to the level of the horde–patrilineal local descent group–estate-group. The problem with this level, drawing on Myers and Hamilton, is that the implied stability and exclusiveness are illusory and critical religious knowledge about the area is likely to be part of a larger, regional religious sphere, subject to its own subtle politics and multifarious opportunities for acquiring knowledge. Some of the potential problems with pitching a title-holding group at this level can be extrapolated from the fate of Layton's attempt to stabilise Western Desert traditional land tenure for the purposes of a claim under the *Land Rights Act* as an ambilineal descent group (see Layton 1983a, 1983b, 1986).

Layton had firmly in his mind the need to establish a 'local descent group' that had primary spiritual responsibility for sites and the land. Like many anthropologists facing this predicament, Stanner's estate–range distinction proved to be irresistible, and there seemed to be an approximate overlap between Stanner's idea of a cluster of main sites and focal waterholes in his Pitjantjatjara material that are more narrowly defined than the much larger foraging range. Thus the estate group is the local descent group. The simplicity and force of this

28 See Douglas (1964, 1971); Merlan (1981); and Miller (1971).

presentation soon broke down under the weight of necessary exceptions and qualifications: traditional rights to estate areas are not exclusive, or exclusively inherited in a patrilineal way. These rights depended on knowledge of Dreaming stories and rituals that are possessed by a wider group of senior men, who came to the knowledge via claims to various kin country, actual residence in a spouse's country or long residence in country (Layton 1983a:23–30). Nevertheless, Layton pursued the estate model with the qualification that affiliation to the focal site could be through either of four lines of descent, hence the phraseology 'ambilineal descent group'.[29]

The anticipated unity of an estate area with its focal waterholes and peripheral water sources did not emerge from the evidence in the hearing of the *Ayers Rock* claim. Instead, different people had different ways of grouping various water sources together, including by their Dreaming affiliations. In later reflections, which would have made sense to Myers, Layton noted that the different groupings related to differing individual life experiences of the sites. Unfortunately for the claim, all the sites on the claim area were peripheral water sources and the apparent confusion of ownership claims was magnified (1983b:229–30).

Similarly, the evidence did not reflect either a consistent distinction between the supposedly separate 'estates' or the relevance of a principle of ambilineal descent to estate group composition. The evidence instead showed a variety of ways of becoming part of the landowning group. In short, the conceptualisation of traditional land tenure in terms of estates—even a modified version of Stanner's original simplicity—put at risk the outcome of the claim because it created difficulties in eliciting evidence and raised unrealistic expectations of coherence at the level of ownership claims and principles of descent. The claim was ultimately successful despite the inadequate anthropological conceptualisations, which were criticised in the Aboriginal Land Commissioner's report (Toohey 1980).

The difficulties of Western Desert land tenure in *Land Rights Act* claims, especially to 'peripheral' areas, continued in the *Lake Amadeus* and *Tempe Downs* land claims (see Gray 1998; Maurice 1989).

Laws and customs

There is a superficial attraction in equating the Aboriginal use of the word 'law', as in Dreaming or 'everlasting', with the requirement in the legal doctrine of native title in order to identify 'traditional laws and customs'. The attraction is that the normative aspect of law—as in correct kinship relations or correct performance of ritual for fear of harsh consequences—coincides with one of the

29 For a critique of Layton's 'ambilineal descent group', see Sutton (1998:32–4, 2003:196–7).

features of law in Western society. The problem, as outlined in the introductory chapter, is that the Aboriginal range of referents for the word 'law' is quite different from the range of referents for the European word. Expressed in an oversimplified way, Aboriginal 'law' can encompass an ontology, a cosmogony, religion, a social norm, a myth, a song, a ritual, a sacred object and a sacred site. European law implies a large-scale constitutional state with a separation of powers; the separation of religion and state; and the positivity of law—that is, the agreed, objectified and precisely defined conventions in statute law that are backed by state sanction (cf. Mantziaris and Martin 2000:35–7).

Like 'Malo's Law' in the first case study, shared beliefs about Aboriginal 'Law' are at a fairly general level that does not itself specify particular owners, even though it is the idiom in which ownership is asserted. Myers codified the more particular shared beliefs about legitimate claims of affiliation to country. His 10-point codification is suggestive of the possibility of identifying 'traditional laws and customs' in the Western Desert cultural bloc at this more specific level of legitimate claims.[30]

Maddock had thought about some of the problems of Western Desert land tenure and the migration of Western Desert people out of their original country in evaluating possible definitions of traditional owner at the time of the Seaman Inquiry into land rights in Western Australia (Maddock 1984b). He suggested that the Western Desert migrants should perhaps be forced to confine their claims to their former homelands in the desert, so that statutory land rights did not precipitate conflict on the fringes of the desert between the migrants and the original owners of those fringe areas. This limitation would be achieved by having a requirement that only those Aboriginal people who were the original traditional owners of the fringe areas at the time of colonisation, and their descendants, would be able to claim primary rights to those fringe areas.[31]

30 There is even an analogue in European bureaucratic processes: the 100-point identification test for opening a bank account. Applying this to Myers' list, one could allocate the full 100 points to conception at place A, say 50 points to conception on the same Dreaming track, 30 points to place of initiation and so on. Thus, if a claimant did not have A as a place of conception, proof of being a native title-holder for that area would involve the need for numerous other links that together would add up to 100 points. As fanciful as it sounds, exasperated land councils have in the past resorted to a similar checklist approach in order to resolve entitlements to disputed royalty payments to traditional owners. Also see the list of 18 bases for affiliation to land compiled by Niblett and Strong and referred to in Justice Michael Maurice's report on the *Lake Amadeus* land claim (Maurice 1989:28–9).

31 Maddock favoured a two-tier system similar to the *Land Rights Act*, which distinguished between traditional owners who had the primary spiritual responsibilities for the land and a wider group who had more circumscribed traditional rights. The potential dual focus of migrants from the Western Desert (their original homelands as opposed to the country on the fringe of the desert where they settled) worried Maddock. He thought that his proposal would prevent some Western Desert peoples, such as Tonkinson's Madudjara and Kolig's Wolmadjeri, from claiming primary traditional ownership rights to two lots of traditional territory. In his view, this constraint would help ensure continuing popular support for land rights in the broader community.

In suggesting this unscrambling of contemporary claims by reference to the pre-contact past, Maddock anticipated the legal doctrine of native title and the potential problems of its application to the Western Desert diaspora.

Change

As we have seen, different conceptualisations of local organisation led directly to opposite interpretations of the implications of big demographic movements for traditional land tenure. Because of his view of tribal territories, Tindale was able to speak of 'usurpation' within the Western Desert cultural bloc, whereas Berndt saw major movements of dialect-identified groups as continuous with past traditions because, in his view, relative stability existed only in the identification between *kapi* and local descent group. A traditional process of succession within the Western Desert cultural bloc, including at the level of a particular *kapi*, could be anticipated from Myers' approach since the relative merits of individual claims to particular places would vary along with births, deaths, absences, breakdown of relationships and the transmission or withholding of sacred knowledge. The lack of such theorising under the explicit heading of 'succession' was to cause problems in the claim.

The interpretation of generational differences in birthplace affiliation also differs according to the range of circumstances in which the Western Desert diaspora found itself and the interests of the various anthropologists. Commonly, the older generation's *kapi* would be hundreds of kilometres away in the desert, while their children were being born on, and gaining traditional affiliations to, its fringes. Tonkinson's 'Mardu' at Jigalong in the mid 1960s were still largely orientated towards their traditional country in the desert. On the other hand, Kolig thought that the Wolmadjeri at Fitzroy Crossing in the early 1970s had no desire to return to their former desert homelands far to the south. Through intermarriage, the birth of children locally, the acquisition of sacred knowledge of the local totemic landscape, and the fact of their numerical superiority over the former locals, the Wolmadjeri had become reorientated to the country of the Fitzroy River Valley (Kolig 1981:10–50, 1987:87). Although she does not refer to Kolig, Doohan (1992) found surprisingly similar processes at work at Finke, an Aboriginal settlement north-east of the claim area.

The story of the initial exodus from the eastern Western Desert had its own peculiarities. The earliest involvement with the European economy was through doggers, who generally travelled to the remote places, where the Aboriginal people lived nomadically, in order to trade rations for dingo scalps. Although there were the early long-distance movements to Oodnadatta, Coober Pedy, Ooldea and Port Augusta, the establishment of a liberal mission at Ernabella in 1937 and the occupation of the eastern extremity of Western Desert country by pastoralists meant that some Western Desert people were able to remain on traditional Western Desert country, even though their *kapi* might have been much further to the west. The mission was liberal in its policy of non-interference in traditional ritual and, as far as possible, in traditional modes of living. The yearly calendar included a long Christmas 'holiday' when the Aboriginal people left the mission to live in the bush (with some supplied rations) and conduct their ceremonies (see Berndt and Berndt 1951:186–90; Hilliard 1968).

The Western Desert people of Ernabella and the eastern pastoral lands suffered the fatal epidemics that killed so many of the Lower Southern Arrernte, Arabana and Wangkonguru to the east, although many would have arrived from the west after the devastating influenza epidemic of 1919–20. Small groups of Aboriginal people clustered around the various sheep and cattle stations, supplying seasonal labour and receiving some rations. They continued some hunting and gathering to make up the shortfall in rations and so maintained their autonomy. This enabled them to continue the performance of ceremony. The life of these small groups and the networks of kin characterised a period of relative predictability that could be called the pastoral era from, say, the 1930s to the late 1960s (Doohan 1992:42–53; Hamilton 1979:3–12).

The particular features of the colonial experience of the eastern Western Desert people have been the basis of various arguments about cultural continuity. From a materialist perspective, Frederick Rose (1965) expressed surprise at the persistence of Western Desert tradition despite the destruction of their traditional economy. Vachon (1982) emphasised the relative unobtrusiveness of pastoralism in relation to the performance of traditional ceremony. Hamilton (1987) saw the intermittent nature of work and rations in the pastoral era as necessitating the development of patterns of mobility among a regional network of mutually supportive kin. She reinterpreted the era as an attempt by Aboriginal people to fit white settlers into their system of kinship and reciprocity, particularly the idea of a boss being the one who looks after subordinates (see Hamilton 1972, anticipating Myers 1986). The nature of the pastoral era meant that Western Desert Aboriginal people were able to hold onto aspects of their traditional culture until the time was ripe for the legal recognition of their traditional land rights in the mid to late 1970s (Toyne and Vachon 1984). Those lands had begun to be resettled through the encouragement of a homeland movement from Ernabella (Wallace 1977b) and the government-sponsored settlements in the 1960s (Woenne 1977).

The late 1960s–1970s was a momentous period in other respects. Within the space of a decade, large-scale Aboriginal involvement in the pastoral industry ceased; there was an expansion of entitlements to social security payments and the granting of drinking–citizenship rights (see Hope 1983). The threat to the continuation of traditional ritual from Aboriginal drunkenness was witnessed firsthand by Sackett in Willuna (Sackett 1977) and Kolig in Fitzroy Crossing (Kolig 1981:122–3), but is less prominent in accounts of the eastern Western Desert in the same period (but see Brady and Palmer 1984).

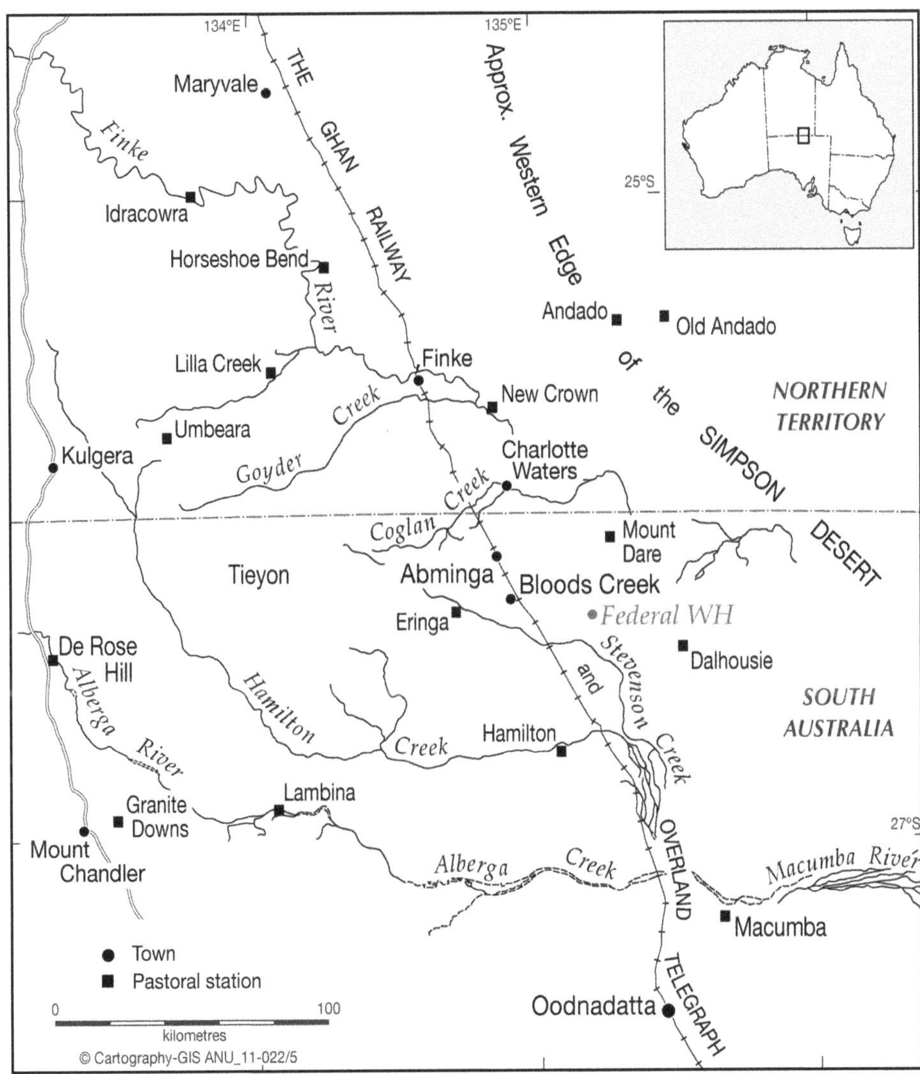

Map 6.5 Historical map of pastoral lands east of De Rose Hill Station

A critical incident in the life of the main claimant in the *De Rose Hill* claim, Peter De Rose, is reflective of this momentous and disruptive period. After an argument with his employer, the owner of De Rose Hill Station, Peter De Rose left the place of his birth, and, in 1978, with all the other Aboriginal people resident at De Rose Hill, went to live at Indulkana, a government settlement on the Anangu-Pitjantjatjara lands. Twenty-three years later, during the hearing of the claim, the question would be asked: did this amount to an abandonment of his traditional country?

The period of the 1980s and 1990s is not well represented in the published anthropological literature on the Western Desert bloc (but see Myers 2002; Poirier 1996, 2005; Willis 1997). It was the era of the homelands movement, the expansion of Aboriginal-controlled service organisations, the Western Desert art movement and the seemingly intractable problems of settlement life: boredom, unemployment, drunkenness, petrol sniffing, domestic violence, poor health and short life expectancy.

One trend that has been documented, though, has been the increasing concentration of attention on initiation ceremonies, and the songs and sites associated with those ceremonies. According to Vachon (1982:484), this focus resulted in a falling away of interest in other sites that were not so linked. Improved communication and availability of transport greatly expanded the 'catchment' area for initiation ceremonies and the area covered by the journeys of the initiates, making circumcision ritual *the* major cultural event of the Western Desert cultural bloc (Peterson 2000; Wallace 1977a). Thus when the lawyers went to Indulkana in 1994 to obtain instructions to use De Rose Hill as the test case for claiming residual native title rights on pastoral leases, interest was sustained largely because one of the Dreaming tracks that went through De Rose Hill—*malu* (kangaroo), *kanyala* (euro) and *tjurki* (fairy owl)—was one of the Dreamings performed at initiation ceremonies.[32]

32 Personal communication from Tim Wooley, 2004. Tim Wooley was the ALRM solicitor working on the *De Rose Hill* claim.

7. Western Desert Ethnography on Trial

Introduction

The significance of the early events, outlined in the previous chapter, for the anthropologists when they eventually began to research the claim was that they were presented with a *fait accompli*. Any doubts they might have had about this area becoming the test case for native title in South Australia were not relevant because the case was proceeding. Also, because it was ALRM's first claim hearing, the case was destined to become one in which ALRM would be learning the pitfalls of claim hearings as they were going along.

Research for the claim

The anthropological research for the claim was largely organised by Susan Woenne-Green, who was appointed senior anthropologist at the Native Title Unit of ALRM in 1994. Woenne-Green was another veteran of anthropology among the eastern Western Desert people. She had, for example, worked on the *Ayers Rock* claim in the late 1970s, assisting the Aboriginal Land Commissioner. In the *De Rose Hill* claim, she planned to take on the role of principal researcher and expert witness for the claimants. In order to overcome the obvious gender difficulties, she engaged a male anthropologist to produce reports of more limited scope on various aspects of the Aboriginal men's evidence.

Craig Elliott, a consultant anthropologist with an MA degree in anthropology based on fieldwork in Arnhem Land (Elliott 1991), was to be her main male counterpart in field research for the claim and chief researcher of the anthropological archive. His involvement actually predates Woenne-Green's, and, between 1994 and 1998, he conducted extensive archival research (150 days) and field research (110 days). The field research involved travelling to various communities on the Pitjantjatjara lands, usually with Woenne-Green and others, who were more familiar with the potential claimants. It also involved site visits to the claim area with the claimants. In December 2000, Elliott was directed to prepare an expert report for the claim. The terms of his brief from ALRM assumed that his report would be subsidiary to the more comprehensive and overarching report that Woenne-Green was preparing, for it directed him to focus on gender restrictions, men's contemporary religious associations, sites and particular Dreamings, associations with wider Western Desert beliefs and practices, and the results of his visit to the Strehlow Research Centre in Alice

Springs. Among other things, Elliott found in Strehlow's diaries details of his 1965 trip through the claim area, where he recorded Dreaming stories and site names—more or less consistent with the claimants' information (see Elliott 2000:71–8, 2001:56–8).

Daniel Vachon, another veteran of eastern Western Desert anthropology, was to provide details of his early research in the region, which, coincidentally, involved Snowy De Rose as one of his main informants during 1977–79. Snowy De Rose was the father of the main claimant in the *De Rose Hill* claim, Peter De Rose.[1]

Dr Jon Willis, the third male anthropologist, was to give evidence about the relationship between ceremony and land affiliation. He was in the unique position of having completed PhD research on Pitjantjatjara ceremony and having been inducted into male initiation rites (Willis 1997, 2003a, 2003b). Although Elliott's research for the claim was extensive, he did not witness any initiation ceremonies (T. 2269) and it was hoped that Willis's evidence could fill that gap.

The SA Crown Law Office, representing the State of South Australia, engaged Professor Ken Maddock to give expert evidence. It was the last native title claim he was involved in before his death in 2003.

Pre-trial processes

Elliott felt that there was a reluctance in ALRM to adopt certain research practices simply because they were used in land claims under the *Land Rights Act* in the Northern Territory. According to him, there was a feeling that native title in South Australia was distinctive and needed to be approached in a different way. He was frustrated that ALRM did not seem to appreciate the need to focus on producing key documents that would inevitably be required: genealogies, site maps, site registers, and concise anthropological reports.

Elliott had initially worked towards a joint expert report with Susan Woenne-Green and had produced a draft in late 1996. About 1998, however, differences developed between Elliott and ALRM about the conduct of the research for the claim, and, between 1998 and 2000, Elliott had nothing to do with the preparations. Meanwhile, Woenne-Green had produced a new expert report under her own name, and this was circulated to the parties along with Elliott's 2000 report. Elliott was not asked to comment on, and in fact never saw, Woenne-Green's circulated report.

---

1 Vachon did not publish from his research with Snowy De Rose and later conducted doctoral research with a different Western Desert group (see Vachon 2006).

The hearing

After considering a number of Adelaide QCs, ALRM eventually decided that Ross Howie SC would lead the legal team in the hearing. He was from the Melbourne Bar and was the most experienced and successful land claim trial lawyer in Australia.[2] When he began working on the case, however, all the extensive pre-trial proceedings had been completed. These proceedings included the provision of detailed further and better particulars of their claim, the circulation of all expert reports and the material on which they were based. Nevertheless, Howie insisted that Elliott be brought back to attend the hearing.

The battlelines were drawn in the opening addresses. Howie encapsulated the claimants' case in the word *'nguraritja'*—a Yankunytjatjara–Pitjantjatjara word for traditional owner.[3] The claimants were part of the Western Desert cultural bloc and under their traditional laws and customs recognise *nguraritja* by criteria of birth at the place, long-term physical association with the place, having geographical and religious knowledge of the area, and descent from an ancestor who was born at the place or who had a long-term physical association with the place. Mr Tony Besanko, senior counsel representing the State of South Australia, argued that the Antakirinya people were separate from the Yankunytjatjara people, and that the Antakirinya people occupied land to the east of the Yankunytjatjara, which included the claim area. He asserted that the Yankunytjatjara claimants could not, therefore, demonstrate continuity of traditional connection since the time of the assertion of sovereignty. In the alternative, he argued that any traditional connection had been lost since 1977, when Aboriginal people no longer permanently resided on the pastoral lease (T. 73–4).[4]

The claimants' evidence

Despite some timesaving measures such as tendering written statements, the evidence of the Aboriginal witnesses was spread over 31 days of the hearing. It involved 13 Aboriginal men and 13 Aboriginal women. There were nine days

2 The other lawyers in the team included Richard Bradshaw and Andrew Collett, both of whom had extensive experience with Western Desert Aboriginal people. John Basten QC was also engaged to argue the legal issue of whether the granting of the pastoral lease extinguished all native title rights.

3 According to Goddard's Pitjantjatjara–Yankunytjatjara dictionary, *ngurara* means 'resident, local, person that lives in a place (placename appears in nominative case—that is, with -nya ending): Paluru Alice Springs-anya ngurara. He's an Alice Springs person (resident) and "*nguraritja*" means "someone that belongs to a place, traditional owner (from *ngurara* plus -(i)tja 'of, from')"' (Goddard 1992:90).

4 Counsel for the pastoralists similarly emphasised loss of traditional connection since the 1970s, denying that the previous Aboriginal occupants had any access problems since the 1970s and emphasising that no traditional ceremonies had been held on the land since the 1970s at least (T. 76–7).

of site visits, including two days of restricted, men-only evidence. The chief claimant and witness was Peter De Rose. His evidence-in-chief lasted for a full one and a half days and he was cross-examined for two and a half days. One feature of all the claimants' evidence was the laborious, sentence-by-sentence processing of objections to hearsay in the witnesses' statements. The judge's early indication was that he would take a liberal view of hearsay in a native title hearing, allowing hearsay into evidence but reserving the right to give it different weight according to its reliability.

For the most part, Peter De Rose's evidence followed a predictable path: his birth on the claim area; his early life with his Aboriginal mother and adoptive Aboriginal father, both of whom worked on the station; hunting and gathering; early travels with family, including visits to the Dreaming sites on or near the claim area; his working life as the station hand employed by Doug Fuller and later his son, Rex Fuller; the stages of his traditional initiation; his gradual acquisition of knowledge of the Dreaming stories associated with the area, including while he was doing mustering work on the station; the various incidents with the Fullers, precipitating the departure of the last Aboriginal people from De Rose Hill Station (his father being run over by Doug Fuller in a car and sustaining a broken leg; feeling that Doug Fuller had delayed giving him news of his brother's death in a motor vehicle accident); setting up a homeland community at Railway Bore on Anangu-Pitjantjatjara lands, close to De Rose Hill; his intermittent return for hunting; and his desire to set up an outstation on De Rose Hill.

He gave extensive evidence about the various Dreamings and sites on the area, although he was reluctant to speak about the *malu, kunyula* and *tjurki* Dreaming in open court with women present, since the Dreaming is associated with male initiation (see, for example, T. 165). He even gave evidence about the meaning of *jukurpa* (Dreaming) and *nguraritja*. Indicative of the multiple pathways to 'country' in the Western Desert, Peter De Rose's explanation of *nguraritja* appeared to go beyond the four criteria emphasised in the opening address and to assert, in a more impenetrable way, a direct relationship between *tjukurpa* and himself.[5]

5 For example:

> PETER DE ROSE: It makes me *nguraritja tjakangka* [our way] because of the *tjukurpa* and the law. (T. 156)

In a similar vein was Whisky Tjukanku's metaphysical challenge to 'criteria for becoming *nguraritja*':

> MR BESANKO: Mr Tjukanku, you were not born on De Rose Hill, were you?
>
> WHISKY TJUKANKU: No, I didn't born there but I am a nguraritja. The land tells me I'm a nguraritja. (T. 951)

(Compare with the limits of the liberal state's recognition of traditional land tenure in Povinelli 2002.)

Where he gave unexpected answers was in response to questions about confrontation with the Fullers and about the rights of the *nguraritja*. Peter De Rose and other witnesses tended to downplay the extent of confrontation with the Fullers and to leave out details. Craig Elliott told me of his own direct observations of the fear that the claimants had of Doug Fuller when taking them on research field trips on De Rose Hill Station. He said that he was well aware of the need to verify any allegations made and in fact he did obtain detailed and, in his view, convincing statements from various claimants. The confirming details, however, tended to disappear from the Aboriginal evidence in the witness box.

Questions designed to elicit evidence about the rights of *nguraritja*, particularly rights of exclusive possession or control of resources, tended to reveal cross-purposes. Questions about rights were answered in terms of responsibilities to care for land. Questions asked to elicit evidence about permission-seeking behaviour were answered in terms of a norm of generosity and, perhaps, the Realpolitik of their current powerlessness. For example, following some strong evidence of *nguraritja* enforcement of their rights against others in the past, the following interchange took place:

> MR HOWIE: What about today? What does the nguraritja do?
>
> PETER DE ROSE: Today the nguraritja they still have their strong law and today also they got on AP lands, Anangu Pitjantjatjara lands, they have got a law and the people go within that rules.
>
> MR HOWIE: I'm not asking you about the law on Anangu Pitjantjatjara lands but I am asking you about the Anangu law on De Rose Hill lands. I'm only asking you about the Anangu law, not about the law for the pastoral lease, today what can nguraritja do if visitors don't behave properly?
>
> PETER DE ROSE: The nguraritja they happy to have visitors who they wanted to show places to the visitors. (T. 166)

Howie, however, made some headway with the example of mining:

> PETER DE ROSE: The nguraritja say no because that sacred site is close. (T. 169)

Riley Tjayrany, Whisky Tjukanku, Witjawara Curtis (an elderly woman), Alec Baker, Peter Tjutatja, Tim De Rose and Owen Kunmanara gave similar evidence to Peter De Rose, if somewhat less detailed. It reinforced the semi-nomadic life of the Aboriginal people living on the station in the early days and included Riley Tjayrany's account of a momentous fight between the original partners, Tom O'Donoghue and Doug Fuller, after which O'Donoghue left (T. 187). The women's evidence tended to be more about family history and hunting, and little about ritual.

One of the questions asked of the Aboriginal witnesses by their lawyers was 'What language do you speak?' The witnesses duly answered Yankunytjatjara, and in some circumstances Pitjantjatjara. In the light of the distinctions in the anthropological and linguistic archives, the answer to such a question has very limited value because it incorrectly assumes monolingualism, and does not distinguish between a dialect and a language (inherently difficult as the Western Desert language does not have a single name), nor does it distinguish language competence, personal identity and group identity. When I asked Elliott about these problems, he agreed that the question suffered from many inadequacies but said that there was a gradual appreciation of the fundamental distinctions among the claimants' lawyers over the course of the hearing.

Another problem was what the Aboriginal witnesses would say about the Antakirinya. They knew that their Aboriginal kin at Oodnadatta and Coober Pedy referred to themselves and their language as Antakirinya, although to them the language was indistinguishable from Yankunytjatjara. Over the course of the preparation for the hearing, however, the claimants became aware of the potential problem Antakirinya posed for the success of their claim[6] and adopted an exaggerated attitude of ignorance of all things Antakirinya, which sometimes was unhelpfully at variance with their written statements:

> PETER DE ROSE: I'm not sure about Antakirinya. I heard about when people talking about. I don't know Antakirinya. I never meet Antakirinya. (T. 849)

Cross-examination

The extraordinarily thorough two-day cross-examination of Peter De Rose raised most of the themes taken up in the cross-examination of all the Aboriginal witnesses. Besanko laboriously went back over the details of Peter De Rose's ancestors and a year-by-year account of Peter's life. Other aspects seemed designed to elicit answers either undermining the witness's credibility or laying the groundwork for specific final submissions. Questions were asked of Peter De Rose and all the Aboriginal witnesses about the birthplace of their parents, demonstrating that they had all come from the west, thereby laying a foundation for the usurpation argument (Pitjantjatjara and Yankunytjatjara usurping the Antakirinya). There were many questions about the Antakirinya, including whether there had been discussions during the research process about Antakirinya on Tindale's map. Excessive denials tended to bring into question the credibility of the witnesses (T. 849–53). Also of relevance to the usurpation argument were questions about boundaries between Pitjantjatjara and Yankunytjatjara country. In his answer, Peter De Rose hinted that the language in Dreaming stories indicated traditional boundaries (T. 880).

6 Tim Wooley (the claimants' solicitor), Personal communication, 2004.

There were questions about the principles by which one became *nguraritja* that seemed designed to emphasise the importance of birthplace and question the weight traditionally given to growing up at a place per se or knowledge of associated Dreaming stories and ritual per se (T. 869–71). There were other questions about why specific individuals, who seemed to meet one of the four proposed criteria for being *nguraritja*, had not been included in the claimant group (T. 889–900). Some other questions were transparently designed to demonstrate loss of traditional connection or general decline in adherence to traditional law—for example, questions about not cleaning sites as they did in the pre-pastoral era (T. 840–4, 864–5).[7]

The restricted sessions

My presentation of the claimants' evidence is not complete. I decided not to request the restricted part of the transcript, as this might have added a layer of complexity that would have threatened my ability to complete the case study. From the open transcript and the judgment, however, it is apparent that the restricted sessions involved taking the judge to gender-restricted sites and the explanation of and performance of gender-restricted songs. This omission from my data was a problem for Howie and Elliott, who thought that these sessions contained the most significant evidence.[8]

The anthropological evidence

Susan Woenne-Green

For reasons that will be explained below, Susan Woenne-Green's report, although circulated, was never tendered in evidence. Some account of it is necessary, however, to understand subsequent events. The largest section of the report described 'the cultural landscape of the claim land' (pp. 58–205). This section

7 They were also questioned about why they had not complained to the Fullers when one site was trampled by cattle (T. 875–7), and why they had not taken up opportunities to hunt on De Rose Hill Station or to teach the younger generation about the sites on the station.

8 The omission of the restricted evidence has caused me some concern because both Ross Howie and Craig Elliott are of the view that it is only by being familiar with the detail and the strength of the evidence given by the claimants in restricted sessions that the scale of the injustice done to them in O'Loughlin's judgment can be fully appreciated. Without revealing specifics, they were impressed with the level of detail, clarity and force of the restricted evidence and were appalled that the judge did not seem to appreciate it or to understand the significance of the concessions that were being made by the claimants in order to present some of their most secret songs to him. I can record their views, but I am in no position to assess them. The focus of this thesis is on anthropology and I have made the assessment that there is sufficient material in the open transcript and the unrestricted parts of Elliott's reports to pursue the case study, notwithstanding that my account of the evidence must necessarily be incomplete.

comprised a comprehensive catalogue of significant sites including photographs, site names, Dreaming associations, kin associations, and quotations from the claimants outlining historical and religious significance—in other words, the kind of evidence one would expect from Aboriginal witnesses on a site visit. It might have served the useful purpose of familiarising the non-Aboriginal participants in the hearing with the way in which the Aboriginal witnesses would speak about the country. The remainder of the report dealt with the way in which the claimants spoke about their connection to the country, including as 'member', *nguraritja*, *ngurawalytja* (family for country) and *waltjapiti* (extended family), and it included 24 examples of how they spoke about *nguraritja*. There was relatively little in the report about historical transformation and the older anthropological sources. Tindale's tribal boundaries were rejected, as was the applicability of the anthropological concept of succession of ownership. Instead, there was an assertion that the claim area is 'Yankunytjatjara country' and that those people currently identifying as Antakirinya are not a separate people. Thus, Woenne-Green's report remained close to the claimants' perspective and tended not to make links to the larger anthropological archive on the Western Desert cultural bloc, or move towards systematising her material into the specifics of 'traditional laws and customs' and the 'rights' of *nguraritja*.

Maddock's first report

Of all the Australianist anthropologists, Ken Maddock has been the most prolific on the interaction of law and anthropology, particularly in the land rights era.[9] This book could be seen as a response to his formulations of the problem (see Chapter 1).

Maddock's tendency to conflate all issues into the polar opposites of expert versus advocate, or science versus sympathy, recalls the structuralist heritage of which he became the main exponent in the Australianist specialisation (see Maddock 1969, 1970a, 1970b). It was his increasingly trenchant criticism of the contamination of the science of anthropology by advocacy that led him to take on a particular role in the native title era. He offered his services to those parties that he thought would have difficulty obtaining the advice of an experienced anthropologist—as if in personal response to criticism of bias in the profession towards working exclusively for Aboriginal interests: 'In proceedings in which expert testimony plays a critical part, the inability to obtain expert advice can be as prejudicial as inability to obtain legal representation' (Maddock 1998c:1–2).

This had been a concern of his from the very beginning, commencing with his analysis of the *Gove Land Rights Case* and continuing throughout the land rights era (see Maddock 1998b:167). In the native title era, it meant, in effect, that he

9 See Maddock (1980a, 1980b, 1981a, 1981b, 1983a, 1983b, 1984a, 1984b, 1998a, 1998b, 1999, 2001b).

was usually called as a witness by State governments that were opposing, or at least testing, native title claims, and his typical role was one of reviewing the work of anthropologists called by claimants.[10]

In terms of both 'scientific' capital and academic capital, Maddock was a formidable presence. He had conducted long-term fieldwork in Arnhem Land for his doctorate. He had combined an original contribution to Australianist ethnography with metropolitan theorising, specifically Lévi-Straussian structuralism at the apogee of its international influence, and published the results in leading academic journals, as well as an introductory text aimed at the general public (Maddock 1972). There are some indications that he did not cope well with the complexifying of theoretical approaches in the 1980s and the anti-colonial challenges to the discipline. Les Hiatt summarised this period in his obituary:

> The fact of the matter is that the profession itself was in a state of crisis, whether as a prelude to death or some unrecognisable metamorphosis no one could confidently say. Topics and issues that had been at the heart of the discipline since its inception, including many of those that Ken had devoted his best years to, no longer seemed to be of interest. More to the point, they were likely to be stigmatised as inappropriate. In the view of a new generation the primary responsibility of anthropologists was not to advance their discipline but to advance its subjects. (Hiatt 2003:404)

Despite his misgivings about the direction of the discipline, Maddock had a long career in academia, commencing as a lecturer in anthropology at Macquarie University in 1969, steadily rising through the ranks to a personal Chair in Anthropology (1991) and, in his retirement, the title of Emeritus Professor (since 1997).[11] This position enabled him to be referred to as 'Professor Maddock' in the *De Rose Hill* hearing. Of additional relevance to his standing as an expert witness was his initial degree in law and his long record of research and publication on land rights and the recognition of customary law.

Maddock's brief from the SA Crown Solicitor's Office called for a review of all the expert reports that had been tendered by the claimants. His report (Maddock 2001a) has the feel of the professor correcting the students' essays as it concentrates on the areas he felt were lacking, principally in Woenne-Green's report: lack of attention to describing the nature of traditional laws and customs, the relevant ethnographic archive and proof of continuity of

10 He was called by the NSW Government in the *Yorta Yorta* claim and by the WA Government in the *Miriuwung Gajerrong* claim (Ward's case: *Ward v. WA* [1998] 159 ALR 483, see description of Maddock's evidence at pp. 528–9).

11 This is not to say that he was always appreciated by his students, one of whom was Elliott himself. He recalled Maddock being 'unengaged and unengaging'.

traditional ownership. But he also seemed not to accept that Elliott and Vachon were circumscribed by their specific briefs from ALRM, for he took them to task for not covering basic matters—Vachon for not relating his fieldwork to the anthropological literature, and Elliott for not clearly describing how one becomes *nguraritja*, for not analysing the ethnographic reality of Antakirinya and for not describing the relationship between the claimants and the surrounding groups.

Maddock was more explicit than the other anthropologists about the translation process involved in searching for relevant concepts in the anthropological archive and the relative lack of guidance from legal doctrine (see para. 12). In seeking further specification of 'Law', 'custom' and 'traditional', Maddock surveyed some anthropological theorising about social order and social control (Berndt 1965; Malinowski 1926) as well as more direct attempts to define law in small-scale societies (Hoebel 1954; Llewellyn and Hoebel 1941; Pospisil 1971; Radcliffe-Brown 1933). He also extended his survey to quasi-legal sources: the Australian Law Reform Commission on the recognition of customary law (Aboriginal customary law as 'a body of rules, values and traditions, more or less clearly defined, which were accepted as establishing standards and procedures to be followed and upheld') and Justice Wootten in his report under the *Aboriginal and Torres Strait Islander Heritage Protection Act 1984* (Cwlth) on the proposed Alice Springs dam ('tradition' as meaning handed down from generation to generation). Having raised the problem of the translation process, though, Maddock did not come to a conclusion about it and introduced his own broad distinctions between living culture and vestiges and between tradition and innovation without a discussion of their problematic nature (para. 34). In the witness box, however, he simply equated 'traditional laws and customs' with traditional Aboriginal culture or 'Blackfella Law' (T. 3450–1).

Presumably in response to the gaps in Woenne-Green's report, Maddock surveyed the literature on local organisation.[12] In the witness box, he elaborated on what Aboriginal 'ownership' might mean, asserting a distinction between an economic and a religious aspect. With regard to local organisation, he favoured Peterson's band perspective—the band as the primary land-occupying and resource-utilising group. Apart from implying that occupation and use per se would eventually be seen as 'rightful use', he did not really explain how the theorising about local organisation related to European concepts of ownership rights (T. 3414–16).

Maddock also surveyed the literature on traditional succession, on Western Desert migration and on Western Desert population movements. He concluded this review by raising the question of whether any change of traditional

12 In his review, he referred to Radcliffe-Brown, Peterson and Long, Strehlow, the Berndts, Elkin, Hamilton and various reports of Aboriginal Land Commissioners in *Land Rights Act* claims.

ownership of the claim area took place according to traditional laws and customs (para. 90). The importance of this question was reinforced by a review of all the references to the Antakirinya in the literature. Again, this was probably in response to Woenne-Green's strong assertion of Yankunytjatjara continuity and her dismissal of Tindale. Although distancing himself somewhat from Tindale's tribes ('whatever might be the precise significance of those labels'), Maddock tended to avoid a thorough critique—for example, avoiding taking a position on Berndt's 1959 critique of Tindale.

At the end of his report, Maddock stated that there were three areas of doubt that the Aboriginal evidence needed to dispel

- the time depth of their association with the claim area
- whether there was significantly more to the claimants' association with the land than spiritual affiliations
- the degree to which traditional laws and customs were currently observed (T. 3418).

Despite Maddock's doubts, both Howie and Elliott thought that his first report was generally helpful to the claimants' case.

In passing, Maddock speculated on the reasons the claimants' experts—principally Woenne-Green at that stage—had not adequately covered the possibility of a change of traditional ownership, returning to one of his longstanding concerns about anthropology in the land rights era: 'The experts may have been prevented from addressing this critical issue by their apparent acceptance of the dogma that the applicants' relation to land is eternal and unchanging' (Maddock 2001a:para. 248).

Critically for the claimants' case, he concluded his review of the literature on the Western Desert cultural bloc by stating that 'the available evidence does not suggest a total rupture of continuity with the pre-contact culture, in spite of territorial shifts, population movements and probable changes in law and custom' (Maddock 2001a:para. 251).

Craig Elliott's second report

During the hearing of the claim, Woenne-Green became ill and had to be taken to hospital. The diagnosis and prognosis were uncertain for some time and during that period the claimants' legal team decided to make a contingency plan. It involved Craig Elliott producing a second report that would take the place of Woenne-Green's report in giving an overview of the anthropology of the whole claim. Susan Woenne-Green was eventually diagnosed as having had three minor strokes. She did not return to the hearing since her condition was stress related.

The plan was a high-risk strategy, but there was not much choice. Without such a report, there would be no expert evidence linking the claimants' evidence to the anthropological archive and the broad requirements of the legal doctrine of native title.

Except for the last item below, Craig Elliott's terms of reference reflected the terminology of the legal doctrine of native title, separated into its constituent elements. They asked him to address

1. the nature of the traditional laws and customs
2. the Aboriginal people who acknowledge and observe the traditional laws and customs
3. the Aboriginal people who have a connection with the claimed land by those laws and customs
4. the nature of the connection of the Aboriginal people with the claimed land by those laws and customs
5. the Aboriginal people who have rights and interests in relation to the claimed land under the traditional laws acknowledged and traditional customs observed
6. the nature of the rights and interests of the Aboriginal people under the traditional laws acknowledged and traditional customs observed
7. whether since the acquisition of sovereignty in 1825 there has been a cessation of the acknowledgment and observance by the community of the traditional laws and customs on which the native title has been founded
8. whether since the acquisition of sovereignty in 1825 there has been a loss of connection with the land by the community which acknowledges and observes the traditional laws and customs
9. an account of the early ethnographic sources.

It can be noted that there is a complete overlap between this list and what one would expect to find in the claimants' final submissions and in the ultimate judgment. When I spoke to Howie in 2005, he did express some misgivings about the questions being exactly like final submissions (advocating a position rather than expressing a balanced expert opinion), but he felt that, considering the problems with Woenne-Green's early report, explicit direction was required to ensure that the resulting report would add something to the overall case.

Elliott had to complete the report under extreme time pressures, during a break in the hearing between the Aboriginal evidence on country and the reconvened hearing in Adelaide for the evidence of the various experts and the pastoral lessees. He produced the report in 10 days (T. 2368–9). He did have his previous report and his accumulated knowledge of the archive to draw on, as well as Maddock's first report and the evidence of the claimants. He told me in 2005 that he had been thinking about the issues for a long time, implying that, although the time frame was tight, it was not impossible. Given the circumstances, however, it is no surprise that this critical report is also very concise.[13] What was left out of the report was to feature prominently in the judge's findings of Elliott's supposed bias. Because of the urgency, there was also no possibility of peer review of the report.

In responding to the issue of the nature of traditional laws and customs, Elliott's report bypassed most of the academic literature on primitive law, legal pluralism and modern law. It took the expedient of approximating 'traditional laws and customs' as 'culture' and adopted Berndt's distinction between the Dreaming law and custom, on the one hand, and kin-based law and custom, on the other. Elliott saw this distinction as one version of the classic formulations of the distinction between 'culture', as a system of ideas and beliefs, and 'society', as governed by principles or laws of social organisation.[14]

It is difficult to see how this distinction advances an understanding of the nature of Aboriginal 'traditional laws and customs', but it did provide Elliott with a framework for outlining the Dreaming as an ontology, cosmogony, system of beliefs, practices and rituals, and a hierarchical economy of sacred knowledge backed by social sanctions, as well as outlining various kinship rules and traditional practices relating to sex segregation, hunting, mourning, visiting sites and so on. His list of traditional 'beliefs, rules and practices', including examples taken from the transcript of the claimants' evidence, was quite extensive (Elliott 2001:3–12).

He identified the Western Desert cultural bloc as the Aboriginal people who acknowledge and observe the traditional laws and customs described, but attempted to identify an eastern subgroup of this cultural bloc. The way he did this became surprisingly controversial in the hearing. He suggested a community of Yankunytjatjara, Pitjantjatjara and Antakirinya-speaking peoples within the Western Desert cultural bloc. He listed 10 features of this 'community', but the distinguishing features seemed to be the last three: residence in the eastern area; shared history, particularly in relation to pastoral leases in the eastern area; and the absence of 'sections, subsections and patrimoieties' (2001:14–15).

Questions 7 and 8 in his brief requested Elliott to consider continuity of traditional connection in terms of whether there had been a 'cessation of the acknowledgment and observances' and whether there had been 'a loss of

13 It was 64 pages, excluding a male-only restricted section.

14 Craig Elliott's comments on my draft chapter, July 2005.

connection with the land'. In comparison with the robust academic model raised in Chapter 1, it can be observed that the form of these questions directs Elliott to come to a judge-like categorical conclusion, rather than explore the nature of the historical transformation of traditions over the period of colonisation. Elliott obligingly responded only to the questions as framed.[15] In brief, his argument was that, at the level of the Western Desert cultural bloc, the writings of Elkin, Tindale, the Berndts and Strehlow, properly understood, demonstrate that there has been no substantial discontinuity of traditional laws and customs. This position involved a critique of Tindale's Western Desert tribal boundaries 'as not having stood the test of anthropological scrutiny and as a cartographical misnomer' (2001:55).

It also involved a critique of the theory that, over the period of colonisation, Aboriginal groups from the west have been usurping the traditional country of eastern groups (2001:43–55). This was an argument based, in part, on an anthropological deconstruction of Tindale's assertions, rather than a detailed historical demographic study, which would have been beyond the resources of the claimants to undertake, even if there were enough Aboriginal people still alive to provide a conclusive answer about early twentieth-century population movements. The argument was that, within the Western Desert cultural bloc, individuals have multiple traditional ties to various places and that usurpation at the level of 'tribe' is highly unlikely:

> Accounts of the Western Desert that interpret population movements in terms of 'displacement' and territorial 'usurpation' overlook a fundamental feature of the traditional system of connection to land, in my view. Namely, that the system has a significant life history or biographical component, chiefly through the mechanism of country of birth. Therefore, people with ancestral connections elsewhere can and do acquire a legitimate, recognised connection to another area, including to an area with different language identity. (2001:54–5)

This was an effective argument against taking tribal usurpation too literally, but has its own problems, perhaps reflecting the general difficulty that anthropology has in grappling with historical transformation. There is a mismatch between the question formulated in terms of historical change and the answer in terms of the synchronic generalising of ethnography. Moreover, if there were in fact unprecedented, relatively large-scale population movements to the fringes of the Western Desert then it would seem that a relatively rapid succession of traditional ownership, consistent with shared traditional principles, could have happened.

With the benefit of hindsight, I asked Elliott why he felt that he had to resolve the question given the lack of conclusive data—in other words, why he could

15 Elliott pointed out in his comments on the draft chapter (July 2005) that he did refer to cultural and historical change in his report (in paragraphs 1.15, 3.14 and 7.4). While this observation is true, those brief comments tend to simply assert the continuity of traditional culture despite historical change, so I think my general point remains valid.

not have said that the current claimants are part of the eastern Western Desert cultural bloc, who have always been the traditional owners *or, alternatively*, that the claimants are people from the west within the Western Desert cultural bloc, who succeeded to traditional ownership of the area according to legitimate traditional principles such as place of birth, descent, long association, knowledge of local Dreaming stories and ceremonies. His answer was that he felt it was incumbent on him as an expert witness to provide a firm opinion and that he had resolved the issue to his own satisfaction.

Under the rubric of 'connection' (Question 8), Elliott traced early Aboriginal occupation of the claim area, drawing on the conclusions of the archaeologist's report, the accounts of early explorers and his older Aboriginal informants. He then narrowed the focus to the eastern Western Desert bloc, his Yankunytjatjara Pitjantjatjara Antakirinya community, again drawing on the anthropological work of Elkin, the Berndts, Tindale, Strehlow (especially his 1965 field trip), and Vachon's fieldwork in 1977–78. Elliott pointed out that the postwar period was also covered in the claimants' evidence and oral history taken by him. He referred to continuing knowledge of the sites, Dreamings and regional ceremonial life to conclude that there had been no loss of traditional connection (2001:32–7).

Maddock's second report

Maddock's second report was essentially a critique of Elliott's second report, particularly the idea of a Pitjantjatjara Yankunytjatjara Antakirinya community. Maddock accused Elliott of not defining what he meant by 'community'—that is, in relation to the various ways in which the word 'community' had been used in the anthropological literature—for example, as a group of tribes (Matthews), as a sub-tribal unit (Meggitt) or as a residential settlement (Doohan, Palmer) (T. 3431–3). He thought that there was no precedent in the anthropological literature for a Pitjantjatjara Yankunytjatjara Antakirinya community. He examined Elliott's 10 criteria individually and concluded that none of them produced a distinctive group that was an ethnographic reality or part of the claimants' consciousness, rather than a construct of Elliott's:

> It is really a topological exercise in which you are seeing how people can be classified in terms of some feature of their language or their social or religious life, which happens to be of interest to you...I would have thought that there must be some sort of structure of authority or structure of organisation which holds it together as a community. (T. 3434)

In his critique, Maddock seems to ignore the legal framing. It is the legal doctrine that requires some sort of title-holding group. In other words, he seems to make no allowance for the imposed artificiality of the claim process. Instead he framed it as an anthropological question independent of the legal framework: what are the features of a group as an ethnographic reality? Even within anthropological discourse, this question does not make much sense without specifying the purpose of the inquiry. Maddock himself demonstrated how the word 'community' could be used in various ways, yet he does not identify how his largely impressionistic ideal of corporate-ness relates to the anthropology of groups generally or the ethnography of the Western Desert cultural bloc, with its rather loose social structures. His expectation of a relatively high degree of corporate-ness is not necessarily required by legal doctrine, which, as we have seen in Chapter 1, is unhelpfully indeterminate.

Maddock also thought that, in listing all the traditional activities mentioned in the evidence, Elliott had not discriminated between activities that really mattered to the claimants and activities that they might not have strong views about, so that he 'overstated the position' (T. 3439). Having heard the Aboriginal evidence, Maddock still had his doubts about the extent to which the applicants observed their traditional laws and customs, as opposed to simply recognising them as being the law. In other words, he wondered whether the evidence he had heard was part of a living culture, whether most boys were still being put through initiation ceremonies, whether other ritual practices were being maintained, whether they related to the claim area itself and how the traditional system of promised marriage was faring (T. 3438). Elliott was incredulous that Maddock still had these doubts, given the evidence in the restricted sessions covering these issues.

Craig Elliott's cross-examination

By any standards, Elliott's cross-examination was a gruelling marathon. His examination-in-chief went for two full days and his cross-examination by two Queen's Counsel lasted eight days—a total of 10 days. This compares with Beckett's total of three days and Sullivan's one and a half days.

Besanko QC for the State and Whittington QC for the owners of the pastoral station had plenty of material on which to base their questions, having undertaken an extensive discovery process.[16] It became apparent in the course of cross-examination that Besanko and Whittington did indeed have the resources

16 Apart from the circulation of the formal reports of Susan Woenne-Green and Craig Elliott, the other parties had obtained all the original fieldwork data, including fieldnotes, tape recordings, transcripts of tape recordings, videos, and photographs. In addition, all the relevant anthropological journal articles had been conveniently collected by Elliott into three folders and copied to all the parties.

between them to exhaustively sift through all the material that was available to them. Moreover, they had two reports from Professor Maddock, in effect critiquing Elliott's first and second reports.

The attack on Elliott's reports can be outlined in a summary way as statements that were implied in the questions he was asked.

- His research methodology did not live up to the ideal of participant observation in anthropology because he relied largely on interviews and did not observe the performance of any ceremonies (T. 2391, 2537).
- He was too reliant on a few key informants rather than testing data with a variety of informants (T. 2541).
- There were inconsistencies between his reports and some of his fieldnotes on which they were based (T. 2613).
- There were inconsistencies between the evidence of the claimants and the transcripts of taped field interviews—for example, about whether there had been discussions with the claimants about the Antakirinya (T. 2619–22).
- He was selective in his use of the older anthropological authorities in a way that was biased towards supporting the claimants' case.
- A fair reading of Elkin, Tindale and the Berndts would indicate that Antakirinya was more than a dialect label applied by others; it was a widespread self-identification of people who had left the vicinity of the claim area (T. 2545–6, 2559–60, 2719–20).
- A fair reading of the anthropological literature would indicate that there had been disputes over territory and there had been a permanent migration out of the desert—that is, the usurpation of Antakirinya territory by Yankunytjatjara or Pitjantjatjara people from the west was plausible (T. 2568–99, 2735–65).
- There is no support in the anthropological literature for the existence of a Yankunytjatjara Pitjantjatjara Antakirinya community (T. 2646–52), nor is it an ethnographic reality (T. 2370–2, 2798–802).
- There is evidence in the anthropological literature for a distinction between Yankunytjatjara and Pitjantjatjara identities and traditional territories that indicates the artificiality of a Yankunytjatjara Pitjantjatjara Antakirinya community (T. 2553–7, 2653–8).

To make these statements, with the benefit of hindsight, is to say nothing of the process involved, the difficulties faced by the witness in responding to questions, their hidden implications and the effect that misjudged answers might have had on the witness's credibility with the judge. The actual cross-examination was conducted at a much more minute level, exemplified by Besanko's early attention to references in a footnote in Elliott's first report. Elliott's footnote referred to a footnote in the Berndts' report on fieldwork at Ooldea and Besanko suggested that Elliott had misrepresented the Berndts' footnote. The footnote was of minor significance to Elliott's report, but the judge, who also had the relevant passage from the Berndts, tended to agree, from his own reading, that there had been a misrepresentation (T. 2376).[17]

This exchange began a long series of questions that examined passages in particular articles in the anthropological literature and questioned Elliott on why his conclusions seemed to be at variance with the quotation. The process of considering each individual item in the archive tends to reinforce the background assumption that the archive is easily accessible to the non-expert and is not a diverse, complex and ever-expanding and continually revised body of knowledge. Then the repetition of each instance that does not directly support the expert's conclusion creates a cumulative effect of the recalcitrance and unreasonableness of the expert.

The only effective way to deal with this kind of cross-examination is to convincingly demonstrate that the passages quoted have been taken out of context and that, given a proper understanding of the totality of the archive, the expert's concluded view is correct. In effect, this means reclaiming mastery over the anthropological archive. Elliott managed to do this on a number of occasions—for example, when Whittington confronted him with one episode,

---

17 The disputed footnote was in an appendix to the Oceania monograph *A Preliminary Report of Fieldwork in the Ooldea Region, Western South Australia*. The appendix described an initiation ceremony held at Macumba Station in 1944 involving 'Antingari, Pidjandja and southern Aranda' people. Following the sentence 'The songs employed referred to the *Ma;lu* and *Kanjala* myth', the footnote reads:

> This Kangaroo and Euro myth belongs partly to the Pidjandja and partly to the Aranda people; it is because of this feature that the ceremony applies appropriately to people of Aranda and Pidjandja (*and hence Antingari, because of its similar cultural background*) extraction, such as are to be found in the Oodnadatta–Macumba area. It further accentuates the fact that it is not only since European times that these two peoples have been in close contact; although each group has maintained a definite pattern of culture clearly dissimilar to that of the other, a certain merging of religious dogma and ritual was unavoidable and was indeed welcome as a means of revivifying certain ceremonies from time to time. In fact the further a certain myth extended, the greater the prestige and sacred aura assumed by the relevant cult lodge; the ceremonies, the ritual, songs and relics (i.e. the sacred objects) developed into a 'big law' or 'big word'; see also Oceania, Vol. XIV, No. 1, p. 42. [Emphasis added]

The footnote then goes on to outline the myth and at various points contrasts 'Pidjandja' and Aranda terminology. Elliott's footnote read:

> In the Berndts' usage, 'Pidjandja' [= Pitjantjatjara] includes 'Antingari' (which I expect denotes Antikirinya). According to the Berndt's [sic], the 'Pidjandja' and 'Antingari', while being 'clearly dissimilar', share a 'similar cultural background' due to close social contact, occupation of an association with nearby areas and the 'merging of religious dogma and ritual' over time (1945:243). (Elliott 2000:35)

Besanko questioned whether the Berndts' footnote supported the assertion in Elliott's footnote, suggesting that the Berndts' footnote was essentially a comparison of Aranda and Pitjantjatjara. The judge tended to agree (T. 2376). In my view, Elliott was correct in his reading of the phrase in brackets, but incorrect in his reading of the remainder of the footnote, which is more consistent with a Pitjantjatjara–Aranda comparison.

supportive of his case, in the long-running Australian local organisation debate. Elliott was able to pinpoint just where Whittington's selective quotation appeared in the broader debate (T. 2712). Many times, however, Elliott's answers were a taciturn denial of the proposition being put to him. In effect, he was standing his ground, but not taking up the opportunity of providing a further explanation of his view.

Elliott faced the dilemma that all expert witnesses face: knowing that the cross-examiner is trying to trap them and having to decide whether to concede a seemingly innocuous proposition or quickly intuit the implied critique and attempt to answer it in advance. To concede too readily will undermine a considered opinion. Not to concede a seemingly obvious proposition might appear to be unresponsive, inflexible and biased. These critical decisions have to be made instantaneously. The experienced expert witness is able to project independence by being able to engage in hypothetical discussions, by readily agreeing to seemingly innocuous propositions, while adding any relevant reservations or qualifications and, generally, by giving expansive answers. Elliott did manage this on occasion with answers in the following form:

> C. N. ELLIOTT: I think that's right but, to be more accurate, I think… (T. 2545)[18]

The rattled, inexperienced expert witness tends to be negative and defensive. Even experienced expert witnesses can be made to appear unresponsive and biased, if they respond to seemingly obvious propositions with the technical reservations that can be portrayed as pedantic, which is so readily perceived as evasiveness (accordingly, accuracy becomes quibbling and pedantry). Elliott's overcautiousness at times exasperated the judge (see T. 2691–2, 2576–7). In this battle of perceptions, there is an obvious mismatch between the field of the academy, in which fine distinctions and counter-intuitive refinements might be rewarded, and the juridical field, in which encapsulating generalisations and agreement to 'commonsense' observations might be more persuasive.

Elliott explained to me that there was another, more compelling, reason why his answers were short; this reason was not reflected in the transcript. He was simply cut off by the judge, who would indicate with a nod that the cross-examining barrister should continue.[19]

Unfortunately, Elliott often tended to anticipate questions rather than answer the question asked, and this had a similar effect of projecting unresponsiveness

18 Elliott thought that he had answered in this form on many more occasions and pointed to examples at T. 2539, 2541, 2563, 2564 and 2700.

19 Craig Elliott's comments on the draft chapter, July 2005.

and inflexibility. One example was Whittington's attempt to engage Elliott in hypothetical discussions about different models of population movements, contrasting peripatetic movements and permanent migration:

> MR WHITTINGTON: The essential difference is this, is it not, Mr Elliott, that in the latter case, the migratory model, the movement is permanent?
>
> C. N. ELLIOTT: No, I don't accept that, I think the record shows that people moved around to settlements such as Ooldea and to the stations on the eastern side of the Western Desert and further to Oodnadatta and Finke...
>
> MR WHITTINGTON: Now, you're there addressing what you considered to be the fact of the matter as opposed to the two models I've put...you would accept that conceptually there are two different models, wouldn't you?
>
> C. N. ELLIOTT: I don't accept that kind of distinction because in this region, a region of great aridity, it's not possible to say that people would move with the intention of migrating to another place. The people moved around in order to sustain life and for other social and religious reasons. There are both similarities and differences in the two processes.
>
> MR WHITTINGTON: So you will not as an expert witness even allow the possibility of those two theoretical models so we can attempt to test what you say? (T. 2741–2)

When the expert witness is being cross-examined, he finds himself alone in the world. He cannot seek safety in having confined himself to the terms of his brief.[20] His own counsel cannot help him, apart from objecting to questions on an extremely limited number of grounds. The judge cannot help him, for fear of unfairly limiting the right of opposing counsel to test his evidence.

Recalling the cross-examination when I interviewed him in 2005, Elliott admitted to a growing feeling of fatalism. He began to feel that any concession would be used against him, that standing by his reports would be portrayed as inflexibility, and that the judge had already taken a negative view of him and was cutting off his answers. This feeling might help to explain the many missed opportunities to attempt to win over the court to his point of view by further explanation. Elliott's feelings are understandable, especially considering that

---

20 There is a legal argument that the terms of a brief would be relevant to the assessment of professional obligations in a non-litigation setting according to Justice von Doussa in *Chapman v Luminis Pty Ltd* (No. 5) [2001] FCA 1106 (21 August 2001). The judge made it clear that these considerations did not apply to an expert witness in court. Even in non-court situations, von Doussa's reasoning has been criticised (see Burke 2002; Edmond 2004; Merlan 2001).

the judge's first intervention in his cross-examination was the negative comment about the footnote mentioned above (T. 2376), and other instances when the judge adopted a sarcastic attitude:

> HIS HONOUR: In 1953 were you engaged in the discipline of anthropology?
>
> C. N. ELLIOTT: No, I wasn't, sir.
>
> HIS HONOUR: I didn't think so. What's your justification for saying that Tindale, who was then engaged in the discipline of anthropology, was wrong to say that Aboriginal groups fought and killed for territory? (T. 2747)

The judge's irritation did on occasion lead him to give Elliott advice on how to better respond to some questions. He advised Elliott that, if a question could not be answered with a 'yes' or 'no', he could say so (T. 2699) and that he should answer a question first then add qualifications, not answer with the qualifications (T. 2683). These seemingly helpful suggestions probably had their own demoralising effect since they provided feedback to Elliott that he was not meeting the judge's expectations of an expert witness.[21]

Daniel Vachon's and Jon Willis's evidence

To keep this case study within reasonable bounds, I have omitted consideration of Vachon's evidence. Willis's evidence, being restricted, is largely inaccessible. There are, however, some references to it in the unrestricted transcript. These references indicate the centrality he gave to the concept of *kuranitja* (spirit essence of the Dreaming ancestors)—a term not mentioned by Woenne-Green or Elliott. It was potentially important in explaining the different pathways to becoming *ngUraritja* in a unified way, based on traditional Aboriginal beliefs—that is, in a way that avoided the complexities of anthropological theories, but at the same time illuminated them. Willis had apparently spoken of birth as a coming into being of local *kuranitja*, particularly entering the body during the period commencing from conception to the dropping of the umbilical stub, but also *kuranitja* entering the body through the water and food taken from the country over the course of a lifetime (T. 3455).

21 Elliott's view was that these seemingly helpful interventions were in fact designed to help the cross-examiners, not him (Comments on the draft chapter, July 2005).

Maddock's cross-examination

Howie's cross-examination of Maddock is reminiscent of the cross-examination of Kolig in *Rubibi*, although it is clear that Howie had a better grasp of anthropology and was able to engage in a more fluid discussion with Maddock. The aim was to neutralise Maddock's most harmful opinions by systematically recounting the evidence in order to demonstrate the observance of tradition and the existence of a Yankunytjatjara Pitjantjatjara Antakirinya community, in the hope of forcing some concessions from him or demonstrating his unreasonableness. Another, more aggressive course would have been to attack his lack of fieldwork experience in the Western Desert. Howie decided against this course because he thought, on balance, that Maddock's evidence was helpful to their case and that his evidence would be influential with the judge.

The strategy was successful up to a point, but on some critical issues Maddock remained unhelpful to the claimants. Adopting a rather strict approach to the requirements of evidence, he was not prepared to include the claimants among the strong ritual community described by Willis because he felt that there was insufficient evidence linking them to the rituals, and he noted that Elliott had not attended any such rituals as part of his research for the claim (T. 3457–62). He was also not prepared to suggest a more appropriate subgrouping, even though he thought that the claimants were within the Western Desert cultural bloc (T. 3492–520). He simply repeated his critique of the Yankunytjatjara Pitjantjatjara Antakirinya community.

The judge

O'Loughlin was a solicitor specialising in taxation law in Adelaide between 1964 and 1984 when he was appointed as a judge of the Supreme Court of South Australia. He was appointed to the Federal Court of Australia in 1989. Besanko and Whittington were both from the Adelaide Bar and Howie detected a degree of camaraderie between them and the judge, including references to cases in which they all had been involved. O'Loughlin had also had previous encounters with Aboriginal issues.[22] Justice O'Loughlin was on the verge of retirement

22 He had been a member of the Full Court bench that decided that the definition of traditional owner in the *Land Rights Act* did not require patrilineal descent groups (*Northern Land Council v Olney* (1992) 34 FCR 470); he had decided that the notice calling for submissions prior to the minister's declaration in the Hindmarsh Island dispute was inadequate and he had set aside the declaration (*Chapman v Tickner* (1995) 55 FCR 316); and he had rejected the *Northern Territory Stolen Generation Case* on both legal and evidential grounds (*Cubillo v Commonwealth* [2000] FCA 1084, 11 August 2000). He had also heard a small native title claim (*The Ngalakan People v Northern Territory of Australia* [2001] FCA 654, 5 June 2001). In *De Rose Hill*, he made a passing reference to his knowledge of anthropology, gained in previous cases (T. 2277).

when he heard this case. A recurrent theme throughout the hearing was his warning about the dreaded prospect of another judge having to hear all the evidence again and his irritation that the case was taking so long.

He also seemed to have difficulty appreciating what the claimants were hoping to achieve through the claim:

> [39] Some, but not all, of the Aboriginal witnesses were asked what it would mean to them if the claimants were to be successful in obtaining a determination of native title. Of those who were questioned on the subject, some did not have an answer. None of them gave detailed evidence that amounted to statements of intention to resume the observance of traditional customs or the maintenance and acknowledgement of traditional laws.[23]

That the judge had difficulties with the merits of the claim was confirmed by the claimants' solicitor, Tim Wooley, who had attended all the preliminary hearings and had tried to explain to the doubtful judge the potential benefits of the right to negotiate under the *Native Title Act*.

One can easily imagine the old judge, trudging around the desert in winter in the cold and rainy conditions, wondering to himself, 'Why are we here; for all the resources put into the hearing how will the claimants benefit and will it be worth the disruption to the pastoralists?' The strategic importance of the case for the whole of the pastoral zone was not something that could legitimately be raised in the case and certainly it could not have been taken into account explicitly by the judge, who was obliged to consider the merits of the case on evidence presented. The broader considerations did enter into the judge's reasons, but in a negative way for the claimants. He seemed to think that De Rose Hill Station had been unfairly targeted since the claimants' traditional country extended beyond the boundaries of De Rose Hill to neighbouring pastoral leases, which had not been claimed (see para. 908).

The judgment

O'Loughlin delivered his exceedingly long judgment on 1 December 2002.[24] In his detailed review of the claimants' case and the course of their evidence, two opposite approaches to the Aboriginal evidence emerged: one sympathetic to the

23 Also see paras 39–47.

24 It was 933 paragraphs long, filling 259 printed pages.

difficulties that the claimants faced as witnesses and another based on a strong belief in the ability of forensic processes to cut through all those difficulties and find the truth.[25]

O'Loughlin had no difficulty in finding that certain monosyllabic answers of Aboriginal witnesses to leading questions in cross-examination completely undermined the position they had taken in their written statement and examination-in-chief (paras 92–3, 95). The judge also took a hard line on the need for a high degree of consistency in Aboriginal evidence. Instead of considering the possibility of contextual factors influencing the naming of different people as *ngureritja*, the judge concluded that Peter De Rose had deliberately lied in his evidence as demonstrated by the inconsistencies in lists of names given to Elliott years before, during the research (para. 85). Moreover, although the judge seemed to be sympathetic to the many difficulties faced by the Aboriginal witnesses, he remained unsatisfied with the level of detail of their evidence in the witness box and he made an invidious comparison with the level of detail he received from Dr Willis, particularly about the laws and customs of male initiation (paras 336–42).

One of the features of O'Loughlin's judgment is how seemingly innocuous pieces of evidence are promoted to centre stage. For example, evidence about the duty of *ngureritja* to clean certain sacred waterholes, which Whittington used in cross-examination as evidence of the decline of tradition, was taken up with a vengeance by the judge. Peter De Rose had explained his neglect of his *ngureritja* duties in terms of the priority given to station work when he was employed by the Fullers. But the judge expected more energy and bravery: 'If Peter and the other witnesses who said that they were *Ngureritja* for De Rose Hill were intent on performing their duties as *Ngureritja*, I am quite satisfied that they would have entered on the land—even surreptitiously if necessary—to perform their duties' (para. 106).

As might be expected, the excessive denials of everything Antakirinya became a major theme for O'Loughlin (paras 117–44). He concluded, however, that

> there was sufficient evidence adduced in this trial for me to conclude that there were (and maybe are) two closely related Aboriginal groups speaking the same language and dialect—the Antakirinya and the

25 The first approach is exemplified by his acknowledgment of the limited value of answers to leading questions and questions containing alternatives (paras 249–59); the futility of cross-examining on Aboriginal Dreaming tracks as if they were compatible with European boundaries (paras 81–2); the acknowledgment that specifying boundaries for one's traditional country in cross-examination was an unnatural exercise for these Aboriginal witnesses (para. 115); and generally acknowledging the limits of the adversarial process in finding answers to questions such as whether in the past, prospective parents would return to a husband's country for the birth of the child (para. 89). It is interesting to note that some of these passages were quoted by Graeme Neate, the President of the National Native Title Tribunal, to demonstrate judicial acknowledgment of the difficulties faced by Aboriginal witnesses (see Neate 2004:20–3). Neate tended to ignore the second tendency in O'Loughlin's judgment.

> Yankunytjatjara. I am not, however, able to make a finding to the effect that the Antakirinya people once inhabited the claim area but were dispossessed by the Yankunytjatjara. (Para. 144)

In relation to the reason for Aboriginal people leaving De Rose Hill Station, the judge recited the conflicting evidence about 'Snowy's accident' but refused to make a finding about whether it had precipitated a walk-off (paras 277–83). He even refused to make a finding that Aboriginal people left De Rose Hill because of perceived hostility by the Fullers, explaining that '[i]f the Aboriginal people left De Rose Hill Station for an unreasonable or illogical reason (even though subjectively they may have thought their departure was necessary) they cannot now turn their lack of reasonableness and lack of logic to their advantage' (para. 291).

The expert anthropologists

The older ethnographic sources were dealt with as a separate issue in the judgment (paras 292–305), demonstrating that they had become dislodged from the umbrella of expert testimony, somewhat like historical documents that are easily accessible to the layperson and could not be claimed as part of the esoterica of an expert anthropologist. Elkin, Tindale, Berndt and Strehlow were all introduced in terms of their academic capital, the position they attained within their various institutions, giving an indication of how the juridical field would reorder the academic field. Unlike historical sources, however, there seems to be a reluctance to reinterpret older anthropological conceptualisations of landowning groups. For example, in relation to Berndt's work the judge stated:

> I do not necessarily regard the evidence of the witnesses as a contradiction of the earlier literature; rather it is explainable, either on the grounds of the evolutionary process, or because the traditional laws and customs of this area are and were at variance with the traditional laws and customs on which the early writers had based their opinions. (Para. 102)

This approach bears many similarities with the way in which later anthropologists have dealt with ethnographic information inconsistent with horde theory (see Chapter 4).

Elliott did not fare well in O'Loughlin's judgment:

> [352] Unfortunately, I have come to the opinion that Mr Elliot became too close to the claimants and their cause; he failed to exhibit the objectivity and neutrality that is required of an expert who is giving evidence before the court. Rather, he seemed—too often—to be an advocate for the applicants.

The examples the judge gave had been passed over in cross-examination uneventfully. Now, they became the prime examples of Elliott's bias and advocacy. At various points during his research, Peter De Rose had given Elliott the names of people whom Peter thought were *ngureritja* for De Rose Hill Station. Some of the people whom Peter De Rose had initially dismissed as not being *nguraritja* were ultimately included in the claimant group. The judge concluded that, because Elliott had not mentioned and explained Peter De Rose's contrary opinions, Elliott had lost his neutrality and become an advocate (paras 353–7). What is difficult to follow in this example is why distancing himself from Peter De Rose could not just as easily be seen as demonstrating Elliott's independence.

The judge gave another example in which he elevated an even more obscure transcribed interview with Riley Tjayranyi, conducted early in Elliott's research. Riley had made an initial denial of being *nguraritja*. Elliott had explained this in cross-examination as being part of an Aboriginal etiquette of preferring such an identification to come from others. On reflection, he explained to me in 2005 that it might have simply been Riley's ironic humour. Now the omission of an explanation of this incident became the example *par excellence* of why Elliott's reports could not be accepted as presenting an accurate picture of the information the claimants had given him (para. 359).

O'Loughlin bolstered these examples with an account of Elliott's cross-examination:

> I must say that Mr Elliot seemed very reluctant to accept, either that such migrations were permanent, or that they were in any way due to the attractions of white settlement. There was ample evidence to warrant a finding that these migrations did occur (most notably as a result of the claimants' own evidence), and his refusal to concede as much indicated, in my view, an obdurate refusal to give ground where appropriate. (Para. 366)

The judge did accept some of Elliott's evidence. He accepted much of the factual information about the various Dreamings and sites in Elliott's reports as corroborative of the Aboriginal witnesses' evidence and as providing contextual detail. Critically for the claimants, he also accepted Elliott's fourfold criteria for becoming a *nguraritja* (para. 897). The judge concluded, however, that 'his partisanship has been his undoing and, as a result, where he has expressed an unsupported opinion that is at odds with Professor Maddock, I rely on the evidence and opinions of the Professor' (para. 367).

The lack of support from Maddock for the concept of a Yankunytjatjara Pitjantjatjara Antakirinya community and the lack of explicit supporting evidence from the Aboriginal witnesses led O'Loughlin to reject Elliott's evidence on this issue (paras 360–5).

In total contrast with the judge's assessment of Elliott was his praise for Maddock: 'Professor Maddock gave his evidence in a forthright and neutral manner. I have had no difficulty in accepting him as an expert, well-qualified to comment on anthropological matters' (para. 369).

O'Loughlin's only reservation was about Maddock's misguided belief in the need to access traditional laws and customs as they existed at the time British sovereignty was asserted. On this issue, Maddock seemed to have assumed a more extreme position than legal doctrine required, for the need to make inferences about the distant past from post-contact sources and archaeology had long been accepted by the courts (paras 369–70).

On everything else, O'Loughlin adopted Maddock's views. Advantageously for the claimants, it meant support for the judge concluding:

> I see no reason why the migratory movements of the Pitjantjatjara to the east—whether as a result of drought or war or marriage—should not be accepted as part of the history and social structure of the Aboriginal people of the Western Desert Bloc. This conclusion, which is no more than an inference that is based more on the evidence of *Anangu* witnesses than it is on the opinions of the experts, gains some support from the frequency of intermarriage and the consequential movement between the Pitjantjatjara and Yankunytjatjara people. (Para. 372)

That conclusion avoided the whole usurpation issue. Adopting Maddock's views also meant, however, adopting his criticisms of the lack of precision in Elliott's reports about the observance of tradition and Maddock's general doubts regarding the adequacy of the claimants' evidence of the current observance of tradition (paras 373–8).

Maddock's doubts were strictly superfluous, for the judge was obliged to make his own assessment of the same evidence that Maddock had heard. Yet Maddock's doubts are given a pivotal position in the structure of the judgment. They seem to justify the remainder of the judgment, which is an evaluation of the observance of traditional laws and customs relating to the claim area following the 1978 exodus.

The long and winding road leading to the judge's eventual negative conclusion can be summarised as follows.

- Belated efforts to protect some sites on De Rose Hill Station raise the question of the claimants' prior inactivity regarding the same sites (para. 402).
- Evidence of older witnesses that ceremonies used to be held at some sites highlighted the absence of those activities since then (para. 429).
- Despite Doug Fuller's 'aggressive, bullying demeanour' and the occasional intimidation of Aboriginal people by the use of firearms, Snowy De Rose, Peter De Rose and others gave evidence that they were not fearful of returning to De Rose Hill (paras 430–48).
- It was difficult to accept that some Aboriginal witnesses genuinely thought that Doug Fuller might shoot them (para. 482).
- Evidence of station gates being locked prior to 1994 was incorrect and not a legitimate excuse for the claimants not returning to De Rose Hill post-1978 (para. 491).
- Peter De Rose did not give any cultural or religious reason for his intermittent visits to De Rose Hill after 1978, save for hunting kangaroos (para. 592); he did not give the detailed evidence about his responsibilities as *nguraritja* for teaching others about the sites on De Rose Hill, including whether he taught his own children and grandchildren; he had not fulfilled his *nguraritja* duties to clean out certain sacred waterholes; all this is evidence of his abandonment of his traditional connection to the area.
- All the other claimants did not demonstrate a strong traditional connection to De Rose Hill as they had also failed to attend to their traditional duties as *nguraritja*, failed to visit or maintain their connection with the land post-1978, and had allowed 'non-Aboriginal factors', such as following work and educational opportunities, to rule their lives (para. 681).

In conclusion, the judge asserted

- gaps in the evidence about the communal and ritual life of the claimants (para. 905)
- lack of evidence that the claimants met each other or participated in the communal or group ceremonies, discussions or projects (para. 910)
- loss of physical connection since 1978
- loss of spiritual connection as demonstrated by the lack of performance of ceremonies on the land and lack of any plans to use the land for traditional purposes if they were successful (paras 906–8).

In short, there had been a loss of traditional connection and there was no longer any native title.

The view of the Full Federal Court

ALRM appealed to the Full Federal Court. The bench consisted of Justices Wilcox, Sackville and Merkel. They proved sympathetic to the claimants' complaints about O'Loughlin's judgment and, ultimately, they overturned it and substituted their own determination of native title.[26]

That the Full Federal Court could overturn Justice O'Loughlin's findings requires us to qualify the idea of fact-finding being the trial judge's empire; it now seems more like a shared responsibility with appeal courts because of the vague fact/law distinction and the fundamental indeterminacies in the key concepts of the legal doctrine of native title. The effect of this qualification is that, although appeals are meant to be restricted to questions of law only, appeals in native title can reopen many issues, to the extent of appearing to be another chance to re-argue final submissions.[27]

Conclusions about the *De Rose Hill* case study

When I made my initial approach to Elliott, explaining that my interest was in the nature of anthropological agency in native title claims, he thought that it was laughable, given his experience. 'What agency?' he asked. Had not the terms of his involvement been dictated by law and lawyers from the very beginning? His relative powerlessness to influence the direction of claim research and the presentation of the evidence does require examination (see below). Within these constraints, however, he did have choices to make about the triangulation of the claimants' likely evidence, the anthropological archive and legal doctrine, as well as choices about the degree of explicit reflexivity regarding key indeterminate terms that he incorporated into his report and evidence (see Chapter 1).

One of his most successful triangulation choices was to avoid the Stanner-inspired ideas of a traditional 'estate' and instead opt for a looser group of *nguraritja* and a list of four principal ways of achieving *nguraritja* status. In terms of the anthropological archive, that choice distanced him somewhat from the more clearly bounded groups of Elkin, Tindale, the Berndts and Tonkinson, and so distanced him from their academic capital. It drew him closer to Myers. Elliott's pathways to *nguraritja*-ship simplified Myers' 10 types of legitimate

26 See *De Rose and others v State of South Australia* [2003] FCAFC 286, 16 December 2003 and *De Rose v State of South Australia (No. 2)* [2005] FCAFC 110, 8 June 2005.

27 This effect was exemplified in this appeal by the extraordinary re-arguing of the usurpation thesis, converted into a legal argument, and the use the Full Federal Court made of Maddock's comments about the Western Desert bloc to justify their fact/inference distinction on the issue of the relevant native title group (paras 279–81). This distinction allowed them to say they were not disturbing a finding of fact but an inference made from the fact.

traditional claims and did not adopt his individual perspective of constant renegotiation.[28] Unlike Woenne-Green's long list of the variety of ways the claimants spoke about country, the identification of the four pathways could be seen as more abstract, stable and law-like. Moreover, it coincided with how the claimants expressed themselves, avoiding the problem in the *Ayers Rock* claim of a divergence between the claimants' evidence and an artificially neat model of estate groups, based on principles of descent alone.

Elliott's least successful triangulation was the idea of a Yankunytjatjara Pitjantjatjara Antakirinya community. Maddock made much of the fact that Elliott's terminology had not previously appeared in the anthropological archive. There was, however, some justification in the anthropological archive for this concept, even if Elliott had not marshalled all the evidence in his second report. Regional cultural differences within the Western Desert cultural bloc had been reported since Elkin and there had been many references to the eastern Western Desert people. Also, Hamilton identified a specific 'network' that is the same as Elliott's Yankunytjatjara Pitjantjatjara Antakirinya community, including references to Aboriginal people at Oodnadatta and Coober Pedy (Hamilton 1987). The claimants themselves did not use the terminology of 'community', and their constant disavowal of all things Antakirinya presented the impression of social distance rather than unity. Part of the problem might have been the word 'community' itself. Elliott was using it in quite a specific sense of the group of people who had in common the characteristics he listed. But the word 'community' has a wide range of references, from abstract commonalities of disparate individuals to intensive face-to-face interaction of groups with a high degree of corporate self-identification and corporate action. Elliott seems to have been pitching his idea of a Yankunytjatjara Pitjantjatjara Antakirinya community somewhere in the middle. But this level was vulnerable to demonstrations by Maddock and the pastoralist's lawyers of a lack of corporate-ness that appealed to an all-inclusive, non-technical understanding of 'community'. This possibility was open, despite the fact that Elliott never asserted a high degree of corporate-ness, and that the whole unsatisfactory enterprise was forced on the claimants by the requirements of the legal doctrine of native title to identify the group under which the claimants held native title rights. One wonders if similar problems would have arisen if it had been called 'the eastern Western Desert cultural bloc' or a 'network' or, perhaps, Berndt's 'society'.

I have already outlined the ways in which Elliott dealt with the key indeterminate concepts in his second report, principally by submerging the issue of indeterminacy, by emphasising the reportage aspect of fieldwork, by equating law and custom with culture and by selecting a title-holding group

28 Elliott pointed out that, although he did not adopt Myers' perspective, his model had a significant 'biographic component' (Comments on draft chapter, July 2005).

that seemed to be justifiable. In his discussion with me in 2005, Elliott spoke of being forced to demonstrate law in native title claims, which I took as an acknowledgment that the anthropologist must choose what is relevant to the court's task. He was also aware of the danger of making anthropology appear too complex. Perhaps he was right. The only time he admitted that it was possible to construct different communities among Western Desert people according to different criteria—'cutting up the pie in a different way'—he was criticised by Maddock for departing from ethnographic reality, a criticism adopted by the judge (judgment para. 363).

In any case, Elliott felt that the content of his second report was dictated by the questions Howie had formulated for him. In the circumstances, Elliott's feelings were understandable. There was a convergence of his own critique of Woenne-Green's early report—that it had failed to come to conclusions—the extreme time constraints and the request being formulated by the most experienced land claim lawyer in Australia. But he still might have underestimated his own influence at that point, because there was really no-one else to whom the lawyers could turn.

Maddock was not in a position to make the triangulations that Elliott made. His lack of relevant fieldwork and reliance on the court evidence of the claimants meant that his role began to approximate that of the judge's. His judge-like approach is also reflected in his lack of reflexivity about the implicit standards he was applying, especially when making statements such as 'I would have liked to see more evidence of the claimants' observance of tradition' and 'I would not call the Yankunytjatjara Pitjantjatjara Antakirinya grouping a community'. These submerged standards approximate a judge's orientation to practical fact-finding and the irrelevance of abstract theorising.

Because he had his own doubts about the case, O'Loughlin did not see Maddock as a competitor, but as someone who could share responsibility with him for the ultimate negative decision. This conclusion might imply that the judge took a strong view of the correct result rather than weighing up the evidence. As usual, things are not so clear cut. The indications in his judgment of his gestalt or hunch about the justice of the case have already been discussed. There is also the evidence of his interventions as recorded in the transcript. His first intervention interrupted Howie's opening address to discuss whether physical separation from traditional country could lead to a finding of loss of traditional connection (T. 23).

On the other hand, O'Loughlin's exhaustive account of the evidence in his judgment, including his acceptance of some of the claimants' arguments, and criticism of some aspects of Maddock's evidence, give the impression of thoroughness and the process of weighing the evidence. Again, for the experienced judgment writer, this is not necessarily inconsistent with having a strong hunch about the preferable outcome of the case from the very beginning.

One of the other impenetrable subtleties raised by this case is the extent to which the judge adopted what I would call the hubris of the superiority of forensic fact-finding. The judicial role requires an attitude of acceptance of legal doctrines about deciding cases on admissible evidence only. But this acceptance can range from the pragmatic (it is necessary and sometimes can reveal the truth) to unswerving belief (it is always the best way of revealing the truth). O'Loughlin seemed to waver between these two positions, as exemplified in his contradictory stances on the difficulties facing Aboriginal witnesses in the witness box.

The professional commitment of anthropology to the value of evidence arising from long-term fieldwork suggests scepticism towards what informants might say under pressure in a one-off court appearance. Elliott commented to me, rather sardonically, that, given all the typical problems with hearings, he was actually surprised that so much of the claimants' evidence did come out in a way that was consistent with what he had previously been told. It is now only possible to wonder how Maddock would have compared the different standards of what counts as evidence. In his published work, he seemed to be quite impressed with forensic standards.

Because of the big differential in academic capital between Elliott and Maddock, this case study raises the issue of the expert's position within the field of the academy, and his broader class position, more starkly than in the other two case studies.

Maddock, at the end of his career, had nothing to lose. He was able to give expansive answers, engage in hypothetical discussion and make concessions while preserving his essential point. My critique of his reports could be summarised as his carelessness about the consequences of his submerged criteria for what constitutes an adequate anthropological explanation in a native title expert report. It was, however, this very carelessness about consequences that was received by the judge as evidence of forthrightness and independence in the witness box. His courtroom performance and his academic capital combined to give him great influence, as evidenced by the judge, the claimants' lawyers and the Full Federal Court all seeking to support their position from his opinions.

Apart from Maddock, there were also the phantom experts, the big names in the anthropological archive: Elkin, the Berndts, Tindale and Strehlow. I have suggested that the separate status they were given in O'Loughlin's judgment reflects a struggle over the 'ownership' of the anthropological archive that is peculiar to native title processes. The early ethnography tends to be treated like historical sources: accessible and open to anyone to interpret. Paradoxically, this also tends to take them out of history, in the sense of the theoretical cross-currents of the time, and their reception and ongoing reassessment within anthropology. The struggle between judge and expert over the prerogative to authoritatively interpret the anthropological archive became even more explicit in the later Western Desert case of *Yulara*, which will be considered in the next chapter.

8. Apocalypse *Yulara*? The emergence of a judicial discourse of 'junk' anthropology

Joining the bruised anthropologists mentioned in the beginning of this book was a battered Peter Sutton, one of the most senior applied anthropologists working in Australia. He was the principal expert witness for the Western Desert applicants in the *Yulara* case and the focus of particularly unrelenting criticism by the trial judge, Justice Sackville.[1] In effect, Sackville blamed Sutton and the applicants' lawyers for what he found to be an unsustainable formulation of the case. To the surprise of many who assumed the applicants to be among the most traditionally orientated Aboriginal people in Australia, the judge decided that the evidence did not support the acknowledgment and observance of the set of laws and customs pleaded in the case. He pointedly suggested that the case might have succeeded had it been formulated in a different way. In a final crushing blow, the judge found that Sutton, a leading anthropologist and champion of strict professionalism in applied anthropology, had himself been biased.

Another participant, Basil Sansom, the anthropologist assisting the Northern Territory Government, published a cantankerous warning about the implications of the case for future expert anthropologists (Sansom 2007). His paper provoked a lengthy response from Sutton (2007) and a briefer one from John Morton (2007), who had been engaged by the Commonwealth to review the first version of Sutton's report.[2] Before attempting some evaluation of this interchange, the background of the case will be outlined.

Background

The claim by Yankunyatjatjara and Pitjantjatjara people for compensation for the extinguishment of native title rights was initiated in 1997 under the *Native Title Act* 1993. It related to a relatively small area of land, —104 sq km—which had been excluded from the much larger area of Aboriginal Land held by the Katiti Aboriginal Land Trust. The excluded land was on the northern border of Uluru National Park, also Aboriginal Land, and had been declared a town. As such it was excluded from claim under the *Land Rights Act*. It was the site

1 *Jango v Northern Territory of Australia* (No. 2) [2004] FCA 1004 (3 August 2004).

2 I also provided a comment on Sansom's paper (Burke 2007), as did Katie Glaskin (2007); Ian Keen (2007); and Lee Sackett (2007).

of the new town of Yulara, proclaimed in 1976, which essentially comprised accommodation and associated facilities for tourists visiting Uluru (Ayers Rock) and Kata Tjuta (the Olgas).

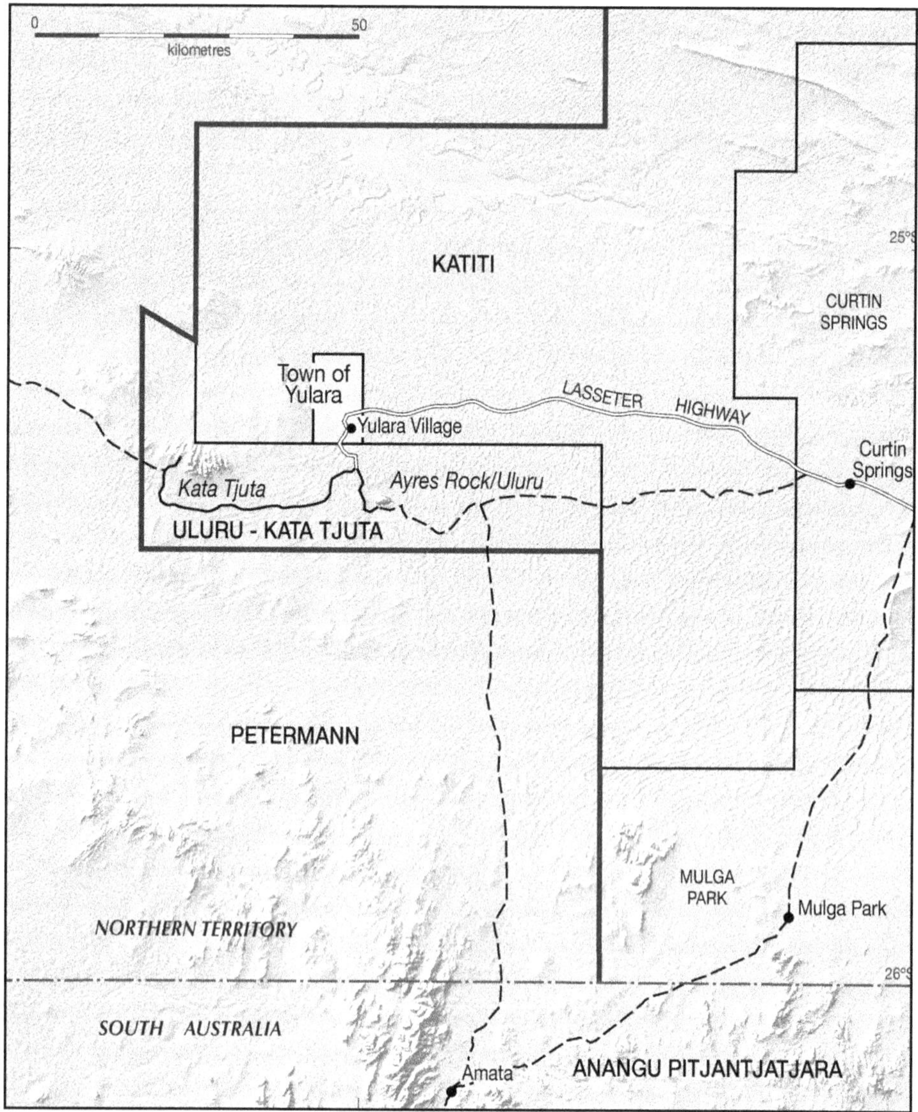

Map 8.1 Yulara location map

Even before the completion of the hearing of the evidence, there were signs that the anthropologists called as expert witnesses by the applicants were not going to have an easy ride. In a preliminary ruling on the evidence, much of the anthropologist's report, authored principally by Sutton, was held inadmissible for not conforming to the rules of evidence and had to be completely rewritten.[3]

3 *Jango v Northern Territory of Australia* (No. 2) [2004] FCA 1004 (3 August 2004).

In essence, the rules of evidence said to be breached were the need for expert reports to distinguish between the facts on which the expert opinion is based and the expert opinions themselves, and to clearly expose the reasoning leading to the opinions. Without this style of writing, it was argued, it would be difficult for a judge to decide whether the opinions really did arise out of specialised knowledge—that is, knowledge based on a person's training, study or experience.

Whether the problems with the form of the report were as dire as indicated by the number of individual objections (more than 1000) is difficult to say. On the other hand, the fact that the applicants' counsel conceded all but one of the objections indicates that there were substantial problems. On the face of it, the judge's criticism and his seeming exasperation were directed towards the applicants' lawyers for not keeping abreast of the developing jurisprudence of expert reports in native title cases and not adequately policing the form of Sutton's report.

If the judge was exasperated, it was perhaps because of the sequence of events leading up to *Yulara*. The Commonwealth's *Evidence Act*, which applied to all Federal Court hearings, had been passed in 1995. The 1998 amendments to the *Native Title Act*, among other things, reintroduced the rules of evidence into native title hearings. There appeared to be a considerable lag in legal and anthropological practice in responding to the changed situation. In 2003, the discrepancy between practice and judicial expectations of a more open and methodical justification of expert opinions became explicit when several expert reports in a native title claim in Western Australia were not admitted into evidence.[4] Coincidentally, soon after that decision, the Chief Justice of the Federal Court issued guidelines for all expert witnesses.[5] The guidelines codified the duty of the expert to the court rather than the party calling them, the need to identify the factual premises of the opinion, and the need to explain the reasoning processes leading to the opinion and warned against involvement in the formulation of the case of a party. The period covered by these developments overlaps with the commencement of Sutton's research for the Yulara claim.

One particular comment in the judge's preliminary decision on the form of Sutton's report must have sounded alarm bells among the applicants' lawyers for its apparent lack of appreciation of applied anthropology. The judge expressed his concern at what he described as unnecessary duplication of anthropologists interviewing claimants for the expert report and the lawyers taking witness statements from the same claimants.[6]

---

4 *Harrington-Smith v Western Australia* (No. 7) [2003] FCA 893.

5 The *Guidelines for Expert Witnesses* were first issued in September 2003 and revised in March 2004.

6 *Jango v Northern Territory of Australia* (No. 2) [2004] FCA 1004 (3 August 2004), para. 15.

Perhaps emboldened by the success of their challenge to the form of the anthropologists' report, lawyers for the Northern Territory later made a rather dramatic challenge to Sutton's report.[7] They argued that because his report contained a broader idea of the native title holders than many of the Aboriginal witnesses, his report should be ruled inadmissible because of irrelevance.[8] While rejecting this global objection and other specific objections, the judge did allow some specific objections. One was to Sutton's assertion that the town would restrict the possibility of Aboriginal people singing particular song verses while they were physically travelling along the Dreaming track. Apparently his informants did not mention this when they gave their evidence at the hearing.[9] Another of their successful objections was to Sutton's commenting on particular examples of lawyers trying to elicit testimony of customary law during the hearing. The judge allowed a general expert opinion to be given about the linguistic and cultural difficulties of Aboriginal witnesses but not a commentary on specific instances. In a familiar, and perhaps inevitable, assertion of his structurally superior position, he stated:

> Insofar as Professor Sutton comments on particular passages of evidence given at the hearing, I do not think that his comments should be admitted into evidence. The evaluation of specific evidence is the task of the trier of fact. In discharging that task, the trier of fact will have to take account of many factors, of which the difficulty of cross-cultural communications is but one. I do not think that the relevant expertise of an anthropologist extends to the evaluation of specific evidence given by particular witnesses at the hearing.[10]

The judgment

The judgment on all the substantive issues in the case was delivered on 31 March 2006.[11] Sackville's problems with the applicants' case started with confusion over what model of traditional laws and customs relating to land was being pleaded. Two different formulations of a Myers-like list of legitimate bases for an individual traditional claim to country seem to have been advanced at different stages of the hearing. One formulation emphasised four certain pathways or 'conditions' to traditional rights to land

1. birthplace near the area

---

7 See *Jango v Northern Territory of Australia* (No. 4) [2004] FCA 1539 (26 November 2004).

8 *Jango v Northern Territory of Australia* (No. 4) [2004] FCA 1539 (26 November 2004), paras 4–7.

9 *Jango v Northern Territory of Australia* (No. 4) [2004] FCA 1539 (26 November 2004), paras 32–5.

10 *Jango v Northern Territory of Australia* (No. 4) [2004] FCA 1539 (26 November 2004), para. 41.

11 *Jango v Northern Territory of Australia* [2006] FCA 318 (31 March 2006).

2. birthplace on a related Dreaming track passing through the area or the birthplace of a parent or a grandparent on a related Dreaming track passing through the area
3. kin links to the area
4. the death of close kin in the area.

This formulation also listed other factors that could bolster a person's claim through the four main pathways. The additional factors included

- taking responsibility for the area
- having traditional knowledge of the area
- identifying with the relevant language group
- long-term residential association with the area
- long-term association with others from the area
- the public assertion and defence of one's connection to the area.

The second formulation listed 11 similar factors without identifying four main pathways. In this formulation, the strength of a person's claim varied according to the number of factors that applied to the individual; the more factors, the stronger was the claim to be a traditional owner. This is similar to the points system referred to in Chapter 6 (p. 204).

Although the full story is not known, there appears to have been a confrontation at some stage in the case preparation over the wording of the pleadings.[12] The original pleadings, drawn up by Ross Howie, the claimants' barrister in *De Rose Hill,* seem to have used *nguraritja,* the Yankunyatjatjara/Pitjantjatjara word for traditional owner, as the umbrella concept of traditional land tenure. If the judge's account of the confrontation is correct, it seems that Sutton thought the use of *nguraritja* as an overarching concept adopted a narrow folk theory that did not accurately represent the ethnographic complexity of the actually recognised claims. In any event, there were some unusually detailed assertions in the amended pleadings that seemed to be transposed directly from the academic debate about traditional land tenure in the Western Desert:

> B1.2 The people of the Western Desert acknowledge and observe a body or system of indigenous laws and customs in relation to land and waters that does not identify country as aggregates of discrete bounded areas or 'estates'. Nor do those laws and customs identify 'clans' or other discrete bounded territorial groupings of people. Personal choice and a level of unpredictability, negotiability and contestation are features of the indigenous laws acknowledged and customs observed by the people of the Western Desert.[13]

12 I include in the word 'pleadings' the 'Points of Claim'; see the discussion of the relationship between formal pleadings and 'Points of Claim' in the Full Federal Court judgment in Jango at paragraphs 75–9.

13 Quoted in *Jango v Northern Territory of Australia* [2006] FCA 318 (31 March 2006), para. 171.

Justice Sackville's objections to Sutton as expert

Before examining the judge's alternative formulation, his reasons for rejecting Sutton's opinions should be outlined, for they do not all depend on inconsistency with other evidence. Sackville made four complaints about Sutton's claim to be an expert

1. although he was an expert on Aboriginal Australia generally, he was not really an expert on the Western Desert
2. he was not engaged in disinterested academic research but research for litigation
3. he was biased in favour of the applicants' case
4. he had misdirected himself on the legal doctrine of native title by adopting an anthropological understanding of 'normative system' rather than a legal one.

Initially there seems to be a contradiction in the judge accepting Sutton as a well-qualified expert anthropologist but then insisting that he was not an expert in the traditional laws and customs of the Western Desert region.[14] In practice, the way this apparent contradiction is resolved is that while Sutton's opinions were regarded as evidence under the rules of expert evidence, the weight given to them, or, in Sackville's words, 'the cogency of certain conclusions', could be diminished.[15]

The strategic redefining of fields of scientific expertise as a means of judges coming to a predetermined conclusion has been part of the sceptical critique of the judicial reception of scientific expert evidence.[16] I have distanced myself from this form of analysis because it seems to assume a strong and unvarying instrumental approach to judging in all cases. Its proponents actually deny that they take a strong view, or indeed any view, of the judge's intention, seeing it more as a logical or literary necessity given the inherent difficulties of certain expert evidence for a particular result.[17]

In any event, there was more to Sackville's insistence on a Western Desert sub-specialisation within Australianist anthropology than discounting inconvenient evidence. Jon Willis was also called as an expert witness and he had the ideal, requisite qualifications for such a sub-specialisation (see Chapter 7). In many ways, Jon Willis's role in the *Yulara* case paralleled his role in the *De Rose Hill* case

---

14 *Jango v Northern Territory of Australia* [2006] FCA 318 (31 March 2006), para. 316.

15 *Jango v Northern Territory of Australia* [2006] FCA 318 (31 March 2006), para. 315.

16 See Edmond (2000, 2001, 2002, 2004).

17 Gary Edmond, Personal communication, 2005.

- his relatively late involvement in the preparation of the case, despite his obvious qualifications
- the very positive reception of his evidence by the judge, but the eventual sidelining of it on the basis that it was more about ceremony and ontology than traditional land tenure.

There were some mysterious tactical decisions made in the *Yulara* case that make one wonder if any of the lessons of *De Rose Hill* had been learnt. One of those lessons must surely have been that Willis, following his long-term and intimate engagement with Yankunyatjatjara and Pitjantjatjara people, had come to some surprisingly different appreciations of land tenure than consultant anthropologists working with the same people but without his intimate experience of ceremony.

In particular, Willis, approaching the issue from knowledge of ceremony and Dreaming stories, saw relatively stable clusters of sites reflecting episodes in Dreaming narratives and those clusters of sites being associated with people born on those Dreaming tracks. In other words, it could easily be interpreted as being at odds with the relatively open-ended flexibility reported by Sutton. In addition, Willis's exploration of Western Desert ontology, including the centrality of *kurunitja* (spirit essence), had the potential to explain disparate and seemingly chaotic rules of traditional land tenure under a unifying, traditional concept that did not have to press *nguraritja* into service as the unifying umbrella. Because the spirit essences of the land enliven the foetus, the significance of birthplace can be seen as fundamentally traditional not 'accidental'. Also, because the same spirits enter the growing person through the food of the land, the importance of long-term residence to traditional land tenure can be seen as a variation on the same theme, not simply some alternative factor. Willis's work explained Tonkinson's remark about 'the bonds of shared spirit and substance' being important in Western Desert traditional land tenure.

Sackville's next complaint—about research for litigation—entirely fulfils the rather dark predictions I made in the introduction of this book, first written in 2005, about the possible emergence of a 'junk anthropology' discourse among Federal Court judges as the concerns about research for litigation and 'junk science', particularly among American judges, carried over to native title cases and anthropological expertise:[18]

> It is significant, in my opinion, that the fieldwork designed to gather that information was undertaken *in the context of the very litigation in which the claims of many of the informants were formulated and assessed.* Professor Sutton did not have the opportunity to carry out fieldwork

18 For an account of the 'junk science' debate, see Black et al. (1994); and Edmond (2000).

> among peoples of the eastern Western Desert in an environment divorced from their pending claims to compensation. Much less did he have the opportunity to study and describe the traditional laws and customs of these peoples as part of what might be described as a disinterested academic endeavour. Many, if not all of Professor Sutton's informants were aware that a compensation claim was pending at the time they spoke to him and were also aware that their observations might be used for the purposes of the litigation. While I do not doubt that Prof Sutton attempted to maintain his independence from the claimants, the fact is that he undertook the fieldwork and other research for the purposes of preparing a report in support of their case and did so while the claim was pending.[19] [Emphasis in original.]

This attitude was perhaps the most dispiriting for all applied anthropologists involved in native title work. What the judge described pejoratively was also the exact and inevitable circumstance in which most anthropological research for native title claims takes place. The expert anthropologists who research a claim for the group among whom they had conducted long-term fieldwork prior to native title are the exception, not the rule.

A further blow to Sutton's applied anthropology, and the least substantiated in the judgment, was the assertion that he was not concerned to test the reliability of informants' statements:

> Despite the contradictions and disputation to which he referred and his 'strong sense' that people were sometimes 'fictionalising', Prof Sutton, understandably enough, did not see it as part of his role to make judgements as to the veracity or reliability of the information on which he acted. It is fair to say (as the Commonwealth argues) that, in effect, Prof Sutton carried out a form of parallel enquiry to that undertaken by the court, but without many of its advantages (such as the opportunity for cross-examination) and without having to make judgements as to the reliability of the information provided.[20]

The fact that the judge's knowledge of 'contradictions and disputation' came from Sutton tends to undermine the main thrust of this criticism. The image of the applied anthropologists as being professionally obliged to accept the truth of anything informants say recalls the whole Hindmarsh Island saga. Whatever was the truth behind the bad press in Hindmarsh Island, one powerful public image to emerge was that of scandalous, fabricated Aboriginal traditions being

19 *Jango v Northern Territory of Australia* [2006] FCA 318 (31 March 2006), para. 319.

20 *Jango v Northern Territory of Australia* [2006] FCA 318 (31 March 2006), para. 321.

accepted too readily by the naive anthropologist.[21] It meant that Sackville and the Commonwealth's counsel had a ready-made image to draw upon as a sort of 'common knowledge' about the methods of anthropology. To this image Sackville added a new characterisation of the anthropologist's native title research as a poor man's judicial hearing. In this characterisation, we see the judge minimising the value of out-of-court interviews and the difficulties faced by Aboriginal witnesses in a formal hearing.

Although I have summarised the third criticism of Sutton as bias, the judge did not use that word. He used the euphemistic and circuitous language common in some legal writing styles that might be an attempt at deftness: 'his role in the case had not been limited to that of a wholly objective expert observer and commentator.'[22]

The evidence cited for this conclusion included Sutton's involvement in redrafting the pleadings, his commentary on draft written statements collected by lawyers, advising on who would be good witnesses, suggesting questions to counsel for the applicants during the hearing and making disparaging remarks about Tindale's qualifications, which the judge labelled as 'defensiveness'.[23]

Needless to say, many of these practices of assisting the conduct of the applicants' case, which had carried over from anthropological practice in *Land Rights Act* claims, are now antithetical to best practice in native title because of the *Yulara* case. They perhaps represent a hysteresis effect, as discussed in Chapter 1—a time lag of habituated practices that do not quite match the new circumstances of the Federal Court hearings. In the new circumstances, pervasive scepticism about all experts called by one party, presenting research undertaken for the litigation, means that every opportunity must now be taken to demonstrate independence.

The questioning of Sutton's independence had particular reverberations among applied anthropologists. He was not just any anthropologist. He was one of the most experienced and highly regarded expert anthropological witnesses in Australia.[24] Within the profession, he had taken a strong public stance against advocacy and for professionalism.[25] 'If Sutton cannot project independence in a Federal Court hearing', it was lamented, 'who can?' His very resistance to the

21 See Bannister (2006); Brunton (1996); Mead (1995); Simons (2003); and South Australia Hindmarsh Island Bridge Royal Commission (1995). Later accounts by some of the key Aboriginal participants indicate that there was probably a diversity of honestly held Aboriginal views about the disputed area, rather than a simple fabrication by one group (see Rowse 2006).

22 *Jango v Northern Territory of Australia* [2006] FCA 318 (31 March 2006), para. 326.

23 *Jango v Northern Territory of Australia* [2006] FCA 318 (31 March 2006), paras 322–5.

24 This impression is gained from talking to colleagues over a long period and to native title lawyers such as Graeme Neate, the President of the National Native Title Tribunal (Personal communication, 2003).

25 See, for example, Sutton (1995b).

initial formulation of the claim under the concept of *nguraritja*, which on the face of it indicates a very assertive independence, had been turned against him as indicating an undue alignment with the applicants' case.

The final criticism was that Sutton had adopted a non-legal interpretation of 'normative' and, in effect, neglected to prove the continuity of a normative system as required by native title legal doctrine. It was suggested that Sutton had an anthropological view of normative as average behaviour, rather than normative as the obligatory. Sutton, in his response to Sansom's commentary, denied this charge and provided a detailed refutation quoting numerous sections of his Yulara report (Sutton 2007). Sutton seems to have a point. One small but telling example is a sentence from his report that Sackville quotes against Sutton: 'The "normative" covers not only explicit rules but also the reflection of the assumptions of a norm, and average or typical behaviour as well as ideal norms.'[26]

A fair reading of this sentence, and the section of the report it comes from, would conclude it is primarily about implicit, obligatory norms. And in any event, why can't average behaviour, along with other evidence, also support the existence of an implicit obligatory norm? Because Sutton's report did not follow exactly the legal formulation of 'normative', it left open the possibility of a literalist misreading and rather tendentious final submissions by the Counsel for the Commonwealth that Sutton had made a fundamental legal error. Another judge might have quickly passed over such a tenuous argument. For whatever reason, however, Sackville was in a mind to accept this and other arguments put to him.

Coherence of the body of laws and customs

Having thus discounted Sutton's expert opinion in a four-pronged attack, a critical link in the applicants' case was missing. The evidence of individual Aboriginal witnesses mentioned a number of the pleaded factors for obtaining rights to land, but the expert testimony was to provide the overview and integrate the divergent emphases into a relatively coherent whole. The judge searched the evidence of the Aboriginal witnesses in vain for an overview that would exactly match the formulation of traditional land tenure in the pleadings: four main pathways plus additional factors. The judge also noted that there was little consistent mutual recognition within the applicant group, with most witnesses nominating themselves and their close relations only, not the entire group.

26 Quoted in *Jango v Northern Territory of Australia* [2006] FCA 318 (31 March 2006), para. 327.

Lest he be thought unappreciative of the difficulties facing Aboriginal witnesses or to be expecting an impossibly high level of technical compliance, he repeated some balancing statements that are typically found in the judgments of trial judges and seem to be pre-emptively addressing a possible appeal court:

> I accept that Aboriginal witnesses cannot be expected to recount their laws and customs with anything like the precision that might reasonably be expected of a lawyer expounding common law principles. I also accept that the fact that there may be disagreement among witnesses as to the relevant rules and practices is not, of itself, surprising and certainly not fatal to the applicants' contentions. Understandably enough, the Aboriginal witnesses are not accustomed to conceptualising their laws and customs in a manner that enables them to respond directly and clearly to the kinds of questions asked by counsel.[27]

As well as the absence of an integrating overview from the Indigenous witnesses, Sackville was also concerned about the level of disputation about the principles of legitimate traditional claims to country and the relevance of language association:

> Some witnesses were adamant that the area was Yankunyatjatjara country. Others claimed that Pitjantjatjara or other non-Yankunyatjatjara speaking people can be and are *ngurraritja* for that country. Some said that a person can take country from either a grandfather or grandmother. Other witnesses appeared to limit the principle to male ancestors. Some supported the principle that country can be taken through a wide range of relatives and indeed claimed that a person can choose his or her country from among the various possibilities. Others recognised a more limited principle of descent and seem to reject the notion that people can choose to be *ngurraritja* for country. Some seem to accept the birth on a Tjukurrpa track travelling to or through a particular site can make a person *ngurraritja* for that site. Others disputed that proposition. Some thought that long residence, or even working in an area for a long period, is sufficient to constitute the person concerned *ngurraritja* for the area. Others denied that there is or was any such custom.[28]

In citing these examples, the judge was suggesting something even more fundamental than lack of conformity to the pleaded system of laws and customs. He found that the lack of consistency and coherence meant that the existence of a body of laws and customs—an essential prerequisite in the legal doctrine of native title—could not be established.[29]

---

27 *Jango v Northern Territory of Australia* [2006] FCA 318 (31 March 2006), para. 407. Also see paras 445–6 and 449.

28 *Jango v Northern Territory of Australia* [2006] FCA 318 (31 March 2006), para. 448.

29 *Jango v Northern Territory of Australia* [2006] FCA 318 (31 March 2006), para. 446.

Having reached the conclusion that the evidence did not reveal any body of laws and customs, let alone the one pleaded, it was technically not necessary for the judge to address the argument that the pleaded laws and customs were in any case not traditional. The alarm in anthropological circles might have been much more muted if he had stopped there. For there is a degree of correspondence between the judicial finding of lack of fundamental coherence of a body of laws and customs and the ethnographic archive that continually emphasised flexibility, negotiation and the significance of context.

Sutton told me that he was quite explicit in his report about the problem of flexibility. He had apparently emphasised the fundamentally biographical nature of the land tenure system and had used the term 'interest-holding set' rather than 'claimant group' to reflect continuing flexibility of identification with country.[30] It remains one of the mysteries of the case that notwithstanding their vulnerability on the central issue of demonstrating a stable, coherent body of traditional laws and customs in relation to land, those running the case decided to go ahead anyway.

Judge as amateur anthropologist

The judge, having disposed of the case on grounds that were to some extent predictable from the ethnography, went on to consider arguments that the pleaded laws and customs were in any event not traditional. Taking that extra step is not only a case of generously responding to the parties who raised the question. Dealing with it further insulated the decision from successful appeal because it provided an alternative ground for the failure of the applicants' case.

The requirement that the contemporary laws and customs relating to land must be traditional goes back to the Brennan formulation of native title in *Mabo*, and it was reinforced in *Yorta Yorta*. In legal doctrine, the critical time is the date of the assertion of British sovereignty—in the *Yulara* case, 1824 or 1825. It must be established that there was a system of traditional laws and customs operating at that time and that the contemporary laws and customs are derived more or less directly from that system, subject to allowable change. The difficulties of proving the content of the system at sovereignty are ameliorated to some extent by the acceptance of inferences drawn from the available post-contact evidence. Thus to follow the requirements of legal doctrine closely would entail a three-stage analysis. The first stage is the reconstruction of the pre-contact system of traditional laws and customs relating to land from all the available evidence. The second stage is to account for the continuity and transformation of that system over the contact period up to the present. The third stage is a description of the contemporary laws and customs and the justification of how they are derived from the pre-contact system within an acceptable degree of change.

30 Peter Sutton, Interview, 8 June 2009.

One of the judge's problems with Sutton's report was that he thought it did not systematically follow the requirements of legal doctrine in this regard. Sutton seems to have evaluated the early anthropological sources as part of a discussion about traditional land tenure in general. Added to this was his problem with Sutton's alleged adoption of a non-legal interpretation of normative as average behaviour. Having discounted Sutton's evidence about the traditional nature of the contemporary laws and customs and having decided that the Indigenous evidence was of limited value in reconstructing the pre-contact era, Sackville could have chosen simply to say that there was not enough evidence about the pre-contact era.

Instead, Sackville, encouraged by similar final submissions made by Counsel for the Commonwealth, decided to treat the early anthropological sources as separate pieces of evidence and make his own evaluation of them outside anthropological expertise. This directly parallels the approach of Justice O'Loughlin in the *De Rose Hill* case, in which I noted the judicial resurrection of phantom experts.[31]

Because Justice Sackville's conclusions are at odds with what I would see as the mainstream of anthropological opinion, it is worth examining in some detail how he came to his conclusion that in the pre-contact era the principal expression of traditional land tenure in the Western Desert was small patrilineal descent groups that had rights to a particular site or cluster of sites connected with the *Tjukurrpa*.[32]

Sackville's first step was to question Sutton's critique of Berndt and Tindale. Sutton had made a rather direct assault on Tindale's conclusions, stating that they were wrong. One wonders whether it would have been sufficient and more tactful for Sutton to simply point out Tindale's reliance on the existing theorising about local organisation in the discipline of anthropology and Tindale's formal qualifications, which made him an outsider to that discipline. Sutton went even further, in what might have been a rhetorical bridge too far, by claiming that Tindale's data, upon reanalysis, did not support Tindale's own conclusions about stable patrilineal descent groups. Sutton put forward what would have been a convincing argument in the field of the academy, but it proved to be a distraction in the highly contested court case.[33]

---

31 Sutton had a similar feeling and called his 2006 Norman B. Tindale Memorial Lecture 'Norman Tindale and Native Title: His Appearance in the Yulara Case'.

32 *Jango v Northern Territory of Australia* [2006] FCA 318 (31 March 2006), para. 497.

33 I find Sutton's reanalysis of Tindale's social-history cards to be convincing as far as it goes. The focus on Tindale's cards does, however, tend to submerge methodological problems of Tindale's whole enterprise. Sometimes we are so grateful that someone was there collecting information that is still available for analysis that problems with its collection tend to be overlooked. The cards themselves project a kind of objective, methodological rigour like a survey questionnaire. But we know there were basic communication problems and it was superficial, expeditionary survey questioning when compared with the Malinowskian ideal of long-term, total-immersion fieldwork. Later research would also suggest that answers to basic questions can be highly contextual and subject to the perceived requirements of the moment. How the question of 'totem' was translated, let alone received, is difficult to imagine given the likelihood of multiple connections to different Dreamings. One unintended consequence of Sutton's detailed reanalysis might have been to reinforce the inflated empirical status of Tindale's data.

The critique of Sutton's reanalysis was the result of a very detailed deconstruction of Sutton's methodology, not by another anthropologist but by the lawyers representing the Commonwealth. It was argued that Sutton's selection of only the most complete social-data cards biased the result against Tindale's conclusions since some of the excluded cards tended to support them. Furthermore, it was argued that Tindale's conclusions could have been based on Tindale's other research, not just the social-data cards. Finally, it was argued that Sutton's rather dismissive view of Tindale was unrepresentative of the general regard in which Tindale's work was held by other anthropologists—an argument that seems to have been derived from the cross-examination of Sutton himself.[34]

Justice Sackville then arrayed against Sutton's critique of the patrilineal descent group model all the literature that seemed to support it. But it was not just the literature; the judge seemed to be treating them as equivalent expert witnesses that could be unproblematically placed on one side of a set of scales to outweigh Sutton's opinion—four professors on one side (Berndt, Munn, Tonkinson and Layton) and one professor (Sutton) on the other side—a very literal interpretation of the idea of the weight of expert opinion. Mysteriously, Sackville identified Berndt's 1959 paper as expressing the conventional view of traditional land tenure in the Western Desert. Nowhere does he explain on what basis this judgment of a disciplinary mainstream was made.

Sackville then moved on to Nancy Munn's unpublished report on her year's fieldwork at Aereyonga in 1964–65. I have not included it in my own selective review of the anthropology of Western Desert land tenure as I did not consider that she had made a substantial contribution. The judge, referring to her as a professor, did find in her fieldwork report to the Australian Institute of Aboriginal Studies references to local landowning units owning relatively discrete estates. Similarly, he refers to passages about traditional estates in Tonkinson's work. In both instances, the context of these passages that could assist in evaluating them is not mentioned. In Munn's case, a relevant context is that traditional land tenure was not a major focus of her research and in Tonkinson's case, as I pointed out in Chapter 6, there was the increasingly loud undercurrent of individual flexibility and fluidity that tended to undermine the passages quoted by the judge.

Sackville then considered the work of Robert Layton and Lee Sackett, who had conducted research among Western Desert peoples for claims under the *Land Rights Act*.[35] Again he found references to patrilineal descent groups but at no time did he avert to the pervasive influence of the descent group requirement in the definition of traditional owner in the *Land Rights Act* and Layton's own reflections on the whole process (see Chapter 6).

34 *Jango v Northern Territory of Australia* [2006] FCA 318 (31 March 2006), para. 475.

35 *Jango v Northern Territory of Australia* [2006] FCA 318 (31 March 2006), para. 448–93.

The judge quickly dispatched Myers. Ignoring the way in which Myers' approach can be seen to synthesise and surpass previous ethnography on traditional land tenure in the Western Desert, Sackville summarily sidelines his contribution on grounds of its geographic and temporal distance from the claim area:

> However, Myers' work has been primarily among the Pintupi people of the northern Western Desert and is relatively recent, having been undertaken in the 1970s and 1980s. Professor Sutton, who acknowledges that Myers 'considered Pintupi land tenure to be an elusive matter', does not attempt in his Report to relate Myers' findings to the laws and customs of the Western Desert at the time of sovereignty or prior to the influence of European settlement.[36]

Finally, the judge dismisses Hamilton. Her discussion of tension between the centrality of place of birth and a patrilineal system ('the system as it was straining to become') he characterises as denying the existence of any settled system of land tenure and hence as being outside the mainstream of anthropology, as construed by him.[37]

The judge then blundered on to his conclusion with only a perfunctory acknowledgment of his own limitations in presenting an alternative view of anthropological opinion, the Commonwealth having failed to call its anthropologist, John Morton, and the Northern Territory having failed to call its anthropologist, Basil Sansom:

> It is not an easy task for a court to assess anthropological evidence on issues as complex and sensitive as the laws and customs of Aboriginal societies. Nonetheless, it seems to me that the weight of the anthropological evidence in this case, which includes the published work of distinguished researchers who have studied the people of the Western Desert, points clearly to a particular conclusion. This is that under the traditional laws and customs (understanding that expression in the sense required by *Yorta Yorta (HC)*) of the Western Desert bloc:
>
> - the land holding units comprised small local groups;
> - each group consisted of people principally recruited or united on the basis of common patrilineal descent; and
> - members of the group had rights and interests (to use the language of the NTA) on a particular site or a particular cluster of sites connected with the Tjukurrpa.

36 *Jango v Northern Territory of Australia* [2006] FCA 318 (31 March 2006), para. 494.
37 *Jango v Northern Territory of Australia* [2006] FCA 318 (31 March 2006), para. 496.

> The evidence, although more equivocal on the point, tends to suggest that the traditional laws and customs of the Western Desert also recognise that in certain circumstances a person could become a member of the local group by being born at a place of significance to the group, at least where a person's claim was acknowledged and accepted by other members of the group.
>
> For the reasons I have given, I am not persuaded by the evidence of Professor Sutton (or Ms Vaarzon-Morel), to the extent that it suggests otherwise. This does not imply that I think that further debate among anthropologists is foreclosed. On the contrary, there may well be room for further scholarly enquiry on the issues canvassed in the evidence in the present case. However, I am bound to decide factual questions on the evidence presented to me. That evidence does not dislodge or rebut the views consistently expressed by the early scholars who carried out field work among Aboriginal people in the Western Desert, including the eastern Western Desert.[38]

Explaining this appearance of the judge as his own expert anthropologist to an incredulous colleague from another regional specialisation within anthropology, my colleague wondered whether a judge would approach an expert physicist in the same way.[39] Would the judge, for example, reject the expert's preference for quantum mechanics, perhaps concluding that Newtonian physics made more sense to him and explained the facts better. This comparison is telling. Apart from highlighting the clumsy judicial dismantling of a disciplinary consensus, it shows that not all disciplines are equally immune from such meddling. I have already noted in the previous case studies how judges tend to feel no compunction in bypassing historians when they are interpreting historical documents, and that, generally speaking, they tended to be a little more wary of anthropological expertise. This kind of continuum from the humanities to the social sciences then to the physical sciences tends to confirm the intermediate position of anthropology that I asserted in Chapter 1.

In the *De Rose Hill* case, counsel for the claimants might have invited and abetted judicial dismantling of disciplinary consensus by tendering separately some of the historical anthropological sources rather than leaving them as references in an expert anthropologist's report. Reacting against the initial anthropologist's dismissiveness of the anthropological archive, the barrister Ross Howie thought that, apart from their anthropological merit, they provided wonderful evidence of traditional continuity and, as part of the overall strategy for winning the case, they deserved greater prominence. In *Yulara*, Sutton was conscientious, to

---

38 *Jango v Northern Territory of Australia* [2006] FCA 318 (31 March 2006), paras 497–8.

39 Don Gardner, Personal communication, 2006.

the point of obsession, about including in annexures all the source material he had considered. He thought that it would assist in demonstrating his openness and independence as an expert. Instead, Counsel for the Commonwealth railed against the difficulty of coming to grips with such a volume of material. But eventually, Counsel for the Commonwealth found in those annexures the material that he used to appeal to the judge to override Sutton's opinion about the pre-contact situation. The appeal was made through final submissions rather than a contrary expert view. The anthropologist engaged by the Commonwealth to review Sutton's report, John Morton, basically agreed with Sutton. Having refrained from calling Morton to give evidence, Counsel for the Commonwealth was free to focus exclusively on Sutton.

There are other aspects of the dismantling of a contemporary disciplinary consensus that are suggested by the judicial treatment of Tindale, particularly in *De Rose Hill*. Tindale, unlike most anthropologists, has a degree of popular recognition and approval.[40] It is interesting to note that the lawyers involved in *De Rose Hill*, especially those from South Australia representing the pastoralists and the State Government, referred to him approvingly in conversation by his nickname 'Tinny'.[41] Is it too fanciful to think that this positive public persona, the simplicity of his notion of the tribe and even his modest academic qualifications enabled him to reach over the heads of his latter-day critics to appeal directly to the lawyers and judges? It is also possible to imagine judges feeling the need to rehabilitate someone whom they think has been unfairly relegated by later, elitist academics who did not do equivalent fieldwork and who were being too clever about him. If these perceptions are real, they present a quandary for the expert anthropological witness of how to be frank about Tindale's limitations. Sutton certainly regretted his offhand remark, strategically quoted by Sackville, that Tindale's major field of expertise was insects.[42] But what is the best tightrope to walk between accurately reflecting the current disciplinary consensus about his contribution to the understanding of traditional land tenure while not appearing to be too dismissive of a sympathetically remembered public figure?

Sutton and the ethics of predigestion

The problem with Tindale is just one aspect of the wider issue of the reformulation of the anthropological archive for native title purposes. For the purposes of my own analysis of that archive for the three main case studies, I proposed a robust academic model of deconstruction of the archive and its reconstruction in terms

40 With the possible exception of Stanner; see Hinkson and Beckett (2008).

41 Craig Elliott's comments on my draft Chapter 7, July 2005.

42 *Jango v Northern Territory of Australia* [2006] FCA 318 (31 March 2006), para. 326; Peter Sutton, Interview, 8 June 2009.

that are relevant to the legal doctrine of native title while acknowledging the indeterminacy of the key terms of the doctrine. This led me to be equivocal about whether Myers' emphasis on the individual perspective would automatically be relevant to native title doctrine, which seemed to assume stable, socio-centric groups and rules. I did acknowledge that his codification of the legitimate bases for traditional claims did approximate socio-centric rules. I was also open, however, to the possibility that earlier accounts that were incorporated into and superseded by Myers' work would be more relevant to native title because they were concerned about identifying relatively stable, socio-centric categories.

Sutton seems to have taken a slightly different view, founding his conclusions about the existence of something like a points system in the complex ethnographic facts that confronted him and which he considered could be adequately encompassed only by such a system. In effect, he de-emphasised the different explanatory purposes and analytical tools of previous researchers and emphasised apparently unmediated ethnographic facts. From this perspective it made perfect sense to Sutton to say that Tindale was wrong about traditional land tenure, rather than to say more diplomatically that Tindale was on a different explanatory mission. Furthermore, it accepts Myers' account of his own work as ethnographic in the sense of describing cultural particularities rather than being a combination of ethnographic description and a strong emphasis on the individual perspective as an analytical tool.

When Sutton read the original points of claim emphasising *ngurraritja*, he tended to see two related ethical dilemmas.[43] One was that it would result in the recognition of a smaller group of Aboriginal people than he thought had legitimate traditional claims. The second was that he felt he would have to curtail his honestly held professional view that *ngurraritja*-ship was an idealised folk theory. That he could insist upon and receive changes to the points of claim to make them more consistent with his views is a testament to his influence and the different circumstances of this case compared with *De Rose Hill*. It will be recalled that Craig Elliott, in effect, received the brief for his report in the middle of the hearing and was in no position to influence the way the case had been framed.

As the dust settles after *Yulara*, the idea that it represents the apocalyptic dismissal of applied anthropology in native title as junk anthropology seems to be receding a little. A number of contested native title hearings were decided while *Yulara* was being heard. In those cases, other judges were very appreciative

43 Peter Sutton, Interview, 8 June 2009.

of the expert anthropologists involved.[44] But this does not mean that *Yulara* was simply an aberration. In those two cases the anthropologists involved had conducted their primary fieldwork with the Aboriginal groups prior to the native title era, so the issue of research for litigation did not arise so starkly. John Morton's assessment of the significance of *Yulara* for anthropological practice is probably closest to the mark:

> [T]he problem was not with the facts, but with their reduction to a transparently convincing narrative ('clearly exposed reasoning')—in other words, a *thesis* that the court would readily accommodate within its peculiar *habitus*. I therefore remain unconvinced that, in the wake of Yulara, anthropologists need to work quickly to shed 'academic habitude' in the preparation of court reports. Rather, it seems to me that we need to refine that 'habitude', because 'forensic indigestibility' is less a matter of not distinguishing between fact and opinion and more a question of making the distinction highly explicit and coherent for legal practitioners, who demand that forensic fare be fastidiously prepared and served to them on a platter. The clearer the story, the more transparent the argument. (Morton 2007:171, emphasis in the original)[45]

44 See the *Ngarinyin* claim (*Neowarra v Western Australia* [2003] FCA 1402 (8 December 2003)), especially paras 71–82 and 112–19; and the *Blue Mud Bay* claim (*Gumana v Northern Territory* [2005] FCA 50 (7 February 2005)), paras 167–78. In the *Blue Mud Bay* claim, Justice Selway was so impressed with Professor Howard Morphy's more than 30-year involvement with the claimants, he stated:

> For the reasons given above notwithstanding the close relationship of Professor Morphy with the claimants over many years his evidence is admissible. Indeed, that close relationship and its duration means that much of his evidence is likely to be admissible as evidence of primary fact, and not just as evidence of opinion. (Para. 168)

45 Sackville's judgment was appealed to the Full Federal Court, the bench consisting of Justices French, Finn and Mansfield. They dismissed the appeal in a joint judgment delivered on 6 July 2007 (*Jango v Northern Territory of Australia* [2007] FCA FC 101). It had been argued, in effect, that the trial judge should not be confined strictly to the case as pleaded because of the inherent difficulties of translating Aboriginal relations to land into European law. This argument was rejected as tantamount to suggesting an inquiry approach rather than the performance of a judicial function, which, as a matter of procedural fairness to opposing parties, involves carefully defining the issues to be resolved and limiting amendment of those issues once adopted (paras 75–85). The issue of whether the Indigenous witnesses had to give evidence of the totality of the system of traditional land tenure that more or less corresponded to the anthropological evidence and the pleadings was subsumed in the full court reasons under the question of whether Justice Sackville had misunderstood the applicants' case. They found that he had understood the case and pointed to Sackville's finding that there was too much variation in the Indigenous evidence to establish the system of law and custom as pleaded (paras 86–92).

9. Conclusion

The essence of this book, and its major claim to originality, is the move to step outside the professional discourse of both law and anthropology so that a more comprehensive account of their interaction in native title might be provided. In other words, it tries to take a genuinely sociological view of the native title encounter. To do otherwise would risk becoming captive of those very professional discourses that need to be seen as part of a bigger picture. The professional discourse of law would tend to collapse the whole of this book into categorical judgments about establishing expertise, the scope of expert testimony and questions of bias. Similarly, to simply adopt the perspective of applied anthropology might have led to a defensiveness that would promote the relevance of anthropology to native title and pass over the significant cracks in establishing a disciplinary consensus about some key issues and downplay the wide range of abilities among expert anthropologists.

To conclude this book, I intend to explore what generalisations can be made from the case studies about the nature of anthropological and judicial agency in the native title encounter—in other words: how have the original ideal models been tested in the case studies? But first I wish to address some methodological issues that emerged during the course of this research.

Agency and method

My discussions with Craig Elliott about the draft of the *De Rose Hill* case study prompted a re-examination of the nature of anthropological agency and the possibility of methodological bias in this research project. In some respects, that case study confirmed the triangulation model of anthropological agency, if in a more diffuse way than Figure 1.1 would suggest. Elliott strongly agreed with my suggestion that Myers' approach to traditional land tenure, as the sum of negotiable individual claims, was inappropriate in the native title context. This would seem to support the process of selection that I attributed to him.

Yet, Elliott thought that my description gave the impression of methodical calculation that was in fact alien to his experience of writing his reports. His recollection was of performing a role, without explicit consideration of all the options available to him. The methodological question that these differences of perspective raises is whether my model of the process of deconstructing the archive and setting out the available choices (as I have attempted in Chapters 2, 4 and 6) produces a systematic bias towards strong, deliberate selection as opposed to a weak, implied selection. This is certainly a possibility and was the basis of my own reservations about the strong, deliberative agency that the sceptical critique of judicial fact-finding seemed to attribute to all judges in all circumstances. As Goffman demonstrated in *Strategic Interactions* (1969), the central problem is that a key part of strategic action is not revealing one's game plan to other participants. This strategy applies to judges who take a strong view about the best outcome of the case and it would also apply to anthropologists who are interviewed by a researcher about their performance as expert witnesses. There is no easy solution to this problem. All attributions of deliberative agency beyond what is admitted are inevitably inferences from all the available information. Ultimately, all that can be done is to carefully compare my interpretation with the subject's interpretation and seek to explain the difference.

In the *Mabo* case study, a similar issue arose over my use of the word 'clever' to describe Beckett's all-inclusive and general formulation of the traditional land tenure principles. In the highly politicised field of native title, 'cleverness' could imply deviousness, whereas all I wanted to imply, at that stage, was the neat fit between his generalisations, the anthropological archive and the assumed requirements of legal doctrine. Beckett's response—to assert that his generalisations were determined by the ethnographic evidence—was more suited to the juridical field. Perhaps, given my legal background, this was how he chose to respond to the question—as if he were being cross-examined again.

In other respects, however, Beckett was happy enough with my adoption of his account of the deliberate choices he made to distance himself from Eddie Mabo's traditionalism and respond to the whole of the anthropological archive, which meant, in effect, describing the contemporary assertion of Malo's Law as neo-traditionalism. I found his account plausible because of his lack of integration into the legal team running the case. Yet, in the back of my mind is also the distant possibility of his having enlisted me in his own project of preserving for posterity his version of the historic case.

The case studies as a test for the model of anthropological agency

Orientation to the juridical field

In relation to Beckett in *Mabo*, I have already indicated that the legal doctrine corner of the triangle needs modification to include more amorphous or global appreciations of the requirements of the juridical field (see Chapter 3). These general appreciations are perhaps evidence of an anthropological gestalt of the juridical field. Even after the High Court's formulation of the legal doctrine and the defining of native title in the *Native Title Act*, anthropological views of the legal requirements were not limited to understanding legal doctrine. Sullivan, for example, was dismayed by the broad terms of the legal doctrine. He and the Kimberley Land Council thought the *Mabo* decision would lead to high-level political negotiations. In fact, it became the inadequate foundation for a court-based land rights scheme. He saw the potentially destructive, regimenting effect of legal recognition and was determined to resist it by arguing for an all-inclusive grouping to become the title-holding group. Elliott seems to have been more focused on the terms of legal doctrine. Even before Howie provided the topics for his second report, Elliott, sensing the rudderlessness of previous research, had been attempting to formulate schematic diagrams of the elements that needed to be proved in order to establish native title.[1]

All the anthropologists in the case studies had a clear idea of the expectations in the juridical field of expert independence and their duty to the court rather than the parties that called them. Both Sullivan and Elliott, however, indicated that their appreciation of the problem of projecting independence, despite their being engaged by the claimants, only developed afterwards. It had not occurred to them that their position was particularly problematic, as a passing acquaintance with the 'junk science' debate would have indicated.[2] Since the jolt of the *Yulara* case, the issue of projecting independence must surely be in the consciousness of all potential expert anthropologists. In that case, practices that seemed innocuous in *Land Rights Act* hearings—such as participating in the overall formulation of the case, suggesting good Indigenous witnesses and suggesting questions to counsel—were all transformed into possible evidence of bias.

Another aspect of anthropological images of the juridical field was revealed in Kolig's high expectations of standards of proof—what should count as convincing evidence (see below).

Orientation to the anthropological archive

As an overarching proposition, the idea of the deconstruction and reconstruction of the anthropological archive in the light of the requirements of the juridical field covers most of the anthropologists in the case studies, but not all. Beckett, Sullivan and Elliott took a broadly evaluative approach to the archive, whereas Maddock, and especially Kolig, adopted a more respectful and protective attitude. In Kolig's case, this attitude seems to have extended to adopting Elkin's

1 Interview with Craig Elliott, 26 March 2005.

2 For the meaning of the 'junk science' debate, see Chapter 1 under the subheading 'Law and scientific expertise'.

dismissive attitude towards Piddington. This difference suggests a continuum of approaches to the anthropological archive. At one end, early ethnography is seen as sealed off from criticism because of a conviction about its methodological rectitude and the fact that the world of the early ethnographers' informants is no longer accessible. At the other end is a view that the whole of the archive, including the methodology used in creating it, is in a process of continual reinterpretation as new material is added. These considerations are suggestive of a more nuanced model than the simple deconstruction–reconstruction that I originally proposed. All anthropological experts have an interest in defending and promoting the value of their disciplinary archive, even if they have come to different conclusions about what is destructive of the general standing of that archive, and what simply represents a new disciplinary consensus about the relative merits of its different parts. Thus the orientation of the expert witness to the anthropological archive should be reformulated as one of deconstruction within the bounds of the perceived disciplinary consensus.

Demonstrating a disciplinary consensus

The case studies in this book draw attention to two vital topics in Australianist anthropology in which a disciplinary consensus has been difficult to find and project in court: the best description of the ownership group in the pre-contact period and what current rules and practices relating to land can be cast as traditional.

The first of these topics has become entangled in what is known in anthropology as 'the local organisation debate'.[3] But for the advent of land rights legislation and native title this arcane debate might have died a natural death long ago because the evidence required to advance its resolution continues to recede into the distant past. This receding evidential base means that expert disagreement about pre-contact land tenure is likely to be a continuing feature of native title claims.

In many parts of Australia there is very limited evidence of the pre-contact era and consequently the task becomes one of extrapolating from other areas. This involves the modification of Radcliffe-Brown's horde model and, for some, the complete rewriting of the horde model. The main conceptual modification has

3 The term 'local organisation debate' refers to the long-running debate over the most appropriate way to generalise, on an Australia-wide basis, about Aboriginal group relations to land in the pre-contact era. It is typified by Hiatt's 1962 critique of Radcliffe-Brown's generalisations and Stanner's 1965 defence and modification of Radcliffe-Brown's generalisations (Hiatt 1962; Stanner 1965). The debate has quite a long history and is ongoing. I did not have the heart to clutter this book with yet another rehearsal of the various positions taken in the debate; there are already many such accounts (see, for example, Hiatt 1996:13–35; Keen 1988:102–4; Maddock 1980b; Peterson and Long 1986:1–25; Sutton 2003:38–53, 68–70, 98–110, 140–58).

been to separate the land-exploiting group (the band) from the ownership group (the patrilineal clan) that owns the sacra for a defined area and has exclusive rights to use the area.[4]

Other modifications will typically make more complex the self-sufficiency of the original theorising of the horde and its all-or-nothing concept of ownership. The supposed self-sufficiency of the horde is made more complex by bringing in the regional systems—for example, trade, shared kinship and section systems, regional initiation rituals, shared long-distance Dreaming tracks, identification of language areas, dispute-resolution procedures and so on. Simple ownership is made complex by providing a grading of different kinds of ownership rights, which minimally mean including secondary rights to mother's father's country. Still further modifications could be extrapolated from Myers' approach to Western Desert traditional land tenure with its variety of legitimate bases for traditional claims leading to a flexible and contingent grouping of owners for any one area. To be clear, Myers never suggested that his approach—of commencing with the terms of legitimate individual claims to traditional country—was a general Australia-wide model; quite the opposite. He presented it as a distinctive regional cultural variation.

Rather than justify a position here, the point I wish to make is that the rather subtle differences of interpretation I have been canvassing tend to be amplified in the adversarial system of native title hearings. This means that anthropologists are sometimes caught in a bind. If the relevant grouping in the pre-contact era is characterised as a regional grouping, it tends to make the argument about continuity with the contemporary era easier but at the risk of undermining key figures in the anthropological archive. Postulating minimal change over the colonial period also challenges credulity because the momentous changes to the lives of Aboriginal people must surely have had their effect. On the other hand, those who characterise the relevant ownership group as the clan with its clan territory then have to explain that the dramatic early collapse of the patchwork of clan territories and the rise to prominence of language group territories are still within the range of acceptable change contemplated by the legal doctrine of native title.

Cultural change and the anthropological archive

Beckett and Kolig stand out among their contemporaries for their interest in the historical transformation of culture, and their approaches in the case studies have exemplified the problems of forming a disciplinary consensus.

4 Because of inconsistencies in Radcliffe-Brown's own terminology, it is also necessary to make some technical clarifications to Radcliffe-Brown's original theorising so that it is clear that out-marrying daughters of the patrilineal clan retain ownership rights to their father's country.

Beckett had developed a comprehensive account of the transformation of island custom under colonial circumstances. In comparison, his account of the Meriam domain changing at a slower pace—while plausible in relation to traditional land tenure—seemed more of an improvisation. By this I mean that it had not previously been analysed in those terms so that the features of a Meriam domain and its relationship to other aspects of Meriam life and the wider world could be specified and come under academic scrutiny. On the mainland, the idea of an Aboriginal domain has been used in a variety of circumstances to denote Aboriginal camps on pastoral stations, remote cultural enclaves or as a deliberate Aboriginal strategy to cope with overbearing missionising in government-sponsored settlements (see overview in Rowse 1992). It is easy to see how such a concept—although not used in the mainland case studies in this book—could be part of an explanation of continuity over the colonial period.

Despite Kolig's longstanding interest in the process of modernisation of Aboriginal religion, cross-examination of his assessment of what constitutes 'reasonable change' revealed a surprising absence of a convincing theoretical position. I explained this absence as resulting from the critiquing role he adopted in the *Rubibi* hearing since it is clear from his published work that he *had* deployed ideas of cultural change such as a generalised Aboriginal consciousness changing as Aboriginal people adopted European daily routines and came into contact with a wider circle of Aboriginal people.

Thus, alongside the process of deconstruction and reconstruction of the existing archive is a process of attempted improvisation where the requirements of legal doctrine reveal a gap in the archive. For a variety of reasons, such gaps are not easily plugged. As in any large field such as Australia, the ethnographic and historical record is likely to be patchy and vary enormously in quality when researching particular claims. Fardon's theorising about the unique development of regional specialisations would suggest that early ideas for a historical anthropology, and later critiques by Wolf (1982) and Fabian (1983), about the pitfalls of ignoring historical context and global interconnections, did not take root as strongly in Australia as in other specialisations. The pre-contact era was still so tantalisingly close—at least in remote areas—during the post-1930s professionalising of anthropology in Australia, it is understandable that the focus was on reconstructing those societies and bracketing what was called 'culture contact'. Even though community studies began to appear with subtitles such as 'tradition and change in an Aboriginal tribe' such concepts remained at an unhelpfully general level. It was not until much later that more complex analytical frameworks and different writing strategies were developed. Merlan's 1998 book *Caging the Rainbow* is a landmark in these developments with its explicit theorising of the intercultural. She fully explored the implications of the reality that all personal identity is relational including in relation to the European colonisers and contemporary state projects to recognise land rights.

These belated advances in the understanding of intercultural history coincide with the belated legal recognition of native title with its seeming emphasis on a relatively complete and separate system of laws and customs that is substantially continuous with the pre-contact system. In other words, there is an anti-intercultural bias in the legal doctrine and this poses particular challenges for anthropologists writing native title reports for groups that have a long contact history. To clarify how anthropologists have chosen to bridge this gap between recent anthropological theorising and legal doctrine, I will outline two broadly opposed possibilities and revisit the approaches taken in the case studies.

The two opposed approaches might be understood as the difference between bookends and the layers of sediment built up over time. The bookends approach is to characterise the elements of the contemporary system of laws and customs and then identify similar elements in the pre-contact system. This approach responds directly to the categorical forms of legal doctrine and to an earlier era of overgeneralised labelling of tradition and change.

The alternative, sedimentary approach would trace cultural changes from the immediate contact generation to the next generation, and so on, to the present. It would demonstrate the evolution to the current system of laws and customs. In doing so, it would respond to that part of the legal doctrine that acknowledges some indeterminate degree of allowable change of traditional laws and customs within substantial continuity. The sedimentary approach allows for a more comprehensive and realistic engagement with intercultural history, which the bookends approach passes over in apprehensive silence. Beckett in *Mabo* was closest to the sedimentary approach with the bedrock of Haddon's *Reports*, the layer of his own fieldwork and his wise distancing of himself from the synthesising projects of a later layer of history. The bookends approach can be seen most clearly in the terms of reference given to Elliot in *De Rose Hill*. They demanded a categorical evaluation of whether there had been a loss of traditional connection since the assertion of sovereignty, and Elliot was not in a position to provide a detailed evolutionary history in response.

What I have been hinting at here is the view that for groups with a long contact history a sedimentary approach to the explanation of change will be more convincing. But there are so few thoroughgoing examples of this in the publicly available anthropological archive for Australia, it is likely that the diversity of approaches exemplified in the case studies in this book will continue. In Chapter 1, I mentioned the assertion of American applied anthropologists that they are the leaders of research into 'change theory' despite the relegation of their work by the pure researchers. In Australia, the writers of anthropological reports in native title cases might be at the cutting edge of the development of historical anthropology within the broader discipline but the reports are generally inaccessible, so it is hard to tell.

Orientation towards the claimants' evidence

While it was true, at a general level, that the Indigenous evidence was broadly consistent with the anthropologists' reports, there were some important examples of divergence. In *Mabo*, there was a key divergence between Beckett and the claimants on whether to characterise Malo's Law as a general precept or as the religious foundation of their land tenure system. In *Rubibi*, there were not so much divergences as gaps: none of the Goolarabooloo group gave evidence, even though they figured prominently in Sullivan's all-inclusive grouping and his report did not include reference to the Leregon group and other dissidents, simply because he was not aware of their views. There were also dramatic divergences between some entries in his fieldnotes and the claimants' evidence. In *De Rose Hill*, the claimants failed to specifically refer to *kuranitja* (spirit essence) even though it was central to Willis's report, and the claimants did not mention Elliott's proposed Yankunytjatjara Pitjantjatjara Antakirinya community as such.

It is interesting to consider the diametrically opposed consequences of these divergences in *Mabo* and *De Rose Hill*. For in *Mabo*, Beckett's credibility was enhanced by the divergence and, in *De Rose Hill*, Elliott's credibility came under question because of the divergences. At one level, these different consequences are easy to explain. Beckett's view aligned him with the judge's own scepticism about claims of direct continuity with the pre-contact significance of Malo's Law. In *De Rose Hill*, Elliott's neologism was not supported by Maddock, whose opinions had been embraced by the judge partly because of Maddock's superior academic capital. Similarly, the limited effect of the embarrassing fieldnotes in *Rubibi* could be seen as a product of the judge's positive disposition towards the claimants' case. It seems more likely, however, that in all cases the judge's general disposition towards the preferred outcome is in tension with a more universal judicial preference for in-court testimony when it diverges from out-of-court statements.

In *Yulara*, divergences and gaps became critical to the outcome in a way that revealed potentially intractable problems for all anthropologists. To what extent should anthropologists go beyond restrictive folk models of traditional land tenure to add additional, more inclusive principles that might not be explicitly objectified but are broadly followed? To what extent should anthropologists limit their own description of the overall system of traditional laws and customs to a version that can also be articulated by at least some of the Indigenous witnesses? The anthropologist is obliged to base any expert opinion on all the information available and not make guesses about what might be said in court. Thus there might be some trepidation before the hearing with the anthropologist wondering whether some small part of what had been told to them will be repeated in court, despite the considerable scope for miscommunication, distortion and gaps in a formal hearing.

Independence and interpretative indeterminacy

In Chapter 1, I imagined an idealised template for an anthropologist's report that projected independence by accepting interpretative indeterminacy and offering plausible alternatives to the judge on the key questions of the title-holding group, 'society', laws and customs, 'normative system' and change (the robust academic model). None of the anthropologists in the three case studies structured their reports in this way. In Beckett's case, his inclination towards inductive generalisation left little room for alternative interpretations. Also, some of the terms of the Statement of Claim already embodied indeterminacy—for example, leaving open the level of the title-holding group (Meriam people or community or family group or individual) and the degree to which relations to land had to be law-like ('laws, customs, traditions and practices'). This relative openness is characteristic of a statement of claim rather than a concluded formulation of legal doctrine. Beckett's corrective stance towards the strong traditionalism of the Statement of Claim also set him on a clear course in explaining continuity at the level of principles of land tenure, rather than in terms of Malo's Law.

In the native title era proper, the indeterminate terms of the legal doctrine did not prompt a radically different approach. In *Rubibi*, Sullivan was guided by his own convictions of the need for the court to recognise the most inclusive group. The narrow focus of the case on rights to conduct ceremony eased the translation problems of identifying 'laws and customs' relating to land, and he took the risk of assuming that only arguments about traditional continuity would be relevant. When I raised the possibility of the robust academic model of report writing, to my surprise, he immediately identified it with aspects of legal discourse, such as the inclusion of contradictory alternatives in a statement of claim or in final submissions. More particularly, he identified it with what he felt was a challenge to his professional integrity when, following the first *Rubibi* claim, lawyers suggested that he modify his firm opinion about the all-inclusive grouping of native title holders to admit to other alternatives. Thus, instead of seeing it as a logical, if risky, means of asserting independence in the legal process, he saw it as the opposite: a challenge to his professional independence.

In response to my questioning about the robust academic model, Elliott emphasised what he took to be the expectations that he, as an expert, would come to a concluded view and be of assistance to the court. It seems to me that these were pervasive expectations in all the case studies. These general expectations seem to flow from a subliminal gestalt of the juridical field to do with expert certainty and finality. Perhaps it is a vaguely apprehended but accurate view that judges want social science expertise to be modelled on that of the physical sciences, rather than be presented with a range of possible interpretations to choose from.

Elliott made the interesting suggestion that, while *he* would not 'get away with' the robust academic model, he thought that others, more senior in the discipline, might. Both Kolig and Maddock were in this position. Kolig tended to avoid interpretative indeterminacy about historical transformation of traditional land tenure even when confronted with it directly—answering legal indeterminacy with anthropological indeterminacy. More than most, Maddock acknowledged the translation problems of identifying traditional laws. Both, however, seem to have been guided by their understanding of their role as corrective to the perceived excesses of the claimants' anthropologists. Accordingly, they gave an alternative view without seeing the need to explore the nature of the indeterminacy or how it might be resolved.

The place of advocacy and the fate of the robust academic model

The whole idea of proposing a triangulation model of anthropologists' agency in native title was to allow a more complex account to be given of what anthropologists do in formulating expert native title reports—an account that transcends a global categorisation as expert *or* advocate. Now that the success or otherwise of that model has been examined, it is time to go back and reconsider that initial move and ask what role simple advocacy of the Indigenous position has played. For even though the advocate/expert dichotomy is a blunt analytical tool, it cannot be denied that there are pervasive social pressures towards advocacy in the social field of anthropology. It is easy to imagine self-imposed pressures coming from the forging of friendships between anthropologists and their informants and the accumulation of intimate local knowledge about the tragedies and injustices of the course of European settlement. It has also been suggested that anthropologists would be wary of exclusion from a long-term research site should they appear to be working against the interests of their original informants (Maddock 1983b:155).

There are also external pressures that could easily become internalised. The anti-colonial critique of anthropology has already been mentioned and there is an even more direct pressure in the expectation of the Aboriginal land councils and representative bodies—which engage and pay for the experts—that they will produce something that is going to advance the recognition of native title rights. Pervasive concerns about advocacy seem to lie behind Kolig's and Maddock's stance of providing a balancing critique of the claimants' anthropologist.

One senior anthropologist thought that the manuscript of this book had underplayed the significance of pressures towards advocacy at every step of the process of formulating an expert report. Through my own belated experience of native title work, I can only agree that such constant pressure does exist and that the issue of avoiding advocacy remains one of the enduring fault lines within native title applied anthropology. By fault line, I mean a matter of internal debate, position taking and a broad criterion in peer assessment. I suspect it is the peculiar collection of case studies I have presented in this book that might have given the impression of underplaying the significance of simple advocacy. For I found the most direct attributions of advocacy and bias—against Elliott in *De Rose Hill* and Sutton in *Yulara*—to be unfair and unwarranted on my reading of the material and from interviews with the people involved. Beckett not only projected independence in the witness box, his estrangement from the legal team removed some of the typical external pressures for advocacy. Sharp, had she been called as a witness in Mabo, would, I believe, have been vulnerable to accusations of advocacy and bias because of the abstract level at which she asserted deep continuities with the pre-contact past. It was Sullivan in *Rubibi* who was most troubled by having to adopt a position of objectivity and distance from his friends in the hard-won Rubibi coalition. His critical concession in cross-examination of possible alternative ways to conceive of the pre-contact era deflected the charge of advocacy that Kolig thought was justified. Other case studies might have produced a different mix, which would have given more prominence to the question of advocacy.

Bringing back the issue of advocacy adds a further layer to the model of the agency of the expert anthropologist that was proposed in Chapter 1. It means that the deconstruction/reconstruction triangulation decisions are being made within a field that also features constant pressure for and against simple advocacy of the Indigenous position. The revised model of anthropological agency could be represented as in Figure 9.1.

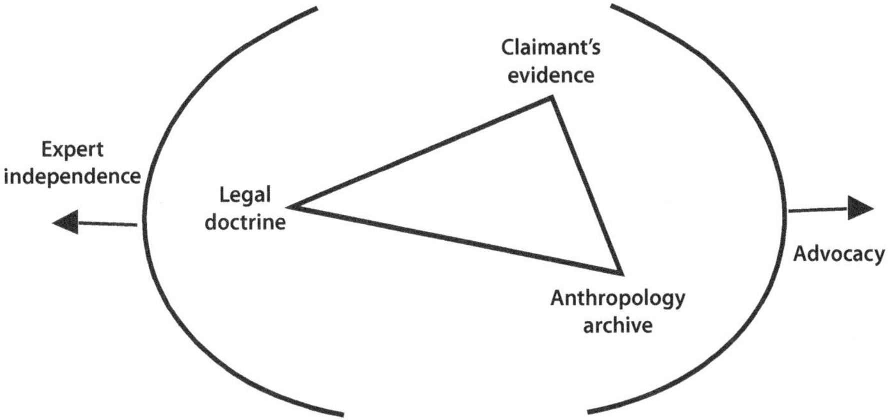

Figure 9.1 Revised idealised model of anthropological agency

Implications for the practice of applied anthropology

The discussion of advocacy has persuaded me to make one final move that I had not anticipated at the beginning of this project, which was not in the first instance aimed at improving applied anthropological practice. The project was always envisaged as a sociological study of applied anthropology. But it seems to me that what I have called the robust academic model of report writing is not only an analytical tool; it can be and should be a model for writing expert reports in future claims. Before I expand upon this, it should be noted that the case studies have in various ways confirmed that there are relatively intransigent features of the social fields that have a substantial impact on the way anthropological evidence is received. Put simply, the opinions of the highly qualified, experienced expert witness who has conducted long-term fieldwork with the claimants prior to the native title era are more likely to be heard. Nevertheless, the content of the anthropological report is still a significant factor.

It will be recalled that what I had in mind was confronting more directly the indeterminacy of the key elements of the legal doctrine of native title, being more explicit about the process of deconstructing and reconstructing the anthropological archive and offering alternative ways to resolve the key indeterminacies. Using Mantziaris and Martin's (2000) terminology, it would mean being more explicit about the process of translation in the recognition space. I am acutely aware of the risks of introducing greater complexity into anthropological reports. I have already agreed with Morton in relation to *Yulara* that one of the implicit expectations of the juridical field is that anthropological evidence will help to simplify ethnographic complexity and so assist the court towards a conclusion. This pressure to simplify was noted by Berndt (1981) in the very first appearance of expert anthropologists in the *Gove* case and will probably always remain. I think, however, the benefits outweigh the risks. The benefits include the more effective projection of expert independence and the return of the responsibility for resolving the indeterminacy of legal doctrine back to the judge.

Judicial agency

Post-hoc reflections by judges about particular cases are rare for obvious reasons: the potential complication of deviating from the formal written judgment might lead to apprehensions of bias and potential decline in public support for the judiciary. I did approach Justice Moynihan, but he could not remember the details of the *Mabo* hearing from 12 years before. I did not approach Justice Merkel because the second *Rubibi* hearing had not been finalised at the time I was completing that case study. He retired from the Federal Court bench in 2006 to pursue public-interest litigation as a barrister. In a radio interview about that time, he took the expected stance of not commenting on individual cases he had heard.[5] Justice O'Loughlin, who had retired also, probably would have taken the same view. In any case, he died in 2005. All this means that there is a different quality to the comparison of my interpretations of the anthropological evidence and the judge's interpretation as revealed in the judgment. I anticipated a certain impenetrability in my account of the juridical field in Chapter 1.

To be clear, what is difficult to penetrate is the judge's performance of the role sanctioned by legal doctrine—deciding whether to accept a witness as an expert, evaluating the expert's evidence in the totality of the evidence and deciding what weight to give it, assessing possible bias—as opposed to deploying legal doctrines about expertise to achieve a predetermined result. Perhaps this is simply a distinction between a judge's official and unofficial agency. But this distinction is problematic as well. First, there is the problem of interpreting the meagre evidence of what the judge's personal views about the justice of the case might have been. Then, it is to be expected that judges will bring, and must bring, their personal knowledge, in the sense of the implicit background that we all share, to fulfil their official role. It is perhaps inevitable that, in the resolution of indeterminate legal doctrine for which there is no official guidance, personality traits, personal values and political opinions will be brought to bear as well.

Despite the methodological difficulties, I have tentatively attributed an active and constructive intervention to the judges in *Rubibi* and *De Rose Hill*. In *Rubibi*, it was the active search for common ground between experts in dispute. The word 'intervention' might imply that Justice Merkel was outside the bounds of acceptable judicial behaviour. This would not be warranted, however, since one overriding judicial obligation is the practical resolution of the case, and finding common ground between the experts certainly assisted a resolution. The argument that the search for common ground is a constructive intervention is really made in comparison with other judges ignoring experts in dispute, as if they cancel each other out.

In *De Rose Hill*, the combination of the judge's publicly expressed doubts about the justice of the case, the unfair treatment of Elliott in the witness box, the judge's adoption of Maddock's doubts, and his high expectations of the claimants' courage and continuing application to traditional duties on De Rose Hill Station all lead to the impression that the judge had taken a strong view about the preferable outcome of the case from a very early stage. For

5 Interview conducted by Damien Carrick, 'Leaving high office for a higher purpose', *Law Report*, ABC Radio National, 23 May 2006. At the time of publication, it was still available on the ABC web site at <www.abc.au/rn/lawreport/stories/2006/1644195.htm> A hard copy of the transcript is in the possession of the author.

understandable reasons, Elliott urged me to call this 'bias', in the same way that he had been accused of bias by the judge. Part of my reluctance to follow his suggestion is to avoid confusion with the legal doctrine of judicial bias, for it is doubtful whether there would be sufficient evidence for a claim of judicial bias to succeed.[6]

The usual difficulties of attributing an active and constructive agency to judges do not apply to Justice Sackville's reconstruction of the anthropological archive on traditional Western Desert land tenure in *Yulara*. It was there in his judgment for all to see. Other choices made to resolve the key indeterminacies of legal doctrine remain implicit because of restrictions on the acceptable ways to state the content of the legal doctrine, as predicted in Chapter 1. But the implied criteria of coherence and completeness in *Yulara* in evaluating whether there was a 'body of traditional laws and customs' are suggestive of one way of reconstructing the choices open to the judge in interpreting that phrase. For the features of modern law have to be adapted to be applied to tribal societies—a process that preoccupied the early theorists of primitive law and comparative law.

There are some distinctive aspects of modern law that are not expected to be found among Aboriginal people: the formal separation of religion from modern law, the completeness and uniformity of modern legal codes within a meta-legal framework (a constitution) formally defining legal authority, the objectified and conventional nature of modern law (positive law), specialised rational adjudication processes and dispute resolution according to well-identified principles and specialised law-enforcement bodies. Some of these features of modern law might be carried over to the search for primitive laws, especially ideas of acknowledged objectified statements of norms, ideas of completeness, coherence and stability (as in *Yulara*), ideas of legitimate authority and ideas of widespread compliance and enforcement. Thus, although the *Mabo* decision legislated primitive law/legal pluralism, there are always implicit judgments being made about how far primitive law can stray from the features of modern law.

---

6 Briefly, bias would be established if a fair-minded person might reasonably apprehend or suspect that the judge has prejudged or might prejudge the case. It might be a prejudgment of fact or law or the determination of fact or credit in a previous case. But it must be more than an apprehension that the judge might decide the case adversely to a party. The making of a series of adverse interlocutory decisions does not of itself warrant disqualification, nor does a judge indicating his thinking in the course of the hearing. In addition, a judge's expressions that are acerbic, or indicative of irritation, do not of themselves justify disqualification (see unattributed case note, 'What is judicial bias', in the *Journal of Judicial Administration*, vol. 7 [1998], pp. 187–8). Thus, the elements that I have used to attribute to Justice O'Loughlin a strong view (see Chapter 7) might not have amounted to the apprehension of bias required by the legal doctrine.

Law's anthropology?

Before turning to my conclusions on the interaction of the two fields, some of the costs of framing the fields as separate should be mentioned. The first is that it tends to obscure the deep homologies between the two fields. At a general level, for example, the persistent distinction between ethnography and theory in anthropology seems to be a counterpart to the fundamental fact–law distinction in the juridical field. So that, at a broad structural level, it could be said that:

ethnography : theory :: fact : law

This general homology could be extended. Just as legal doctrine tends to mould facts despite their clear separation in legal theory, in anthropology, theory either explicitly or implicitly moulds ethnography. These deep homologies are perhaps what allow a recognition in the juridical field of native title of the centrality of anthropological expertise among the range of available experts and the unusual discussions that sometimes occur between judge and expert anthropologist during the latter's evidence. On closer inspection, these basic distinctions operate in different ways in the two social fields. In the juridical field, the fact–law distinction is pervasive and relentless, even forcing anthropological evidence to become more fact-like by announcing a lack of interest in the theoretical entanglements of ethnographic facts. While this structuralist approach is of interest, a comprehensive explanation requires that these broad structures be linked to individual agency. I have sought to do this by invoking habitus and, more generally, by viewing structures as resources that can be manipulated and as constraints that can be partially evaded because of the ambiguity of language.

The other cost of separating the two fields too sharply is the underplaying of the circulation of ideas between the two fields. Anthropological borrowing from legal theory occurred most directly in primitive law and legal pluralism, but also in the language of rights and duties, and the distinction between rights *in personam* and rights *in rem* (for example, see Meggitt 1962). Because of this borrowing, Mantziaris and Martin referred to the structural–functionalist era as 'the jural paradigm' (2000:33–5). Arguably, there are even more subtle influences of legal theory—for example, the idea of the self-contained constitutional state might lie behind Radcliffe-Brown's theorising about the horde and Tindale's theorising about the tribe (cf. Gumbert's characterisation of Radcliffe-Brown's theorising of the horde as a 'mini-state' theory).

Legal borrowing from anthropology has a different character. The ties to the anthropological origin of some terms in the definition of traditional owner in the *Land Rights Act* and the mention of 'clans or groups' and 'society' in native title legal doctrine seemed to be severed once these terms became part of legal doctrine and subject to the norms of legal interpretation in the juridical field. Also, broad judicial assessments of Aboriginal relations to land as spiritual–religious, drawing principally on Stanner's work, tend to take on the form of a precedent, or judicial notice of a widely accepted fact, and are continually quoted by later judges who require some introductory remarks or to deploy a standard of authenticity.[7]

There are plenty of examples in the case studies of law swallowing and digesting anthropology: the disregarding of Beckett's central argument about the Meriam domain changing at a slower rate than other parts of the society; the dismantling of Sullivan's umbrella grouping in favour of a narrower Yawuru group; the disregarding of Elliott's theorising about the Yankunytjatjara Pitjantjatjara Antakirinya community; and the extraordinary reconstruction of the ethnography of traditional Western Desert land tenure in *Yulara*. To extend the metaphor, there is also a dawning realisation that one way to view the anthropologist's task is one of predigestion of the anthropological archive to aid its digestion by the legal system.

The evidence that could be interpreted as collusion or the sharing of responsibility is also there, if not so directly accessible. It can be seen in *Mabo* in Justice Moynihan's discussions with Beckett, testing his own half-formed opinions in discussions with Beckett; in *Rubibi*, in Justice Merkel's search for common ground between anthropologists in dispute, to support his own conclusion; and in *De Rose Hill*, in Justice O'Loughlin's adoption, as his own, of Maddock's doubts about the case. In a variation on this theme, Sackville sought to share responsibility with the phantom experts, rather than with Sutton.

One feature of the interaction I did not fully anticipate in my original theorising has been the struggle between judge and anthropologist over the authoritative interpretation of the anthropological archive as occurred in *De Rose Hill* and, in its most extreme form, in *Yulara*. In both cases, most items in the anthropological archive directly relating to the claim area were tendered in evidence separately to the anthropologist's report thus providing the raw material for the judge to

7 Although the characterisation of Aboriginal relations to land as essentially religious was more widespread than Stanner's writings, his personal influence, as an expert witness in the *Gove* case and as a public intellectual, can be directly traced. One of the most quoted parts of the *Gove* decision was Justice Blackburn's conclusion on the facts of that case, including the facts of expert opinion, that 'the fundamental truth about aboriginals' [sic] relationship to the land is that whatever else it is, it is a religious relationship' (*Milirrpum v Nabalco Pty Ltd* 17 FLR 141, Blackburn J. at p. 167). The most recent use of that quotation was in the critical decision of the High Court in *Ward*, where the majority explicitly stated: 'As is now well recognised, the connection which Aboriginal peoples have with "country" is essentially spiritual' (*Western Australia v Ward* 213 CLR 1, para. 14). Part of Stanner's Boyer Lectures in which he describes Aboriginal relations to land in terms of an everlasting spiritual home was adopted by Justice Brennan (as he then was) in *The Queen v Toohey; Ex Parte Meneling Station Proprietary Limited* (1982) 158 CLR 327 at 356. Having received this judicial imprimatur, later judges have referred to it frequently via the *Meneling* case, the latest example being Justice Merkel in the first *Rubibi* decision.

form his own view about them. There is no legal rule of evidence preventing a judge from doing this since the weight to be given to each piece of evidence is for the judge to decide. On my reading, though, there was a tendency for the judges to give undue weight to anthropologists in the archive who had a high public profile or high academic capital. That is why I used the terms 'phantom experts' and 'big names'. Unsullied by an account of the reception of their work by other anthropologists or by contrary findings from other locations or by more recent syntheses, the opinions of the big names seemed to rise from their graves and be afforded similar or even greater status than those of the living experts who have the benefit of later research and debate and can also be cross-examined.

As the case studies have demonstrated, to prevail in the struggle over the anthropological archive requires more than being qualified as an expert witness. At a minimum it requires a complete mastery of the archive and an ability under cross-examination to quickly and convincingly contextualise each individual item that might be deployed separately to undermine a considered opinion.

This book in the fields of anthropology and law

One way of bringing the consideration of these issues to a close is to outline how the results of this project might be received in the two social fields described. In the field of anthropology certain complexities arise because of the unusual nature of this research project. It is anthropology at home—exceedingly close to home—but which does not use classic participant-observation methodology. Yet, it is still seeking to be a 'pure' approach to applied anthropology. As such, it falls on the 'pure' side of the pure–applied divide. From an applied perspective, it does not seem to offer many solutions to the practical problems of performing well as an expert witness. Instead, it tends to confine what experts can directly influence (triangulation decisions, courtroom technique), by emphasising the powerful effect of the more immutable constraints in the encounter. These constraints include the level of scientific and academic capital within the field of anthropology, hysteresis effects (time lags in learning to function effectively in a new social field), the general disposition of the judge to the justice of the case and judicial scepticism about research for litigation.

In the juridical field, the attribution of active and constructive intervention to an identified judge in a particular case would be grounds for a contempt charge, if made in court, and goes beyond the usual bounds of acceptable legal commentary in most academic legal journals. With the exception of the analysis of the reception of expert scientific testimony, the analysis of fact-finding is relatively rare in that literature; it typically concentrates on developments in legal doctrine. Leaving the possibility of defamation to one side, I have struggled with the issue of what terminology of agency to use—'forming a gestalt', 'having a hunch', 'forming a strong view', 'unofficial agency', 'bias', 'prejudice'. Even though I have distanced myself from the sceptical critique of judicial fact-finding, I have adopted some of its terminology as a partial explanation of what occurred in *De Rose Hill* and *Rubibi*. After all these years, however, such terminology still tends to be a dangerously personal affront to the integrity of the judge, not merely a challenge to greater reflexivity and openness, as was originally intended.

Bibliography

Books, journal articles, theses

Abbott, A. 1988. *The System of Professions: An Essay on the Division of Expert Labour*. Chicago: The University of Chicago Press.

Altman, J. C. 2001. Can quality independent research in Indigenous affairs be influential? Personal reflections on the Reeves Land Rights Inquiry and its aftermath. *Australian Aboriginal Studies* 2:12–17.

Appadurai, A. 1986. Theory in anthropology: centre and periphery. *Comparative Studies in Society and History* 28:356–61.

Asad, T. 1973. *Anthropology and the Colonial Encounter*. London: Ithaca Press.

Attwood, B. and J. Arnold (eds), 1992. *Power, Knowledge and Aborigines. Journal of Australian Studies*. Melbourne: La Trobe University Press.

Baer, H. A. 1995. Commentary: elitism and discrimination within anthropology. *Practicing Anthropology* 17:42–3.

Bannister, J. K. 2006. Secret Business and Business Secrets: The Hindmarsh Island Bridge Affair, Information, Law and the Public Sphere. Unpublished PhD Thesis, The Australian National University, Canberra.

Barnes, J. A. 1962. African models in the New Guinea Highlands. *Man* 62:5–9.

Basedow, H. 1904. Anthropological notes made on the South Australian Government North-West Prospecting Expedition, 1903. *Transactions and Proceedings of the Royal Society of South Australia* XXVIII:12.

Basedow, H. 1914. *Journal of the Government North-West Expedition*. Adelaide: Royal Geographical Society of Australasia, South Australian Branch.

Bates, D. 1914. Social organisation of some Western Australian tribes. *Reports of the Australia and New Zealand Association for the Advancement of Science* 14:387–400.

Bates, D. 1915. Few notes on some south-western Australian dialects. *Journal of the Royal Anthropological Institute of Great Britain* 44:65–82.

Bates, D. 1918. Aborigines of the west coast of South Australia: vocabularies and ethnological notes. *Transactions and Proceedings of the Royal Society of South Australia* XLII:152–67.

Bates, D. 1938. *The Passing of the Aborigines*. London: John Murray.

Bates, D. 1985. *The Native Tribes of Western Australia*. Canberra: National Library of Australia.

Beckett, J. R (ed.), 2000. *Wherever I Go: Myles Lalor's 'Oral History'*. Melbourne: Melbourne University Press.

Beckett, J. R. 1958. Marginal men: a study of two half-caste Aborigines. *Oceania* 29:91–108.

Beckett, J. R. 1959. Further notes on the social organisation of the Wongaibon of New South Wales. *Oceania* 29:200–7.

Beckett, J. R. 1963. Politics in the Torres Straits Islands. Unpublished PhD Thesis, The Australian National University, Canberra.

Beckett, J. R. 1965. Kinship, mobility and community among part-Aborigines in rural Australia. *International Journal of Comparative Sociology* 6:2–23.

Beckett, J. R. 1967. Elections in a small Melanesian community. *Ethnology* 6:332–44.

Beckett, J. R. 1971. 'Rivalry, competition and conflict among Christian Melanesians', in *Anthropology in Oceania: Essays Presented to Ian Hogbin*. Edited by L. R. Hiatt and C. Jayawardena. Melbourne: Melbourne University Press.

Beckett, J. R. 1983. 'Ownership of land in the Torres Strait Islands', in *Aborigines, Land and Land Rights*. Edited by N. Peterson and M. Langton, pp. 202–10. Canberra: Australian Institute of Aboriginal Studies.

Beckett, J. R. 1987. *Torres Strait Islanders: Custom and Colonialism*. Cambridge: Cambridge University Press.

Beckett, J. R. 1989. Meriam land tenure. Unpublished report.

Beckett, J. R. 1994. Review of Nonie Sharp's *The Stars of Tagai: The Torres Strait Islanders*. *Canberra Anthropology* 17(2):128–30.

Beckett, J. R. 1995. The Murray Island Land Case. *The Australian Journal of Anthropology* 6:15–31.

Beckett, J. R. 1996. Against nostalgia: place and memory in Myles Lalor's 'Oral History'. *Oceania* 66:312–22.

Beckett, J. R. 1998. 'Haddon attends a funeral: fieldwork in Torres Strait 1888, 1899', in *Cambridge and the Torres Strait: Centenary Essays on the 1898 Anthropological Expedition*. Edited by A. Herle and S. Rouse, pp. 23–49. Cambridge: Cambridge University Press.

Beckett, J. R. 2001. 'Against the grain: fragmentary memories of anthropology in Australia, 1956–1970', in *Before It's Too Late: Anthropological Reflections, 1950–1970*. Edited by G. Gray, pp. 83–98. Oceania Monographs. Sydney: University of Sydney.

Beckett, J. R. 2002. Some aspects of continuity and change among anthropologists in Australia or 'He-Who-Eats-From-One-Dish-With-Us-With-One-Spoon'. *The Australian Journal of Anthropology* 13:127–38.

Bell, D. 1998. *Ngarrindjeri Wurruwarrin: A World That Is, Was, and Will Be*. Melbourne: Spinifex Press.

Bennett, J. W. 1996. Applied and action anthropology: ideological and conceptual aspects. *Current Anthropology* 36:S23–53.

Benterrak, K., S. Muecke and P. Roe. 1984. *Reading the Country: Introduction to Nomadology*. Fremantle, WA: Fremantle Arts Centre Press.

Bern, J. 1979. Ideology and domination: towards a reconstruction of Australian Aboriginal social formation. *Oceania* 50:118–32.

Berndt, R. M. 1941. Tribal migrations and myths centring on Ooldea. *Oceania* 12:1–20.

Berndt, R. M. 1959. The concept of 'the tribe' in the Western Desert of Australia. *Oceania* 30:81–107.

Berndt, R. M. 1965. 'Law and order in Aboriginal Australia', in *Aboriginal Man in Australia: Essays in Honour of Emeritus Professor A. P. Elkin*. Edited by R. M. Berndt and C. H. Berndt, pp. 167–206. Sydney: Angus & Robertson.

Berndt, R. M. 1972. 'The Walmadjeri and Gugadja', in *Hunters and Gatherers Today*. Edited by M. G. Bicchieri, pp. 177–216. New York: Holt, Rinehart and Winston.

Berndt, R. M. 1981. A long view: some personal comments on land rights. *Australian Institute of Aboriginal Studies Newsletter* 16:5–20.

Berndt, R. M. 1982. 'The changing face of Aboriginal studies—some personal glimpses', in *Anthropology in Australia: Essays to Honour 50 Years of 'Mankind'*. Edited by G. McCall, pp. 49–65. Sydney: Anthropological Society of New South Wales.

Berndt, R. M. and C. H. Berndt. 1945. *A Preliminary Report of Fieldwork in the Ooldea Region, Western South Australia*. Sydney: University of Sydney/ Australian Medical Publishing Company.

Berndt, R. M. and C. H. Berndt. 1951. *From Black to White in South Australia*. Melbourne: Cheshire.

Bernstein, D. E. 1996. Junk science in the United States and the Commonwealth. *Yale Journal of International Law* 21:123-182.

Bicchieri, M. G. (ed.), 1972. *Hunters and Gatherers Today: A Socioeconomic Study of Eleven Such Cultures in the Twentieth Century*. New York: Holt, Rinehart and Winston.

Birdsell, J. B. 1970. Group composition among the Australian Aborigines: a critique of the evidence from fieldwork conducted since 1930. *Current Anthropology* 11:115–42.

Bischofs, P. J. 1908. Die Niol-Niol, ein Eingeborenenstamm in Nordwest-Australien. *Anthropos* 3:32–40.

Biskup, P. 1973. *Not Slaves, Not Citizens: The Aboriginal Problem in Western Australia 1898–1954*. Brisbane: University of Queensland Press.

Black, B., F. J. Ayala and C. Saffran-Brinks. 1994. Science and the law in the wake of *Daubert*: a new search for scientific knowledge. *Texas Law Review* 72:715–802.

Blackburn, J. 1994. *Daisy Bates in the Desert*. London: Secker & Warburg.

Blake, T. 1998. Deported…At the sweet will of the government: the removal of Aborigines to reserves in Queensland 1897–1939. *Aboriginal History* 22:51–61.

Bohannan, P. J. 1957. *Justice and Judgment Among the Tiv*. London: Oxford University Press/International African Institute.

Bohman, J. 1991. *New Philosophy of Social Science: Problems of Indeterminacy*. Cambridge: Polity Press.

Bohman, J. 1999. 'Practical reason and cultural constraint: agency in Bourdieu's theory of practice', in *Bourdieu: A Critical Reader*. Edited by R. Schusterman, pp. 129–52. Oxford: Blackwell.

Bourdieu, P. 1987. The force of law: towards a sociology of the juridical field. *The Hastings Law Journal* 38:814–53.

Bourdieu, P. 1988. *Homo Academicus*. Cambridge: Polity Press.

Bourdieu, P. 1990. *The Logic of Practice*. Cambridge: Polity Press.

Bourdieu, P. 1991. *Language and Symbolic Power*. Cambridge: Polity Press.

Bourdieu, P. 2000. *Pascalian Meditations*. London: Polity Press.

Brady, M. 1986. Leaving the spinifex: the impact of rations, missions, and the atomic tests on the Southern Pitjantjatjara. *Records of the South Australian Museum* 20:35–45.

Brady, M. and K. Palmer. 1984. *Alcohol in the Outback: Two Studies of Drinking*. Darwin: North Australia Research Unit, The Australian National University.

Brown, A. R. 1913. Three tribes of Western Australia. *The Journal of the Royal Anthropological Institute of Great Britain and Ireland* 43:143–94.

Brunton, R. 1996. The Hindmarsh Island Bridge and the credibility of Australian anthropology. *Anthropology Today* 12:2–7.

Brunton, R. and L. Sackett. 2003. Anthropologists in the hot tub. *Native Title News* 6:86–8.

Buckley, R., C. J. Ellis, L. Hercus, L. Penny and I. M. White. 1967. *Group Project on Andagarinja Women, Volume 1*. Adelaide: Private Publication, University of Adelaide Library.

Buckley, R., C. J. Ellis, L. Hercus, L. Penny and I. M. White. 1968. *Group Project on Andagarinja Women, Volume 2*. Adelaide: Private Publication, University of Adelaide Library.

Burke, P. 2002. *The Legal Implications of Chapman v Luminis for Anthropological Practice*. Australian Anthropological Society web site. <http://www.aas.asn.au>

Burke, P. 2007. The problem when flexibility *is* the system. *Anthropological Forum* 17(2):163–5.

Burke, P. 2010. 'Overlapping jural publics: a model for dealing with the "society" question in native title', in *Dilemmas in Applied Native Title Anthropology in Australia*. Edited by T. Bauman, pp. 55–71. Canberra: Australian Institute of Aboriginal and Torres Strait Islander Studies.

Burton, J. 2005. 'The people remember and the government forgets: the last 100 years of land disputes at Mer, Torres Strait', in *Native Title, Decision-Making and Conflict Management Seminar Series*. Canberra: Native Title Research Unit, Australian Institute of Aboriginal and Torres Strait Islander Studies.

Burton, J. 2007. 'Determinacy of groups and the "owned commons" in Papua New Guinea and Torres Strait', in *Contemporary Land Tenure and Registration in Australia and Papua and New Guinea: Anthropological Perspectives*. Asia-Pacific Environment Monographs 3. Edited by J. F. Wiener and K. Glaskin, pp. 175–98. Canberra: ANU E Press.

Campbell, C. M. 1974. Legal thought and juristic values. *British Journal of Law and Society* 1:13–30.

Cane, S. 2002. *Pila Nguru: The Spinifex People*. Fremantle, WA: Fremantle Arts Centre Press.

Capell, A. 1940. Classification of languages in north and north-west Australia. *Oceania* 10:241–72, 404–43.

Capell, A. 1964. Obituary: the Reverend E. A. Worms. *Oceania* 34:155–6.

Cassell, J. 1995. Caste and class in anthropology. *Practicing Anthropology* 17:43–4.

Chaney, F. M. 1994. *The Particular Significance to Aboriginals of Land Near Broome to be Leased for the Purpose of a Crocodile Park: Report to the Minister for Aboriginal Affairs under s.10(4) of the Aboriginal and Torres Strait Islander Heritage Protection Act 1984*. Perth: The Graduate School of Management, University of Western Australia.

Clarke, P. A. 1996. Response to 'Secret women's business: the Hindmarsh Island affair'. *Journal of Australian Studies* 50–1:141–49.

Clifford, J. 1986. 'Introduction', in *Writing Culture: The Poetics and Politics of Ethnography*. Edited by J. Clifford and G. E. Marcus. Berkeley: University of California Press.

Clifford, J. and G. E. Marcus (eds), 1986. *Writing Culture: The Poetics and Politics of Ethnography*. Berkeley: University of California Press.

Comaroff, J. and J. Comaroff. 1991. *Of Revelation and Revolution: Christianity, Colonialism and Consciousness in South Africa. Volume One*. Chicago: University of Chicago Press.

Connelly, J. F. 1932. Distribution of tribes in Western Australia. *Mankind* 1:101.

Connolly, A. 2006. Judicial conceptions of tradition in Canadian aboriginal rights law. *The Asia Pacific Journal of Anthropology* 7(1):27-44.

Cooper, R. E. 1997–98. Federal Court expert usage guidelines. *Australian Bar Review* 16:Extra-Traditional Notes 2–10.

Cotterrell, R. B. M. 1986. Law and sociology: notes on the constitution and confrontations of disciplines. *Journal of Law and Society* 13(1):9–34.

Cotterrell, R. B. M. 1999. *Emile Durkheim: Law in a Moral Domain*. Edinburgh: Edinburgh University Press.

Cove, J. J. 1996. Playing the devil's advocate: anthropology in *Delgamuukw*. *Political and Legal Anthropology Review* 19:53–8.

Cruickshank, J. 1992. Invention of anthropology in British Columbia's Supreme Court: oral tradition as evidence. *BC Studies* 95:25–42.

Culhane, D. 1992. Adding insult to injury: Her Majesty's loyal anthropologists. *BC Studies* 95:66–92.

Culhane, D. 1994. *Delgamuukw* and the People Without Culture: Anthropology and the Crown. Unpublished PhD Thesis, Simon Fraser University, Burnaby Mountain, BC.

Culhane, D. 1998. *The Pleasure of the Crown: Anthropology, Law and First Nations*. Vancouver: Talon.

Curr, E. M. 1883. *Recollections of Squatting in Victoria, then called the Port Phillip District (1841 to 1851)*. Melbourne: G. Robertson.

Curthoys, A. and J. Docker. 1996. Is history fiction? *The UTS Review* 2(1).

Dagmar, H. 1989. Review of *Torres Strait Islanders: Custom and Colonialism*. *American Ethnologist* 16:800–1.

Dalton, P. 1964. Broome—A Multiracial Community: A study of social and cultural relationships in a town in the West Kimberleys, Western Australia. Master of Arts Thesis, University of Western Australia, Perth.

Dalton, P. 1965. 'The two men', in AIATSIS Library, Australian Institute of Aboriginal and Torres Strait Islander Studies, Canberra.

Davis, S. L. and J. R. V. Prescott. 1992. *Aboriginal Frontiers and Boundaries in Australia*. Melbourne: Melbourne University Press.

De Vries, S. 2008. *Desert Queen: The Many Lives and Loves of Daisy Bates*. Pymble, NSW: HarperCollins Publishers.

Diamond, S. 1969. 'Anthropology in question', in *Reinventing Anthropology*. Edited by D. Hymes, pp. 401–29. New York: Pantheon Books.

Dobyns, H. F. 1978. 'Taking the witness stand', in *Applied Anthropology in America*. Edited by E. M. Eddy and W. L. Partridge, pp. 261–74. New York: Columbia University Press.

Doohan, K. 1992. *One Family, Different Country: The Development and Persistence of an Aboriginal Community at Finke, Northern Territory*. Oceania Monographs 42. Sydney: University of Sydney.

Douglas, W. H. 1964. *An Introduction to the Western Desert Language of Australia*, Second edition. Oceania Linguistic Monographs No. 4. Sydney: Sydney University.

Douglas, W. H. 1971. Dialectic differentiation in the Western Desert—a comment. *Anthropological Forum* 3:79–82.

Dumont, L. 1971. 'Marriage alliance', in *Readings in Kinship and Social Structure*. Edited by N. Graburn. New York: Harper and Row.

Durkheim, E. [1893] 1984. *The Division of Labour in Society*, Translated by W. D. Halls. London: Macmillan.

Dussart, F. 2000. *The Politics of Ritual in an Aboriginal Settlement: Kinship, Gender, and the Currency of Knowledge. Smithsonian Series in Ethnographic Inquiry*. Washington, DC: Smithsonian Institution Press.

Dwyer, K. 1979. The dialogic of ethnology. *Dialectical Anthropology* 4:205–24.

Dwyer, K. 1982. *Moroccan Dialogues*. London: Johns Hopkins University Press.

Edmond, G. 2000. Judicial representations of scientific evidence. *Modern Law Review* 63(2):216–51.

Edmond, G. 2001. The law-set: the legal-scientific production of medical propriety. *Science, Technology and Human Values* 26(2):191–226.

Edmond, G. 2002. Legal engineering: contested representations of the law, science (and non-science) and society. *Social Studies of Science* 32:371–412.

Edmond, G. 2004. Thick decisions: expertise, advocacy and reasonableness in the Federal Court of Australia. *Oceania* 74:190–230.

Edmond, G. and D. Mercer. 1997. Keeping 'junk' history, philosophy and sociology of science out of the courtroom: problems with the reception of *Daubert v Merrell Dow Pharmaceuticals Inc. University of New South Wales Law Journal* 20:48–100.

Elkin, A. P. 1931. The social organisation of South Australian tribes. *Oceania* 2:44–73.

Elkin, A. P. 1932. Social organisation in the Kimberley Division, north-western Australia. *Oceania* 2:296–333.

Elkin, A. P. 1933. Totemism in north-western Australia. *Oceania* 3:257–96, 435–81.

Elkin, A. P. 1937. Kinship in South Australia (Part 1). *Oceania* 8:419–52.

Elkin, A. P. 1939. Kinship in South Australia (Part 2). *Oceania* 10:196–234.

Elkin, A. P. 1943. *The Australian Aborigines: How to Understand Them*, Second edition. Sydney: Angus & Robertson.

Elkin, A. P. 1964. *The Australian Aborigines: How to Understand Them*, Fourth edition. Sydney: Angus & Robertson.

Elliott, C. 1991. Mewal is Merri's Name: Form and Ambiguity in Marrangu Cosmology, North Central Arnhem Land. MA Thesis, The Australian National University, Canberra.

Elliott, C. 2000. Anthropological Report De Rose Hill Native Title Claim.

Elliott, C. 2001. Supplementary Anthropological Report De Rose Hill Native Title Claim.

Ellis, C. J. and L. Barwick. 1989. 'Antikirinja women's song knowledge 1963–72: its significance in Antikirinja culture', in *Women, Rites and Sites: Aboriginal Women's Cultural Knowledge*. Edited by P. Brock, pp. 21–40. Sydney: Allen & Unwin.

Fabian, J. 1983. *Time and the Other: How Anthropology Makes its Object*. New York: Columbia University Press.

Fardon, R. 1990. 'General introduction: localising strategies, the regionalisation of ethnographic accounts', in *Localising Strategies: Regional Traditions of Ethnographic Writing*. Edited by R. Fardon, pp. 1–37. Edinburgh: Scottish Academic Press.

Fergie, D. 1996. Secret envelopes and inferential tautologies. *Journal of Australian Studies* 48:13–24.

Finlayson, J. 2001. Anthropology's contribution to public policy formulation: the imagined other? *Australian Aboriginal Studies* 2:18–26.

Fish, S. 1980. *Is There a Text in this Class: The Authority of Interpretive Communities*. Cambridge, Mass.: Harvard University Press.

Fisher, R. 1992. Judging history: reflections on the reasons for judgment in *Delgamuukw v BC*. *BC Studies* 95:43–54.

Fiske, J.-A. 2000. Positioning the legal subject and the anthropologist: the challenge of *Delgamuukw* to anthropological theory. *Journal of Legal Pluralism* 45:1–17.

Fitzpatrick, J. 1989. Review of *Torres Strait Islanders: Custom and Colonialism*. *American Anthropologist* 91:812–13.

Folds, R. 2001. *Crossed Purposes: The Pintupi and Australia's Indigenous Policy*. Sydney: UNSW Press.

Frank, J. 1949. *Courts on Trial: Myth and Reality in American Justice*. Princeton, NJ: Princeton University Press.

Freckleton, I. and H. Selby. 2009. *Expert Evidence: Law, Practice, Procedure and Advocacy*, Fourth edition. Sydney: Lawbook Company.

Freckelton, I. R., P. Reddy, H. Selby and Australian Institute of Judicial Administration. 2001. *Australian Magistrates' Perspectives on Expert Evidence: A Comparative Study*. Carlton, Vic.: Australian Institute of Judicial Administration Incorporated.

Freckelton, I. R., H. Selby, P. Reddy and Australian Institute of Judicial Administration. 1999. *Australian Judicial Perspectives on Expert Evidence: An Empirical Study*. Carlton, Vic.: Australian Institute of Judicial Administration Incorporated.

Gailey, C. W. 1992. 'Introduction: civilisation and culture in the work of Stanley Diamond', in *Dialectical Anthropology: Essays in Honour of Stanley Diamond. Volume 1: Civilisation in Crisis: Anthropological Perspectives*. Edited by C. W. Gailey, pp. 1–35. Gainesville, Fla: University of Florida Press.

Garfinkle, H. 1967. *Studies in Ethnomethodology*. Englewood Cliffs, NJ: Prentice-Hall.

Gibson, J. 1989. 'Digging deep: Aboriginal women in the Oodnadatta region of South Australia in the 1980s', in *Women, Rites and Sites: Aboriginal Women's Cultural Knowledge*. Edited by P. Brock, pp. 60–75. Sydney: Allen & Unwin.

Glaskin, K. 2002. Claiming Country: A Case Study of Historical Legacy and Transition in the Native Title Context. PhD Thesis, The Australian National University, Canberra.

Glaskin, K. 2003. Native title and the 'bundle of rights' model: implications for the recognition of Aboriginal relations to country. *Anthropological Forum* 13:67–88.

Glaskin, K. 2007. Manifesting the latent in native title litigation. *Anthropological Forum* 17:165–8.

Glowczewski, B. 1983. Manifestations rituelles d'une transition economique: 'Le Juluru', Culte intertribal du cargo. *L'Homme* 23:7–35.

Glowczewski, B. 1991. *Du Rêve à la Loi Chez les Aborigènes—Mythes, Rites et Organisation Sociale en Australie*. Paris: PUF.

Glowczewski, B. 1998. The meaning of 'one' in Broome, Western Australia: from Yawuru tribe to Rubibi Corporation. *Aboriginal History* 22:203–22.

Glowczewski, B. 2000. Au nom du père et de la terre: Les Aborigènes aux prises avec le passé. *L'Homme* 154–55:409–30.

Gluckman, M. 1955. *The Judicial Process Among the Barotse of Northern Rhodesia (Zambia)*. Manchester: Manchester University Press.

Goddard, C. 1992. *Pitjantjatjara/Yankunytjatjara to English Dictionary*. Alice Springs, NT: Institute for Aboriginal Development Press.

Goffman, E. 1969. *Strategic Interactions*. Philadelphia: University of Pennsylvania Press.

Gould, R. A. 1969a. Subsistence behaviour among the Western Desert Aborigines of Australia. *Oceania* 39:253–74.

Gould, R. A. 1969b. *Yiwara: Foragers of the Australian Desert*. London: Collins.

Gray, G. 1994. 'Piddington's indiscretion': Ralph Piddington, the Australian National Research Council and academic freedom. *Oceania* 63:217–45.

Gray, G. 1997. 'Mr Neville did all in [his] power to assist me': A. P. Elkin, A. O. Neville and anthropological research in northwest Western Australia, 1927–1928. *Oceania* 68:27–46.

Gray, G. (ed.), 2001. *Before It's Too Late: Anthropological Reflections, 1950–1970*. Oceania Monographs. Sydney: University of Sydney.

Gray, G. 2007. *A Cautious Silence: The Politics of Australian Anthropology*. Canberra: Aboriginal Studies Press.

Gray, P. 1998. *Report of the Aboriginal Land Commissioner on the Tempe Downs and Middleton Ponds/Luritja Land Claim*. Report No. 53. Canberra: Aboriginal and Torres Strait Islander Commission.

Gumbert, M. 1984. *Neither Justice Nor Reason: A Legal and Anthropological Analysis of Aboriginal Land Rights*. Brisbane: University of Queensland Press.

Habermas, J. 1984. *The Theory of Communicative Action. Volume 1: Reason and the Rationalization of Society*. Boston: Beacon Press.

Habermas, J. 1987. *The Theory of Communicative Action. Volume 2: Lifeworld and System: A Critique of Functionalist Reason*. Boston: Beacon Press.

Hacking, I. 1999. *The Social Construction of What?* Cambridge, Mass.: Harvard University Press.

Haddon, A. C. 1901. *Head-Hunters: Black, White, and Brown*. London: Methuen & Company.

Haddon, A. C. (ed.), 1904. *Sociology, Magic and Religion of the Western Islanders. Volume V. Reports of the Cambridge Anthropological Expedition to Torres Straits*. Cambridge: Cambridge University Press.

Haddon, A. C. (ed.), 1908. *Sociology, Magic and Religion of the Eastern Islanders. Volume VI. Reports of the Cambridge Anthropological Expedition to Torres Straits*. Cambridge: Cambridge University Press.

Haddon, A. C. and C. S. Myers. 1908. 'The cult of Bomai and Malu', in *Sociology, Magic and Religion of the Eastern Islanders. Volume VI. Reports of the Cambridge Anthropological Expedition to Torres Straits*. Edited by A. C. Haddon, pp. 281–316. Cambridge: Cambridge University Press.

Hamilton, A. 1972. Blacks and the whites: the relationships of change. *Arena* 30:34–48.

Hamilton, A. 1979. Timeless Transformations: Women, Men and History in the Australian Western Desert. PhD Thesis, The University of Sydney, Sydney.

Hamilton, A. 1982a. 'Anthropology in Australia: some notes and a few queries', in *Anthropology in Australia: Essays to Honour 50 Years of 'Mankind'*. Edited by G. McCall, pp. 91–106. Sydney: Anthropological Society of New South Wales.

Hamilton, A. 1982b. 'Descended from the father, belonging to country: rights to land in the Australian Western Desert', in *Politics and History in Band Societies*. Edited by E. Leacock and R. Lee, pp. 83–108. Cambridge: Cambridge University Press.

Hamilton, A. 1987. Coming and going: Aboriginal mobility in northwest South Australia, 1970–71. *Records of the South Australian Museum* 20:47–57.

Hamilton, A. 2003. Beyond anthropology, towards actuality. *The Australian Journal of Anthropology* 14:160–70.

Harris, M. 1972. *The Rise of Anthropological Theory: A History of Theories of Culture*. London: Routledge and Kegan Paul.

Harrison, F. V. 1995. Auto-ethnographic reflections on hierarchies in anthropology. *Practicing Anthropology* 17:48–50.

Heine-Geldern, R. 1964. One hundred years of ethnological theory in German-speaking countries: some milestones. *Current Anthropology* 5:407–18.

Hemming, S. J. 1996. Inventing anthropology. *Journal of Australian Studies* 48:25–39.

Hemming, S. J. 1997. Not the slightest shred of evidence: a reply to Philip Clarke's response to 'Secret women's business'. *Journal of Australian Studies* 5:130–45.

Henderson, J. and D. Nash (eds), 2002. *Language in Native Title*. Canberra: Aboriginal Studies Press.

Hiatt, L. R. 1962. Local organisation among the Australian Aborigines. *Oceania* 32:267–86.

Hiatt, L. R. 1966. The lost horde. *Oceania* 37:81–92.

Hiatt, L. R. (ed.), 1984. *Aboriginal Landowners: Contemporary Issues in the Determination of Traditional Aboriginal Ownership*. Oceania Monographs 27. Sydney: University of Sydney.

Hiatt, L. R. 1996. *Arguments About Aborigines: Australia and the Evolution of Social Anthropology*. Cambridge: Cambridge University Press.

Hiatt, L. R. 2003. Obituary for Kenneth Maddock, 1937–2003. *The Australian Journal of Anthropology* 14:402–4.

Hill, B. 2002. *Broken Song: T. G. H. Strehlow and Aboriginal Possession*. Sydney: Knopf.

Hilliard, W. M. 1968. *The People in Between: The Pitjantjatjara People of Ernabella*. London: Hodder and Stoughton.

Hinkson, M. and J. Beckett. 2008. *An Appreciation of Difference: WEH Stanner and Aboriginal Australia*. Canberra: Aboriginal Studies Press.

Hodge, B. and V. Mishra. 1990. *Dark Side of the Dream: Australian Literature and the Postcolonial Mind*. Sydney: Allen & Unwin.

Hoebel, E. A. 1954. *The Law of Primitive Man: A Study in Comparative Legal Dynamics*. Cambridge: Harvard University Press.

Hogbin, H. I. and B. Malinowski. 1934. *Law and Order in Polynesia: A Study of Primitive Legal Institutions*. London: Christopher.

Holcombe, S. 2004. The politico-historical construction of the Pintupi–Luritja and the concept of tribe. *Oceania* 74:257–75.

Hope, D. A. C. 1983. Dreams Contested: A Political Account of Relations Between South Australia's Pitjantjatjara and the Government 1961–1981. PhD Thesis, Flinders University, Adelaide.

Hosokawa, K. 1991. The Yawuru Language of West Kimberley: A Meaning-Based Description. PhD Thesis, The Australian National University, Canberra.

Hosokawa, K. 1994. Retribalisation and language mixing: aspects of identity strategies among the Broome Aborigines, Western Australia. *Bulletin of the National Museum of Ethnology (Kokuritsu Minzokugaku Hakubutsukan)* 19:491–534.

Huber, P. W. 1991. *Galileo's Revenge: Junk Science in the Courtroom*. New York: Basic Books.

Idriess, I. L. 1933. *Drums of Mer*. Sydney: Halstead.

Imwinkelried, E. J. 1997. *The Methods of Attacking Scientific Evidence*. Charlottesville, Va: Michie Company.

Jackson, J. 1988. 'Hart and the concept of fact', in *The Jurisprudence of Orthodoxy: Queen's University Essays on H. L. A. Hart*. Edited by P. Leith and P. Ingram, pp. 61–84. London: Routledge.

Jackson, S. 1996. *When History Meets the New Native Title Era at the Negotiating Table: A Case Study in Reconciling Land Use in Broome, Western Australia*. Darwin: North Australia Research Unit, The Australian National University.

Jasanoff, S. 1995. *Science at the Bar: Law, Science, and Technology in America*. Cambridge, Mass.: Harvard University Press.

Jebb, M. A. 1984. 'The Lock Hospital experiment: Europeans, Aborigines and venereal disease', in *European–Aboriginal Relations in Western Australian History*. Edited by B. Rees and T. Stannage. Perth: University of Western Australia Press.

Johannes, R. and J. MacFarlane. 1984. Traditional sea rights in the Torres Strait Islands, with emphasis on Murray Island. *Senri Ethnological Studies* 17:253–66.

Johnson, J. M. 2002. 'In-depth interviewing', in *Handbook of Interview Research: Context and Method*. Edited by J. F. Gubrium and J. A. Holstein, pp. 103–19. Thousand Oaks, Calif.: Sage Publications.

Johnston, B. R. 1995. Notes and reflections on life in the margins. *Practicing Anthropology* 17:46–8.

Jolly, M. and T. Jamieson. 2002. 'Anthropology: reconfiguring a Janus face in a global epoch', in *Investing in Social Capital: Postgraduate Training in the Social Sciences in Australia*. Edited by S. Marginson, pp. 45–72. Brisbane: Queensland University Press/Academy of the Social Sciences, Australia.

Jones, J. A. 1956. Problems, opportunities and recommendations. *Ethnohistory* 2:347–56.

Jones, P. G. 1987. South Australian anthropological history: the Board for Anthropological Research and its early expeditions. *Records of the South Australian Museum* 20:71–92.

Kandel, R. F. (ed.), 1992. *Double Vision: Anthropologists at Law*. Washington, DC: National Association for the Practice of Anthropology, American Anthropological Association.

Keeffe, K. 2003. *Paddy's Road: Life Stories of Patrick Dodson*. Canberra: Aboriginal Studies Press.

Keen, I. 1988. 'Twenty-five years of Aboriginal kinship studies', in *Social Anthropology and Australian Aboriginal Studies*. Edited by R. M. Berndt and R. Tonkinson, pp. 79–123. Canberra: Aboriginal Studies Press.

Keen, I. 1994. *Knowledge and Secrecy in an Aboriginal Religion*. Oxford: Oxford University Press.

Keen, I. 2007. Sansom's misreading of 'The Western Desert vs. the Rest'. *Anthropological Forum* 17:168–70.

Kenny, C. 1996. *Women's Business*. Sydney: Duffy & Snellgrove.

Keon-Cohen, B. A. 2000. The Mabo litigation: a personal and procedural account. *Melbourne University Law Review* 24:893–951.

Kitaoji, H. 1977. The myth of Bomai: its structure and contemporary significance for the Murray Islanders, Torres Strait. *Minzokugaku Kenkyu (Japanese Journal of Ethnology)* 42:209–12.

Kitaoji, H. 1978. Culture of the Torres Strait people. *Arena* 50:54–63.

Kitaoji, H. 1980. Meriam perceptions of themselves and those around them: cognitive ordering after one hundred years of culture contact. Australian Anthropological Society Conference, University of Queensland, Brisbane, 1980.

Kolig, E. 1972. *Bi:n* and *Gadeja*: an Australian Aboriginal model of the European society as a guide in social change. *Oceania* 43:1–18.

Kolig, E. 1973a. Aboriginal land rights, policies, and anthropology: an anthropological dilemma. *Bulletin of the International Committee on Urgent Anthropological and Ethnological Research* 15:57–69.

Kolig, E. 1973b. The future begins now: the role of the missions in Aboriginal advancement. *Aboriginal Affairs Planning Authority Newsletter* 1:4–10.

Kolig, E. 1973–74a. Glaube als Rechtsmittel: anatomie eines Landanpruchs moderner Schwarzaustralier. *Wiener Volkerkundliche Mitteilungen* 20–1.

Kolig, E. 1973–74b. Tradition and emancipation: an Australian Aboriginal version of 'nativism'. *Aboriginal Affairs Planning Authority Newsletter* 6.

Kolig, E. 1974. Kerygma and grog. *Aboriginal Affairs Planning Authority Newsletter* 1.

Kolig, E. 1977. 'From tribesman to citizen?', in *Aborigines and Change*. Edited by R. M. Berndt. Canberra: Australian Institute of Aboriginal Studies.

Kolig, E. 1978. 'Dialectics of Aboriginal life-space', in *Whitefella Business*. Edited by M. C. Howard. Philadelphia: Institute for the Study of Human Issues.

Kolig, E. 1979a. 'Captain Cook in the western Kimberleys', in *Aborigines of the West: Their Past and Their Present*. Edited by R. M. Berndt and C. H. Berndt, pp. 274–82. Perth: University of Western Australia Press.

Kolig, E. 1979b. Djuluru: ein synkretistischer Kult Nordwest-Australiens. *Baessler Archiv* 27.

Kolig, E. 1980. Noah's Ark revisited: on the myth–land connection in traditional Aboriginal thought. *Oceania* 51:118–32.

Kolig, E. 1981. *The Silent Revolution: The Effects of Modernisation on Australian Aboriginal Religion*. Philadelphia: Institute for the Study of Human Issues.

Kolig, E. 1982. Anthropology: anybody's whore? *Australian Anthropological Society Newsletter* 14:16–27.

Kolig, E. 1987. *The Noonkanbah Story*. Dunedin: University of Otago Press.

Kolig, E. 1988. 'Mission not accomplished', in *Aboriginal Australians and Christian Missions: Ethnographic and Historical Studies*. Edited by T. Swain and D. B. Rose. Adelaide: The Australian Association for the Study of Religions.

Kolig, E. 1989. *Dreamtime Politics: Religion, Worldview and Utopian Thought in Australian Aboriginal Society*. Berlin: Dietrich Reimer Verlag.

Kolig, E. 1995a. A sense of history and the reconstitution of cosmology in Australian Aboriginal society. *Anthropos* 90:49–67.

Kolig, E. 1995b. 'Durrugu: sacred objects in a changing world', in *Politics of the Secret*. Oceania Monographs. Edited by C. Anderson. Sydney: University of Sydney.

Kolig, E. 1996. 'Aboriginal worldview and oral traditions: the case of myth versus history', in *Kimberley Languages—In Honour of Howard Coate*. Edited by W. McGregor. Munich: Lincom Europa.

Kolig, E. 2003. Legitimising belief: identity politics, utility, strategies of concealment, and rationalisation in Australian Aboriginal religion. *The Australian Journal of Anthropology* 14:209–28.

Kolig, E. and H. Mueckler. 2002. *Politics of Indigeneity in the South Pacific*. Munster: LIT.

Kuper, A. 1996. *Anthropology and Anthropologists: The Modern British School*, Third edition. London: Routledge.

Laade, W. 1969. Ethnographic notes on the Murray Islanders, Torres Strait. *Zeitschrift fur EthnologieBand* 94:3–46.

Laade, W. 1971. *Oral Traditions and Written Documents on the History and Ethnography of the Northern Torres Strait Islands: Saibai, Dauan, Boigu. Volume 1*. Wiesbaden: F. Steiner.

Langton, M. 1981. Anthropologists must change. *Identity* 4:11.

Latour, B. and S. Woolgar. 1979. *Laboratory Life: The Social Construction of Scientific Facts*. London: Sage.

Lawrie, M. 1970. *Myths and Legends of Torres Strait*. Brisbane: Queensland University Press.

Layton, R. 1983a. 'Ambilineal descent and traditional Pitjantjatjara rights to land', in *Aborigines, Land and Land Rights*. Edited by N. Peterson and M. Langton, pp. 15–32. Canberra: Australian Institute of Aboriginal Studies.

Layton, R. 1983b. 'Pitjantjatjara processes and the structure of the *Land Rights Act*', in *Aborigines, Land and Land Rights*. Edited by N. Peterson and M. Langton, pp. 226–37. Canberra: Australian Institute of Aboriginal Studies.

Layton, R. 1986. *Uluru: An Aboriginal History of Ayers Rock*. Canberra: Australian Institute of Aboriginal Studies.

Lee, R. 1976. '!Kung spatial organisation: an ecological and historical perspective', in *Kalahari Hunters-Gatherers*. Edited by R. Lee and I. De Vore. Cambridge, Mass.: Harvard University Press.

Lee, R. and I. De Vore. 1968. 'Problems in the study of hunters and gatherers', in *Man the Hunter*. Edited by R. Lee and I. De Vore. Chicago: Aldine.

Lévi-Strauss, C. and R. Needham. 1973. *Totemism*. Harmondsworth, UK: Penguin Books.

Lilley, I. (ed.), 2000. *Native Title and the Transformation of Archaeology in the Postcolonial World*. Oceania Monograph 50. Sydney: University of Sydney.

Llewellyn, K. N. 1960. *The Common Law Tradition: Deciding Appeals*. Boston: Little Brown.

Llewellyn, K. N. and E. A. Hoebel. 1941. *The Cheyenne Way: Conflict and Case Law in Primitive Jurisprudence. Civilization of the American Indian Series*. Norman, Okla.: University of Oklahoma Press.

Long, J. 1989. Review of *Torres Strait Islanders: Custom and Colonialism*. *Oceania* 60:63–5.

Lucas, R. 1996. The failure of anthropology. *Journal of Australian Studies* 48:40–51.

Luhmann, N. [1972] 1985. *A Sociological Theory of Law*, Second edition. London: Routledge and Kegan Paul.

Lurie, N. O. 1955. Problems, opportunities and recommendations. *Ethnohistory* 2:357–75.

Lurie, N. O. 1956. A reply to 'The land claims cases: anthropologists in conflict'. *Ethnohistory* 3:256–79.

McCall, G. (ed.), 1982. *Anthropology in Australia: Essays to Honour 50 Years of 'Mankind'*. Sydney: Anthropological Society of New South Wales.

McCalman, I. and A. McGrath. 2003. *Proof & Truth: The Humanist as Expert*. Canberra: The Australian Academy of the Humanities.

McCoy, B. F. 2008. *Holding Men: Kanyirninpa and the Health of Aboriginal Men.* Canberra: Aboriginal Studies Press.

McKenna, M. 2005. The potential utility of delivery of decisions to facilitate mediation. *Native Title News* 7:66–8.

Maddock, K. 1969. Necrophagy and the circulation of mothers: a problem in Mara ritual and social structure. *Mankind* 7:94–103.

Maddock, K. 1970a. Imagery and social structure at two Dalabon rock art sites. *Anthropological Forum* 2:444–63.

Maddock, K. 1970b. 'Myths of the acquisition of fire in northern and eastern Australia', in *Australian Aboriginal Anthropology: Modern Studies in the Social Anthropology of the Australian Aborigines.* Edited by R. M. Berndt, pp. 174–99. Canberra: Australian Institute of Aboriginal Studies/University of Western Australia Press.

Maddock, K. 1972. *The Australian Aborigines: A Portrait of Their Society.* Melbourne: Penguin.

Maddock, K. 1980a. Anthropologists and their ethical problems. *Australian Anthropological Society Newsletter* 9:4–13.

Maddock, K. 1980b. *Anthropology, Law and the Definition of Australian Aboriginal Rights to Land.* Nijmegen, Netherlands: Institute voor Volksrecht, Faculty of Law, Catholic University Nijmegen.

Maddock, K. 1981a. Professor Tatz on anthropology and land rights. *Australian Anthropological Society Newsletter* 12:27–33.

Maddock, K. 1981b. Warlpiri land tenure: a test case in legal anthropology. *Oceania* 52(2):85–102.

Maddock, K. 1983a. '"Owners", "managers" and the choice of statutory traditional owners by anthropologists and lawyers', in *Aborigines, Land and Land Rights.* Edited by N. Peterson and M. Langton, pp. 211–25. Canberra: Australian Institute of Aboriginal Studies.

Maddock, K. 1983b. *Your Land Is Our Land: Aboriginal Land Rights.* Melbourne: Penguin Books.

Maddock, K. 1984a. 'Aboriginal customary law', in *Aborigines and the Law: Essays in Memory of Elizabeth Eggleston.* Edited by P. Hanks and B. A. Keon-Cohen, pp. 212–37. Sydney: George Allen & Unwin.

Maddock, K. 1984b. How to do legal definitions of traditional rights. *Anthropological Forum* 5:295–308.

Maddock, K. 1998a. Anthropologists in native title claims. *Anthropological Forum* 8:85–90.

Maddock, K. 1998b. 'Involved anthropologists', in *We Are Here: Politics of Aboriginal Land Tenure*. Edited by E. N. Wilmsen, pp. 155–76. Berkeley: University of California Press.

Maddock, K. 1998c. The dubious pleasures of commitment, (Editorial). *Anthropology Today*.

Maddock, K. 1999. Bearing witness. *Australian Anthropological Society Newsletter* 75:23–5.

Maddock, K. 2001a. Anthropology Report on the De Rose Hill Native Title Application.

Maddock, K. 2001b. 'Sceptical thoughts on customary law', in *Waking Up To Dreamtime: The Illusion of Aboriginal Self-Determination*. Edited by G. Johns, pp. 152–71. Singapore: Media Masters.

Malinowski, B. 1926. *Crime and Custom in Savage Society*. London: Kegan Paul, Trench, Trubner & Company.

Manners, R. A. 1956. The land claims cases: anthropologists in conflict. *Ethnohistory* 3:72–81.

Mantziaris, C. and D. Martin. 2000. *Native Title Corporations: A Legal and Anthropological Analysis*. Sydney: The Federation Press.

Marchand, S. 2003. 'Priests among the pygmies: Wilheim Schmidt and the counter reformation in Austrian ethnology', in *Worldly Provincialism: German Anthropology in the Age of Empire*. Edited by H. G. Penny and M. Bunzl. Ann Arbor: The University of Michigan Press.

Marcus, G. and D. Cushman. 1982. Ethnographies as texts. *Annual Review of Anthropology* 11:25–69.

Martin, D. F. 2004. *Capacity of Anthropologists in Native Title Practice: Report to the National Native Title Tribunal*. Anthropos Consulting, Dickson, ACT.

Maurice, M. 1989. *Report by the Aboriginal Land Commissioner on the Lake Amadeus Land Claim*. Report No. 28. Canberra: Australian Government Publishing Service.

Mead, G. 1995. *A Royal Omission: A Critical Summary of the Evidence Given to the Hindmarsh Island Bridge Royal Commission with an Alternative Report*. Adelaide: Greg Mead.

Mead, G. H. 1934. *Mind, Self and Society: From the Standpoint of a Social Behaviourist*. Chicago: The University of Chicago Press.

Meggitt, M. J. 1962. *Desert People: A Study of the Warlpiri Aborigines of Central Australia*. Sydney: Angus & Robertson.

Merlan, F. 1981. Land, language and social identity in Aboriginal Australia. *Mankind* 13:133–48.

Merlan, F. 1989. The objectification of 'culture': an aspect of current political process in Aboriginal affairs. *Anthropological Forum* 6:105–16.

Merlan, F. 1995. The regimentation of customary practice: from Northern Territory land claims to *Mabo*. *The Australian Journal of Anthropology* 6(1–2):64–82.

Merlan, F. 1998. *Caging the Rainbow: Place, Politics, and Aborigines in a North Australian Town*. Honolulu: University of Hawai'i Press.

Merlan, F. 2001. Assessment of von Doussa on anthropology. Unpublished address given at a Centre for Aboriginal Economic Policy Research seminar, 31 October 2001.

Merlan, F. 2002. What is the 'inter-' in 'intercultural'? Australian Anthropological Society Annual Conference, 2002.

Merlan, F. 2005. Explorations towards intercultural accounts of socio-cultural reproduction and change. *Oceania* 75:167–82.

Michaels, E. 1987. 'If all anthropologists are liars…' Review article. *Canberra Anthropology* 10:44–62.

Miller, B. 1992. Common sense and plain language. *BC Studies* 95:55–65.

Miller, W. R. 1971. Dialect differentiation in the Western Desert language. *Anthropological Forum* 3:61–78.

Mills, A. 1994. *Eagle Down is Our Law: Witsuwit'en Law, Feasts and Land Claims*. Vancouver: University of British Columbia Press.

Mills, A. 1996. Problems of establishing authority in testifying on behalf of the Witsuwit'en. *Political and Legal Anthropology Review* 19:39–51.

Moore, C. 1990. Review of *Torres Strait Islanders: Custom and Colonialism*. *Journal of Pacific History* 25:131–2.

Morphy, F. and H. Morphy. 1984. 'Owners, managers, and ideology: a comparative analysis', in *Aboriginal Landowners*. Edited by L. R. Hiatt, pp. 46–66. Sydney: University of Sydney.

Morris, B. 2004. 'Anthropology and the state: the ties that bind', in *Expert Knowledge: First World Peoples, Consultancy and Anthropology*. Edited by B. Morris and R. Bastin, pp. 102–15. New York: Berghahn Books.

Morton, J. 1987. Review of *Pintupi Country, Pintupi Self: Sentiment, Place and Politics Among Western Desert Aborigines*. *Oceania* 57:304–13.

Morton, J. 1988. 'Introduction: Géza Róheim's contribution to Australian ethnography', in *Children of the Desert II: Myths and Dreams of the Aborigines of Central Australia*. Edited by J. Morton and W. Muensterberger, pp. vii–xxx. Sydney: Oceania Publications, University of Sydney.

Morton, J. 1999. Anthropology at home in Australia. *The Australian Journal of Anthropology* 10:243–58.

Morton, J. 2007. Sansom, Sutton and Sackville: three expert anthropologists? *Anthropological Forum* 17:170–3.

Mountford, C. P. 1937. Aboriginal crayon drawings from the Warburton Ranges in Western Australia, relating to the wanderings of the two ancestral beings, the Wati Kutjara. *Records of the South Australian Museum* 6:5–28.

Mountford, C. P. 1976. *Nomads of the Australian Desert*. Adelaide: Rigby.

Moyle, R. M. 1979. *Songs of the Pintupi: Musical Life in a Central Australian Society*. Canberra: Australian Institute of Aboriginal Studies.

Muecke, S. 1992. *Textual Spaces: Aboriginality and Cultural Studies*. Sydney: UNSW Press.

Munn, N. D. 1987. Review of *Pintupi Country, Pintupi Self: Sentiment, Place, and Politics Among Western Desert Aborigines*. *American Anthropologist* 89:497–8.

Myers, F. R. 1976. To Have and to Hold: A Study of Persistence and Change in Pintupi Social Life. Unpublished PhD Thesis, Bryn Mawr College, Bryn Mawr, Pa.

Myers, F. R. 1980a. A broken code: Pintupi political theory and contemporary social life. *Mankind* 12:311–26.

Myers, F. R. 1980b. The cultural basis of politics in Pintupi life. *Mankind* 12:197–214.

Myers, F. R. 1982. 'Always ask: resource use and land ownership among Pintupi Aborigines of the Australian Western Desert', in *Resource Managers: North American and Australian Hunter-Gatherers*. Edited by N. M. Williams and E. S. Hunn, pp. 173–95. Boulder, Colo.: Westview Press.

Myers, F. R. 1986. *Pintupi Country, Pintupi Self: Sentiment, Place, and Politics Among Western Desert Aborigines*. Washington, DC/Canberra: Smithsonian Institution Press/Australian Institute of Aboriginal Studies.

Myers, F. R. 1987. Representing whom? Privilege, position and posturing. A rejoinder. *Canberra Anthropology* 10(1):62–73.

Myers, F. R. 1989. 'Burning the truck and holding the country: Pintupi forms of property and identity', in *We Are Here: Politics of Aboriginal Land Tenure*. Edited by E. N. Wilmsen, pp. 15–42. Berkeley: University of California Press.

Myers, F. R. 2002. *Painting Culture: The Making of an Aboriginal High Art*. Durham, NC: Duke University Press.

Nachman, S. R. 1989. Review of *Torres Strait Islanders: Custom and Colonialism*. *Journal of Anthropological Research* 45:339–42.

Nader, L. 1995. Grumblings about elitism in anthropology. *Practicing Anthropology* 17:52–3.

Nash, J. 1997. When isms become wasms: structural functionalism, Marxism, feminism and postmodernism. *Critique of Anthropology* 17(1):11–31.

Neate, G. 2004. 'Speaking for country' and speaking about country: some issues in the resolution of Indigenous land claims in Australia. Paper delivered to the Joint Study Institute, Sydney, 21 February 2004.

Niblett, M. 1992. Text and Context: Some Issues in Warlpiri Ethnography. PhD Thesis, The Australian National University, Canberra.

Ortner, S. B. 1984. Theory in anthropology since the Sixties. *Comparative Studies in Society and History* 26:126–66.

Ortner, S. B. 2006. *Anthropology and Social Theory: Culture, Power and the Acting Subject*. Durham, NC, and London, UK: Duke University Press.

Paine, R. (ed.), 1977. *The White Arctic: Anthropological Essays on Tutelage and Ethnicity*. Newfoundland Social and Economic Papers No. 7. Toronto: Institute of Social and Economic Research, Memorial University of Newfoundland.

Paine, R. (ed.), 1985. *Advocacy and Anthropology, First Encounters*. St John's: Institute of Social and Economic Research, Memorial University of Newfoundland.

Paine, R. 1996. In Chief Justice McEachern's shoes: anthropology's ineffectiveness in court. *Political and Legal Anthropology Review* 19:59–70.

Palmer, K. 1984. 'Aboriginal land ownership among the southern Pitjantjatjara of the Great Victoria Desert', in *Aboriginal Land Owners: Contemporary Issues in the Determination of Traditional Aboriginal Land Ownership*. Oceania Monographs No. 27. Edited by L. R. Hiatt, pp. 123–33. Sydney: University of Sydney.

Palmer, K. 2001. 'Never ask a question unless you know the answer': anthropology and the formation of public policy. *Australian Aboriginal Studies* 2:4–11.

Paredes, J. A. 1995. Notes for a manifesto on working-class anthropology. *Practicing Anthropology* 17:55–6.

Paul, M. and G. Gray (eds), 2003. *Through the Smoky Mirror: History and Native Title*. Canberra: Aboriginal Studies Press.

Peterson, N. 1976. 'Introduction', in *Tribes and Boundaries in Australia*. Edited by N. Peterson, pp. 1–11. Canberra: Australian Institute of Aboriginal Studies.

Peterson, N. 1983. 'Rights, residence and process in Australian territorial organisation', in *Aborigines, Land and Land Rights*. Edited by N. Peterson and M. Langton, pp. 134–45. Canberra: Australian Institute of Aboriginal Studies.

Peterson, N. 1985. Capitalism, culture and land rights: Aborigines and the state in the Northern Territory. *Social Analysis* 18:85–101.

Peterson, N. 1990. 'Studying man and man's nature': the history of the institutionalisation of Aboriginal anthropology. *Australian Aboriginal Studies* 1990(2):3–19.

Peterson, N. 2000. An expanding Aboriginal domain: mobility and the initiation journey. *Oceania* 70:205–18.

Peterson, N. and M. Langton (eds), 1983. *Aborigines, Land and Land Rights*. Canberra: Australian Institute of Aboriginal Studies.

Peterson, N. and J. Long. 1986. *Aboriginal Territorial Organisation: A Band Perspective*. Oceania Monographs. Sydney: University of Sydney.

Petri, H. 1939. Mythische Heroen…im nordliche Dampierland, nord-west Australien (map). *Paideuma* 1:217–40.

Petri, H. and G. Petri-Odermann. 1970. 'Stability and change: present-day historic aspects among Australian Aborigines', in *Australian Aboriginal Anthropology: Modern Studies in the Social Anthropology of Australian Aborigines*. Edited by R. M. Berndt, pp. 248–76. Canberra/Perth: Australian Institute of Aboriginal Studies/University of Western Australia Press.

Piddington, M. and R. Piddington. 1932. Report of the field work in north-western Australia. *Oceania* 2:342–58.

Piddington, R. 1932a. Karadjeri initiation. *Oceania* 3:46–87.

Piddington, R. 1932b. Totemic system of the Karadjeri tribe. *Oceania* 2:373–400.

Piddington, R. 1950. *An Introduction to Social Anthropology: Volume One*. Edinburgh: Oliver and Boyd.

Piddington, R. 1971. A note on Karadjeri local organisation. *Oceania* 41:239–43.

Poirier, S. 1996. *Les jardins du nomade: Cosmologie, territorie, et personne dans le désert occidental australien*. Münster, Germany: Lit Verlag.

Poirier, S. 2005. *A World of Relationships: Itineraries, Dreams, and Events in the Australian Western Desert*. Toronto: University of Toronto Press.

Pospisil, L. J. 1956. *Law Among the Kapauku of Netherlands New Guinea*. New Haven, Conn.: Yale University Press.

Pospisil, L. J. 1971. *Anthropology of Law: A Comparative Theory*. New York: Harper & Row.

Povinelli, E. A. 2002. *The Cunning of Recognition: Indigenous Alterities and the Making of Australian Multiculturalism*. Durham, NC: Duke University Press.

Rabinow, P. 1986. Discourse and power: on the limits of ethnographic texts. *Dialectical Anthropology* 10(1):1–13.

Radcliffe-Brown, A. R. 1931. *The Social Organisation of Australian Tribes*. Oceania Monographs No. 1. Sydney: University of Sydney.

Radcliffe-Brown, A. R. 1933. 'Primitive law', in *Encyclopaedia of the Social Sciences, Volume IX*, pp. 202–6. New York: Macmillan.

Radin, P. [1920] 1963. *The Autobiography of a Winnebago Indian*. New York: Dover Publications.

Reece, B. 2007. *Daisy Bates: Grand Dame of the Desert. An Australian Life 3*. Canberra: National Library of Australia.

Ribeiro, G. L. and A. Escobar. 2006. *World Anthropologies: Disciplinary Transformations Within Systems of Power*. Wenner-Gren International Symposium Series. Oxford: Berg.

Ridington, R. 1992. Fieldwork in Courtroom 53: a witness to *Delgamuukw v BC*. *BC Studies* 95:12–24.

Rigsby, B. 1995. 'Anthropologists, land claims and objectivity: some Canadian and Australian cases', in *Native Title: Emerging Issues for Research, Policy and Practice*. Edited by J. Finlayson and D. E. Smith, pp. 23–38. Canberra: Centre for Aboriginal Economic Policy Research, The Australian National University.

Rigsby, B. 1997. 'Anthropologists, Indian title and the Indian Claims Commission: the Californian and Great Basin cases', in *Fighting Over Country: Anthropological Perspectives*. Edited by D. E. Smith and J. Finlayson, pp. 15–45. Canberra: Centre for Aboriginal Economic Policy Research, The Australian National University.

Rivers, W. H. R. 1908. 'Social organisation', in *Sociology, Magic and Religion of the Eastern Islanders, Volume VI, Reports of the Cambridge Anthropological Expedition to the Torres Straits*. Edited by A. C. Haddon, pp. 169–84. Cambridge: Cambridge University Press.

Robbins, D. 2004. The transcultural transferability of Bourdieu's sociology of education. *British Journal of Sociology of Education* 25:415–30.

Roberts, S. 1979. *Order and Dispute: An Introduction to Legal Anthropology*. Harmondsworth, UK: Penguin Books.

Rose, D. B. 1987. Representing the Pintupi. *Canberra Anthropology* 10:35–43.

Rose, D. B. 1996. 'Histories and rituals: land claims in the Territory', in *In the Age of Mabo: History, Aborigines and Australia*. Edited by B. Attwood, pp. 35–53. Sydney: Allen & Unwin.

Rose, F. G. G. 1965. *The Winds of Change in Central Australia: The Aborigines of Angas Downs*. Berlin: Akademie-Verlag.

Rosen, L. 1977. The anthropologist as expert witness. *American Anthropologist* 79:555–78.

Rowse, T. 1992. *Remote Possibilities: The Aboriginal Domain and the Administrative Imagination*. Darwin: North Australia Research Unit, The Australian National University.

Rowse, T. 2002. *Indigenous Futures: Choice and Development for Aboriginal and Islander Australia*. Sydney: UNSW Press.

Rowse, T. 2006. Public occasions, Indigenous selves: three Ngarrindjeri autobiographies. *Aboriginal History* 30:187–207.

Rumsey, A. 1989. Language groups in Aboriginal land claims. *Anthropological Forum* 6:69–79.

Rumsey, A. 1996. Aspects of native title and social identity in the Kimberleys and beyond. *Australian Aboriginal Studies* 1996(1):2–10.

Sackett, L. 1977. 'Liquor and the law', in *Aborigines and Change: Australia in the '70s*. Edited by R. M. Berndt, pp. 90–9. Canberra: Australian Institute of Aboriginal Studies.

Sackett, L. 2007. A potential pathway. *Anthropological Forum* 17:173–5.

Sahlins, M. 1981. *Historical Metaphors and Mythical Realities: Structure in the Early History of the Sandwich Islands Kingdom*. Ann Arbor: University of Michigan Press.

Sahlins, M. 1983. Other times, other customs: the anthropology of history. *American Anthropologist* 85(3):517–44.

Said, E. W. 1978. *Orientalism*. New York: Routledge.

Salter, E. 1971. *Daisy Bates: The Great White Queen of the Never Never*. Sydney: Angus & Robertson.

Sansom, B. 1980. *The Camp at Wallaby Cross: Aboriginal Fringe Dwellers in Darwin*. Canberra: Australian Institute of Aboriginal Studies.

Sansom, B. 1985. 'Canons of anthropology', in *Advocacy and Anthropology, First Encounters*. Edited by R. Paine, pp. 3–12. St John's: Institute of Social and Economic Research, Memorial University of Newfoundland.

Sansom, B. 2007. *Yulara* and future expert reports in native title cases. *Anthropological Forum* 17:71–92.

Sharp, N. 1980. *Torres Strait Islands 1879–1979: Theme for an Overview*. La Trobe Working Papers in Sociology. Melbourne: Department of Sociology, School of Social Sciences, La Trobe University.

Sharp, N. 1989. Review of *Torres Strait Islanders: Custom and Colonialism*. *Journal of the Polynesian Society* 98:215–17.

Sharp, N. 1993. *Stars of Tagai: The Torres Strait Islanders*. Canberra: Aboriginal Studies Press.

Sharp, N. 1996. *No Ordinary Judgment*. Canberra: Aboriginal Studies Press.

Shaw, B. 1995. *Our Heart is the Land: Aboriginal Reminiscences from the Western Lake Eyre Basin*. Canberra: Aboriginal Studies Press.

Shnukal, A. 1998. 'At the Australian–Papuan linguistic boundary: Sidney Ray's classification of Torres Strait languages', in *Cambridge and the Torres Strait: Centenary Essays on the 1898 Anthropological Expedition*. Edited by A. Herle and S. Rouse, pp. 181–200. Cambridge: Cambridge University Press.

Simons, M. 2003. *The Meeting of the Waters: The Hindmarsh Island Affair*. Sydney: Hodder Headline.

Singer, M. 1995. Reflections on elitism in American anthropology. *Practicing Anthropology* 17:44–6.

Smith, B. R. and F. Morphy (eds), 2007. *The Social Effects of Native Title: Recognition, Translation, Coexistence*. Centre for Aboriginal Economic Policy Research, Research Monograph No. 27. Canberra: ANU E Press.

Smith, M. E. 1995. Core and periphery in anthropology. *Practicing Anthropology* 17:53–5.

South Australia Hindmarsh Island Bridge Royal Commission. 1995. *Report of the Hindmarsh Island Bridge Royal Commission*. Adelaide: Government of South Australia.

Spencer, B. and F. Gillen. 1899. *The Native Tribes of Central Australia*. London: Macmillan.

Spicer, E. H. 1976. Beyond analysis and explanation? Notes on the life and times of the Society for Applied Anthropology. *Human Organization* 35:335–47.

Stanner, W. E. H. 1965. Aboriginal territorial organisation: estate, range, domain and regime. *Oceania* 36:1–26.

Steward, J. H. 1968. Review of the current status of anthropological research in the Great Basin: 1964. *American Antiquity* 33:264–7.

Steward, J. H. 1977. 'The foundations of basin–plateau Shoshonean society', in *Evolution and Ecology. Essays on Social Transformation by Julian H. Steward.* Edited by J. C. Steward and R. F. Murphy. Urbana: University of Illinois Press.

Stewart, O. C. 1966. 'Tribal distributions and boundaries in the Great Basin', in *The Current Status of Anthropological Research in the Great Basin: 1964.* Technical Report Series S-H, Social Sciences and Humanities Publications No. 1. Edited by W. L. d'Azevedo. Reno, Nev.: Desert Research Institute.

Stocking, G. W. 1983. *The Ethnographer's Magic: Fieldwork in British Anthropology from Tylor to Malinowski.* Madison: University of Wisconsin Press.

Stocking, G. W. 1996. *After Tylor: British Social Anthropology 1888–1951.* London: The Athlone Press.

Strehlow, C. 1907–20. Die Aranda- und Loritja-Stämme in Zentral-Australien. Translated by C. Chewings. Manuscript from the Barr Smith Library, University of Adelaide.

Strehlow, T. G. H. 1965. 'Culture, social structure, and environment in Aboriginal Central Australia', in *Aboriginal Man in Australia: Essays in Honour of Emeritus Professor A. P. Elkin.* Edited by R. M. Berndt and C. H. Berndt, pp. 121–45. Sydney: Angus & Robertson.

Strehlow, T. G. H. 1970. 'Geography and the totemic landscape in Central Australia: a functional study', in *Australian Aboriginal Anthropology: Modern Studies in the Social Anthropology of the Australian Aborigines.* Edited by R. M. Berndt, pp. 92–140. Perth: University of Western Australia Press/ Australian Institute of Aboriginal Studies.

Sullivan, P. 1986. The generation of cultural trauma: what are anthropologists for? *Australian Aboriginal Studies* 1:13–23.

Sullivan, P. 1988. 'Aboriginal community representative organisations: international cultural processes in the Kimberley region, West Australia', in *East Kimberley Impact Assessment Project.* Working Paper No. 20. Canberra: Centre for Resource and Environmental Studies, The Australian National University.

Sullivan, P. 1995a. *Beyond Native Title: Multiple Land Use Agreements and Aboriginal Governance in the Kimberley.* Discussion Paper No. 89. Canberra: Centre for Aboriginal Economic Policy Research, The Australian National University.

Sullivan, P. 1995b. 'Problems of mediation in the National Native Title Tribunal', in *Anthropology in the Native Title Era*. Edited by J. Fingleton and J. Finlayson. Canberra: Native Title Research Unit, Australian Institute of Aboriginal and Torres Strait Islander Studies.

Sullivan, P. 1996a. *All Free Man Now: Culture, Community and Politics in the Kimberley Region, North-Western Australia*. Report Series. Canberra: Australian Institute of Aboriginal and Torres Strait Islander Studies.

Sullivan, P. 1996b. 'All things to all people: ATSIC and Australia's international obligation to uphold Indigenous self-determination', in *Shooting the Banker: Essays on ATSIC and Self-Determination*. Edited by P. Sullivan. Darwin: North Australia Research Unit, The Australian National University.

Sullivan, P. 1997a. *A Sacred Land, A Sovereign People, An Aboriginal Corporation: Prescribed Bodies and the Native Title Act*. Report Series No. 3. Darwin: North Australia Research Unit, The Australian National University.

Sullivan, P. 1997b. 'Dealing with native title conflicts by recognising Aboriginal authority systems', in *Fighting Over Country: Anthropological Perspectives*. Edited by D. E. Smith and J. Finlayson, pp. 129–40. Canberra: Centre for Aboriginal Economic Policy Research, The Australian National University.

Sullivan, P. 1998. 'Salt water, fresh water and Yawuru social organisation', in *Customary Marine Tenure in Australia*. Edited by N. Peterson and B. Rigsby, pp. 96–108. Oceania Monographs. Sydney: University of Sydney.

Sullivan, P. 2002. Don't educate the judge: court experts and court expertise in the social disciplines. Native Title Conference, Geraldton, WA, 2002.

Sutton, P. 1987. Review of *Pintupi Country, Pintupi Self: Sentiment, Place, and Politics Among Western Desert Aborigines*. *American Ethnologist* 14:588–9.

Sutton, P. 1990. 'The pulsating heart: large-scale cultural and demographic processes in Aboriginal Australia', in *Hunter-Gatherer Demography Past and Present*. Edited by B. Meehan and N. White, pp. 71–80. Oceania Monographs. Sydney: University of Sydney.

Sutton, P. 1995a. *Country: Aboriginal Boundaries and Land Ownership in Australia*. Aboriginal History Monograph Series. Canberra: Aboriginal History Incorporated.

Sutton, P. 1995b. 'Forensic anthropology in Australia: does it have a case to answer?', in *Native Title: Emerging Issues for Research, Policy and Practice, Volume 10*. Research Monographs. Edited by J. D. Finlayson and D. Smith, pp. 83–100. Canberra: Centre for Aboriginal Economic Policy Research, The Australian National University.

Sutton, P. 1998. *Native Title and the Descent of Rights*. Perth: National Native Title Tribunal.

Sutton, P. 2001. Ronald and Catherine Berndt: an appreciation. *Anthropological Forum* 11:121–4.

Sutton, P. 2003. *Native Title in Australia: An Ethnographic Perspective*. Cambridge: Cambridge University Press.

Sutton, P. 2007. Norms, statistics and the *Jango* case at Yulara. *Anthropological Forum* 17:175–92.

Sylvain, R. 1996. Leo Frobenius: from Kulturkreis to Kulturmorphologie. *Anthropos* 91:483–94.

Tamanaha, B. Z. 1995. An analytical map of social scientific approaches to the concept of law. *Oxford Journal of Legal Studies* 15(4):501-535.

Tashima, N. and C. Crain. 1995. Determining our future: addressing elitism in anthropology. *Practicing Anthropology* 17:50–2.

Teubner, G. (ed.), 1988. *Autopoietic Law: A New Approach to Law and Society*. Berlin: Walter de Gruyter.

Teubner, G. 1993. *Law as an Autopoietic System*. Oxford: Blackwell.

Thomas, N. 1989. *Out of Time: History and Evolution in Anthropological Discourse*. Cambridge: Cambridge University Press.

Tindale, N. B. 1934. Anthropological expedition to the north-west of South Australia, 1933. *Oceania* 4:99–105.

Tindale, N. B. 1935. Initiation among the Pitjantjara natives of the Mann and Tomkinson ranges in South Australia. *Oceania* 6:199–225.

Tindale, N. B. 1936. General report on the Anthropological Expedition to the Warburton Range, Western Australia, July–September, 1935. *Oceania* 6:481–5.

Tindale, N. B. 1937. Legend of the Wati Kutjara, Warburton Range, Western Australia. *Oceania* 7:169–85.

Tindale, N. B. 1953. Tribal and intertribal marriage among the Australian Aborigines. *Human Biology* 25:169–90.

Tindale, N. B. 1972. 'The Pitjandjara', in *Hunters and Gatherers Today: A Socioeconomic Study of Eleven Such Cultures in the Twentieth Century*. Edited by M. G. Bicchieri, pp. 217–68. New York: Holt, Rinehart and Winston.

Tindale, N. B. 1974. *Aboriginal Tribes of Australia: Their Terrain, Environmental Controls, Distribution, Limits, and Proper Names*. Canberra: Australian National University Press.

Tonkinson, R. 1966. Social Structure and Acculturation of Aborigines in the Western Desert. MA Thesis, University of Western Australia, Perth.

Tonkinson, R. 1974. *The Jigalong Mob: Aboriginal Victors of the Desert Crusade*. Menlo Park, Calif.: Cummings.

Tonkinson, R. 1978. *The Mardudjara Aborigines*. Fort Worth, Tex.: Holt, Rinehart and Winston.

Tonkinson, R. 1988. 'One community, two laws: aspects of conflict and convergence in a WA Aboriginal settlement', in *Indigenous Law and the State*. Edited by B. Morse and G. Woodman, pp. 395–411. Dordrecht, Netherlands: Foris.

Tonkinson, R. 1989. 'Local organisation and land tenure in the Karlamilyi (Rudall River) region', in *The Significance of the Karlamilyi Region to the Martujarra of the Western Desert*. Edited by WDWGPA Corporation, pp. 99–114. Perth: WA Department of Conservation and Land Management.

Tonkinson, R. 1990. *The Mardu Aborigines: Living the Dream in Australia's Desert*, Second edition. Fort Worth, Tex.: Holt, Rinehart and Winston.

Tonkinson, R. 1996. The dynamics of Aboriginal identity in remote Australia. *Anthropological Notebooks* 11:27–42.

Tonkinson, R. 1997. Anthropology and Aboriginal tradition: the Hindmarsh Island Bridge affair and the politics of interpretation. *Oceania* 68:1–26.

Tonkinson, R. 2002. Spiritual prescription, social reality: reflections on religious dynamism. Second Berndt Memorial Lecture, 31 October 2002.

Tonkinson, R. 2007. Aboriginal 'difference' and 'autonomy' then and now: four decades of change in a Western Desert society. *Anthropological Forum* 17:41–60.

Tonkinson, R. and M. Howard. 1990. 'The Berndts: a biographical sketch', in *Going it Alone? Prospects for Aboriginal Autonomy: Essays in Honour of Ronald and Catherine Berndt*. Edited by R. Tonkinson and M. Howard, pp. 16–43. Canberra: Aboriginal Studies Press.

Tonkinson, R. and M. Tonkinson. 1991. Obituary for Ronald Murray Berndt (1916–1990). *Aboriginal History* 15:1–3.

Toohey, J. 1980. *Uluru (Ayers Rock) National Park and Lake Amadeus/Luritja Land Claim: Report by the Aboriginal Land Commissioner*. Canberra: Australian Government Publishing Service.

Toussaint, S. (ed.), 2004. *Crossing Boundaries: Cultural, Legal, Historical and Practice Issues in Native Title*. Melbourne: Melbourne University Press.

Toussaint, S. and J. Taylor (eds), 1999. *Applied Anthropology in Australasia*. Perth: University of Western Australia Press.

Toyne, P. and D. Vachon. 1984. *Growing Up The Country: The Pitjantjatjara Struggle for Their Land*. Melbourne: McPhee Gribble/Penguin.

Twining, W. 1973. *Karl Llewellyn and the Realist Movement*. London: Weidenfeld and Nicholson.

Urry, J. 1989. Review of *Torres Strait Islanders: Custom and Colonialism*. *Man* (NS)24:533.

Urry, J. 1998. 'Making sense of diversity and complexity: the ethnological context and consequences of the Torres Strait expedition and the Oceanic phase of British anthropology 1890–1935', in *Cambridge and the Torres Strait: Centenary Essays on the 1898 Anthropological Expedition*. Edited by A. Herle and S. Rouse, pp. 201–33. Cambridge: Cambridge University Press.

Vachon, D. 2006. The Serpent, the Word and the Lie of the Ground: The Discipline of Living in the Great Sandy Desert of Australia. Unpublished PhD Thesis, University of Toronto.

Vachon, D. A. 1982. 'Political consciousness and land rights among the Australian Western Desert people', in *Politics and History in Band Societies*. Edited by E. Leacock and R. Lee, pp. 463–90. Cambridge: Cambridge University Press.

van Willigen, J. 1993. *Applied Anthropology: An Introduction*, Revised edition. Westport, Conn.: Bergin and Garvey.

Veit, W. 1991. 'In search of Carl Strehlow: Lutheran missionary and Australian anthropologist', in *From Berlin to the Burdekin: The German Contribution to the Development of Australian Science, Exploration and the Arts*. Edited by D. Walker and J. Tamke. Sydney: UNSW Press.

Wallace, N. M. 1977a. 'Change in spiritual and ritual life in Pitjantjatjara (Bitjantjatjara) society, 1966–1973', in *Aborigines and Change: Australia in the '70s*. Edited by R. M. Berndt, pp. 74–89. Canberra: Australian Institute of Aboriginal Studies.

Wallace, N. M. 1977b. 'Pitjantjatjara decentralisation in north-west South Australia: spiritual and psycho-social motivation', in *Aborigines and Change: Australia in the '70s*. Edited by R. M. Berndt, pp. 124–35. Canberra: Australian Institute of Aboriginal Studies.

Warren, C. A. B. 2002. 'Qualitative interviewing', in *Handbook of Interview Research: Context and Method*. Edited by J. F. Gubrium and J. A. Holstein, pp. 83–101. Thousand Oaks, Calif.: Sage Publications.

Weber, M. [1925] 1978. *Economy and Society: An Outline of Interpretive Sociology*. Berkeley: University of California Press.

Weiner, J. F. 1995. Anthropologists, historians and the secret of social knowledge. *Anthropology Today* 11(5):3–7.

Weiner, J. F. 1999. Culture in a sealed envelope: the concealment of Australian Aboriginal heritage and tradition in the Hindmarsh Island Bridge affair. *Journal of the Royal Anthropological Institute* 5:193–210.

Weiner, J. F. 2001. 'Strangelove's dilemma: or, what kind of secrecy do the Ngarrindjeri practice?', in *Emplaced Myth: Space, Narrative, & Knowledge in Aboriginal Australia and Papua New Guinea*. Edited by A. Rumsey and J. F. Weiner. Honolulu: University of Hawai'i Press.

Weiner, J. F. 2002. Religion, belief and action: the case of Ngarrindjeri 'women's business' on Hindmarsh Island, South Australia, 1994–1996. *The Australian Journal of Anthropology* 13(1):51–71.

Weiner, J. F. and K. Glaskin (eds), 2007. *Customary Land Tenure and Registration in Australia and Papua New Guinea: Anthropological Perspectives*. Asia-Pacific Environment Monograph 3. Canberra: ANU E Press.

Wellborn, O. G. 1990–91. Demeanor. *Cornell Law Review* 76:1075–105.

White, I. 1981. Generational moieties in Australia: structural, social and ritual implications. *Oceania* 52:6–27.

White, I. 1985. 'Introduction', in *The Native Tribes of Western Australia*. Edited by I. White, pp. 1–35. Canberra: National Library of Australia.

White, I. 1993. 'Daisy Bates: legend and reality', in *First in Their Field*. Edited by J. Marcus, pp. 47–65. Melbourne: Melbourne University Press.

Wilkin, A. 1908. 'Property and inheritance', in *Sociology, Magic and Religion of the Eastern Islanders, Volume VI, Reports of the Cambridge Anthropological Expedition to Torres Straits*. Edited by A. C. Haddon, pp. 163–8. Cambridge: Cambridge University Press.

Williams, N. M. 1986. *The Yolngu and Their Land: A System of Land Tenure and the Fight for its Recognition*. Canberra: Australian Institute of Aboriginal Studies.

Williams, N. M. 2008. 'Stanner, Milirrpum, and the Woodward Royal Commission', in *An Appreciation of Difference: WEH Stanner and Aboriginal Australia*. Edited by M. Hinkson and J. Beckett, pp. 198–216. Canberra: Aboriginal Studies Press.

Willis, J. 1997. Romance, Ritual and Risk: Pitjantjatjara Masculinity in the Era of AIDS. Unpublished PhD Thesis, University of Queensland, St Lucia.

Willis, J. 2003a. Condoms are for whitefellas: barriers to Pitjantjatjara men's use of safe sex technologies. *Culture, Health & Sexuality* 5:203–17.

Willis, J. 2003b. Heteronormativity and the deflection of male same-sex attraction among the Pitjantjatjara people of Australia's Western Desert. *Culture, Health & Sexuality* 5:137–51.

Wise, T. 1985. *The Self-Made Anthropologist: A Life of A P Elkin*. Sydney: George Allen & Unwin.

Woenne, S. T. 1977. 'Old country, new territory: some implications of the settlement process', in *Aborigines and Change: Australia in the '70s*. Edited by R. M. Berndt, pp. 54–64. Canberra: Australian Institute of Aboriginal Studies.

Wolf, E. R. 1982. *Europe and the People Without History*. Berkeley: University of California Press.

Wolfe, P. 1999. *Settler Colonialism and the Transformation of Anthropology: The Politics and Poetics of an Ethnographic Event*. Writing Past Colonialism Series. London: Cassell.

Woolgar, S. 1988. *Science: The Very Idea*. London: Tavistock Press.

Worms, E. A. 1938a. Die Initiationsfeiern Einiger Kusten und Binnenlandstamme in Nord-Westaustralien. *Annali Lateranensi* 2:147–74.

Worms, E. A. 1938b. Onomatopeia in some tribes of north-western Australia. *Oceania* 8:453–7.

Worms, E. A. 1940. Religiose Vorstellungen und Kultureiniger Nordwestaustralischen Stämme in fünfzig Legenden. *Annali Lateranensi* 4:213–82.

Worms, E. A. 1942. Sense of smell of the Australian Aborigines: a psychological and linguistic study of the natives of the Kimberley. *Oceania* 13:107–30.

Worms, E. A. 1944. Aboriginal place names in Kimberley, Western Australia: an etymological and mythological study. *Oceania* 14:284–310.

Worms, E. A. 1947a. 'Modern ethnology confirms Catholic belief', in *The Advocate*, 26 February, p. 11. Melbourne.

Worms, E. A. 1947b. 'Primitive as believed in one god not many', in *The Advocate*, 5 March, p. 11. Melbourne.

Worms, E. A. 1947c. 'Primitive man had but one wife, not many', in *The Advocate*, 12 March, p. 15. Melbourne.

Worms, E. A. 1949. An Australian migratory myth. *Primitive Man* 22:33–8.

Worms, E. A. 1950. Djamar, the creator. *Anthropos* 45:641–58.

Worms, E. A. 1952. Djamar and his relation to other culture heroes. *Anthropos* 47:539–60.

Worms, E. A. 1953. H. Nekes' and E. A. Worms' Australian languages. *Anthropos* 47:539–60.

Worms, E. A. 1954. Prehistoric petroglyphs in the Upper Yule River, north-western Australia. *Anthropos* 49:1067–88.

Worms, E. A. 1957. The poetry of the Yaora and Bad. *Annali Lateranensi* 21:213–29.

Worms, E. A. 1970. 'Observations on the mission field of the Pallottine Fathers in north-west Australia', in *Diprotodon to Detribalisation: Studies of Change Among Australian Aborigines*. Edited by A. R. Pilling and R. A. Waterman, pp. 367–79. East Lansing: Michigan State University Press.

Worms, E. A. and H. Petri. 1998. *Australian Aboriginal Religions*, Second edition. Nelen Yubu Missiological Series No. 5. Sydney: Spectrum Publications/Nelen Yubu Missiological Unit.

Yabuuchi, Y. 1977. Preliminary Reports of Field Research on Torres Strait Islands.

Yengoyan, A. 1968. 'Demographic and ecological influences on Australian Aboriginal marriage sections', in *Man the Hunter*. Edited by R. Lee and I. DeVore, pp. 185–99. Chicago: Aldine.

Yengoyan, A. 1970. 'Demographic factors in Pitjandjara social organisation', in *Australian Aboriginal Anthropology: Modern Studies in Social Anthropology of the Australian Aborigines*. Edited by R. M. Berndt, pp. 70–91. Perth: University of Western Australia Press/Australian Institute of Aboriginal Studies.

Yin, R. K. 2003. *Case Study Research: Design and Methods,* Third edition. *Volume 5: Applied Social Research Methods.* Thousand Oaks, Calif.: Sage.

Zucker, M. 1994. *From Patrons to Partners: A History of the Catholic Church in the Kimberley.* Fremantle, WA: University of Notre Dame.

Reasons for judgment, cases and transcripts

Mabo

The transcript of the hearing of the facts before Justice Moynihan of the Supreme Court of Queensland appears to have been produced by the Supreme Court staff and printed by the Queensland Government Printer. The formal title of these proceedings is:

> *Eddie Mabo, David Passi and James Rice v State of Queensland and the Commonwealth of Australia* Writ No. 1594 of 1986 in the Civil Jurisdiction of the Supreme Court of Queensland.

There is a copy of the transcript in the Australian Institute of Aboriginal and Torres Strait Islander Studies (AIATSIS) Library and in the Bryan Keon-Cohen Papers in the Manuscript Section of the National Library of Australia (MS 9518).

Justice Moynihan's Determination of Facts as presented to the High Court has not been published. The title of the document is:

> *Determination Pursuant to Reference of 27 February 1986 by the High Court of Australia to the Supreme Court of Queensland to hear and determine all issues of fact raised by the pleadings, particulars and further particulars in High Court Action B11 of 1982.*

Again, there is a copy of the Determination of Facts in the AIATSIS Library and in the Bryan Keon-Cohen Papers in the Manuscript Section of the National Library of Australia (MS 9518).

The official report of the High Court's *Mabo* decision is in the *Commonwealth Law Reports* (*CLR*):

> *Mabo v Queensland (No. 2)* 175 CLR 1.

Rubibi

The transcript of hearing of the first *Rubibi* claim was produced by a separate organisation called Transcript Australia. The official title of the proceedings is:

Felix Edgar, Frank Sebastian & Others on Behalf of the Rubibi Community v The State of Western Australia, No. WG 90 & 91 of 1998 in the Western Australia District Registry of the Federal Court.

A copy of the transcript can be purchased from Transcript Australia. Alternatively, one of the parties may lend a copy of the transcript to a researcher. Usually there is a copy of the transcript on the court file and it may be possible to obtain access to it at the Federal Court Registry in Perth.

Justice Merkel's reasons for judgment were reported in the *Federal Court Reports* (*FCR*):

Rubibi Community v Western Australia (No. 2) (2001) 112 FCR 523.

They are also available on the Internet via the Austlii web site <www.austli.edu.au> under the title:

Rubibi Community v Western Australia (2001) FCA 607 (29 May 2001).

De Rose Hill

The transcript of the *De Rose Hill* native title claim was produced by the company Spark and Cannon of Adelaide. The official title of the proceedings is:

Peter De Rose and Others v State of South Australia and Others No. SG 6001 of 1996 in the South Australia District Registry of the Federal Court.

A copy of the transcript can be purchased from Spark and Cannon. Alternatively, one of the parties may lend a copy of the transcript to a researcher. Usually there is a copy of the transcript on the court file and it may be possible to obtain access to it at the Federal Court Registry in Adelaide.

As far as I am aware, Justice O'Loughlin's reasons for judgment have not been reported in the law reports. They are available on the Internet via the Austlii web site <www.austli.edu.au> under the title:

De Rose v State of South Australia (2002) FCA 1342 (1 November 2002).

The Full Federal Court's consideration of the appeal has been reported in the *Federal Court Reports* (*FCR*) in two separate reports:

De Rose v South Australia (2003) 133 FCR 325.

De Rose v South Australia (2005) 145 FCR 290.

Both judgments are also available on the Internet via the Austlii web site <www.austli.edu.au> under the titles:

De Rose v State of South Australia (2003) FCAFC 286 (16 December 2003).

De Rose v State of South Australia (No. 2) (2005) FCAFC 110 (8 June 2005).

Yulara

Within the time constraints of my consideration of the *Yulara* case it was not practical for me to attempt to read the transcript of the hearing. For researchers wishing to view the transcript, the most practical course might be to approach one of the parties. The preliminary decisions on the anthropological reports are available on the Internet via the Federal Court home page <www.fedcourt.gov.au> or via the Austlii web site <www.austlii.edu.au> under the titles:

Jango v Northern Territory of Australia (No. 2) [2004] FCA 1004 (3 August 2004).

Jango v Northern Territory of Australia (No. 4) [2004] FCA 1539 (26 November 2004).

The later decision was also reported in the *Australian Law Reports* (*ALR*):

Jango v Northern Territory of Australia (No. 4) (2004) 214 ALR 608.

The judgment on the substantive issues in the case is entitled:

Jango v Northern Territory of Australia [2006] FCA 318 (31 March 2006).

It was reported in the *Federal Court Reporter*:

Jango v Northern Territory of Australia (2006) 152 FCR 150.

The Full Federal Court's judgment is entitled:

Jango v Northern Territory of Australia [2007] FCAFC 101 (6 July 2007).

It was reported in the *Federal Court Reporter* and the *Australian Law Reports*:

Jango v Northern Territory of Australia (2007) 159 FCR 531.

Jango v Northern Territory of Australia (2007) 240 ALR 432.

Index

www.ingramcontent.com/pod-product-compliance
Lightning Source LLC
Chambersburg PA
CBHW061242270326
41928CB00041B/3369